Urban Masses and Moral Order
in America,
1820—1920

Urban Masses and Moral Order in America,

1820—1920

Paul Boyer

HARVARD UNIVERSITY PRESS
Cambridge, Massachusetts
and
London, England

First Harvard University Press paperback edition, 1992

Library of Congress Cataloging in Publication Data

Boyer, Paul S
  Urban masses and moral order in America, 1820–1920.

  Includes bibliographical references and index.
  1. Urbanization—United States—History.
  2. United States—Moral conditions. I. Title.
HT123.B67   301.36'3'0973   78–15973
ISBN 0–674–93109–2 (cloth)
ISBN 0–674–93110–6 (paper)

This book has been digitally reprinted. The content remains
identical to that of previous printings.

For my mother and father

Preface

"To produce a mighty book," said Herman Melville (who was in a position to know), "you must choose a mighty theme." While I have no grandiose illusions about the mightiness of this book, I am fairly certain about the mightiness of the theme: America's moral response to the city.

In the hundred years between the election of James Monroe to a second term as President and the elevation of Warren Harding to the same office, the United States underwent the most profound of transformations: it changed from an agrarian to an urban society. Throughout this century-long period, the process of urbanization functioned as a potent catalyst for social speculation and social action. Fears about industrialization, immigration, family disruption, religious change, and deepening class divisions all focused on the growing cities. Social thinkers, reformers, philanthropists, and others whose assumptions and activities seemed otherwise very different were often linked by a shared preoccupation with the city and, more specifically, by a common interest in controlling the behavior of an increasingly urbanized populace.

In this book I have attempted to unravel some of the central threads of this urban social-control effort. The book is less an excavation of new historical material than an effort at a fresh synthesis of familiar material. It is an attempt to establish meaningful intellectual relationships between movements that are usually treated separately, by clarifying the common concerns and objectives that underlay surface differences.

At first glance, what may strike one about the various endeavors examined in these chapters is how little they have in common, beyond the obvious and rather banal fact that all were concerned in one way or another with the city. Between the moral reformers of the Jacksonian era, with their quaint fustian about wickedness in the city, and the Progressive environmentalists, with their soaring rhetoric of civic idealism and their confidence in the transforming power of parks, playgrounds, and city plans, the gap seems almost unbridgeable.

Yet beneath the differences run powerful currents of ideological continuity. Common to almost all the reformers considered in this book was the conviction—explicit or implicit—that the city, although obviously different from the village in its external, physical aspects, should nevertheless replicate the moral order of the village. City dwellers, they believed, must somehow be brought to perceive themselves as members of cohesive communities knit together by shared moral and social values. In their bleaker moments, the only alternative they saw to such a cohesive order was anarchy and chaos. These were the first tentative explorers of modernity, and it is hardly surprising that they confronted the new order with a set of social assumptions rooted in the world they were leaving behind. The driving thrust behind this century-long effort to impose moral conformity on urban America ultimately diminished—as a different set of controlling assumptions about the nature of the city gained currency—but for at least three generations it provided a powerful stimulus to reform effort, and one cannot fully understand vast stretches of American social and intellectual history without coming to grips with it.

A word about the phrases "social control" and "moral control" —terms that are used nearly interchangeably in this study—may be in order. My focus in this book is not on the prosecution of statute-book crime, or on efforts to constrain the urban populace by force of law. (When such efforts are examined, as in chapters 13 and 14, it is primarily for their symbolic meaning.) Nor have I attempted a sociological analysis of the many subtle and largely unconscious ways by which all social groups, including those in cities, shape those who fall within their orbits. My area of interest lies between these two poles. I have concentrated on individuals and groups who sought through consciously planned and organized (but voluntarist and extra-legal) effort to influence that range of social behavior usually considered outside the purview of criminal law, yet not entirely private and personal.

It follows, then, that in speaking of "urban morality" or the "urban moral order," I mean something more than simply the absence of the various human vices and failings so frequently catalogued by the reformers who populate these pages. I use the word "moral" in the sense of its Latin root *mores:* the accepted usages and common behavior patterns of a people. Even when the reformers were concentrating their fire on specific evils, their underlying purpose—or so I would contend—was to win adherence to a general standard of right conduct upon which an enduring urban moral order could be built.

It is easy to ridicule these earnest uplifters, as Mark Twain did with his sly comment, "Nothing so needs reforming as other people's habits." But although their social outlook is alien to our contemporary ethos, it becomes more comprehensible when the larger concerns that underlay it are understood. These men and women were experiencing the final breakup of a social order that had endured for centuries, and it was not yet at all clear to them (as it would become in retrospect) that even as urbanization was sweeping away the old order, it was also, through its own internal dynamic, generating powerful new forces of social cohesion.

I should add, finally, that I have not dealt extensively with some subjects obviously germane to my theme: the asylum movement and the public-school reform, just to name two examples. These subjects have already been explored so comprehensively by others that it would be redundant to retrace their steps and rehearse their conclusions. In general, I have found these related studies quite compatible with my own findings. Nor is this yet another history of the response of the Protestant churches to the city. I have profited by the work of John R. Bodo, Timothy Smith, Robert T. Handy, Henry F. May, and others, but my focus is primarily on men and women who, although firmly rooted in the Protestant moral tradition, labored outside the framework of organized religion. Indeed, it was precisely the *failure* of the Protestant churches to exert decisive leverage in the cities that impelled the search for alternative approaches.

I am happy to be able to acknowledge some of the obligations I have incurred in the writing of this book. Wendell Harmon, my friend and former mentor, now at Mount San Antonio College in Pomona, California, introduced me to the study of American intellectual history in 1955, bringing to the subject his characteristic blend of thoughtful inquiry and gentle wit. I hope that Frank Freidel of Harvard University does not find reason here to regret his role in nurturing my interest in urban social control some years ago. More recently, but still as far back as 1970, Frederic C. Jaher of the University of Illinois turned my thoughts to the possibility of writing a broad-scale book on the subject. A fellowship from the John Simon Guggenheim Memorial Foundation in 1973–74 allowed me to begin work in earnest, and subsequent grants from the University of Massachusetts Research Council provided help along the way.

A careful and insightful reading of the manuscript by Henry F. May significantly strengthened the book in both detail and overall conception. Leonard L. Richards and Jack Tager, colleagues at the University of Massachusetts, and Bertram Wyatt-Brown of Case Western Reserve University read and commented helpfully on portions of the manuscript. I have benefited, too, from the suggestions and critical insights of other colleagues, including Mario DePillis, Bruce Laurie, Gerald McFarland, and Stephen Nissenbaum, to mention only those whose fields bear most closely on the subject of this book. Though Stephen Nissenbaum and I have returned to our respective areas of specialization after collaborating on a study of Salem witchcraft, I continue to be challenged by his probing mind, his stimulating historical imagination, and his unfailing intellectual generosity.

My wife, Ann, again providing the unsparing stylistic criticism I have come to depend on in my writing, read the entire manuscript, and is responsible for improvements at many points. Alex and Katie, although finding the subject matter of the book somewhat arcane, entered enthusiastically into the process of trying to select a title.

Jay Newsome, an uncommonly skilled and helpful undergraduate research assistant, checked hundreds of quotations and bibliographical notes, saving me from an embarrassing number of errors. (For any that remain, of course, I bear entire responsibility.)

Although the secondary sources upon which I have drawn are acknowledged in the notes, I wish here to credit the host of scholars whose work served to illuminate aspects of my subject. In some instances, works published after my own manuscript was essentially complete have confirmed or run counter to my conclusions in ways that make me regret that I did not have the opportunity to read them sooner. I am thinking, for example, of Thomas Bender's *Toward an Urban Vision: Ideas and Institutions in Nineteenth-Century America*; Thomas W. Laqueur's *Religion and Respectability: Sunday Schools and Working Class Culture, 1780–1850*; Park Dixon Goist's *From Main Street to State Street: Town, City, and Community in America*; Joseph F. Kett's *Rites of Passage: Adolescence in America 1790 to the Present*; and Don S. Kirschner's "The Ambiguous Legacy: Social Justice and Social Control in the Progressive Era" (*Historical Reflections*, summer 1975).

I find myself particularly beholden to many members of the library profession—thanks, then, to the library staffs of the University of Massachusetts, Amherst College, Smith College, Mount

Holyoke College, and, further afield, Harvard University, Clark University, Johns Hopkins University, the Bancroft Library of the University of California at Berkeley, the Moody Bible Institute, the Gordon-Conwell Theological Seminary, the Young Men's Christian Association national headquarters in New York, and the public libraries of Boston, Baltimore, Saint Louis, and Dayton. All of the above treated me with courteous helpfulness on my visits, or responded graciously to written requests for assistance. Daniel Boorstin, the Librarian of Congress, most helpfully passed along to the appropriate staff member a last-minute request for assistance with a small but thorny research problem. My special thanks go to the women of the interlibrary loan office at the University of Massachusetts who processed what must have seemed an endless stream of requests with good-natured efficiency and a genuine interest in facilitating my research. The staff at the University of Massachusetts photographic center was similarly helpful.

I would like to express appreciation, too, to the editorial staff at the Harvard University Press and especially to Aida DiPace Donald, editor for the social sciences, whose early and sustained confidence in the work, not to mention specific suggestions for improvement, had much to do with bringing this book to fruition.

And lastly I wish to make a personal observation. In 1911, my grandfather William H. Boyer founded a mission in a working-class district of the industrial city of Dayton, Ohio. I grew up attending that mission, with its revivals, its tract rack, and its Sunday school. I also frequented a playground near my home under the watchful eye of summer supervisors hired by the city. And I took swimming lessons at the local YMCA, where, though I never advanced beyond the Minnow Club, the slogan painted on the locker-room wall was indelibly engraved on my memory: "You Are Never Fully Dressed until You Are Wearing a Smile." Just as deeply embedded in my consciousness are two other anonymous imperatives that leaped out from the sides of downtown refuse containers and the garbage trucks that plied the city's streets: "Dayton, the City Beautiful" and "Let's Make Dayton America's Cleanest City!"

Not yet having had the benefit of graduate training in history, I did not then realize that I was in my own boyish experience recapitulating a century or more of urban moral-control effort. But, in retrospect, I can see that the experiences of those years, no less than the books and articles I have read since, have had their part in shaping what I say in this book.

P.B.

Contents

PART THREE
The Gilded Age:
Urban Moral Control in a Turbulent Time

PART FOUR
The Progressives and the City:
Common Concerns, Divergent Strategies

Illustrations

Between pages 36 and 37:

Lyman Beecher. From *The Autobiography of Lyman Beecher*, ed. Barbara W. Cross (Cambridge, Mass., Harvard University Press, 1961), I, 153.

Lewis Tappan. From Bertram Wyatt-Brown, *Lewis Tappan and the Evangelical War Against Slavery* (Cleveland, The Press of Case Western Reserve University, 1969), frontispiece.

Tract illustrations. From *Tracts of the American Tract Society: General Series* (New York, n.d.), vols. I, nos. 19 and 35; II, no. 41; VI, frontispiece; XI, no. 444.

William E. Dodge. From D. Stuart Dodge, *Memorials of William E. Dodge* (New York, Anson D. F. Randolph, 1887), frontispiece.

Eleazer Lord. From Kenneth Lord, *Certain Members of the Lord Family Who Settled in New York City in the Early 1800's, Descendants of Thomas Lord of Hartford, Conn.* (privately printed, 1945), p. 40. Reprinted courtesy of Arthur S. Lord.

Model Sunday school. From *The Teacher Taught: An Humble Attempt to Make the Path of the Sunday-School Teacher Straight and Plain* (Philadelphia, American Sunday School Union, 1839), p. 46.

Shame as a mode of Sunday school discipline. From *Plain and Easy Directions for Forming Sunday Schools* (New York, New-York Sunday School Union Society, 1826), p. 72.

A city Sunday school of the 1950s. From Emmett Dedmon, *Great Enterprises: 100 Years of the YMCA of Metropolitan Chicago* (New York, Rand McNally, 1957), p. 43. Reprinted by permission of Emmett Dedmon.

Between pages 94 and 95:

Draft riots of July 1863. From Joel Tyler Headley, *The Great Riots of New York, 1712–1873* (New York, 1873; reissued, New York, Dover Publications, 1971), p. 169. Reprinted by permission of Dover Publications, Inc.

Marketing the "Wicked City." From George Ellington, *The Women of New York; or, The Underworld of the Great City* (New York, The New York Book Co., 1869), title page.

The murder of Helen Jewett. From *The Truly Remarkable Life of the Beautiful Helen Jewett* (New York, 1878), reproduced in James L. Crouthamel, "James Gordon Bennett, the New York Herald, and the Development of Newspaper Sensationalism," *New York History*, 54 (July 1973), 304. Reprinted by permission of the New York State Historical Association.

Robert M. Hartley. Reprinted by permission of the New York Historical Society.

An 1849 Philadelphia riot. From *The Life and Adventures of Charles Anderson Chester, The Notorious Leader of the Philadelphia "Killers" Who Was Murdered While Engaged in the Destruction of the California House* (Philadelphia, 1850), reprinted in David Grimsted, "Rioting in Its Jacksonian Setting," *American Historical Review*, 77 (April 1972), 391.

Charles Loring Brace. From *The Life of Charles Loring Brace Chiefly Told in His Own Letters*, Edited by His Daughter (New York, Charles Scribner's Sons, 1894), p. 209.

*The city reveals the moral ends of being,
and sets the awful problems of life.*
　　　　—Edwin H. Chapin, *Moral Aspects of City Life* (1853)

It was in the 1820s that Americans began to awake to a fundamental transformation that was going on around them: a society that had been overwhelmingly rural since its foundation in the seventeenth century was entering a period of explosive urban growth. For many—churchmen, moralists, members of old elites, and even well-to-do and upwardly aspiring city dwellers—this development was profoundly disturbing. Would religion and morality find nurture in the cities? Indeed, would the social order itself be able to survive this transformation?

The first organized response to the urban moral challenge was that of American evangelicalism—one of the more dynamic and expansive social forces of the early-nineteenth-century era. Though the evangelical churches and revivalists were frustrated in their efforts to influence urban America directly, the great evangelical voluntary organizations that flourished in these years —especially the Bible societies, the tract societies, and the Sunday schools—moved into the cities in a major way. Although these undertakings did not ultimately live up to their leaders' expectations, they were nevertheless extremely important. They influenced countless numbers of Jacksonian city dwellers—not only the poor at whom they were particularly aimed but also the thousands of volunteers who represented the bones and sinews of these efforts. Further, the leaders of these undertakings articulated assumptions and developed strategies that would, under various guises, remain influential throughout the entire hundred-year span of urban moral-control effort in America. The most basic of these assumptions was that the key to dealing with the urban challenge lay in re-creating in the cities the moral order of the village. The varied and resourceful attempts of these early-nineteenth-century evangelicals to accomplish this objective remains one of the most fascinating chapters in the history of urban reform in the United States.

1

The Urban Threat Emerges

A STRATEGY TAKES SHAPE

"I look upon the size of certain American cities, and especially on the nature of their population, as a real danger." In penning these words after a visit to the United States in 1831–1832, Alexis de Tocqueville expressed a viewpoint widely held among the well-to-do Americans with whom he had conversed. For earlier generations, "the city" had typically figured either as a metaphor (John Winthrop's "We shall be as a city upon a hill") or as a distant, somewhat hypothetical menace. When Thomas Jefferson in 1785 denounced city mobs as the social equivalent of bodily sores, he clearly believed that with timely forewarning, the new nation could avoid such hazards. And with reason: in 1785 America's largest city, Philadelphia, had only about 40,000 residents, and the fourth largest, Charleston, perhaps 15,000.[1]

But even then, portents of change were gathering. Although well over 90 percent of Americans still lived on farms or in villages and small towns, the rural/urban ratio was already beginning to tilt. From 1790 to 1840, every decade but one saw a rate of urban growth nearly double that for the population as a whole, and greater than *any* post–Civil War decade![2] In its earliest stages, urbanization was most vividly evident in four major coastal centers—Boston, New York, Philadelphia, and Baltimore—and in such lesser Atlantic ports as Portland, Salem, Providence, New Haven, and Charleston. In the forty years from 1790 to 1830, Philadelphia more than tripled in size, and New York experienced a more than sixfold increase, from 33,000 to 215,000.[8] Modest enough by later standards (New York's 1830 population would have placed her sixty-first among American cities in 1970, just ahead of Corpus Christi, Texas), such growth was impressive indeed to the men and women who lived through it.

The rural population was increasing, too, of course, but the cities, unlike the farms, were changing qualitatively as well as quantitatively. Until the late eighteenth century, the coastal cities of British America were compact and comparatively stable places where merchants, artisans, clergymen, lawyers, and laborers lived in close proximity to each other and to their shops, churches, and taverns. (Benjamin Franklin's nearest neighbors in Philadelphia were a merchant, a cooper, and a plumber.)[4] Pauperism, drunkenness, bawdy houses, and occasional rowdyism were a part of the prerevolutionary urban scene—but a familiar and tolerable part, usually found near the wharves or in distinct outlying districts.

The surge of urban growth after 1790 unleashed social forces that would ultimately shatter this cohesive pattern forever. As newcomers crowded in, long-settled families pulled up stakes, merchants moved away from their shops, and shipmasters fled the congestion of the wharves for more distant residences, leaving what had been stable, socially diverse neighborhoods to begin the long decline into slums.[5] The protracted period of business depression and unemployment that has been labeled the "Panic of 1819" hastened this process of urban decay and also contributed to a high rate of population turnover: that ceaseless flow of people into and out of the cities which has from the beginning been a central feature of the American urban experience.[6] And if the foreign immigrants arriving in steadily growing numbers were less numerous and less alien-seeming than those of later periods, they nevertheless reflected a wide ethnic, linguistic, and religious spectrum. (The number of Roman Catholics in America grew from 30,000 in 1790 to 600,000 in 1830.) Of the native-born Americans moving into the cities, many were youthful, unmarried males—those "young men from the country" who would soon figure prominently in sermons and tracts as a rootless, unstable element particularly vulnerable to the city's temptations.[7]

But the strangeness of the city was not simply a matter of size, physical expansion, or even of a shifting demographic profile. The very rhythm and pace of life differed in ways that were as unsettling as they were difficult to define. From the early 1800s on, observers commented on the impersonality and bustle of urban existence, the lack of human warmth, the heedless jostlings of the free-floating human atoms that endlessly surged through the streets. Very early, the realization dawned that the urban order represented a volatile and unpredictable deviation from a familiar norm. As early as 1818, a visitor commented on the "unsocial indifference" of New Yorkers; that same year, an observer of life in Pittsburgh wrote: "A next door neighbor is, with them, frequently unknown, and months and years pass, without their exchanging with each other the ordinary compliments of friendship and goodwill."[8]

Among Americans of the early national period, this first wave of urban growth, with its attendant social dislocations, aroused feelings that were decidedly mixed, not to say contradictory. To many an insecure democrat, the vision of a nation criss-crossed by a network of great cities was a source of vicarious pride. Foreign visitors noted with amusement the prevailing national assumption that the size of a New York or a Philadelphia somehow proved that Americans were virtuous and their system of government sound.[9] But beneath the bravado eddied currents of apprehension. This generation sensed that in ways as yet unclear, urbanization posed profound threats to the social and moral order they knew. As they attempted to reduce this apprehension to manageable terms, some observers singled out the more obvious surface features of urban life. In sermons, speeches, and periodical literature, one begins to encounter somber warnings about the prevalence of intemperance, gambling, sexual immorality, profanity, and Sabbath breaking in the cities.

In fact, of course, all these manifestations of human perversity had been prevalent enough in the villages and towns of colonial America, as the most casual dip into the court records makes clear. But in the unfamiliar urban setting, they took on a more menacing aspect. The bawdy servant girl was transformed into the painted prostitute soliciting on the street. The village tavern became the beer cellar in the slum; the neighborly wager on a horse race or a cockfight, the organized gambling of the city. The unruly child and the discontented farm youth quarreling with his father became the multiplied thousands of street arabs and young urban newcomers who seemed to have broken free of all familial control.

Would Jefferson's forebodings come true? Would the web of community restraint be utterly swept aside, turning the emerging cities into seething cauldrons of licentious, brutalized creatures contemptuous of morality, responsible to no one, owning no master but the lustful dictates of their own wicked flesh? A lurid prospect, but no more so than it appeared to some in the opening years of the nineteenth century. The outrages and debaucheries that had engulfed Paris in 1789 were fresh in memory, and who could be sure that American cities were immune to such outbreaks? It was in these decades that the clichés which would dominate a century of writing about the city were minted. Big cities, announced a New York journalist of the 1830s, obviously convinced that he was offering a keen and fresh insight, were "hotbeds of vice and immorality."[10]

It would be misleading to insist on either the intensity or the prevalence of such fears in this earliest phase of America's long struggle to come to terms with the city. The threat was still finite; the emergence of a few big cities on the Atlantic coast hardly made the United States an urban nation. For many, perhaps a majority, pride won out over apprehension.

But for an influential segment of the population—Protestant churchmen, members of the upper class whose status was rooted in a preurban order, members of an emerging urban commercial class whose religious outlook and economic interest converged at this point—the immorality and social volatility of the cities became matters of compelling concern. Although these groups will figure prominently in the chapters that follow, it is important to stress that they were not alone. Behind them were innumerable rural folk and city dwellers of the middle and even the poorer ranks who shared their fears, anxiously read their grim pronouncements, and supported the reform efforts they initiated.

The city, of course, was not the only source of concern in these years. The westward movement was also, for many, a matter of profound anxiety. If the pioneers pouring into the upper Mississippi Valley in the post-1815 years outran the social and religious restraints of the settled East, might not social chaos and political disintegration result? Some feared that the vast interior would succumb to Roman Catholicism or sink into barbarism—a prospect the Connecticut theologian Horace Bushnell considered entirely possible as late as the 1840s.[11]

As sources of apprehension, the West and the cities had much in common. Indeed, they sometimes merged completely, for "the West" included not only isolated settlements but such emerging urban centers as Pittsburgh, Buffalo, Saint Louis, and Cincinnati.[12] And even when not so obviously linked, the two fears were really but facets of a single fundamental concern. The burgeoning interior and the burgeoning cities both represented massive challenges to the established social order, and fears about the menace of the city were reinforced and intensified by the parallel menace of the wilderness.

What was to be done? One natural response of those troubled by urban vice and social disorder was to call upon the civil authorities. After all, in the colonial town the magistrates had played an important role in upholding the moral order, and it was reasonable to expect them to perform a comparable function in the cities. To the dismay of many, however, it early became evident that municipal officialdom was going to be hard pressed just to maintain essential services and control out-and-out crime, let alone oversee the morality of the general populace. And even had city governments been up to the task, they would in most instances not have been accessible to would-be moral reformers for such purposes. For this first great era of urban growth was also (by no coincidence, of course) the period when an older political order based on deference to elite figures gave way to a system based on the manipulation of a mass electorate.[13]

In the larger cities, this meant the emergence of political organizations that drew their strength from precisely those who (from the reformers' perspective) represented the greatest menace: the poor, the immigrants, the laboring masses. The politicians who surfaced in the wake of these developments were often men for whom preservation of a traditional moral code was not a matter of high priority. In Philadelphia, the 1820s saw the rise of Joel Barlow Sutherland, a corrupt and demagogic political boss who represented, for conservatives, an ominous portent of the future of urban politics. In 1829, the Philadelphia Quaker reformer Roberts Vaux, distressed by moral conditions in his city, announced his support for President Jackson, in hope that Old Hickory's personal rectitude would inspire a general moral rebirth. His reward was to find himself at odds with Jackson's great Philadelphia enemy Nicholas Biddle, who proceeded to engineer his removal from every moral-uplift society in which he held office! Vaux died in 1836, having learned a bitter lesson in the difficulty of achieving urban moral reform through politics.[14]

New York City reformers were learning the same lesson. In 1821, the year the New York electorate was enlarged by some 30 percent through enfranchisement of the poorer classes, a Manhattan moral-reform society complained of the "total aversion" of elected authorities toward their proposals for combating gambling, intemperance, and other evils. A veteran of many urban moral-uplift struggles in New York later recalled how in these years "profligate jurors, unprincipled attorneys, and debauched judges" repeatedly thwarted his efforts. The turbulence of New York City politics in the late 1820s and 1830s—the rise of Tammany Hall, the election of a Tammany-backed mayor in 1834, and the emergence of radical Tammany splinter groups like the anticlerical Workingmen's party—did little to dispel such gloomy assessments.[15]

In Boston, the legal transition from town to city in 1822 underscored the break with the past, and the mayoral election of 1823 was widely viewed as evidence of the break-up of the old governing elite and the emergence of a new and somewhat disreputable political group described by one observer—the young Boston schoolteacher Ralph Waldo Emerson—as "a parcel of demagogues . . . hoping for places as partisans which they could not achieve as citizens."[16]

Nor was the national political scene much more promising. Occasionally, moral reformers called for a direct entry into the national political arena, but the response was not encouraging. In 1827 the Reverend Ezra Stiles Ely, a Philadelphia Presbyterian, urged the formation of a Christian party in politics ("the Presbyterians alone could bring half a million electors into the field"), but his proposal was ridiculed in the press and even dismissed as impractical by many of his fellow clerics.[17] The uselessness of the federal government as a moral-control instrument was heavily underscored by the failure of a massive evangelical effort in 1828–1829 to force the discontinuation of Sunday mail delivery. Under the leadership of the General Union for Promoting the Observance of the Christian Sabbath set up by the Reverend Lyman Beecher and others, church members bombarded Congress with Sabbatarian petitions. The Jacksonian-dominated Senate post-office committee rejected them in a strongly worded report in 1829, however, and three years later the General Union disbanded.[18]

This embarrassing debacle had a traumatic effect on moral reformers: "At one time, Christians were much engaged in petitioning Congress to suspend the Sabbath Mails," the evangelist Charles G. Finney observed later, "and now they seem to be ashamed of it"; in 1839 a Philadelphia minister, the Reverend John Todd, vividly recalled the "stream of invective and obloquy" that had engulfed "the good of the land" a decade before. As a test of the political system's viability as an agency of moral oversight, the Sabbatarian campaign had provided a clear and discouraging answer. Sabbath neglect was symptomatic of a larger "moral desolation" in America, wrote Todd, and Washington had proved unable even to deal with the symptom! It was "perfectly obvious," he concluded, that on moral issues "legislation and laws are impotent."[19] The denial of a charter to the American Sunday School Union by the Pennsylvania legislature in 1828— amid cheers in Philadelphia's poor wards and Democratic charges that the ASSU wished to become "dictator to the consciences of thousands"—underscored the bleak truth: with traditional modes of moral restraint crumbling under the pressure of urban growth and frontier expansion, elected public officials could not be depended upon to step into the breech.[20]

If not politics, what of the church? Evangelical Protestantism was a powerful institutional force in Jacksonian America, and determined efforts were made to bring its influence to bear upon the burgeoning cities. As early as 1816 a Female Missionary Society launched religious work among the poor of New York City, and similar groups emerged in Philadelphia, Charleston, and Boston. In 1817 the missionary supported by the New York ladies, the Reverend Ward Stafford, warned that the city's poor wards harbored "a great mass of people beyond the restraints of religion," including "thousands who are grossly vicious." Sharing Stafford's concern, a group of New York Presbyterian evangelicals led by merchants William E. Dodge and the brothers Arthur and Lewis Tappan in the early 1830s established a string of missions in rented storefronts, theaters, public halls, and even warehouse lofts throughout the city. By 1832 these "free churches" (no pew rent was required) had attracted about 4,000 members. Some churches in New York and other cities established "satellite" branches in underchurched neighborhoods, supported by volunteers from the parent congregation. Not to be outdone by the evangelicals, Unitarian leader William Ellery Channing in 1826 designated the Reverend Joseph Tuckerman as minister to Boston's poor. With neither meetinghouse nor specific parish bounds, Tuckerman was soon pursuing a busy schedule of visitation and extemporaneous preaching in the city's slums.[21]

Much energy was expended, too, in channeling cityward the waves of revivalism that periodically swept over America in the early nineteenth century. Early Methodist evangelists included New York, Providence, Baltimore, and other cities on their itineraries; by 1820, an estimated 6,000 Methodist revival converts in New York had become regular churchgoers. The English visitor Mrs. Frances Trollope was much impressed by the impact of a Cincinnati revival in 1828. Three years later, in the wake of a revival in Rochester, New York, an enthusiast reported that the city's "grog shops" had closed, the theater had been converted into a livery stable, and the circus arena into a soap and candle factory! The evangelist who achieved this feat, the famed Charles G. Finney, campaigned in Philadelphia and New York City as early as 1827–1828 and in 1832 established a kind of permanent revival center in a rented theater near Five Points, the heart of New York's worst slum.[22]

But the overall result of these early efforts to win for the church in the cities the moral hegemony it enjoyed in rural and small-town America was discouraging. With its ministers, its meetinghouses, and its numerical strength still overwhelmingly concentrated in the country, Protestantism found it exceptionally difficult to keep pace with the urban surge. In New York, the growth rate of Methodism, despite its early successes, lagged far behind the city's population increases after 1820. The unsettledness of city life continually undermined the efforts of the churches. In letters of 1836–1839, Philadelphia's John Todd, pastor of the Clinton Street Congregational Church, expressed his frustration: "Let no man who values his soul, or his body, ever go into a great city to become a pastor . . . You cast the salt into the water, and soon see that you are trying to salt a river; it all runs away at once."[23]

Nor did revivalism prove the hoped-for panacea. "Cities are poor places to promote Revivals," complained one evangelical leader in a letter to Finney, and fellow laborers such as Asahel Nettleton and Jacob Knapp, frustrated in repeated assaults on the major urban centers, shared his pessimism. In an 1830 novel of New York life, an emotional revival is dismissed as "a passing fervor, a gust of passion." Even in the generally receptive Middle West, notes Richard Wade, revival fires "licked very close to the towns, but could not find inflammable material in them."[24]

Not even Finney could prevail in the metropolis. On his first visit to New York, his supporter Lewis Tappan was forced to concede (in the privacy of his diary) that his preaching "did not so affect the audience or have so great an impression of abilities as I had expected." The Reverend Gardiner Spring of the city's Brick Presbyterian Church, though eager enough to promote revival, found himself repelled by Finney's country coarseness and "vulgarity."[25] The anticipated revival still did not materialize after Finney began preaching full-time in New York in 1832, and in a series of "Lectures on the Revival of Religion" late in 1834, he betrayed his mounting frustration. Recalling the outpourings he had witnessed elsewhere, Finney concluded that the reason "we never have such things here in New York" lay in the "pride" of the city's professing Christians. With urban church members so "worldly," so given over to "the vanity of earthly things," the masses naturally remained cold to religion's appeal. As the lectures progressed, Finney became almost strident in berating his middle-class listeners. "It is easy to see why revivals do not prevail in a great city. How can they? Just look at God's witnesses . . . They . . . go bowing at the shrine of fashion, and then wonder there are no revivals . . . Do you suppose . . . I can promote a revival by preaching over your heads, while you live as you do? . . . [M]ost of you are right in the way of revival. Your spirit and deportment produce an influence on the world against religion."[26] Soon after, Finney left New York for a teaching position at Oberlin College in Ohio.

Despite his self-justificatory tone, Finney had put his finger on a key issue in the urban religious situation: social class. Such success as urban Protestantism did enjoy in these years was primarily among the more settled and comfortable ranks: the families of professional men, merchants, clerks, and skilled artisans; the more successful of the native-born newcomers. The masses below that level—the unskilled laborers, the destitute, the transient, the immigrants—remained largely outside the fold. Even so evangelistic a congregation as Gardiner Spring's Brick Presbyterian Church drew its membership almost entirely from "the middle ranks of life." In Rochester, scene of Finney's greatest urban success, it was not the laboring classes but those higher on the scale who mainly responded. And, despite the efforts of some female members of Finney's Five Points tabernacle to "gather in all classes, from the neighborhood round about," his 1834 lectures made clear that the poor did not flock in.[27]

Nor was it just hardened sinners who stayed away from the city churches. The New York Female Bible Society in 1822 reported a case that probably reflected the experience of many newcomers. "An interesting family in Elm-street, who arrived here from Scotland last July, showed us certificates of their having been members of the Presbyterian church there. Since their arrival in this country they had never attended public worship, not from any want of inclination, but on account of pecuniary inability to purchase or hire seats, as they had been told that without so doing, they would not be admitted into our churches."[28]

Finney, as we have seen, attributed this exclusiveness to middle-class snobbishness, and other frustrated churchmen shared his view. "Should Christians, all cleansed by the same blood and Spirit, treat other Christians as 'common'?" cried one minister in these years.[29] No doubt many urban churchgoers of the upper and middle ranks did shrink from sharing a pew or communion cup with shabby laborers or impoverished immigrants, but even with the best will in the world, it would have been difficult for the established city churches, with their limited capacity, settled membership, parish orientation, and traditional pew-rental system of support, to absorb the massive influx of Protestant newcomers. (Catholic immigrants, of course, posed an even more insurmountable challenge.) There were psychological barriers as well, related to social class but not necessarily rooted in mere snobbery. For the urban middle class, the church represented one of the few islands of stability and moral authority in an unsettled social environment. To have flung open its doors to all comers or attracted throngs of seekers and new converts through vigorous evangelistic effort would have jeopardized its already existing social and religious function. In a sense, the churches' failure to play a larger urban role was the price they paid to continue the limited, but not insignificant, role they were already playing.

For a variety of reasons, then, the Protestant churches failed to emerge as dominant centers of moral authority or social cohesion for the expanding urban population of the Jacksonian era. With the dawning realization of this fact came the first great innovative phase of the long effort to devise alternative mechanisms of moral control for urban America.

Evangelical Voluntarism and the City

Although American Protestantism proved frustratingly unable to exert its influence directly in the cities of the 1820s and 1830s, the evangelical impulse played a crucial role in shaping the voluntarist urban moral-control strategies that did emerge and in inspiring the thousands of volunteers who implemented those strategies.

Early-nineteenth-century evangelical voluntarism was a product of the broader religious situation of the period. To be an evangelical leader or devout layman in these years was often to feel oneself under siege. The cities and the West loomed as threatening imponderables. Politically, the century was ushered in by the triumph of Jeffersonian Republicanism, with its whiff of sansculotte anticlericalism and moral laxness. The disestablishment of Congregationalism in New England in the wake of Jeffersonian advances showed the vulnerability of even the strongest bastions of piety. Then came Jacksonianism—hardly more congenial, as we have seen, to the social and political objectives of evangelical activists. On the religious front, not only did Rome seem a growing menace, but Unitarianism and other heresies were seducing many from the very heart of the fold.

Far from being disheartened, however, American evangelicals reacted with an aggressive counter thrust. Revivalism was one expression of this response. Another was a lush flowering of voluntary moral and religious societies led by evangelicals, financed by evangelicals, and dedicated to furthering evangelical purposes. Transcending denominational bounds and closely patterned on British precedents, these associations promoted a wide variety of causes: training foreign missionaries; printing Bibles, tracts, and uplifting books; founding domestic missions and Sunday schools; marshaling public opinion against a broad range of moral evils.[30] But although not initially directed exclusively or even primarily at the city, evangelical voluntarism early emerged as a powerful and versatile weapon in the intensifying struggle against urban immorality and social disorder.

In promoting voluntarism as a moral-reform strategy, no one played a more crucial role than Lyman Beecher. It was at the initiative of this indefatigable revivalist and churchman, then a thirty-seven-year-old minister in Litchfield, Connecticut, that some thirty Congregational clergymen met at New Haven in October 1812 to establish a statewide society for the "Suppression of Vice and the Promotion of good Morals." The immediate impetus, as Beecher later acknowledged, was the disturbing political situation in Connecticut, where not only were the Republicans making inroads but the Federalists were ending their long-standing practice of consulting the state's ecclesiastical leadership in the selection of candidates.[31]

Although these political developments were troubling, Beecher's sermon inaugurating the Good Morals Society placed the issue in a broader context and invoked a vision of the power of voluntarism that would inspire evangelicals for generations. Detailing a large catalogue of alarming moral trends—public inebriation, profanity, Sabbath desecration—and blaming them in part on the rise of cities, Beecher declared: "The mass is changing. We are becoming another people. Our habits have held us long after those moral causes that formed them have ceased to operate. These habits, at length, are giving way . . . We have always been so accustomed to restraint that we had imagined human nature in our nation incapable of the violence manifested in other nations."[32] People who once would have been deterred from wrongdoing by "shame alone," Beecher went on, now flaunted their contempt for the established order and the proprieties. If action were not taken quickly, society would succumb to "Sabbath-breakers, rum-selling, tippling folk, infidels"—and a catchall category he labeled the "ruff-scruff."[33] (In another sermon of the period, he warned that without vigorous countermeasures hordes of urban poor would soon "swarm in your streets, and prowl about your dwellings . . .")[34]

The task of the moment, Beecher insisted, was to revive the power of shame through organized social disapproval. With old communal patterns breaking down and the political influence of the ministry crumbling, "local voluntary associations of the wise and the good" must step in to exert a moral force "distinct from that of the government, independent of popular suffrage, superior in potency to individual efforts, and competent to enlist and preserve the public opinion." Such associations—"a sort of disciplined moral militia"—would discountenance individual vice and bring collective pressure to bear against organized evil.[35] Warming to his theme, Beecher envisioned a nationwide network of voluntary moral-control societies to "exert a salutary, general influence . . . ; retrieve what we have lost; and perpetuate forever our civil and religious institutions."[36]

In Beecher's scheme it was crucial that the "wise and good" also be the influential, and as head of the Good Morals Society he installed his Litchfield parishioner Tapping Reeve, a jurist of national repute. The goal, of course, was to maintain elite moral hegemony by playing upon ingrained habits of deference—but now by voluntaristic means rather than through legal coercion or a formal religious establishment. Indeed, Beecher in 1818 professed to believe that disestablishment was "the best thing that ever happened to the state of Connecticut," since moral leadership could be more effectively exercised through voluntary effort than through such external badges of status as "queues, and shoe-buckles, and cocked hats, and gold-headed canes."[37]

Lyman Beecher did not invent the voluntary moral-control society. Such groups had emerged in England in the eighteenth century; Yale president Timothy Dwight had established a student Moral Society to marshal college sentiment against vice in 1797 (Beecher's senior year); and short-lived societies for the "suppression of vice" were founded as early as 1809–10 in New York City, Philadelphia, and Pittsburgh.[38] But it was he who emerged as the most articulate spokesman for this highly adaptable new instrument of social control. His initiative in Connecticut clearly influenced the founding of similar groups elsewhere, including the Massachusetts Society for the Suppression of Intemperance (1813), an association of prominent citizens (mostly conservative Federalists) who hoped through their "example and influence" to combat not only intemperance but "every kind of vice and immorality."[39]

Although these early moral-reform associations included rural as well as urban America within their purview, it was the city that would prove their natural habitat, as Beecher himself demonstrated when he moved from Litchfield to Boston in 1826. Distressed to find that "evangelical people had no political influence," he organized an Association of Young Men to combat Boston's more glaring moral defects. To protest liquor sales on the Common, for example, the association drew up a petition, secured the endorsement of numerous religious and civic notables, and "carried into the city council the largest number of signatures ever known before that time to any such document." Similar campaigns were waged against lotteries and Sunday excursion boats.[40]

The 1820s and 1830s saw the emergence in city after city of such voluntary associations to combat urban vice. In Louisville in 1824, for example, a committee of thirty local dignitaries led a campaign against "gambling, drunkenness, and other practices subversive to the peace, comfort, and good order of society." One historian, having listed 158 such societies dating from the early 1800s, warns that this is "by no means an exhaustive listing."[41]

Who were the key figures in this effort? Predictably, the evangelical clergy (and their wives) played an important catalytic role.

And occasionally, one finds a national figure—a Tapping Reeve, Benjamin Rush, Francis Scott Key, or John Quincy Adams— lending the luster of his' name. More typically, however, the founders, directors, and principal financial backers of these voluntary moral-uplift societies were locally prominent bankers, merchants, editors, and professional men. Evangelical in religion and conservative in politics, they were usually men of recent wealth who were also comparative newcomers to the cities where they were forging their careers.[42]

Below this relatively small circle was a vast second tier of volunteers who provided the sinews of these societies through financial contributions; day-to-day clerical work; and service on the exposed front lines of the struggle as Sunday school teachers, Bible and tract distributors, crusaders against vice, and laborers in campaigns to elevate the physical and moral condition of the urban poor.

Forgotten today, this dedicated army of urban-morality foot soldiers played a crucial role. Without them, these early voluntarist efforts would have remained mere paper schemes; with them, some at least assumed major importance in the antebellum years. Like junior versions of the top leaders, these volunteers were often first-generation urbanites active in evangelical churches and holding what would later be called white-collar jobs—clerks, accountants, bank tellers—on the lower rungs of the business or professional ladders. Typical of this group are the otherwise obscure Boston youths who joined Lyman Beecher's Association of Young Men: Amasa Walker, for example, a shoe salesman who had migrated from a Connecticut farm; or Julius Palmer, a Rhode Island farm boy working in Boston as a hardware clerk.[43]

An important niche at this organizational level was filled by women: not only ministers' wives but the wives and daughters of strivers in all walks of city life. No longer bound by the domestic routine of rural life, many middle-class women turned with enthusiasm to benevolent and moral-reform societies, which welcomed their support and made good use of their energies.[44]

One way to convey something of the human dimension of these efforts is to consider for a moment a remarkable pair of brothers we have already encountered as supporters of the "free-church" movement and the Finney revivals, Arthur and Lewis Tappan. Natives of the small western Massachusetts town of Northampton, they were the products of a pious late-eighteenth-century Calvinist upbringing. Their father, a dry-goods dealer, also owned some twenty acres of orchard and pastureland where his children loved to roam. In the Northampton of their boyhood, morality rested upon the interconnected influence of family, church, established local elite, and such archaic Puritan social-control devices as the gallows in front of the schoolhouse where noosed wrongdoers were still occasionally compelled to stand as a public example.[45]

The early days in Northampton remained a vivid memory, and in 1848 Arthur and Lewis Tappan and their seven brothers and sisters, all now advanced in years, returned for a family reunion. They visited the "old haunts" where they had "skated, slid downhill, played ball, trundled hoops, and gathered nuts." But the community of their memory had vanished. The town was much bigger, and seemed "full of strangers." Only the great elms and the names on weathering slate tombstones recalled the past. After a few days the nine old people scattered, never again to reassemble.[46]

Despite the nostalgia of their reunion, all of the Tappans had long since abandoned Northampton for larger urban centers. In 1801, at fourteen, Arthur had become a dry-goods clerk in Boston, where he lived in a boardinghouse. A few years later he went into business for himself, first in Portland, Maine, and then in Montreal. Driven from Canada by the War of 1812, he passed three years of "restless inactivity" and then moved to New York. Here he established a fabric-importing business that within a decade became a million-dollar-a-year enterprise. In 1828, having lived in four different locations in the city, he purchased a house in New Haven where his family settled and where he himself spent occasional weekends to gain "respite from the turmoil of the mercantile metropolis." His daughter later recalled how rarely she saw her father in these years; his immersion in commerce was almost total. To conserve time, he ate crackers and water for lunch; to discourage idle conversation, he conducted business standing up. His principal traits, his brother later noted, were "seriousness, dispatch, [and] impatience at non-observance of rules."[47]

The career of Arthur's younger brother Lewis Tappan followed a similar trajectory. In 1805, at seventeen, he, too, left Northampton to become a dry-goods apprentice in Boston. His initial impression was not favorable: the city presented, he wrote home, "a picture of dissipation and laxness in principles, astonishing to any, who does not consider himself the child of chance, and a votary of vice. Decency and order are thought obsolete by these sons of folly." Briefly seduced by Unitarianism, Lewis soon returned to the evangelicals' fold, primarily because of their readiness to "stand up for morality and piety in all places, fearlessly, and at the risk of unpopularity."[48]

Marrying well, he moved to suburban Brookline where he built a large house on a seventeen-acre tract near his wife's family. But for all his qualms about urban immorality, the city exerted a pull Lewis could not resist. In 1828 he entered partnership with his brother Arthur. Moving to New York initially without his family, he lodged in a boardinghouse where he persuaded the landlady to institute regular prayers and religious observances. (One boarder left in disgust.) On the Fourth of July, 1828, Lewis was tempted by the fireworks display in Battery Park, but instead remained at the boardinghouse to organize an evening's hymn-sing from a collection called *Village Favorites*.[49]

With their small-town roots, their suspicions of the city where they were making their fortune, and their own periodically disrupted family and community ties, the Tappans threw themselves into a succession of organized efforts to re-create in New York City the kind of moral order they had known in Northampton. Through the 1820s and 1830s they contributed organizational talent and thousands of dollars to a wide range of moral-reform associations. Nor was their commitment merely one of leadership and money. Busy as he was, Arthur Tappan also spent many hours, his brother later recalled, "distributing religious tracts, exploring the destitute portions of the city for scholars for the Sunday-School, visiting prisoners, and endeavoring to allure the young and their parents to church."[50] In many ways, the Tappans epitomize thousands of middle-class, evangelical men and women of the Jacksonian period—a few well known, most obscure—for whom the moral condition of the city was a matter of earnest concern, and who expressed that concern through a variety of voluntary moral-uplift endeavors.

Initially, many of these organizations, like Beecher's Association of Young Men in Boston, concentrated on specific urban evils: gambling, profanity, prostitution, Sabbath breaking, and the other vices in the litany with which we are becoming familiar. Such single-issue crusades had pitfalls, however, as a group of antiprostitution volunteers in New York City learned to their sorrow.

Of all the evidences of the city's corrosive effect on the traditional order, none was more shocking to evangelical newcomers than the prevalence of organized prostitution. In the preurban world, extramarital sexuality had normally been contained within a larger framework of strict social control. It was tolerated as long as the primacy of the community's moral standard was ultimately asserted: through public confession and the marriage rite for the wayward young, periodic prosecution and rituals of public shame for chronic offenders. But brothels that operated openly and prostitutes who brazenly walked the city streets were flagrant reminders of the ineffectiveness of such traditional restraints in the urban setting. They showed how readily, in the anonymity of the city, men and women could break free of community control.

Nor was it mere chance that the first antiprostitution campaign arose in New York City. New York had surpassed Philadelphia as the nation's largest city by 1810, and with the opening of the Erie Canal in 1825, its primacy was assured. As in many other areas of endeavor, we shall find New Yorkers time and again taking the lead in urban social-control undertakings.

In 1830 John R. McDowall, a twenty-nine-year-old Canadian studying at Princeton Theological Seminary, came to New York for a summer of voluntary religious work. Quickly, however, his attention was riveted upon a single issue: prostitution. Conducting a one-man investigation of this "gangrenous canker," McDowall in 1831 published his *Magdalen Report,* an exposé alleging that New York harbored 10,000 prostitutes. "How long," he cried in a second tract, "will the people suffer their families to be exposed to the deadly, unchecked tide of moral contagion that is rolling as the waves of the ocean over our city?"[51] Securing financial backing from Arthur Tappan and other evangelical merchants, McDowall transformed a run-down Five Points boardinghouse into the Asylum for Females Who Have Deviated from the Path of Virtue—or, for brevity's sake, Magdalen Asylum. Few prostitutes responded, however, and Tappan soon withdrew his support; "we saw no fruits of our labors," declared the always profit-conscious merchant.[52]

But McDowall's crusade gained a significant if brief new lease on life in May 1834 when several New York City women founded the New York Female Moral Reform Society, with Mrs. Charles G. Finney as "directress." John McDowall was hired as agent; a journal, the *Advocate of Moral Reform,* was founded; and auxiliaries sprang up in Boston and elsewhere in New York and New England. Under female sponsorship the movement's focus shifted in subtle ways. Whereas McDowall had dwelt on the danger that "depraved and abandoned females" represented to innocent young men, the Female Moral Reform Society portrayed the prostitutes as innocent victims of male lust. From this perspective they crusaded against the double sexual standard and supported a revived Magdalen Asylum to rescue their exploited sisters and train them as domestics or for some other acceptable social role.[53]

In focusing on the prostitute's male patron, these reformers went to the heart of a dilemma confronting those troubled by moral conditions in the city: the fact that the cloak of anonymity permitted city dwellers to commit all manner of moral transgressions without fear of exposure or censure. It was a problem that had been articulated as early as 1817 by New York City missionary Ward Stafford. In the "well-regulated village," he told the

Female Missionary Society that year, "the character, and circumstances of every family are almost necessarily known"; in the city, by contrast, "there are, strictly speaking, no neighborhoods . . . [W]e do not expect that all who live near each other should enter into habits of intimacy." If patterns of village moral oversight could be re-created in the city, Stafford suggested, the transformation would be dramatic.

> Were those who are pious and in comfortable circumstances to become so much acquainted with those who live near them as to ascertain their character and condition, . . . it would produce the most salutary effects . . . The very sight of the moral and pious is a check to the wicked. Should respectable persons simply *pass through* particular streets every day, and *look* at those who now exhibit in those streets all the degradation of their character, it would soon cause them to hide their heads.[54]

Needless to say, such sidewalk patrols had not materialized in the intervening years; indeed, with continued urban expansion, the "respectable" and the "vicious" had grown still more remote from each other, permitting—so it seemed—prostitution and other vices to proliferate. The Female Moral Reform Society's plan for dealing with this problem at least had the virtue of simplicity: it proposed that "companies of pious males or females" be organized to station themselves outside brothels and that the *Advocate of Moral Reform* publish the names of men (especially the socially prominent) observed entering and leaving! If "the licentious . . . are not ashamed of their debasing vice," the *Advocate* declared, "we will not be ashamed to expose them." Through "fear of detection," urban sexual vice would be curbed.[55]

The social dynamic underlying this scheme is clear enough. It was an attempt to devise an urban analogue to the informal, but continuous and pervasive, scrutiny of behavior upon which the preurban moral order rested. What had been an organic feature of village life would be re-created in the city through voluntary organized effort, systematic surveillance, and journalistic publicity. Though the tactics differed radically, the underlying aim was the same: to introduce a public dimension into even the most intimate private realm; to reassert society's right to oversee every facet of personal behavior.

This imaginative proposal, however, got nowhere. Indeed, the entire antiprostitution drive of the 1830s proved short-lived. With the premature death of John McDowall in 1836, the Magdalen Asylum closed. Circulation of the *Advocate of Moral Reform* dwindled, and by the end of the decade overt interest in the issue was at a low ebb.[56]

The reasons for the failure were complex. The most obvious was McDowall himself, whose sensationalized approach repelled many. The *New York Observer*, a leading religious periodical of the day, was sharply critical of his methods. A grand jury cited McDowall's writings as a public nuisance in 1834, and soon after, he was suspended by his presbytery. Increasingly gripped by his monomania, McDowall found vice everywhere, recording in his diary that an Erie Canal boatman had "confessed that he was lewd and . . . that most of those who navigated boats were licentious." He welcomed New York's periodic cholera epidemics because they carried off so many evildoers. Toward the end, his attention shifted to obscene books, and he carried about a valise of works like *Fanny Hill* to prove their full horror to doubters.[57] By the time of his death, this wandering fanatic had become an embarrassment even to his supporters.

Furthermore, the antiprostitution campaign had offended an unlikely but powerful coalition of New Yorkers, including not only religious leaders disturbed by the open discussion of sexual matters but also an influential coterie of the old New York elite who resented outsiders' attacks on "their" city. It was they for whom the former mayor and patrician man-about-town Philip Hone spoke when he dismissed the *Magdalen Report* as a "disgraceful document."[58] At the other end of the social scale, the opposition included Tammany Hall and its various radical factions. With their power base among immigrants and laboring men (including a growing number of Catholics), and their suspicion of "special privilege" in religion and morals as in business and politics, these groups intensely mistrusted all Protestant and merchant-supported moral-reform efforts.

However, the central reason for the collapse of the antiprostitution crusade was the impracticality of its urban analogue to preurban mechanisms of social control. Street-hardened New York prostitutes were not to be forced into ersatz "homes" like wayward daughters. (Of the few who did enter the Magdalen Asylum, the sponsors confessed, only four proved "serious and industrious.") Similarly, the proposal to publish the names of men observed entering brothels was an impossibly harsh and rigid substitute for the more subtle social-control methods of the small community. With chance observation, word-of-mouth gossip, and informal social censure as well as legal retribution among its resources, the preurban community could quietly overlook occasional lapses, delicately calibrate the punishment to the circumstances, and, since it involved people who knew each other and would continue to live together, take extenuating considerations into account. The mechanical surveillance-and-exposure system proposed by the Female Moral Reform Society lacked such flexibility and human dimension. This was evidently recognized even by the society itself, for the teams of "pious males or females" to spy on brothels never materialized, and the lists of names never appeared.[59]

Such a heavy-handed attempt to control a specific facet of urban moral behavior could probably have arisen only when urbanization was in its infancy, with memories of preurban modes of social control still fresh. In the prostitution investigations of the early twentieth century, interestingly, the published reports were strictly impersonal, with neither prostitutes nor patrons identified by name. By that time, as we shall see, the hope of achieving large-scale urban moral reform by a literal re-creation of village social-control techniques had been supplanted by a quite different set of assumptions.

Although they hardly represented the wave of the future, the single-issue crusades of the 1820s and 1830s remain interesting, for they reveal this first generation of urban reformers struggling to translate their social-control impulses into workable strategies. Men like Lyman Beecher and the Tappan brothers demonstrated what a powerful instrument the voluntary moral-reform association could be in a pluralist society, but how to utilize it effectively in the city was to prove a chronically troublesome problem. "An annual report, or a public meeting once in twelve months," commented the *New York Post* in an 1821 article on the failure of a short-lived society that had set out to elevate moral standards among the poor, were simply not enough to "arouse the attention and command the zeal and confidence of a great and slumbering metropolis." A New York City organization dedicated to the advancement and moral welfare of young men, observing its fourteenth anniversary in 1834, noted that it was "one of the few exceptions to the multitude of associations which start up around us, and after a short-lived pursuit of unattainable objects, perish and pass to forgetfulness."[60] As a succession of campaigns against one urban vice or another sputtered and collapsed, moralists and reformers became increasingly convinced that the answer did not lie in short-term, whirlwind crusades. The magnitude of the challenge demanded more comprehensive responses.

2

The Tract Societies

TRANSMITTING A
TRADITIONAL MORALITY BY
UNTRADITIONAL MEANS

As awareness of the social implications of urban growth deepened in the Jacksonian period, and the futility of single-issue reform crusades became evident, interest turned toward broader efforts to reshape—more gradually, perhaps, but also more decisively—the fundamental moral contours of the emergent cities. What was needed, many became convinced, were *sustained* undertakings that would be firmly grounded institutionally, adapted to urban realities, not too forbidding economically, and independent of passing gusts of reformist excitement.

For many urban reformers of evangelical leanings, the humble religious tract seemed to fit these specifications precisely. Thanks to a variety of social and technological developments—the spread of literacy, the invention of the steam-driven rotary press, the prolongation of reading time through improved whale-oil lamps and then illuminating gas—the volume and variety of cheap reading matter took a great leap forward in the early nineteenth century.[1] One by-product of this development was the mass-produced religious tract—an innovation whose moral potential in a modernizing society was quickly recognized. Mention of the tract movement may conjure up images of musty, execrably printed leaflets distributed by the nineteenth-century equivalents of little old ladies in tennis shoes: daffy enthusiasts like the character in Wilkie Collins's 1868 mystery novel *The Moonstone*, who rushes through a house stuffing tracts into flower pots, vases, umbrella stands, and every other available orifice. Or it may recall the crusty old Nantucket Quaker Captain Bildad in Melville's *Moby Dick,* pressing a tract entitled "The Latter Day Coming; or No Time to Lose" on the cheerful, uncomprehending pagan Queequeg. In fact, the tract movement in its vigorous early years was a large-scale, coordinated national effort led by prominent public figures and employing strikingly sophisticated techniques of persuasion. Improbable as the fact may seem today, the lowly tract was once welcomed as an important and exciting innovation in the campaign to shore up a threatened moral order.

The tract movement was the child of the Bible society movement, and some attention to the latter is necessary to an understanding of the former. For evangelical Protestants, the Bible itself was the central repository of moral truth, and in the early nineteenth century, much energy went into the printing and mass distribution of the Scriptures. Local groups for this purpose were organized soon after 1800 in Philadelphia, Boston, and New York, and in 1816, emulating London's British and Foreign Bible Society, representatives of these local bodies came together to form the American Bible Society.[2]

In a quite literal sense, the Bible society movement was a product of the rise of the city. The ABS was founded in New York; its headquarters were in New York; and by constitutional provision, two-thirds of its thirty-six directors had to be New Yorkers. The first directors were almost all prominent Manhattan figures, including real-estate developer Henry Rutgers and merchants Divie Bethune and Zechariah Lewis. The first treasurer was Richard Varick, lawyer and former New York mayor. The brisk confidence of urban leaders accustomed to managing complex affairs pervades the society's initial statements. "Concentrated action" to develop a "great system" of Bible production combining "energy of effect with economy of means," asserted the ABS constitution, was essential to assure the "moral cultivation" of a population breaking free of traditional restraints.[3] Furthermore, added an early report, such "concerted action" required a centralization of the enterprise in a single city: the "great commercial metropolis" of New York. "We cannot manufacture missionaries, but we can manufacture Bibles," asserted an ABS spokesman—and manufacture they did! By 1849, nearly six million Bibles and Testaments had poured from Bible House, the ABS's New York City headquarters.[4]

Tirelessly, the ABS insisted that America's greatest moral challenges were her unchurched frontier and her cities. The annual reports of the local ABS auxiliaries and branches make clear that the most active were those of New York, Boston, Philadelphia, Baltimore, and other principal cities. These big-city Bible societies repeatedly stressed that immigrant-fueled population increases made their task especially urgent, and time and again they devised elaborate schemes for dividing up their cities into small subunits and sending out volunteers to distribute the Scriptures on a saturation basis. Every incoming immigrant in New York City received an ABS Bible.[5]

These groups took it as axiomatic that the distribution of God's Word in the cities would have a "restraining effect on vicious habits" and thereby "strengthen the fabric of civil society." Through citywide Bible distribution, asserted the Philadelphia Bible Society in 1822, vice was abating and the "haunts of wickedness" were being abandoned. The Young Men's Bible Society of New York reported in 1835 that a slum ward "destitute of moral culture" had exhibited "decided improvement" following a Bible distribution campaign.[6]

A key role in urban Bible distribution was played by women. "This work is peculiarly fitted to her nature," noted a historian of the ABS in 1849, "and assorts most beautifully with the character given of devoted females in the time of Christ." In Boston, eighty women volunteers, working in teams of two, regularly canvassed the city throughout the 1820s. In 1832 the ABS praised New York's Female Bible Society as one of its "most efficient" auxiliaries. In part this reflected a shrewd recognition by male leaders that women could be invaluable assets in the work; "men might be regarded as intruders," noted the Baltimore Bible Society in 1822, "but what door would be rudely closed against female loveliness; what heart so hard, as to be insensible to the soft and imploring tones of her voice?"[7]

Even when accompanied by "female loveliness," however, the Bible as an instrument for the moral guidance of the masses had certain disadvantages. Its length and the difficulty of its prose diminished its impact when isolated from a liturgical context. In 1827 the American Sunday School Union went so far as to call the Bible "a very unfit book for children to read promiscuously." By 1839 the ABS itself was lamenting the "lack of novelty" in its single publication: "The Bible, though infinitely the best of all books, is ever the same; it ministers little to that spirit of these days which calls for something new and stirring."[8]

As early as the 1820s, though Bibles continued to pour from the ABS presses, increasing interest focused on the *tract*, that versatile little missive which could be written in the vernacular, cheaply printed, easily distributed, and quickly read. By 1832 the Bible Society of Providence conceded that it was not they, but the local tract society volunteers, who were now the leaders in reaching the city's poor.[9]

Though polemical tracts had played a role in Christian history since the Reformation, the modern movement dates from 1799, when the Religious Tract Society was founded in London to systematize the work of British evangelicals like Hannah More and the Reverend George Burder who had earlier begun to publish brief treatises for the moral edification of the masses. The idea crossed the Atlantic with the founding of the New York Religious Tract Society in 1812, when the outbreak of war interrupted the flow of tracts from London. A New England society was established two years later; similar bodies soon emerged in Philadelphia, Baltimore, Providence, and elsewhere; and in May 1825 representatives of these local groups met to form the American Tract Society.[10]

Like the Bible society, the ATS was very much a New York City organization. The headquarters was established in New York; Manhattan notables like textile importer Arthur Tappan and banker Moses Allen were among the principal backers; and the six ministers who composed the first board of directors included the pastors of four major New York Protestant churches. These were, in short, vigorous and energetic young urban evangelicals, convinced that by decisive action they could play a role in shaping America's moral development in their generation and beyond. The Reverend Justin Edwards, a Massachusetts tract society leader, expressed the prevailing confidence when, in an address to an early ATS gathering, he glowingly described the "ease and effect" with which tracts could "speak at the same time to millions"—especially the millions in the West and in the great cities "destitute of that influence which is so essential to the preservation of all our social, civil, and religious blessings." Edwards went on to relate the experience of a New York City volunteer who had left a tract in the sordid slum household of a drunkard. Returning some time later, he had found the place transformed: fighting, disorder, and the bleak stigmata of poverty had disappeared; now "neatness and comfort characterized the dwelling, and peace smiled on every countenance." The drunkard's wife joyously explained the change: "O, the Tract—the Tract—the Tract has got all these nice things! My husband never drank after you gave him the Tract."[11]

Visions of innumerable social transformations like this underlay the vigorous introductory address issued by the ATS directors in 1825. Describing the urgent need to " 'lengthen the cords and strengthen the stakes' that bind together the body politic," the directors confidently asserted that among the most effective means to this end, especially in influencing the poor, were "short, plain, striking, entertaining, and instructive Tracts." Tracts, they continued, were especially well adapted to an emerging nation

of cities, railroads, and commerce. Indeed, the same developments that were eroding older modes of social control simply enhanced their effectiveness. Men and women on journeys could
"scatter them along the roads and . . . spread them before the eye
of the thoughtless traveller; [m]erchants . . . distribute them to
shipmasters, and shipmasters to seamen; men of business . . .
transmit them with every bale of goods." And—a clinching argument: "All this may be done . . . with no loss of time."[12]

Nor did the tract's effectiveness depend on the authority of a
religious establishment or settled patterns of deference: "The
obscure in the meanest condition, can give away a Tract, and,
perhaps, accompany it with a word of advice or admonition . . .
All this may be done in the most inoffensive and unobtrusive
way; with no magisterial authority; no claims of superior wisdom
or goodness; and no alarm to human pride or frowardness."[13]

While the moral implications of urbanization were being contemplated uneasily in many quarters, the ATS directors took a
positive view, assuring potential supporters that concentrating
the endeavor in a single urban center would vastly enhance its
effectiveness. The keys to success, they argued, were mass production, efficient management, and the centralized distribution
of tracts "supplied . . . from one general establishment, one set
of stereotype plates, and one set of engravings, one Board of Managers and Officers, and one centre of transportation." And it was
New York City, they concluded bluntly, that was "destined, in
the wisdom of Divine Providence, to become the centre of these
extended operations."[14] The ATS, in short, was offering a specific
blueprint for harnessing the voluntarist energies whose importance Lyman Beecher had early recognized, linking them to the
technological resources of a major urban center, and marshaling
them against the centrifugal forces of the frontier and the city.

This confidence was soon translated into impressive results.
From its headquarters on Nassau Street in lower Manhattan, the
ATS launched an ambitious publication program. Nearly 700,000
tracts were printed the first year, and that number was soon multiplied many times over. By 1846, in a new five-story, fifty-six
room ATS headquarters, a crew of thirty printers was operating
seventeen late-model steam presses, and nearly a hundred more
employees were at work in the bindery room. By 1850 the ATS
had built up a back-list of more than 500 titles and was annually
producing over 5 million tracts and other publications. Subsidized
by thousands of dollars in annual contributions and endowment
income, these publications were attractively printed, well illustrated, and made available either free or at a nominal cost.[15]

Distribution was as efficient as production. A network of
branches and auxiliaries served as outlet centers, supplying thou-

sands of agents and volunteers. Bulk shipments went to Sunday schools, poorhouses, prisons, orphanages, and immigration depots. In city after city, local tract societies conducted systematic, house-by-house distributions. In 1829, for example, New York City was divided into districts of about sixty families each, with a team of tract volunteers assigned to each. These volunteers visited every household monthly, leaving an ATS tract, offering moral counsel, and gathering data ·to be filed in the district tract society office. (Arthur Tappan helped cover the tough waterfront district.) Other volunteers met incoming ships, seeing to it that immigrants began life in the New World with a tract in their hands. By 1831, according to a contemporary estimate, 6 million tracts had been distributed in New York City alone. At about the same time, the tract agency of the Society of Friends complained that so many tracts were flooding Philadelphia that it was having difficulty disposing of its own output![16]

But to understand the importance of the tract as an instrument of social control in the early republic one must go beyond organizational history and numbing statistics to look at the tracts themselves. What did the urban slum dweller actually read when he opened the tract handed to him by an earnest volunteer? In the 150-year-old bound volumes of early ATS tracts gathering dust in library basements, one may begin to find an answer.

What first strikes one in these tracts is their authors' urgent desire to communicate with an unknown—but vast and threatening—public that lies outside the range of their personal experience. Over and over again, the authors betray an almost poignant wish to break through the barrier of print to the immediacy of a direct encounter. "My dear friend," begins one tract, "Will you permit one, with the best of intentions, to converse with you a few moments on a very important subject? As a friend, I feel interested in your welfare." Another, an "Appeal to Youth,"' concludes somewhat defensively: "And now my young friend, I bid you an affectionate farewell . . . When we meet [in Eternity] if this Tract should rise up in judgment against you . . . , I think you will allow that I have acted the part of a kind friend, and done what I could for your spiritual welfare."[17]

Other tract writers tried to maximize their fleeting claim on the reader's attention by using precisely such an ephemeral encounter as the setting for their narrative. Many tracts take the form of a dialogue between two strangers—one invariably pious, the other not—who meet on a trip or in some other casual way. The author of one such tract begins by establishing the unpromising setting with some care. "Every one has remarked the mixed, and often ill-assorted company which meets in a public packet or stage coach. The conversation . . . is commonly insipid, frequently disgusting, and sometimes insufferable . . . A few years ago, one of the stages which ply between our two principal cities was filled with a group which could never have been drawn together by mutual choice."[18] Despite the frustrating distractions of the situation—so sadly typical of the bustling impersonality of the new order—this author managed to engage a young fellow passenger in a conversation (minutely reported in the tract, of course) that ended with his conversion.

The desire to bridge the chasm of anonymity is revealed, too, in the many tracts written for specific categories of readers—a tactic that enabled the volunteer to select one aimed at the situation of the person at hand. There were tracts for children, young men, young women, parents, the ill, the aged, the bereaved, the poor, and those in "Fashionable Life." There was even one addressed "To a Person Engaged in a Law Suit." ("A spirit of litigation is not a spirit to die in. Consider that you may soon die.")[19]

Another of these special-audience tracts urges the newly arrived immigrant to abandon any "vice or impropriety"—intemperance is particularly stressed—that he may have acquired in the Old World, and ends with a variant of the grim warning found in many tracts of this period. "God has brought you across the Atlantic, but this is not your home. You will remain here but a little while, and then you will take another voyage. The passage will be short; but whether it shall . . . safely conduct you to the realms of never-ending bliss, or . . . cast [you] into a gulf of tumultuous flame without a bottom and without a shore, depends upon the question whether you consecrate . . . your heart and life to Christ."[20]

Despite such efforts to create the aura of a personal encounter, these tracts often betray their authors' keen awareness that a printed leaflet was a poor substitute for the face-to-face remonstrance of a friend or neighbor. The above-quoted author who tries so hard to convince the reader (and himself) that he has "acted the part of a kind friend" goes on to ruminate bleakly, "Very probably what I have written will be hastily read by you, and afterward unheeded, uncared for, and but little thought of." Another tract begins on a similarly pessimistic note: "Friend, before you throw these pages aside, permit one word with you."[21]

The frustrations inherent in this new mode of depersonalized social control is revealed in the authors' uncertainty when they do attempt to confront the reader directly:

Reflect, Sir (for I address myself to every particular person) . . .

Reader, is this, or something like it, your case? Permit a well-wisher of your soul to be free with you.

The stranger who puts this into your hand is anxious to promote [your welfare]. Accept this tract as a proof that, though unfortunate, you are not without a friend.

O man or woman, youth or child, whoever you are.

Were I, indeed, acquainted with the peculiar circumstances of your loss [in a tract for the bereaved], I should employ particular considerations; but my present address can have only a *general* aim.[22]

The awkward fumbling of such phrases, contrasting so sharply with the brisk optimism of the ATS's introductory address, suggests an underlying recognition, even at the high tide of tract enthusiasm, that these ephemeral leaflets were no match for the changes overtaking American society. But still the earnest authors kept writing, the presses kept rolling, and the tracts—with what effect no one really knew—continued to rain down by the million upon the burgeoning cities.

Although the task was often a thankless one, the contents of these tracts demonstrates the American Tract Society's determination to mold "popular feeling" by the most persuasive techniques it could devise. To be sure, some of them, especially the early ones, were simply theological treatises heavily laced with Biblical passages confirming the doctrines on which the ATS directors—mainly Congregationalists and Presbyterians—could agree. And others denounced specific vices. Benjamin Rush's classic temperance disquisition, "The Effect of Ardent Spirits upon the Human Mind and Body" (with its famous account of the drunkard who belched near an open flame and exploded) was reissued as an ATS tract. Another offered grim warnings about the dangers of neglecting the Lord's Day, including a pioneering foray into historical quantification: "Records which have been kept in a place near one of our large rivers [show that] more than twice as many have been drowned there on the Sabbath as on any other day of the week."[23]

More typically, however, the tracts take the form of brief, readable narratives whose moral is woven into the story itself. In narrative after narrative, a central message is driven home: the individual who breaks free of the web of moral restraint to pursue his personal interests and pleasures, or who indulges "sensual lusts" and "malignant passions" in "violation of the rules of sobriety and chastity," faces a grim fate. Young men "thrown out upon the open bosom of our city" confront special hazards. Lonely and isolated, they all-too-easily plunge into the "fatal vortex of licentious dissipation" where their doom is sealed. "Reduced to penury, stript of character, and corrupted by sensuality," they quickly progress from "the dram-shop [and] the brothel" to "the prison, the gallows, or some other miserable end." Similarly, *"lawless ambition"* and the *"spirit of enterprise and of change"* can lead the unwary to "the abandonement of all moral principle." In a "delusive, unstable, uncertain" age, only the moral precepts of evangelical Protestantism offer a sure anchor. "Tired of perpetual change, the soul may fix here." Sobriety, diligence, piety, contentment with one's station in life, loyalty to one's parents and their values—only by remaining faithful to these old verities can one maintain sure footing across the treacherous void and achieve "the dignified enjoyment of cultivated life."[24]

How were these exhortations to be brought alive? How could the tract writers reanimate traditional social values that had found natural nutriment in village America but that seemed increasingly irrelevant to the temper of the Jacksonian age? In trying to identify potential sources of institutional support for their values, the tract writers frequently turned to the one social institution that seemed—to some extent at least—to be resisting the centrifugal forces of the age: the family. Scores of tracts proclaimed the importance of home and family in promoting social stability and urged parents to create the kind of domestic environment that would help their children resist the morally corrosive power of the larger society. "The relation between parents and children involves all the relations of human society," noted one. "If your children . . . prove the curse of their country," added another sternly, "as well as the torment and ruin of those most intimately related to them, the guilt is in part yours."[25] Still another, "The Christian Minister's Affectionate Advice to a Married Couple," spelled out in no uncertain terms the broader social obligations of parenthood. "You are . . . not to consider yourselves merely as two friends, who have agreed to share each others' trials or enjoyments; but as the founders of a little community of rational and immortal creatures, who may hereafter found other small communities, and from whom in process of time, a *multitude* may spring."[26]

However important the strengthening of family bonds as a long-range objective, the immediate problem in Jacksonian America, from the tract writers' perspective, was that millions of people had already broken free of traditional constraints. In their appeals to these millions, the strategy was to awaken inner checks on behavior to replace the external checks that had been left behind. One frequently employed tactic, for example, was to remind the reader that, although he may have escaped the eyes of village neighbors, there remained a higher realm where all was observed, and where the concealing cloak of anonymity would someday be pulled aside. The sinner in this life may be able to conceal his "real character and condition" from those around him, but at the Last Judgment will come the moment of shameful public exposure. "If a man be on trial for a single crime of which he is guilty, he turns pale at the sight of a well-known witness . . . But how much more must the sinner's attention be fixed upon himself, when he stands arraigned before the infinitely holy and omniscient God! . . . Among millions and millions I am forced to appear . . . Awful moment! . . . Oh for a hiding place under the rocks or caves! But no; I must appear."[27]

A parallel and probably even more effective strategy for adding emotional force to the tract's moral exhortations was to link them to family and community ties that had been left behind, but which still remained alive in memory. Think of the friends and neighbors back home, one tract urged; though physically distant, they "still affectionately regard your spiritual and eternal welfare."[28]

In a manner reminiscent of Jonathan Edwards's sermons, the tract writers did not simply assert the moral claim of the old order; they made it real by linking it to tangible images calculated to have a strong emotional effect. Although city dwellers were a major target of these tracts, urban life is rarely portrayed. Most have village settings, with the preurban aura reinforced by bucolic engravings. (Some of the early ATS tracts were simply reprints of older ones with English village settings, and thus twice removed from the contemporary American urban experience.) When poverty is depicted, it is invariably in a country context and suffused with a sentimental glow: "The furniture was very simple and poor, hardly indeed amounting to bare necessaries. It consisted of four brown wooden chairs, which, by constant rubbing were become as bright as a looking-glass."[29] A typical tract of this type, "David Baldwin; or, The Miller's Son," recounts the story of a Long Island village youth who drifts into infidelity (through reading David Hume) but is lovingly drawn back to the fold by his pastor and his parents. Though David dies an early death (on April 5, 1833, notes the tract, adding a telling note of contemporary authenticity), he does so once again secure in the faith of his family and neighbors.[30]

This seemingly anachronistic preoccupation with a village world far removed from the actual life of many of the readers was, of course, quite deliberate. It was a means of reawakening memories of that world, and of reasserting the claim of the moral order associated with it. "Need you be reminded of the tender anxieties of your parents on your behalf?" asks a tract aimed at young people—and proceeds to remind them in graphic detail.

Another reports "A Dying Mother's Counsel to Her Only Son," and a third relates the experiences of a city youth who succumbs to drink and other urban evils that ruin both his health and his career. Vowing at last to mend his ways, he remembers "a precious treasure he had preserved from the wreck of all his earthly fortune. 'Ah,' said he, 'to MY MOTHER'S BIBLE I will apply: here I may obtain relief from my bitter anguish.' " With this beacon from the past as his guide he returns to the path of virtue and soon decides to enter the ministry.[31]

Two popular English tracts selected for reissue by the American Tract Society, "The Dairyman's Daughter" and "The Widow's Son," offer perhaps the best instances of the use of village nostalgia to add emotional intensity to the conservative social message. In the former, the poor heroine—basically good but "proud," "thoughtless," and "fond of dress and finery"—abandons her village for the city. Here, rather than seeking lodging with a pious family, she joins a fast and "worldly" crowd, and soon falls victim to a variety of unspecified but debilitating vices.[32] In "The Widow's Son," the hero, a lad named Lewellin, similarly leaves his rural home and goes, at seventeen, to London and a position as an accountant. He initially leads a sober and well-regulated life as a boarder with a religious family but is gradually drawn into loose habits by his fellow workers. In a crucial development, he abandons his surrogate family and moves to a hotel. "The line was now passed; and Lewellin, having tasted of the forbidden fruit, resolved to rid himself of his puritanical notions, (as he began to term his religious sentiments,) that he might enjoy life." His moral standards now collapse completely as he discovers in turn the amusement park (where he goes with girls on Sundays), the theater, the billiard hall, and the brothel.[33]

The climax of both tracts comes when the central character, broken in body and spirit and deeply contrite, flees the city to return to family and native village. The dairyman's daughter, having contracted tuberculosis in the city, dies peacefully in her parents' humble cottage (soothed by "the gentle lowing of cattle") and is borne to the village burying ground by her grieving family and neighbors—a member of the community again at last.[34]

In "The Widow's Son," it appears for an alarmingly long time that Lewellin will meet the same fate when he returns to his mother mired in debt and wracked by horrible city diseases. One night as he seems near death the neighbor standing watch proposes to awaken his mother for a last farewell, but he thoughtfully responds: "No; let her sleep on, and take her rest, and I will die alone, and spare her the agony of hearing the last tremendous groan which is to announce my entrance into hell." But the renewal of familial and communal ties does its work: Lewellin recovers and returns to the city—this time full of sober purpose. He rejoins the family with whom he had originally boarded, attends church faithfully, and begins a busy round of benevolent activity as a "Sunday-school teacher, . . . visitor of the sick, [and] agent of the Tract Society." Triply supported by the institutional framework of family, church, and voluntary moral-uplift society, he finds the order and purpose so sadly lacking in his initial, near-fatal encounter with the city.[35]

The village funeral, which terminates the saga of "The Dairyman's Daughter" and very nearly ends Llewellin's career as well, is a prevailing motif in these tracts. Deathbed scenes, funeral rites, and country burials are described in minute detail. In part, of course, this preoccupation simply reflected the Victorian sentimentalization of death, which Philippe Ariès, Ann Douglas, and others have explored, but in the tracts it served the more specific purpose of adding force to the image of a unified, morally cohesive community. "The stroke of death makes a wide space in the village circle," one author noted, "and is an awful event in the tranquil uniformity of rural life." Another tract writer described in detail the stones in a village graveyard with their somber carvings and memento mori inscriptions. "Such an association of objects," he noted, "produced a powerful effect on my thoughts"— an effect he clearly wished to reproduce in his readers.[36] In the solemn rituals of death, when the moral unity of the village was graphically dramatized, the strategists of the American Tract Society found a compelling symbol for the central message they wished to impart to Jacksonian America.

In studiously ignoring the complex and ambiguous urban reality in these tracts and instead conjuring up an idealized "village" as the setting for so many of the moral dramas that unfold in their pages, they were attempting to revive the moral authority of a communal order that for many Americans was no more than a memory. The point of tracts like "David Baldwin" or "The Widow's Son" was not to trigger a stampede back to actual villages but rather to give emotional immediacy to a set of values and moral constraints associated with the village order. The enormous support the tract movement was for a time able to generate in the antebellum period reflected a supreme—or perhaps desperate?—faith in the power of the printed word to reshape social reality. In the clear-cut moral world of the tracts, if nowhere else, the old-time verities endlessly triumphed.

3

The Sunday School in the City
PATTERNED ORDER IN A
DISORDERLY SETTING

The American evangelical writer of the late 1820s who described his era as "an age of Sabbath schools" was making no idle boast.[1] Like the tract, the Sunday school was a response to the social dislocations of the early-nineteenth-century. But though the Sunday school sprang from the same evangelical soil as the tract societies and reflected the same concerns, it utilized a far more innovative strategy. Whereas the tract used words and pictures to evoke the moral order of the village, the Sunday schools actually re-created such an order. The young scholar was not simply instructed in the values of the preurban community; he actually witnessed such a community, for a brief time each week, take shape before his eyes.

From small beginnings in England in the 1780s, the Sunday school movement quickly crossed the Atlantic, and by 1824, when the American Sunday School Union (ASSU) was founded in Philadelphia, state and local societies that were sponsoring more than 700 Sunday schools enrolling some 50,000 children were brought under one organizational umbrella. Six years later enrollment in ASSU-affiliated schools stood at about 350,000, and in succeeding years the number rose still higher.[2] Thousands more attended denominational Sunday schools not associated with the ASSU, especially those of the Methodists, who in the 1830s and early 1840s founded new Sunday schools at the rate of 150 a year. In 1833, marveling at "the great and increasing demand for the

Scriptures for the use of the Sunday Schools," the American Bible Society offered to supply Bibles to the schools for forty cents each, with a special discount for those in cities.[3]

As the Bible society's announcement suggests, the moral threat of the city loomed large in the thinking of the early Sunday school leadership. The Sunday school was not, of course—any more than was the tract movement—solely a response to urbanization. The ASSU from the first dedicated itself to "planting a Sunday-school wherever there is a population," and an 1826 handbook called for Sunday schools "in all places, cities, villages, or country." Indeed, in the 1830s the challenge of the unchurched West sometimes appeared to overshadow that of the unchurched cities. But from the time the earliest American Sunday schools were established in New York, Philadelphia, Boston, Baltimore, and other coastal cities around 1815, the surging pace of urban growth was a matter of profound and continuing concern. "Vice is pouring into the city like a torrent, the population is wonderfully increasing," said the New York *Christian Observer* in 1827, "and the best shield against immorality is the sabbath school institution."[4]

The Sunday school literature of the period is full of apprehension about the urban menace. "In every large city," declared the ASSU in the early 1830s, "there is a frightful amount of population, who, if left to themselves, will never enter the door of a church, or come within the hearing of religious instruction." Sunday schools were especially needed, warned a prominent Lutheran churchman, among the debased population of "a few of our prominent cities"—a population swelling daily with "the vast and increasing influx of foreigners, especially of the poorer and vicious class." Another Jacksonian Sunday school publicist described the "torrents of vice and iniquity" in the cities, and the author of an 1839 Sunday school manual, while conceding that cities included good as well as evil, dwelled on the "frightful mass of depravity hidden from public observation" in the "confusion and bustle" of urban life.[5]

The note of urban concern was particularly insistent, as one would expect, in the Sunday school reports from specific cities. "A moral desolation broods over the scene of our exertions," reported the Philadelphia Association of Male Sunday School Teachers in 1826. A writer in the ASSU magazine that same year evoked a Poe-like image of masses of city dwellers "hastening their steps with the rapidity of lightning, to the vortex of eternal perdition."[6]

Like their associates in the Bible and tract societies, most of the early leaders of the movement were big-city men who knew at first hand the social ramifications of urban growth. In New

York, Eleazer Lord, William E. Dodge, and Divie Bethune are typical. Lord, born in 1788 in a small town in Connecticut, came to Manhattan as a young man and launched a business career that in 1833 brought him the presidency of the newly founded Erie Railroad. In 1816, at twenty-eight, he founded and became secretary of the New York Sunday School Union. Dodge, another Connecticut boy, went into the metals business and eventually became one of New York's richest men. Having taught his first Sunday school class over a livery stable in New York as a young man around 1820, he remained a lifelong and generous supporter of the movement. Divie Bethune had launched himself successfully in the mercantile world upon his arrival from Scotland in 1792, at the age of twenty-one. As early as 1803 he conducted a Sunday school in his home, and he actively supported the movement until his death in 1824. (So did his wife, Joanna, who in fact established the Female Union for the Promotion of Sabbath Schools in 1816 a few months before Eleazer Lord founded his organization.)[7]

In Philadelphia, the cause was championed by men like Alexander Henry, a Scotch-Irishman who arrived in Philadelphia as a seventeen-year-old in 1783 and had made, lost, and regained a fortune as a fabric importer by 1818 when he retired to devote himself to philanthropy and public endeavors. The first president of the ASSU, he held that post until his death in 1847. The pattern was similar in Massachusetts, where the early Sunday school leadership included Alfred D. Foster, who was brought up in a village in the western part of the state and subsequently became a lawyer and Whig leader in the emerging industrial center of Worcester, and Samuel T. Armstrong, reared in a town near Boston and in his adult years a prominent printer and Whig politician who served briefly as governor of Massachusetts and mayor of Boston.[8]

Inextricably bound to the cities where they were carving out substantial places for themselves, these men were at the same time troubled by the social unsettledness and rampant moral evils those cities seemed to spawn—so different from the communities they remembered from their earlier years. The author of an obituary tribute to Divie Bethune, describing his initial reaction to New York City, might have been writing of many of Bethune's colaborers in the Sunday school movement: "Although he was not at that time decidedly religious; yet he was seriously exercised, and felt a horror of profanity and vice."[9]

For individuals of this stripe who took up the Sunday school reform, generalized concern over urban immorality and social fragmentation quickly found specific focus in anxiety about the city child. At a time when the street arab was making his appear-

Lyman Beecher. As early as 1812, while a minister in Litchfield, Connecticut, he formulated the fundamental voluntarist strategy that would influence generations of urban moral-control effort.

Lewis Tappan. New York textile importer who, with his brother Arthur,
supported a variety of antebellum urban moral reform causes.

In their illustrations as in their prose, the early tracts evoked an orderly, family centered, pre-urban world.

WIDOW'S SON.

William E. Dodge (1805-1883), millionaire capitalist who for more than half a century helped finance city revivals, Sunday schools, YMCAs, tract societies, and numerous other urban moral uplift endeavors.

Eleazer Lord, railroad executive and founder of the New-York Sunday School Society.

In this model Sunday school floor plan recommended by the American Sunday School Union in 1839, every detail serves to remind scholar and teacher alike that this was to be an orderly, cohesive, and strictly hierarchical little community.

Shame as a mode of Sunday school discipline: In the "lock bench" (top), the hinged door could be locked. In "the stocks" (below), the faces of children guilty of "lesser offences" could be hidden by a movable screen.

A city Sunday school of the 1850s. In this frequently reprinted (and subtly retouched) photograph, Dwight L. Moody (*left*) and John V. Farwell pose with a picturesque group of urchins from Moody's mission Sunday school in Chicago.

ance in American popular fiction, travel narratives, and moral-reform literature, the early Sunday school spokesmen endlessly discussed the hoardes of city children "without moral culture" who were becoming "pests to society, and ruinous to their families."[10] The movement's English founder, Gloucester newspaper editor Robert Raikes, had been concerned about the poor children of his town who were kept busy in a local pin factory during the week but on Sunday ran wild "free from every restraint," and the same fears pervaded the American movement in its early years. The Massachusetts Sabbath School Society described the vulnerability of "wandering, ignorant" children amid the "moral darkness" of the city; the Troy, New York, Sunday school association called attention to the "companies of noisy wandering boys" who infested Troy's streets on Sundays; and even in far-off Detroit the founders of the first Sunday school, in 1818, warned of children growing up "in the practice of vice without restraint."[11]

The ambivalent blend of sympathy, revulsion, and fear these reformers felt toward street urchins was nicely conveyed by the Boston minister who confessed in an 1839 address to the city's Sabbath School Union that when he heard their "profane and impious language" he simultaneously experienced "compassion" and a strong impulse "to look upon them as monsters." One reason for these intense reactions was that the street arab's behavior was not only alarming in itself but also a disquieting omen. The children the Sunday school sought to reach, noted Samuel Miller of the Princeton Theological Seminary, would all too soon be in a position to "sway the affairs both of church and state."[12]

Another urban group that loomed large in the thoughts of this first generation of Sunday school leaders comprised the young men pouring into the cities from America's farms and small towns. The Philadelphia Sunday School Union explored the moral hazards confronting city apprentices in 1827, and by 1837 the ASSU was portraying this as one of the nation's urgent social problems.

Hundreds come in from the country in pursuit of trades and employment, who are thrown into promiscuous association in boarding-houses, over whom there is no sort of supervision whatever except during the working hours of the day ... The excitements and allurements of their new situation and the connection they instantly form with the thoughtless, if not with the licentious, soon break up their good habits, unless there is something at hand in the form of a Sunday School, Bible class, or family influence to restrain and guide them.[13]

As this passage suggests, the Sunday school seemed to many a heaven-sent means of giving moral shelter to vulnerable children and youth in the city—a practical alternative to traditional modes of oversight either missing or severely weakened in the urban setting. Only the Sunday school, declared the ASSU, could prevent the slum urchin from graduating to "the class of youth who crowd the streets, free from the restraints of a proper guardianship, and without the powerful influence of a settled, quiet, well ordered home." Prematurely confident, New York's Female Union for the Promotion of Sabbath Schools rhetorically inquired two years after its founding: "Where now are those groups of idle children who formerly met to profane the Sabbath and take God's name in vain? All is now still." For older youth, too, contended the ASSU, the Sunday school offered "the best guaranty of . . . moral safety." Following a plan adopted in Philadelphia in 1828, a number of urban Sunday school societies introduced "apprentice classes" aimed specifically at this needy group.[14]

Such optimism seemed justified, for if the young were especially vulnerable to the urban moral threat, they were also the most malleable group within the city population: "docile, susceptible, unprejudiced," and as yet "free from the defilements of the flesh."[15] Though in mortal jeopardy, they had not yet been destroyed by the corrupting power of the city. At this time theologians like Nathaniel W. Taylor were moderating orthodox Calvinism with a more hopeful view of man's innate moral capacity, and Sunday school proponents were quick to see the implications of "Taylorism" for their own reform. "The soul of the child is empty, and you may fill it with the treasures of life," noted one. "The wax is more soft, and you may mould it as you will." The Sunday school, agreed another, was such a potent "engine of good" because its influence was exerted "at the threshold of being; and before vice has confirmed its habits, while the heart is tender, and sensitive to any impression."[16]

Implicit in all this was the assumption that in the city the traditional agencies of child nurture were failing. Indeed, in the early Sunday school periodicals one finds repeated complaints that masters were ignoring the moral welfare of apprentices, that city churches were neglecting the poor, and that parents were shirking their spiritual duty. Particular attention was given to the urban family, for it was here that Sunday school apologists confronted a troublesome ambiguity in their position. As social conservatives, they espoused an organic, family-centered view of the social order, and vehemently denied any intention of detaching children from "the care of their natural guardians." Sunday school instruction, they insisted, was "given in aid of that of the parents, and never as a substitute for it." New York City Sunday school teachers were cautioned that they should never condescend to a scholar's parents but treat them as "co-labourers" in the child's upbringing. Sunday school propaganda aimed at parents reinforced this theme. Permit the Sunday school to share in your offspring's nurture, parents were urged, and "you will not have the trouble to scold and beat them, in order to keep them from doing what is wrong. They will remember that *God* always sees them, and . . . will behave well to you, and to every body . . . [W]hen you are old and feeble, they will be glad to support and comfort you under your infirmities."[17]

For all their efforts to portray the Sunday school and the parents as partners in a common effort, Sunday school spokesmen often betrayed hostility and even contempt toward the parents of their scholars, especially those of the urban poor, and the conviction that the Sunday school was much the superior socializing agent. At best, they suggested, slum parents were either guilty of "indifference" toward their offspring or the hapless victims of a disordered social environment where a child could go bad before his parents were even aware of the danger. At worst, they were an actively destructive agent in their children's lives. Jacksonian Sunday school literature is full of references to the "ruinous" influence of "intemperate," "profane," "dishonest," "brawling," "licentious," "profligate," and "vicious" parents. The evils by which "the peace of society is broken up" and "its heaviest burdens accumulated," the ASSU insisted sternly in 1835, "may usually be attributed to something wrong *at home*." A passage in an 1826 Sunday school report from New York City could be endlessly reduplicated in the urban Sunday school literature of these years. "Frequently we have seen the intoxicated parent stagger about the room, . . . utter[ing] expressions of obscenity with the most dreadful oaths. The children too would probably contract the same habits were they not prevented by the influence of our schools."[18]

Such hostility not only reflected prevailing middle-class perceptions of lower-class life but also served an additional function for Sunday school apologists. For the period of the Sunday school's emergence was also the point at which "the Home," presided over by a saintly wife and mother, was beginning to be idealized as a haven where moral values and the gentler virtues could be cherished and transmitted, secure from the buffetings of the competitive world outside. Thus, the Sunday school movement proposed to take over part of the family's child-nurturing function just as its importance was being magnified by moralists and social thinkers. As the ASSU acknowledged in 1831, the early Sunday schools were in fact widely criticized for poaching on the parental role.[19]

To counteract such criticism and justify what in fact was an infringement on the parental (especially the maternal) prerogative as it was coming to be defined, Sunday school leaders dismissed with growing asperity the domestic environment from which many of their scholars came as shocking travesties of "true" homes. Households where "no pious counsel ever flows from parental lips" were "abodes of moral death," insisted the ASSU, and the children of such households, having been spiritually "deserted" by their parents, were in reality "moral orphans." If this were the case, wise social policy clearly demanded that they be led out of "degradation and squalor" into a purer moral environment—one that would provide an antidote, as the Reverend John Todd put it in 1837, to *the poison of wrong example and wrong teaching at home.* The "machinery of a Sabbath school," boasted the ASSU, could "humanize and beautify the moral deformities which are to be met with in many families."[20]

The conclusion was inescapable. If the homes of slum children were so corrupt, the only solution was "ingrafting them into a new family": the Sunday school.[21] Mesmerized by their own arguments, Sunday school apologists began to portray the Sunday school as itself a home—a purified alternative to degraded and disordered slum households. The Sunday school teacher, they contended, though "unprompted by natural affection, and unconstrained by social laws," could often provide a more worthy model for the child than the debased creatures who were his actual parents. By 1848, abandoning its earlier defensive tone, the ASSU was assiduously enveloping the Sunday school in the sentimental haze through which Victorians viewed the domestic sphere. "The Sunday-school," it declared, "is the nearest approach to the family that human wit has yet devised. It separates groups of children into small companies, and gives to each of them one who . . . will act the part of a faithful, intelligent, Christian parent or elder brother or sister."[22]

At an early date in America's urban history, then, a significant group of reformers had dismissed the slum family as a social failure and a moral disaster—a flawed institution that could, in all good conscience, be thrust aside in favor of new instrumentalities of moral nurture.

The issue was not merely theoretical, for the Sunday school did touch the lives of substantial numbers of city children—though probably still a minority—in these years. As early as 1817, a Female Missionary Society Sunday school on Henry Street in lower Manhattan drew 400–600 children each week. By 1840, a vast network of Sunday schools existed in the major East Coast urban centers and many interior cities as well: places like Albany, Utica, Pittsburgh, Cincinnati, and Chicago. As for actual attendance, the

ASSU reported in 1825 that about one-third of the children of Philadelphia in the six to fifteen age group were Sunday school scholars. An 1829 survey in New York City revealed that some 9,000, or about 41 percent, of all children aged four to fifteen were in Sunday school. (The same survey found that only about 5,700 youngsters were enrolled in the public schools.) Similarly impressive statistics were recorded for Boston and other cities.[23]

Dramatic visual evidence of the Sunday school's role in the city (or at least the role to which it aspired) was provided by the great annual Sunday school rallies and parades in all the big cities. In New York, the scholars would march down Broadway, each Sunday school bearing its flag, their "neat and uniform" ranks a pointed contrast to the usual throngs of urchins. Assembling in Battery Park, the marchers would sing Sunday school songs and hear speakers expound the significance of the movement. In 1829 some 12,000 scholars and 8,000 teachers and sympathizers took part in this display, inspiring one observer to comment: "Nothing can exceed, I think, the interesting sight of these companies of children, . . . accompanied by thousands of spectators, with banners inscribed with holiness to the Lord."[24]

To be sure, such enthusiasm was often tempered by bleaker reflections. One 1827 *Christian Advocate* writer boasted of the great numbers of "wretched" New York City children in the Sunday schools yet reflected gloomily on the magnitude of the task remaining. "Twenty thousand degraded children, still belong to no school and have no instructions . . . Last week while searching for children, I suppose that I saw more than eighty heathen families."[25] In 1825 the Philadelphia Sunday School Association lamented the thousands in Philadelphia and its working-class suburbs "still without the pale of these benign institutions"; by the mid-1830s, Massachusetts Sunday school leaders were commenting uneasily on the "rather gloomy" Boston situation, and the ASSU was acknowledging that its efforts were encountering "indifference" and even "reproaches" among the urban masses.[26] Nevertheless, thousands of Sunday school teachers and superintendents remained faithful to the task through the antebellum period and beyond, convinced that the moral destiny of the city was riding on their efforts.

How did the Sunday school's broad aspirations translate into practice? It is in its actual structure and week-by-week operations, more than in its leaders' rhetoric, that the innovative aspects of the early Sunday school movement, and the intensity of its concern over the social disruptions of the Jacksonian era, most clearly emerge.

A central fact to be noted is that the objectives of the early movement went well beyond mere conversion and religious instruction. To be sure, Sunday schools from the first had a strongly Protestant cast: they sometimes met in churches; the lessons were based on the King James Bible; the songs and prayers were those of evangelicalism; and the teachers, superintendents, and national leaders were often members of one or another of the Protestant denominations—usually Presbyterian, Congregational, or low church Episcopal. (The Methodists, while not active in the ASSU, had their own vigorous Sunday school organization.)[27] But while the movement was eventually absorbed into the larger program of the church, it initially maintained a quite distinct identity, both organizationally and ideologically.

Indeed, the early movement aroused suspicion and even hostility within the American Protestant establishment—hostility rooted not only in institutional rivalries but in the fact that the Sunday school's objectives included explicit and overt social goals as well as religious ones. As one Sunday school writer put it, the aim was not only to prepare the scholar for eternity, but to train him in those "*safe and permanent principles of conduct*" that would fit him for a life of "respectability and usefulness" here on earth. An 1839 handbook went so far as to suggest that *unconverted* Sunday school teachers might be preferable to more pious ones, if they possessed the qualities of "diligence, sobriety, and punctuality"![28] The endlessly reiterated goal was to bring about the "transformation of character" that would turn the younger generation from "the grossness of sensuality to the dignified enjoyment of cultivated life" and thereby transform what threatened to be "a public nuisance into a public blessing." The ASSU, attempting in 1828 to set forth its objectives systematically, gave only oblique attention to religious concerns. The central aims, it declared, were "to lay in the children's minds the foundation of obedience to their governors in church and state, to make them contented with the station which providence has appointed to them in the world, to teach them the subjugation of their passions, and the avoiding the company of dissolute and profligate and vicious characters."[29] The complex blend of religious, humanitarian, and social-control impulses that fueled the early movement is well revealed in an 1818 address by the Reverend James Milnor, a New York Presbyterian leader, to the New York Sunday School Union. Describing the Sunday school as "a necessary link in the chain of our social institutions," Milnor proceeded to detail its varied facets:

> As a friend of civil order, I congratulate you on the assurance which these institutions are calculated to give to the preservation of the peace and order of society; as a philan-

thropist, I congratulate you on that increase which they promise by the diffusion of knowledge, and the inculcation of virtue to the sum of human happiness. As a moralist, I congratulate you on their past effects and their benefits in prospect, to the private and social habits of the poorer classes. Above all, as a Christian, I congratulate you on the accessions they have already furnished to the family of the Redeemer.[30]

"The God we serve," said the ASSU in 1849, "is a God of order, and not of confusion."[31] These words hold the key to understanding the antebellum Sunday school. Its central impetus was not simply to enlarge the spiritual ministry of the church but also to promote deferential and disciplined patterns of behavior based on an image of society as stable, orderly, and securely hierarchical. It sought, in short, to serve as a counterweight to the centrifugal forces that were at work in Jacksonian America—and nowhere more so than in the cities.

Variously formulated, this goal appears everywhere in the Sunday school literature of these years, from the teachers' instructions issued by the New York Sunday School Union in 1816 ("instill in their young minds the duty of contentment in the stations allotted to them by Providence . . . , filial obedience, and . . . respect to superiors") to the ASSU teachers' handbook of 1839, with its insistence that "industry," "sobriety," "civility," "subordination," and "obedience" were essential to "the peace and indeed to the very existence of society." The ASSU summed matters up in 1849: the supporters of Sunday schools, it declared, "must be regarded as holding a very high place among the friends of social order."[32]

One way to achieve these social-control objectives was to use the Sunday school lessons themselves to indoctrinate the child in what one manual called "all the social and relative duties."[33] The uniform ASSU lessons used by most local Sunday schools from the mid-1820s on included a heavy emphasis on each person's economic, social, and civic obligations. One cycle of nine study topics, each buttressed by appropriate Biblical passages, included the duties of husbands, wives, parents, children, masters, servants, magistrates, and subjects, as well as "duties under affliction."[34] The cumulative message is clear: no one is a free moral agent; everyone exists in complex relationships to others; society's well-being depends upon each person's submission to the web of social obligations that binds him.

The message was made plain, too, in the flood of tracts, weekly papers, and library books upon which the early Sunday school movement swept forward. Pervading this literature were all the familiar themes: self-restraint, deference, loyalty to kin and community, attention to duty, satisfaction with one's lot in life. The message was sometimes accompanied by hints that good fortune would bless the child who remained faithful to the code, and sometimes by warnings of retribution, in this world and the next, for deviations from the proper path. Sunday school literature was drenched with grim reminders of the imminence of death, often including graphic narratives of Sunday school children who met violent or unexpected ends. In 1825 the *American Sunday School Magazine* advised teachers to address their classes this way:

> Many little children who used to go to Sunday School and to Church, as you do, grew sick and died; their eyes were shut, and their mouths were shut, and they could not breathe any more, and they were cold and stiff, and people nailed them up in a coffin, and dug a deep hole in the ground, and put them in and covered them up—and then their souls went up to God: and if they were good children they are in heaven now, but if they were bad, where are they? Remember, as these children died, so must you; the time will come when you will be cold and dead, and put in a coffin, and buried deep in the ground and your soul go to God.[35]

As with the tracts, such morbid exhortations represented an effort to reintroduce under altered circumstances a weapon from the preurban social-control arsenal. In the colonial community, death was a shared social occasion and an obvious time for solemn moral warnings. In the cities, by contrast, although death was a frequent visitor, its moral penumbra was often missing. The graphic reminders of mortality in the antebellum Sunday school were attempts to establish in advance an intellectual context for death, so when children encountered it they would feel its moral power and social meaning.

Important as the lessons and reading matter were in their cumulative effect, the principal means by which the antebellum Sunday school achieved its purpose was through its very organization and routine. In the first place, the fact that in the city Sunday school the staff was drawn from the middle class and the scholars often from the lower ranks not only meant that the urban poor would be exposed to "a new world of thought, and feeling, and moral influence" but it also held out hope that the widening chasm between the social classes could be bridged. Through the Sunday school, predicted an ASSU speaker in 1826, "the two extremes of society" would develop "a mutually kind feeling and interest in each other's behalf"; the poor child would form a "strong attachment" to his teachers, based on "gratitude . . . for their generous labours in his behalf," and the teachers, experiencing firsthand the "deplorable ignorance of the poor and indigent" would be awakened to a sense of Christian compassion and social obligation. Taking a slightly different tack, another Sunday school spokesman that year saw the "kindly collision" between the classes in the Sunday school as a force for social stability: the poor would "cease to feel their inferiority so galling . . . , [as] they perceive that all do not consider them as the mere instruments of labour, or the tools of interest," and the middle-class teachers would be made aware that "the sons and daughters of indigence have the same nature and capacities as themselves."[36] The Sunday school, in other words, would provide a setting for those encounters between people of different social station which were a natural feature of village life but which were becoming increasingly rare as the village grew into a town, and the town into a city.

But the urban role of the Sunday school was not simply to facilitate harmonious cross-class contacts. Its advocates envisioned for it a far more active function in transmitting traditional values, and they planned its every detail with this aim in view. In the struggle against urban depravity and disorder, noted the ASSU in the 1820s, "the machinery of a Sabbath school" represented "one of the mightiest engines ever put in operation." In the 1830s, the Reverend John Todd's son later recalled, Todd's Philadelphia Sunday school was "so perfect in its machinery as to attract visitors from all parts of the land, and even from Europe." Sunday school work, observed the ASSU in 1849, was "like the endless web of the machinist. The revolution of successive years bears to our hands a constant succession of materials on which to exert the moulding influence of the Sunday-school." The Episcopal clergyman Stephen Tyng, writing in 1860 after a lifetime of involvement in Sunday school work in Philadelphia and New York, turned to a different branch of modern industry for his imagery. "Like the fingers of one of those beautiful power-presses," the teachers in the Sunday school sponsored by his church "take up the very pages which I desire to impress, and smoothly and quietly spread them out before me, prepared to receive the blessed communications from on high which I long to stamp on their minds and hearts forever." Who, continued Tyng, extending his analogy, having witnessed the "glowing regularity" of such a process, "would desire to go back to the single hand-press of the individual laborer, toiling, with far greater weariness, to accomplish but a small portion of the result?"[37]

Such mechanical imagery, which pervades the literature of the early Sunday school movement, graphically conveys the degree to which antebellum urban reformers drew upon the age's technological achievements in formulating and rationalizing their moral-control strategies. It also reveals, unintentionally, the extent to which the Sunday school was recognized, even by its partisans, as a contrivance for producing an artificial version of a social order whose natural roots were withering.

When this point is understood, the seemingly excessive attention given to details of procedure, routine, and physical layout begins to make more sense. "The machinery of a Sabbath school" was in fact designed with scrupulous care to assure the successful functioning of a miniature community in which a strict social hierarchy would prevail; lines of authority would be unambiguous; everyone would know his station; and the rules of behavior would be clear, explicit, and strictly enforced. The Sunday school, in short, would be everything the city was not.

This carefully patterned order began with the school's physical arrangement, to which the handbooks and manuals gave minute attention. Usually it was recommended that all the classes meet in one large room, with each class seated on a single, high-backed bench, each pupil at a numbered seat on that bench. (Ideally the bench would be curved, to focus all eyes on the teacher.) At precise points around the room were the stations of the librarian, secretary, and monitors. At the front, on an elevated platform, stood the desk of the superintendent.[38] These details of arrangement were not matters to be settled casually. They gave immediate visual notice that this was to be an orderly social environment in which every individual had a clearly defined place: again, the antithesis of the sprawling and unsettled city.

The physical layout established, the first step in actually launching a new Sunday school and organizing a rowdy throng of children into a cohesive and disciplined community was a public reading of the regulations.

I must always mind the superintendent, and ALL the teachers of this school.
I must go to my seat as soon as I come in.
I MUST ALWAYS BE STILL.
I must take good care of my book.
I must behave well in the street.
I must not LEAN on the next scholar.
I must be clean, neat, and industrious.[39]

Then the formal, public assent: "On concluding the reading of these rules the Superintendent says, 'you have heard these good rules—if you agree to them and will strive to mind them all, please to hold up your right hand.' " Having owned the covenant, the children were divided into classes, and the names of their respective teachers announced. "This formal method of appointing them . . . will have a good effect on the order of the school," noted one manual. "Whatever is methodically arranged and systematically begun is likely to proceed with good order and precision."[46]

The same themes dominate the instructions for the week-by-week Sunday school routine. The requirement that "every hour and moment . . . be rigidly economized" was elevated to almost cosmic significance.

> Suppose a [Sunday] school consist of 150 scholars and the teachers 25. Suppose several teachers come so late that the Superintendent must delay opening the school for five minutes. This seems a short time to wait. Take the 175 which compose the school and multiply it by five, and you have 875 minutes lost. Suppose this take place once on every Sabbath; the loss for one year is 758 hours; and suppose the same set of teachers continue this for five years, it would be 3,790 hours. If, now, we suppose the habit to be by them perpetuated in the school, and transmitted down, and above all, be woven into the habits of the hundreds of pupils, and become a part of their character, no arithmetic can compute the evils of such a habit.[41]

The obsession with punctuality was simply one manifestation of the larger preoccupation with order and regularity. That preoccupation crops up everywhere: Philadelphia's Sunday school teachers' association warned its members against any "want of system" in their efforts; the ASSU endlessly emphasized the importance of adopting a "uniform method"; an 1839 manual insisted that a "fixed . . . system of discipline" was the essential first step to the ultimate goal, "*a well regulated Sunday-school.*" A strict routine was especially important, added the Reverend John Todd, in *city* Sunday schools.[42]

Every aspect of the Sunday school program was considered with an eye to its impact on the child's future social behavior, and particularly its effectiveness in promoting decorum and restraint. The recommended class opening, for example, went like this:

> As soon as the opening exercises of the school are over, the Teacher says, "Attention!" "Hands before." (Here they are directed to fold their arms together, and so come to order.) Then the Teacher, if he keeps a class book, will call the names of his scholars . . . , requiring each scholar to answer "Sir!" as his name is called, and at the same time lift his right hand . . . The roll being called, the teacher gives the following orders, "Rise up," "Hands behind," "Hands before," "Hands down," "Sit down," "Hands before." This exercise prepares them the better for their lesson, and is a means at all times of bringing them to immediate order. It

may sometimes be repeated during the time of instruction, particularly if the class should get out of order, or if any of the children should be dull or sleepy.[43]

The distribution of the lesson booklets provided another opportunity for a quasi-military drill. "Here they are instructed to bring the flat of the hand on the knee, and to remain so till receiving their book, which they should receive in their right hand, and bringing it to their left, should put the book on the knee before them, with both hands, awaiting the order to 'Open books.' "[44]

The diary of one Michael Floy, a Manhattan florist and Methodist Sunday school superintendent of the 1830s, vividly conveys the dominant concerns of the Sunday schools of the period. "Truly thankful am I that union prevailed among us," runs a typical entry; "Had a very orderly school both in the morning and afternoon," goes another. Many stratagems were employed to reinforce the prevailing social values. One manual advised that a large clock be prominently displayed, with the placard "I Am Late" placed beneath it at the scheduled moment of opening. A Baptist Sunday school in Boston noted that "order and solemnity" had been greatly improved by having "all the recitations made in whispers." The practice of encouraging Sunday school children to put aside a penny a week toward purchase of a Bible was not only a way of spreading God's Word; it also taught the "self-denial" and "habits of economy" that would lay "the foundation of their future dignity."[45]

The centrality of order was reinforced, too, by an elaborate system of record keeping involving six separate books: the register, containing the students' names, ages, parents' names and occupations, and "such remarks concerning them as may be thought useful"; the secretary's class roll, with the names of all teachers and scholars arranged by class; the journal, chronicling the "transactions of every Sabbath"; the superintendent's directory, a geographically organized list of all scholars (to aid visitation); the class book, where teachers recorded attendance and conduct; and the librarian's register. When a child left a Sunday school district he was given a letter of dismissal, and if possible a Sunday school in his new city or neighborhood was notified of his arrival.[46]

Supervising these procedural and clerical matters was an elaborate and highly visible official hierarchy. At the bottom were the scholars themselves, carefully divided into classes on the basis of age and ability. Next came the monitors: trusted older scholars who helped distribute books, transmit messages, maintain records, and keep order at the opening and dismissal; they were the wardens and constables of the little Sunday school community.

Enjoying a great vogue in both the Sunday schools and the public schools in the 1820s, the monitorial system threatened for a time to overwhelm the entire operation by its sheer complexity. In 1826, the New York Sunday School Union advised that every well staffed Sunday school should have class monitors, a librarian's monitor, a secretary's monitor, a "monitor of order," "monitors of dismission," and a superintendent's monitor to oversee all the other monitors.[47]

Above the monitors were the teachers, young men and women, usually in their early twenties, whose task was to maintain "unyielding discipline" over their scholars, and see to it that "the vivacity and mischievous propensities of the youthful mind" were "carefully *watched* and constantly *checked.*" During opening and closing exercises, teachers were to maintain "*profound silence*" among their pupils by keeping "their right hand raised, with the palm outward, and their eyes constantly traversing the class."[48]

At the pinnacle of this complex hierarchy was the superintendent, who was assigned a most exalted role in antebellum Sunday school literature. He was the Sunday school's "directing, presiding mind"; upon him rested "all responsibility for [its] outward conduct and discipline." His authority as "the executive officer of the little community" had to be supreme, wrote Stephen Tyng. "Any other view . . . would convert the school into a mob."[49]

The superintendent opened and closed the school by delivering moral homilies to the scholars, but these were only the beginning of his duties. His was the task of keeping the entire mechanism in adjustment and of responding decisively, by either private admonition or public reproval, to any breach of decorum or infraction of the rules. Eternal vigilance was the watchword. The superintendent, said the ASSU, "should pass continually from class to class, to observe their arrangement and order." To fulfill this important function, he obviously had to be a man of superior qualifications: dignified, judicious, self-controlled, and of "influential standing" in society.[50]

As with all details of the Sunday school operation, the object of this elaborate hierarchy was not simply to assure the school's smooth functioning but to further its larger social purpose: to inculcate within young scholars habits of deference, restraint, and self-control that would last a lifetime. In a revealing section of its 1848 annual report, the ASSU defended its seemingly excessive emphasis on organizational detail and procedural routine. The most important means of influence available to the Sunday school, declared the ASSU directors, was "association"—the child's personal involvement with the Sunday school as a social organism. "Association," they went on, "brings each child into such relations with others, that the power and influence of every well-taught lesson may be tested at once."

> It subjects every mind and breast to wholesome but not irksome restraint, and environs it with moral and religious habits, which will be as its shield and buckler when assailed by foes without or within . . . It brings children and youth into social relations with each other, which cannot but exert a powerful influence in the formation of character, and . . . introduce[s] the elements of a WHOLESOME SOCIAL ORGANIZATION into a society of children and youth.[51]

But the Sunday school's effectiveness as a social-control instrument depended entirely upon the willingness of children to submit to its regimen. As a voluntary institution, the Sunday school had to develop strategies for attracting and holding those it sought to reach. Corporal punishment not only smacked of despotism, noted the ASSU, but it alienated the child rather than reforming him. The "children of poverty" were still "free agents" and would never be permanently influenced by "threats" or "coercive stripes." Far preferable was a system based on "moral control" in which the child would be "compelled only by love."[52]

Applying this strategy, American Sunday school leaders (drawing on British precedents) devised an elaborate system of rewards and sanctions designed to gain emotional leverage over the child without either spoiling him or driving him away. The tangible rewards included elaborately embellished enrollment certificates and tickets distributed each Sunday for attendance, punctuality, good decorum, and so forth, and redeemable for Bibles, Testaments, and books. The intangible rewards included promotion to monitorial rank and other signs of favor, vague promises of prosperity and advancement in later life, and the excitement of the frequent parades and rallies.[53]

Of the sanctions, the mildest was simply deprivation: withholding tickets, for example, or even requiring a child to forfeit those already held. For chronic failure to conform, ostracism was advised. "Let the child have his place in the class, and on the roll, but let him be entirely unnoticed . . . [L]et him be treated as one whose repentence and submission are desired and expected, but who cannot be treated as a member of the school until they are shown."[54] One way of dramatizing this shunning was "to reverse a child's position . . . , obliging him to face outward from the teacher." Some schools had a bench with a partial screen before it, upon which troublemakers were seated in full view, bodies visible, but faces hidden.[55]

If temporary ostracism failed, there remained the ultimate punishment: banishment. In the *Sabbath School Teacher*, the Reverend John Todd offered a rather harrowing account of how this punishment was imposed on a "very rude and unmanageable boy" in one city Sunday school.

> As all mild measures failed . . . , it was determined that he should be sent away . . . To make a deeper and more lasting impression upon himself and all present, it was also determined that this act of discipline should be administered in a formal and solemn manner. Accordingly, whilst the exercises of the school were going on, the Superintendent knocked upon the table and called for attention. He directed the teacher of the class to which the little culprit belonged, to take him by the hand, and lead him out into the view of the whole school. This done, the Superintendent, in a solemn manner, told him that he had been so bad a boy, the teachers were under the painful necessity of sending him away from the school, and go he must. After a few words of admonition and advice, he gave out an appropriate hymn, and the whole school sang it standing. The teacher, by the direction of the Superintendent, then took the boy by the hand, led him out of the school, through the vestibule, through the enclosure, and through the gate; then closing the gate upon him, let him go. The boy wept; the teachers and scholars wept; the whole scene was most affecting.[56]

This incident goes to the heart of the social-control strategy of the antebellum Sunday school. The point was not simply to discipline individuals, but to influence the social development and moral outlook of the entire group—not merely to punish the misbehaving child for a specific infraction, but to make him feel profound shame for his behavior, and to *will* the desired reformation. As Unitarian leader William Ellery Channing told a group of Boston Sunday school teachers in 1837, the aim was not to impose external conformity upon the scholars, but "to train them to control themselves"; not merely "to form an outward regularity, but to touch inward springs."[57] Certainly this strategy succeeded in the episode recounted by John Todd: the little lad returned to the Sunday school the very next week, "entreating with tears that he might be taken back, and promising that he would henceforward be a good boy." His request granted, he proved "no trouble" from that day onward.

By such tactics, it was hoped, the movement's larger purposes would be realized. For an hour or two each week, thousands of Sunday schools would function as so many carefully fabricated little "communities." Here children would experience in their quintessential form those social norms that seemed most in jeopardy on the frontier and in the city. As a member of such a community, the Sunday school scholar would imperceptibly absorb its values and shape his own behavior and attitudes accordingly.

As early as 1788, visiting a Methodist Sunday school in an English industrial center, John Wesley had praised it as "a pattern to all the town," and countless early nineteenth-century American Sunday school leaders echoed his thought and even his words. In the useful phrase of Arthur E. Bestor, Jr., the Sunday school was seen as a kind of "patent-office model" of a stable, moral community.[58] But in contrast to the remote utopian experiments to which Bestor applied the term, the Sunday school would function within the very heart of the larger society.

Anticipating John Dewey's vision of the role of the public school two generations later, the Sunday school pioneers consciously designed their institutions as miniature but functioning models of the society they wished to achieve. Like Dewey, too, they hoped that their little communities, by influencing the young, would ultimately transform the larger society.[59] But the differences were important as well: whereas Dewey looked forward to an open, egalitarian society prizing reason, scientific method, and creative individual expression, the Jacksonian Sunday school leaders harked back to a time when life had been characterized by a familiar and predictable routine, a stable structure of authority and status, and the subordination of individual impulses to the well-being of the group.

The effort was demanding, but the possibilities were great. Not only would Sunday school literature find its way to "ignorant and depraved families," declared the ASSU, but as the scholars themselves were gradually transformed, they would become living models of respectable, orderly behavior. "Parents cannot escape the society and the example of their offspring," a Baltimore minister told a gathering of Sunday school teachers in 1828. "Thus you will penetrate the hearts of fathers and mothers through their children." Sunday school periodicals were full of accounts of children who tearfully reproved their parents and other adults for intemperance, profanity, rowdiness, and other behavior alien to the sober world of the Sunday school. In the homes of many scholars, the New York Sunday School Union reported, "filthiness and confusion" had yielded to "cleanliness and regularity."[60] All of this, of course, was a striking inversion of the traditional order in which parents were seen as the transmitters of the community's moral values to their offspring. Now it would be the child, shaped and molded by his Sunday school experience, who would have a transforming influence on his elders.

For some, this belief helped generate an enormous confidence in the power of the Sunday school to bring about a fundamental moral transformation in urban America. If the movement's influence continued to grow, the *American Sunday School Magazine* predicted in 1831, cities could soon "lock up every gaming-house, and theatre, and brothel"; the "whole army of drunkards and paupers" would be transformed into "useful and independent members of society"; and urban America would become "chaste, moral, and religious." Whereas other reformers simply tried to cope with already existent evils (this same periodical had euphorically declared a few years earlier), the Sunday school was "a system of prevention" that with sufficient support could "make prisons and almshouses and poor-laws almost unnecessary."[61]

As we shall see, this bright vision soon became clouded. But in the early decades of the nineteenth century, it was still possible to believe that in the patterned order of the Sunday school lay the means of gaining a decisive moral leverage on the city.

4

Urban Moral Reform in the Early Republic

SOME CONCLUDING
REFLECTIONS

As we replace upon the shelves the stout and sober volumes of sermons by Lyman Beecher and Charles Finney; the sexual-purity appeals of John R. McDowall and the Female Moral Reform Society; and the annual reports of the Bible, tract, and Sunday school societies, what conclusions may we draw about the great wave of urban moral reformism, beginning in the early nineteenth century and cresting in the 1830s, in which these men and women, and these organizations, played so crucial a part?

To begin, it is clear that one could hardly overstate how thoroughly these reformers were steeped in the moral earnestness of evangelical Christianity. For them, the city was a mission field—an arena where the nation's moral destiny would be decided. Even when (as in the Sunday school movement) the objectives were not exclusively or even primarily religious, the moral intensity of evangelicalism remains undiminished.

Obviously, matters involving the destiny of immortal souls and the spiritual fate of a whole people could not be heedlessly dismissed or coped with through halfway palliatives. One can only stand in awe at the zeal with which countless urban moral reformers, from the national leaders down to the local volunteers, pursued their chosen mission.

But this same evangelical fervor, with its individualistic theology and its well-worn moral rubrics, blunted the capacity of this generation to respond to the profound transformations that underlay urbanization or to recognize that what they confronted was nothing less than the emerging contours of an entirely new social order. The ASSU leaders who in 1849 ridiculed those who made "the invisible, intangible and irresponsible composition which we call SOCIETY the scape-goat for the sins and sufferings of the visible, tangible and responsible individuals who compose it" were clearly defining the bounds of their social vision.[1]

Responding to the surface turbulence and disarray of the commercial city, Jacksonian evangelicals found it easier to blame individuals than to explore the complex forces underlying that turbulence. It is easy in retrospect to share Marx's contempt for "hole-and-corner reformers of every imaginable kind" whose simplistic panaceas revealed their obliviousness to all but the most superficial aspects of urban-industrial change.[2] Yet what in its experience had prepared this generation to react other than it did? Shaped by a preurban social order far different from the one now confronting them and eager to re-create in the city some semblance of that order, these reformers turned to the narrowly focused moral crusade, the nostalgia of the tract, and the mechanically contrived "community" of the Sunday school.

Nor was the unfamiliarity of the threat the only problem. A radical analysis of the deeper sources of urban social disruption would have forced the leaders of these reforms to confront the degree to which they themselves—these merchants, lawyers, bankers, and real-estate developers—shared complicity for the very conditions whose moral consequences they so earnestly deplored.

Even if we accept the goals of these reformers at face value, it is difficult to measure their success. What was the impact on the city's moral life of those millions of tracts and thousands of Sunday schools? The reformers' own self-evaluation, as we have seen, fluctuated between euphoric optimism and bleak discouragement. When in the latter mood, they berated themselves for their failure to influence, or even reach, more than a fraction of the urban population, and ultimately this seems the more realistic assessment.

In the quixotic strategies of the single-issue crusades, the tract writers' sedulous avoidance of the realities of city life, and the fearful hostility of the Sunday school spokesmen toward the urban poor, one gains a compelling sense of the degree to which the urban population was already divided into distinct and mutually uncomprehending groups. "Those whose walks are limited to the fairer parts of our city," a speaker told the New York Society for the Prevention of Pauperism in 1823, "know nothing of the habits, the propensities and criminal courses, of a large population in its remote and obscure parts." A few years later, the

Boston city missionary Joseph Tuckerman wrote that the laboring and indigent classes of the major cities were essentially "living as a *caste*—cut off from those in more favoured circumstances."[3] Instead of "union and sympathy," agreed William Ellery Channing in 1841, one found in most urban centers "different ranks so widely separated as, indeed, to form . . . two nations, understanding as little of one another, having as little intercourse, as if they lived in different lands." (A few years earlier, Channing had offered an even more disturbing picture of the urban poor as too remote from the well-to-do for "spiritual communication" but "near enough to inflame appetites, desires, [and] wants which cannot be satisfied.")[4]

The stock phrases used by these reformers to describe the urban masses—"vicious," "abandoned," "debased"—convey by their very conventionality the extent to which firsthand knowledge of actual human beings was being replaced by abstractions. They help us gauge the distance the reformers had already come from the order they hoped to re-create. Here are "we," striving valiantly to uphold the moral order; over there the sinister, faceless "they" gnaw away at its foundations.

To be sure, efforts were made to bridge the abyss. The ladies of New York's Female Missionary Society visited poor neighborhoods to purvey the sort of counsel that "might be given by a kind and judicious neighbor." Sunday school teachers were endlessly urged to visit the homes of their scholars, and tract volunteers to utilize "the living voice, as well as the written word."[5] But the gap remained. The missionary society visitor who vanished to another part of the city after a fleeting encounter in the slums was patently not a neighbor motivated by personal interest in a specific family but an emissary from a different social class impelled by more abstract concerns. The tract, for all the efforts to personalize it, remained by nature an impersonal medium—a lifeline flung by middle-class volunteers to people on the other side of "the great gulf which they would never pass" (as a New York City tract society leader put it in 1835). And how many teachers or superintendents in city Sunday schools could maintain a close or continuing relationship with the children they encountered for an hour or two each week? The contrived social order of the Sunday school remained little more than a caricature of an authentic community. Indeed, one Sunday school writer in 1836 acknowledged that many potential teachers were evading this service out of unwillingness to "mingle with those beneath [them] in rank."[6]

Much of this early urban moral-reform effort, then, simply underscored the erosion of an organic sense of community in a period of urban growth. An abstract concern for the moral welfare of "vicious slum dwellers" or "the city's poor" was a far cry from the efforts of a village elite to deal with old Goodman Buckley, who was spending too much time in the tavern; to look out for the children of Widow Putnam, whose husband had perished in the Indian wars; or to admonish young Abigail Walcott, who had been observed in the company of Thomas Fuller's hired man. The tie had snapped, and it was not to be restored by impersonal moral crusades, printed exhortations, ersatz "communities," or fleeting encounters between strangers.

Was cynical self-interest as well as wishful thinking involved? Some historians of antebellum moral reform, noting its manipulative features and its frequently hostile references to the poor, have portrayed it as little more than a ruse contrived by a once-dominant elite to thwart the powerful democratic currents of the age—a means by which frustrated Federalists and Whigs tried to regain, in the moral realm, the power they had lost in the political. (This line of interpretation typically emphasizes the disestablishment of New England Congregationalism as a particularly dramatic instance of the status upheavals that gave rise to the moral-control societies.)

As Lois W. Banner has characterized this interpretive approach, it assumes that what the early-nineteenth-century moral reformers really wanted "was to gain power over society for their own conservative, if not reactionary, ends." One recent historian, for example, has portrayed the Jacksonian Sunday school movement as part of a coordinated "moral attack on the poor"; the tract movement, charges another, represented "bald social aggression"; the central purpose of the entire effort, declares a third, "was to make men conform to particular interpretations of morality and decency."[7]

Without question, this interpretation is a persuasive one. Indeed, it cropped up frequently enough in the Jacksonian period itself, especially in the literature of the New York Workingmen's party for whose leaders the city's tract and Sunday school societies represented a presumptuous meddling by the monied interests in the lives of the poor. And it is the theme of *Protestant Jesuitism*, an 1836 polemic by Calvin Colton, a somewhat eccentric New York pamphleteer and unsuccessful clergyman convinced that a small cabal was trying to use "moral and religious organizations of various names" to gain a "controlling influence" in society, "leaving the great mass in subjection to the will and control of select, and often self-elected individuals."[8]

Nor is it difficult in the voluminous literature of the moral-reform societies themselves to unearth blunt assertions of the need to gain mastery over what the New York Sunday School

Union called the "depraved and uneducated part of the community." The publicists for these organizations were quite willing to appeal to conservative fears in their quest for support. In 1826, for example, an ASSU writer contended that self-interest alone should compel the wealthy to back the Sunday school movement. While Sunday schools could not by themselves assure "the peace and tranquility of society," he wrote, "the danger to be apprehended from the vices and evil propensities of a great part of the community [would] be much diminished" through their influence. Two decades later the ASSU was still soliciting the support of "discerning . . . men of the world as well as men of God."[9]

The difficulty with this interpretive framework, then, is not that it is wrong but that it obscures important nuances and necessary qualifications. For example (as Lois Banner goes on to point out), the sustaining drive behind these urban moral-control efforts was not the status anxieties of a disestablished New England Congregational clergy or any other "declining" group. Typically, as we have seen, they were led by successful and prosperous merchants, lawyers, bankers, and other high-status or upwardly mobile groups in the major cities of the mid-Atlantic region, together with their wives and the clergymen (more often Presbyterian than Congregational) whose salaries they paid.[10]

A similar distortion creeps in when these movements are portrayed as nothing but bald social coercion. Part of the confusion arises over the use of the term "social control" to characterize their aims. Loosely applied, social control may suggest an image of would-be moral dictators deviously scheming to clamp their own rigid and puritanical code upon the more easygoing and unsuspecting masses. Certainly, from our contemporary perspective it is easy to view these efforts in just such terms.

From another perspective, however—and certainly from the reformers' own vantage point—these activities represented a public-spirited attempt to develop new supports for a community order which the reformers' experience led them to think of as the normal one—perhaps even as the only alternative to chaos. Watching as the traditional buttressing elements of that order buckled under the combined battering of immigration, the westward movement, and urban growth, they strove somehow to restore social equilibrium by assuming in a responsible way the moral leadership that men and women of their station (or the station to which they aspired) had customarily exercised. Not coercive repression or even "reform," they would have insisted, but the preservation of the moral order amid vastly altered social conditions was the aim of their effort. A degree of self-delusion, perhaps, but certainly not total cynicism, underlay William Ellery Channing's instructions to two young men he was ordaining as "ministers-at-large" to Boston's poor in 1840: "Do not go as representatives of the richer classes, to keep them in order; but go in the name of Christians to make them partakers of the highest distinctions and blessings in which·any of us rejoice."[11]

The concept of social control is often equated with involuntary manipulation; sociologists, however, emphasize that except in totalitarian situations it usually involves considerable mutuality, with a nexus of shared social assumptions and aspirations linking the "controllers" and the "controlled."[12] Certainly, in considering the Jacksonian city, it would be a mistake to assume that the wish to re-create a cohesive moral order was confined to the well-to-do or that the urban poor always greeted the social-control efforts of the voluntary societies with hostility. To be sure, the reformers sometimes found their city Sunday schools dwindling; their efforts to combat prostitution, drunkenness, and Sabbath violation attacked; and their tracts ridiculed by the "vicious" and "depraved" among the masses of slum dwellers.

The literature of the moral-reform societies is also full, however, of stories of Bible and tract distributors, antivice crusaders, and Sunday school visitors eagerly welcomed in the slums as allies in the shadowy but desperate struggle to maintain respectability and reestablish familiar moral landmarks in an alien environment. We have already seen the newly arrived New York immigrant family who warmly welcomed the Bible society visitor in 1822, proudly showed her a church membership certificate, and emphasized that their failure to attend church in New York was not from "want of inclination, but on account of pecuniary inability." In 1845 a New York City Tract Society visitor reported that the response he most frequently encountered in the slums was not hostility but despair: "Oh, we are so poor—we have such trouble to get our daily bread, so destitute of comfortable and decent apparel, that we have no time to think about religion." A recent study of Lynn, Massachusetts, suggests that workers in the shoe factories there supported the local Society for Industry, Morality, and Temperance no less strongly than did the factory owners and ministers who founded it in 1826.[13]

Such fragmentary evidence must be treated cautiously, since it obviously served the interests of the reformers, but it cannot be dismissed. To the poor of the Jacksonian city—many of social backgrounds hardly distinguishable from those of the reformers —prostitution, drunkenness, and family disintegration were not abstract symptoms of urban disruption but the stuff of day-to-day existence. It should hardly surprise us that they sometimes gave at least cautious support to organized efforts to erect a shield against these threatening features of city life, or at least to inoculate the young against their ravages.

That these efforts eventually faltered is not necessarily proof of the hostility of the masses to their social aims or of a narrow coercive intent lying behind them. In large part, the difficulty lay in broader social realities beyond the control or sometimes even the comprehension of either the reformers or the people they sought to influence: the divergent religious traditions separating Protestant reformers from Catholic immigrants, the subtly corrosive effects of class differences on the attempt to create a common moral and social ethos, the unremitting dynamic of urbanization itself.

The social-control model is misleading, too, if it is interpreted to mean that representatives of a stable, cohesive, and sharply delineated middle class were doing the controlling. Unquestionably, these movements did have a class dimension. As early as 1818 the *Sunday School Repository* noted that the Sunday school movement was sustained mainly by "persons of the middle class of society," and similar observations dot the literature of antebellum urban moral reform.[14]

But who were the members of this "middle class"? Shading off from a small patrician elite of aristocratic old families, extremely wealthy merchants, and leading professional men, this broad middle range of the urban population blended imperceptibly at its lower levels into the ranks of the laboring poor.[15] It included within its capacious bounds great numbers of marginal people whose middle-class status was less a matter of measurable attainment than of hope and psychological orientation. For them, the city posed at least as great a threat as it did to the slum dweller. The young man who turned his steps cityward in these years had no assurance of his future rank. He might move upward through successive levels of the middle class, eventually perhaps to enter the rarefied ranks of the elite. Or, he might slide downward into poverty through illness, business failure, bad luck, or the influence of "evil companions," those shadowy emissaries from the city's vast underside ever lurking to entice the newcomer down to their own submerged level. In an 1830 novel about New York City life, Catharine Sedgwick noted how readily a "sudden reverse of fortune, one of the most common accidents of a commercial city," could plunge the well-to-do into "irretrievable obscurity and insignificance."[16] Even the seemingly established middle-class family faced the ever present possibility that a beloved son or daughter might sink to the city's lowest depths. The ubiquitous saloons, brothels, theaters, and gambling halls—even the boarding houses and the streets themselves—offered the aspiring young merchant, clerk, artisan, or shop girl many seductive exits from the confines of middle-class respectability. (One of Lyman Beecher's major objections to theaters was that they forced the respectable to mingle with "the most debased and wretched portion of the community.")[17]

From this perspective, the decision to participate in an urban moral-reform society might reflect less the wish to control others than an impulse toward self-definition, a need to avow publicly one's own class aspirations. The Bible, tract, and Sunday school societies enabled would-be members of this still inchoate middle class to seek each other out, join together in purposeful common effort, and submit to the oversight of others who shared their aspirations. In becoming a volunteer in such an organization, and thereby forging a link with a great national society led by prominent directors and endorsed by prestigious figures of national repute, one ceased to be simply a drifting molecule in an impersonal city; one now had a meaningful role in a significant social undertaking.

Surely such considerations influenced the thousand-odd New Yorkers who volunteered as tract distributors in the wake of Finney's revival of 1834–35 and the green country youths who joined Lyman Beecher's Hanover Street Association of Young Men with its well-orchestrated campaigns against urban vice. We have seen how the aspiring bank clerk of the ATS tract "The Widow's Son," returning to the city that had almost spelled his ruin, became a tract volunteer, a Sunday school teacher, and a visitor to the poor, thereby managing to organize his life and armor himself against a second moral collapse.[18]

The literature of the early Sunday school movement illustrates with particular clarity the role of the Jacksonian urban moral-reform societies in helping an embryonic urban middle class define itself. By the 1830s some 100,000 Americans—most of them young people and many of them city dwellers—had volunteered as Sunday school teachers, yet little attention has been paid to their experience or its meaning. The decision to become a Sunday school teacher was no light matter for the young city dweller of the 1820s or 1830s: it meant giving up a large measure of personal autonomy; adopting a regime of "*hard, persevering, untiring labor*"; faithfully and punctually attending Sunday school even if "alluring novelties" had to be sacrificed; and repressing everything in one's behavior that might seem (as one teachers' handbook put it) "queer," "odd," or "eccentric." It meant, too, submitting to a routine almost as strict for the teachers as for the scholars:

Teachers should not be allowed to remain at the door, or in any part of the [Sunday] school-room, but should go directly to their station, and be seated . . . At roll-call they should give a respectful attention, . . . answer in the same manner as required of the scholars . . . , "Sir!", and raise the right hand . . . The methods of instruction adapted to each class should be written down: and each teacher should strictly adhere to it, introducing no new plan without the advice and consent of the Superintendent . . . and unless sanctioned by the regulations of the school, the motto of which should ever be, "Let all things be done in order."[19]

As we have seen, the young city dweller knew that in assuming the avocation of Sunday school teacher he was associating himself with an institution holding at its command disciplinary mechanisms that exerted (in the words of one proponent) a "silent but powerful influence" over everyone connected with it, teachers no less than scholars. According to the manuals, the would-be teacher was placed on three-month probation, after which the other teachers voted whether to retain him. At any time, a teacher could be dismissed or fined by vote of his colleagues. He could also be disciplined by the superintendent, who was advised to record each teacher's absences, lateness, or "neglect of duty" in a "Docket of Discipline" and then to deal with the waverer through fines; "kindly but decided" public rebuke at the teachers' meetings; or, if all else failed, dismissal.[20]

Beyond such institutionalized regulatory techniques lay the informal but close mutual scrutiny that Sunday school teachers were expected to exercise. The ASSU in 1830 urged teachers to observe each other's behavior "with a degree of anxiety," since "an incompetent, careless, unfaithful teacher is like Achan in the camp of Israel—the whole army . . . falls before its enemies, because the accursed thing is in the midst of it." Making the same point more positively, the ASSU noted that since Sunday school teachers shared "a community of interest," it was only natural that they should "sustain each other in . . . all things that are pure, honest, lovely, and of good report." One outlet for this ceaseless surveillance was the regular teachers' meetings, at which mutual criticism was encouraged.[21]

The teachers were watched by their scholars as well, and here the scrutiny took on added significance, for (as teachers were endlessly reminded) they were to be models to the children in their care. "You have not a single habit, good or bad," teachers were cautioned by the Reverend John Todd, "with which your class will long be unacquainted." A "well regulated class," the ASSU noted in 1828, "must depend upon a well regulated teacher." The "fretful, peevish, hasty teacher can do no good," agreed the Reverend Stephen Tyng, urging teachers to cultivate a "sunny" and "genial" manner.[22]

This constant awareness of one's exemplary role operated with redoubled force upon the superintendent. "If he speak harshly, or quickly, or peevishly, to the teachers or the scholars, if his color comes and goes, and the school is expecting some outbreaking of impatience, he has not self-government . . . [T]o train the teachers to habits of regularity, and punctuality, the Superintendent must be a pattern himself [cultivating] *evenness of temper*, that the school may feel that the hand which holds the helm never varies."[23]

As with the children, the underlying assumption was that what began as external restraint would be internalized, so that the teachers would become their own best moral watchdogs. "Keep your temper and feelings . . . under absolute command," John Todd admonished them. "Cultivate the habit of watchfulness over yourself." The "discipline of every *Teacher*," advised another manual, "should begin with HIMSELF."[24]

But as always in the moral calculus of the Sunday school, sacrifices were balanced by gratifications. The role of the Sunday school teacher might be demanding, but it enabled the urban newcomer unsure of his status or his future to feel "honest and becoming" satisfaction "at the thought of being a useful member of society." And although continual surveillance by one's fellow teachers could become oppressive, the compensatory opportunities for companionship were great. "There is something disheartening to work alone, and to feel that you have not anyone to sympathize in your trials and difficulties," wrote John Todd, but "it is not thus with the Sabbath School teachers." Another writer, describing the rewards of Sunday school work, included this imaginary reverie by a prospective volunteer: "It must be very pleasant to be a Sunday school teacher. They seem to form a company by themselves."[25]

Monthly citywide meetings of Sunday school teachers and tract volunteers allowed lonely urban young people to find companionship, mutual support, and emotional warmth. The ASSU magazine regularly reported the lively and well-attended meetings of the Philadelphia Association of Male Sunday School Teachers and similar groups in other cities. An 1827 Sunday school report from New York City noted: "The teachers here have become an army . . . At their monthly association for discussion, we find six or eight hundred of them present." As the ASSU observed with satisfaction in 1844: "In one way or another, every teacher is drawn out of his privacy."[26]

For many early-nineteenth-century young people starting out in New York, Philadelphia, Boston, or Providence, becoming a tract volunteer or Sunday school teacher was a crucially important step. It provided trustworthy companionship, a sense of worthwhile social involvement, and above all a voluntary means whereby flaws or weaknesses of character that might jeopardize one's chances for upward mobility could be identified and corrected. Sunday school teaching, declared the ASSU in 1828, "is undoubtedly the best guaranty we can have for the morals of those who are not pious. It brings them into immediate connexion with *safe* companions of their own age."[27]

We are left, then, with a perhaps ironic conclusion: the most lasting effects of the Jacksonian urban moral-reform movements may not have been upon the lower classes who figured so prominently in their pronouncements, but upon the volunteers themselves as they groped for institutional supports and moral anchors in a new and unsettling social environment.

PART

Two

The Mid-Century Decades

YEARS OF FRUSTRATION
AND INNOVATION

The city was never far from the center of the American consciousness in the middle decades of the nineteenth century. Despite the
distractions of sectional controversy and the trauma of war itself, the nagging preoccupation with urbanization and its consequences steadily intensified. Indeed, it was in these years that a
stereotyped image of the "wicked city"—purveyed through many
channels and underscored by periodic outbursts of urban violence and disorder—penetrated deep into the national consciousness and lent fresh urgency to the urban social-control movement.

Although the tract and Sunday school movements fell prey
to doubt and discouragement in these years, new organizations
emerged to take their place. Three of these—the Association for
Improving the Condition of the Poor, the Children's Aid Society,
and the Young Men's Christian Association—were particularly
important new departures. In contrast to the earlier evangelical
efforts, they defined their respective target groups with considerable precision, they brought a new level of professionalization
(and secularization) to the movement, and they concentrated
their energies exclusively on the cities. Further, they produced
brilliant and innovative leaders who made significant contributions to the movement's developing strategies. In Charles Loring
Brace of the Children's Aid Society, for one, the urban social-
control movement produced a highly original theoretician. Although they devised new tactics and forged a new ideological

framework for the movement, the earnest determination of these mid-century reformers to forge a cohesive moral order in the sprawling immigrant cities proved them the legitimate heirs of their Jacksonian predecessors.

5

Heightened Concern,
Varied Responses

Once again the ineluctable reality of urban growth—compellingly evident to all who lived through it and confirmed by federal censustakers as each new decade rolled around—is the essential starting point for an understanding of the social-control initiatives to which we now turn. In the thirty years preceding the outbreak of the Civil War, the urban population increased by over 700 percent, from about 500,000 to 3.8 million. Much of this growth occurred in the older coastal cities: Philadelphia grew from 161,000 to well over 500,000, Boston from 61,000 to 133,000, and New York from about 200,000 to more than 800,000. Increasingly, this surging growth was fueled by foreign immigration. Over 540,000 immigrants arrived in the 1830s (about four times as many as in the 1820s), and in the 1840s and 1850s Ireland's devastating potato famine, coupled with economic and political upheavals in Europe, drove the totals far higher. Of the 1.2 million Irish immigrants who arrived during the peak famine years (1847–1854), most huddled down exhausted within a few miles of the docks, and by 1860 the slums of New York, Baltimore, Philadelphia, and especially Boston were heavily Irish.[1]

Reeling under this influx and the pressure of commercial expansion, the big coastal cities were almost literally demolished and rebuilt in these years. "The pulling down of houses and stores in the lower parts [of the city] is awful," noted New York's Philip Hone in 1839; "it looks like the ruin occasioned by an earthquake." By 1860 Boston and Philadelphia had been so totally re-built and enlarged that a Rip Van Winkle from 1830 would have had difficulty orienting himself. It was in these years that bird's-eye views, allowing one to apprehend at least on paper the city's formless sprawl, began to appear in urban guidebooks.[2]

Important as was the growth of the older eastern cities, the mid-century decades were especially notable for the emergence of urbanization as a national phenomenon. In the Midwest, this development was particularly dramatic along the network of riv-ers, lakes, canals, and railroads that transported the goods and produce of a burgeoning population. First came the river cities— Pittsburgh, Cincinnati, Louisville, Memphis, Saint Louis—thrust-ing "a broad wedge of urbanism" into the heart of the transappa-lachian wilderness. Then came the lake cities: Buffalo, Cleveland, Detroit, Milwaukee, and Chicago. A wilderness fort in 1832, Chi-cago became a city of 109,000 in thirty years' time. By 1870, the population of these five lake cities was over sixteen times their 1840 total![3] Wherever Americans looked in these years (includ-ing, after 1849, the Pacific coast) they confronted cities.

With each passing year, these expanding urban centers—espe-cially those with heavy immigrant concentrations—came to seem increasingly sinister and menacing. Turbulent, crime-ridden hot-beds of "popery," they were also places of desperate poverty where thousands endured a barely human existence in decaying tenements, stinking hovels, and damp cellars. The compiler of Boston's first atlas, unable even to map the worst slums, simply wrote them off as "full of sheds and shanties."[4] While overall urban crime statistics are sketchy, a recent study of arrests for major crimes in Boston concludes that the rate was markedly higher in the mid-nineteenth century than it would be a century later. These years, too, saw an intensification of what Stephan Thernstrom and Peter R. Knights have called the "extraordinar-ily volatile" pattern of geographic mobility among the urban pop-ulation. In Boston (where this phenomenon has been studied most fully), the annual rate of population turnover in the 1850s ap-proached an almost incredible 40 percent![5]

All these unsettling urban realities emerged with horrifying starkness in those notorious districts in every big city where vice, drunkenness, crime, and pauperism were concentrated: Philadel-phia's Dandy Hill, for example, described by a journalist in the 1840s as "the rottenest and most villainous neighborhood ever peopled by human beings," or New York's Five Points, a fright-ening warren of brothels, low-grade dives, decayed tenements, street gangs, and—so wrote Charles Dickens in 1842—all that was "loathsome, drooping, and decayed" in the city. If the newer western cities did not yet present so sinister an aspect, they, too, had their slums and their "districts" where lurked gamblers, prostitutes, drifters, and out-and-out criminals.[6]

These regions were the spawning ground of the riots and bloody street brawls that emerged as another alarming feature of urban life in these years. In the textbooks, this disorder is often reduced to a few memorable but isolated outbreaks: the burning of an Ursuline convent by a Boston mob in 1834; the 1835 Baltimore riot over a defaulting bank that left five dead and helped give Baltimore the nickname "Mob City"; New York's 1837 "flour riot" when slum dwellers enraged by soaring bread prices stormed a warehouse, defied the police and the mayor, and destroyed hundreds of barrels of flour; the armed confrontations between Protestants and Irish Catholics in Philadelphia in 1844; the 1849 Astor Place riot in New York between partisans of two rival actors (twenty-two killed); the Five Points gang war of July 1857, "the most ferocious free-for-all in the history of the city"; or, more terrible still, the 1863 antidraft riots that for several days reduced New York City to virtual anarchy as Irish immigrant mobs roamed the streets, pillaging houses and public buildings, lynching blacks, and ultimately yielding only to an overpowering force of federal troops at a cost of over 100 lives.[7]

In fact, these well-known riots were only the tip of the iceberg. The period from the 1830s to the 1850s was a time of almost continuous disorder and turbulence among the urban poor. The 1834–1844 decade saw more than 200 major gang wars in New York City alone, and in other cities the pattern was similar. By the 1850s, writes James F. Richardson, police were practically helpless against the "mobs and gangs [that] often controlled the streets of New York, Philadelphia, and Baltimore." Nor were the western cities immune. Throughout the 1840s and 1850s, Saint Louis was in a state of continual uproar over the brawling of rival volunteer fire companies.[8]

In recent years, American social historians, influenced by the work of George Rudé and Eric Hobsbawm on European mobs in the early industrial era, have probed the internal dynamics of this antebellum urban disorder and concluded that it was often "goal-oriented violence"—a rational response to identifiable grievances marked by a considerable degree of organization, planning, and collective consciousness.[9] To many who lived through them, however, these outbreaks presented no such rational pattern. They seemed simply part of a frightening, intensifying cycle of violence—a cycle perhaps presaging that cataclysmic social collapse which some believed the inevitable result of urbanization.

In the urban commentary of these years, expressions of dismay over the turbulence of the cities recur with almost monotonous regularity. "Great cities have ever been, and probably ever will be, . . . the theatre of the mob," concluded one writer. An American theologian, addressing the faculty of the University of Berlin in 1854 on conditions in the United States, began with a discussion of the "disgraceful scenes of rowdyism" and what they portended.[10] "Riot, disorder, and violence increase in our city," complained Philip Hone in 1840; "every night . . . gangs of young ruffians . . . prowl the streets . . . making [the] night hideous by yells of disgusting inebriety." Philadelphians complained in angry newspaper letters of street gangs in the city's working-class districts who were assailing passersby with "the most obscene and profane language" and even insulting "unprotected females, going [to] and returning from Church." In Saint Louis, the outrages of the fire companies were attacked in a stream of newspaper comment and by the mayor, who warned that good order in the city was being gravely jeopardized by "a sett of Wild men and half grown boys." The draft rioters of 1863, charged New York's mayor, represented "the scum of this great city."[11]

In short, the quickening pace of urbanization, with its concomitants of poverty, vice, crime, and disorder, was a source of intense concern in the middle decades of the nineteenth century. That such conditions also afflicted the cities of the West was doubly disturbing, for many Americans had imagined that the virgin interior, while posing its own moral challenges, would nevertheless provide an ethical counterweight to the urbanizing East. Now this region, too, was becoming pockmarked with cities in whose wake could be found all the familiar evidences of moral degeneration and social disruption.

At once reflecting and exploiting these fears, there emerged in the literature and art of this period, at all cultural levels, a strong current of hostility to the city—a current which helped shape the urban moral-control impulse in this generation and the next. Sometimes this was no more than an allusive antiurban undercurrent: the callousness and deceitfulness of colonial Boston in Hawthorne's 1851 story "My Kinsman, Major Molineux"; Thomas Cole's vision of urban cataclysm and decay in the final canvas of his famous series *The Course of Empire;* Thoreau's fantasy that the trains rumbling past Walden Pond toward Boston were "long battering-rams going twenty miles an hour against the city's walls"; Emerson's youthful journal musing that "destruction of a city" would make a good subject for a poem, and his 1844 Boston lecture welcoming whatever would "disgust men with cities and infuse into them a passion for [the] country."[12]

But when the city does make a direct appearance, it almost invariably has a menacing if not loathsome aspect. In Catharine Sedgwick's *Clarence* (1830), a novel set in New York City, the isolation and hazards of lodging house life are vividly portrayed, and the city's destructive impact upon family cohesion and parental responsibility is symbolized in the death of the principal character's son from an infected cut that his father, involved in a busy round of urban preoccupations, has neglected. In Herman Melville's *Pierre* (1852), the hero no sooner arrives in New York for his first visit, late one night, than he finds himself the victim of a misadventure that lands him in a police station with the drunken, brawling inmates of a "stew" that has just been raided. Subhuman creatures, Melville calls them, "poured out upon earth through the vile vomitory of some unmentionable cellar." As a theme in American fiction, concludes Eugene Arden, "the Evil City" loomed large throughout the later antebellum period, cresting in the 1850s.[13]

Even more influential in shaping the wicked-city stereotype was a torrent of sensational stories that poured forth in newspapers, popular magazines, and pulp novels, as editors, publishers, and hack writers discovered the commercial potential of sin in the city. James Gordon Bennett's *New York Herald*, a penny daily founded in 1835, and the *National Police Gazette*, established in 1845, led the way. Bennett's coverage of such sensational crimes as the 1836 murder of the young prostitute Helen Jewett, and the 1841 rape and murder of Mary Rogers, a tobacco-shop clerk whose body was found floating in the Hudson, was a potent blend of factual reporting, prurient innuendo, and sanctimonious moralizing.[14]

Of the pulp fiction writers dealing in melodramatic portrayals of urban vice and crime, one of the most prolific was Joseph Holt Ingraham, whose many works included *Frank Rivers; or, The Dangers of the Town* (1843), a thinly disguised account of the Helen Jewett murder. In the 1850s one lurid, crime-drenched novel entitled *Life in the Great Metropolis* extended to three volumes, and Osgood Bradbury's *Female Depravity; or, The House of Death* painted the city as a hotbed of prostitution and sexual license.[15] The most popular author in this vein was George Lippard, a Philadelphia newspaper reporter who developed a compulsion to expose the sordid reality behind the city's sedate facade and to show that despite its "regular streets and formal look" it was in reality a "Whited Sepulcre" concealing "rottenness and dead men's bones." In Lippard's *The Quaker City*, an 1844 novel which quickly went through twenty-seven editions, a steamy blend of gothic horror and urban realism transforms Philadelphia into a chillingly sinister place. In *Empire City* (1850) and *New York: Its Upper Ten and Lower Million* (1853), Lippard shifted the locale but continued to exploit the same dark themes.[16]

Closely related were the gaudy journalistic exposés of the city's seamier side that began to appear in the 1840s. The first work in this vein, *The Mysteries and Miseries of New York* (1848) by Ned Buntline [E. Z. C. Judson], was inspired by Eugène Sue's *Les Mystères de Paris*, published a few years earlier. Heavily promoted in small-town and rural America, and featuring lurid illustrations of urban wickedness and crime, Buntline's book and its numerous imitators played their part in shaping mid-nineteenth-century perceptions of the city.[17]

Most of these writers, to be sure, adopted a stance of severe disapproval toward the material they described. Occasionally, as in *Moral Aspects of City Life* (1853) and *Humanity in the City* (1854) by the New York Universalist minister Edwin H. Chapin, the moral-uplift purpose was quite sincere. Neither the melodramatic accounts of prostitution and crime that filled Horace Greeley's moralistic *New York Tribune* nor the reports of mob violence regularly published in the conservative *Niles' Weekly Register* reflected a conscious desire to exploit the wicked-city theme for profit or titillation.[18] But in a sense, the motive made little difference. Sensationalists, reformers, opportunists, and conservatives alike contributed to the stereotype. Cities represented social upheaval, moral collapse, and an undifferentiated, omnipresent menace. Beneath their showy facade lay traps ever ready to ensnare the unsuspecting; in their unholy glare, village innocence withered. Joseph Ingraham's fictionalized account of the Helen Jewett murder drew upon what was, by 1843, already a stock explanation: the young murderer had committed the horrible deed because the "quiet routine of country life" had not prepared him for the city and, like Lewellin in the tract, he had fallen victim to "the intoxicating pleasures and dazzling temptations of this great Babel of enjoyment."[19]

All these themes were fully orchestrated in the Reverend John Todd's *Moral Influence, Dangers, and Duties, Connected with Great Cities* (1841). A facile writer on religious and social themes (including the Sunday school movement), Todd was keenly sensitive to the shifting preoccupations of his middle-class evangelical audience, and in this work he unleashed a vehement attack on cities as "gangrenes on the body politic," "greenhouse[s] of crime," and centers of "all that demoralizes and pollutes." On page after page, Todd catalogued the appalling varieties of urban vice: prostitution, "licentiousness," gambling, theatergoing, Sabbath desecration, the neglect of parental wisdom. To understand the noxious moral effect of urban life, he cried, "go to the sweet country village [and watch] as the poor weeping mother hangs over her boy who has returned from the city to die."[20]

In part this book represented the accumulated bitterness of Todd's own unhappy urban experience. Born in 1800 in Vermont, he held several small-town New England pastorates before coming to Philadelphia in 1837 at the invitation of some disaffected Presbyterians seeking to establish a Congregational church. At first all went well: his membership grew, his Sunday school flourished, the "young and enterprising business men" of his congregation launched an ambitious building program, and he himself bought (on credit) a large house for his growing family. But difficulties soon arose. His revival efforts failed, he was treated as an interloper by the city's established ministers, and the aftermath of the Panic of 1837 wrecked the church's building program and his own finances. His letters became increasingly bleak—"If there be a spot on earth full of pitfalls and death-holes, it is the city"—and in 1841, discouraged and exhausted, he left Philadelphia to take a pastorate in the western Massachusetts town of Pittsfield.[21]

What is perhaps most striking in Todd's book is the absolute quality of its denunciations: every city is not only totally evil but completely depersonalizing. In the country, a dead man "lives in the memory of all the generations who knew him." Not so in the city: "Today you see a man who seems to be the centre of a vast circle, the main-spring of a great business. Tomorrow he drops into the grave,—the crowd pauses a moment, and then the tide rolls on as if he had never lived." In the country, successive generations occupy the same cottage and cultivate the same soil; the city dweller moves from house to house "without reluctance and without emotion. In a little while, you pass and re-pass your former dwelling, and hardly recollect that you ever lived there." In the country, tradition and continuity mean something; in the city, "our attachments, so to speak, are to things in general . . . The waves roll too rapidly to allow us to love any one very strongly."[22]

The theme that beneath the obvious, brazen wickedness of the city lurks an even more insidious power to dissolve the social bond entirely is a dominant one of the period. Lydia Maria Child, for example, who chronicled New York City life in several volumes of *Letters From New-York* in the 1840s, knew from her consultations with phrenologists that her sympathetic capacity was highly developed, and yet in the city's bustling impersonality, she felt it atrophying: "For eight weary months, I have met in the crowded streets but two faces I had ever seen before . . . At times, I almost fancy I can feel myself turning to stone by inches." Another writer made the same point succinctly in 1859: in the city a man "loses his own nature and becomes a new and artificial creature—an inhuman cog in a social machinery."[23]

In Poe's "The Man of the Crowd" (1840), the narrator on impulse begins to follow a man he has randomly singled out from the human mass surging along a great urban thoroughfare. All evening, all night, and into the next day this "man of the crowd" drifts and bobs along on a "tumultuous sea" of humanity, never stopping, never acting purposively as an individual, never encountering a single friend or familiar face. The city's power to disintegrate the social bond takes a different form in Melville's "Bartleby the Scrivener" (1853), whose dim hero reacts not with aimless, frenetic activity but with a hermitlike withdrawal from all social encounters. A man without a past (a "vague report" has it that he once worked at the dead letter office in Washington) and almost without a present, he passes his minimal existence in a gloomy cubbyhole in a Wall Street office, gradually severing all human ties and finally dying, alone, in the Tombs prison. For all its apparent vibrancy, the city is a destroyer: first undermining the sense of community, it finally shatters the human personality itself.

Some, of course, resisted this grim stereotype. If viewed with "comprehensive eyes" and "not to prop up a theory," insisted Edwin Chapin in his 1853 work *Moral Aspects of City Life,* the city presented the usual mixture of good and bad. Nor was the bad entirely a matter of blatant vice and slum disorder. Chapin gave equal attention to the civic withdrawal of the well-to-do, the "masked insincerity" of fashion, and the heartless "metallic men" so caught up in business that should they ever reach Heaven they "would only compute the worth of the golden streets and the jasper walls." Above all, he sought to resist the prevailing tendency to view urbanization as some monstrous aberration. The city, he insisted, "is not an abnormal world—it is not a world outside the Divine sphere, as some would seem to imply . . . No, my friends, it is the great appointed sphere of human endeavor."[24]

In Chapin's view, what made the city seem such a threat to the moral order was that in contrast to the predictable routine of the village, it posed issues, offered choices, and forced decisions. Yet in this very fact lay its profound ethical significance: "The city reveals the moral ends of being, and sets the awful problems of life . . . When men are crowded together, the good and evil that are in them are more intensely excited and thrown to the surface . . . Innocence may thrive in the sweet air of the country, but . . . that which is strongest and noblest in our nature is illustrated in the city . . . The city is a great school for principle, because it affords a keen trial for principle."[25] But Chapin was bucking a powerful current. For many of his generation, the city was, indeed, an abnormal world, if not wholly excluded from the Divine sphere, then surely on its outermost fringes.

This sinister stereotype gained such currency in these years in part because for millions still living on farms and in small towns, the printed word represented practically their only window on urban America. And even within the cities themselves, deepening class stratification and greater spatial separation of the classes—a process well under way by the 1850s—meant that men and women of the elite or the middle class could hold fixed opinions about the moral character of the city as a whole based on the most limited and fleeting firsthand experience. The situation Stephan Thernstrom has found in a relatively small urban center like Newburyport, Massachusetts, was vastly intensified in the larger cities. "The 'teeming lanes and alleys' of these [poor] districts, with their floating population," he writes, "were becoming unknown territory to most middle class citizens. Since less was known of the people who resided there, it was natural to view them in invidious stereotypes. Lower-class neighborhoods were portrayed as breeding grounds of drinking, crime, fornication, and other immoral activities."[26]

Under such circumstances, a single vivid account of some gruesome crime, riot, or notorious sink of urban iniquity could permanently fix a general image of "the city" in the minds of thousands. "Saturate your handkerchief with camphor, so that you can endure the horrid stench, and enter," began an 1854 description of one of the alleys of Five Points.

Grope your way through the long, narrow passage . . . up the dark and dangerous stairs; be careful where you place your foot around the lower step, or in the corners of the broad stairs, for it is more than shoe-mouth deep of steaming filth. Be careful, too, or you may meet someone, perhaps a man, perhaps a woman, who in their drunken frenzy may thrust you . . . headlong down, those filthy stairs . . . [O]pen that door—go in, if you can get in . . . There is no bed in the room —no chair—no table—no nothing—but rags, and dirt, and vermin, and degraded, rum-soaked human beings.[27]

Such accounts, obviously designed to arouse maximum revulsion, captured only a fragment of the total urban reality, yet for many, that fragment became the whole. Morally, the city was becoming an abstraction: a problem to be dealt with in isolation from the economic transformation of which even so sweeping a process as urbanization was merely a side effect.

The Frustrations of Urban Moral Control at Mid-Century

As anxiety about urban disorder mounted and the wicked-city stereotype gained currency in the late antebellum period, the moral-control impulse became, for some, correspondingly more urgent. As in earlier decades, however, efforts to use the machinery of the law for this purpose achieved little. To the reformers' chagrin, municipal authorities consistently failed to exert the moral leadership that men in their position had exercised in an earlier era. Some critics attributed this to their personal moral deficiencies or even their collusion with the forces of vice. Philip Hone in 1838 saw it as yet another proof of New York City's general "depravity . . . of morals." The New York Association for the Suppression of Gambling in 1851 accused the authorities of "frigid indifference" to their cause, and Charles Loring Brace, looking back in 1872 on twenty years of moral-uplift work by his New York Children's Aid Society, described it with some asperity as "a few heroic laborers" trying to do what "legislation and the government" had conspicuously failed to do.[28]

Instances of official corruption and malfeasance can certainly be found in the municipal record of this period, but even with the best will in the world it was no easy matter to translate moral concern for the city into official action. Out-and-out criminality might be combated by strengthening and professionalizing the police (as many cities did in these years); particular sources of disorder might be eliminated by, for example, doing away with the rambunctious volunteer fire companies.[29] But how could the law be marshaled against the ubiquitous evidences of a more insidious moral breakdown: the neglect of the Sabbath; the brothels, gambling halls, and saloons; the pervasive rowdyism and disorder; the young men who lounged on street corners; the children who roamed free of all control?

Proposals to use the law to regulate such areas of personal conduct invariably aroused intense partisan controversy in these years. Political conservatives generally defended the right and duty of society to oversee individual behavior, rejecting what Horace Greeley called the "Loco-Foco" notion that legal prohibitions on alcohol, gambling, and prostitution were "gross usurpations" on individual liberty. "The fallacy here . . . ," Greeley argued in 1845, "lies in the assumption that the perpetrators 'injure nobody but themselves.' They do injure others; they bring scandal and reproach to their relatives; they are morally certain to prove unfaithful to their duties as parents, children, etc., and they corrupt and demoralize those around them."[30]

But a powerful countercurrent of laissez faire political thought in these years continued to see all efforts at coercive moral oversight as simply another manifestation of the arrogance of privilege. In 1838, when a New York City alderman tried to ban Sunday newspaper sales in his ward, Philip Hone sighed: "I do not approve of Sunday papers . . . , [b]ut I think it indiscreet in the alderman to meddle with the matter. It is the very thing they wish. It takes the form of persecution, and . . . thousands of persons who never read a Sunday paper . . . will now espouse its cause."

A would-be moral reformer in New York expressed similar frustrations in 1845. It was "delicate indeed," he wrote, "to interfere with the private concerns of any individual, however poor he may be—that claims to be *one of the independent citizens of the United States—one of the sovereign people!*"[31]

Even had the ideological objections to imposing a moral code by legislative fiat been overcome, a practical difficulty remained: How was a heterogenous urban population to decide which specific forms of behavior were proper subjects for legal restraint? The patrician elites often took a more relaxed attitude toward alcohol, gambling, and the pleasures of the flesh than did the rising commercial class with its evangelical creed and self-disciplined habits. And the immigrant perspective on these matters frequently differed from that of the native-born; one man's vice was another man's folkway. In 1847 Irish spokesmen in Philadelphia denounced the city's Sabbath laws as the product of the same "fanatical, persecuting spirit" that had condoned the hanging of Quakers in seventeenth-century Massachusetts. Even the proverbially stolid and law-abiding German immigrants could react violently—as a "New York Sabbath Committee" discovered in 1857—if anyone tampered with their traditional "Continental" Sunday featuring a family visit to the neighborhood beer garden.[32]

As a means of elevating the city's moral tone and promoting urban stability, law was not the answer. "It requires something more than legislation to convince the judgment," observed a New York tract volunteer in 1845; "no legislation, though based upon the soundest principles, will be generally respected, if it be opposed to popular error." Edwin H. Chapin made the same point, as did Lydia Maria Child. "In the moral world," she wrote in her *Letters From New-York*, coercive legislation was "as useless . . . as machines to force water above its level are in the physical world."[33]

This conclusion was heavily underscored by the fate of the antebellum prohibition movement. Dating from the early nineteenth century, the temperance reform steadily won adherents in the Jacksonian period and for a time, under the general leadership of the American Temperance Union (founded in 1836), it appeared destined to play a major role in shaping the mores of urban America. By the end of the 1830s most cities had thriving temperance societies, and temperance parades (including Sunday schools marching as the Cold Water Army) were a familiar sight. In New York, one temperance leader personally secured some 180,000 total-abstinence pledges, including several fire companies who signed up en masse, in the years from 1833 to 1842.[34]

In the 1840s popular temperance orators like reformed drunkard John Gough attracted large urban audiences, as did the entertaining speakers of the Washington Temperance Society, or Washingtonians, founded in Baltimore in 1840. Four thousand persons took the pledge during a Washingtonian rally in New York City in 1841, and at a Washingtonian parade in Boston that year women crowded the sidewalk "weeping for joy as they beheld their husbands and sons marching onward in sobriety and moral dignity." The Sons of Temperance, a fraternal society founded in 1843, soon boasted 250,000 members, many of them

in cities. At last, one temperance leader later recalled, the "great barrier" separating the urban masses from their would-be moral benefactors seemed to be crumbling. For many urban workingmen, as Norman H. Clark has persuasively argued, the temperance cause offered a means of bringing a degree of order and stability into their lives at a time when so many of the forces buffeting them lay outside their control.[35]

But when the temperance leaders attempted to translate mass enthusiasm into law, the cities turned against them. In state after state in the 1850s, efforts to enact prohibition laws were thwarted by urban opposition. When such legislation was finally passed in New York in 1855, it aroused such hostility in New York City that Mayor Fernando Wood refused to enforce it. In 1856 the state appellate court declared the law unconstitutional. Similar mass opposition, some of it violent, effectively nullified state prohibition legislation in Indianapolis and Chicago. A more moderate measure enacted by the New York legislature early in 1857 to regulate liquor sales and the proliferation of saloons was one of the causes of the New York City riots which broke out that summer.[36] Even in Portland, Maine, where Mayor Neal Dow, a well-known temperance leader, tried vigorously to enforce the state law, saloon keepers found ways of circumventing it—sometimes by giving their customers a "free" drink and then charging for the accompanying cracker. By the 1860s, the American temperance movement, according to its own historian, was "crippled and . . . rapidly disintegrating."[37] The central role cities had played in that process offered persuasive evidence that if urban moral decay were to be stemmed, it would not be through legislative coercion.

With one significant exception: in a few mill towns where most of the inhabitants were dependent upon a single powerful employer, individual behavior was minutely regulated—not by law, perhaps, but by company fiat. The most comprehensive such effort occurred in Lowell, Massachusetts, where the textile operatives—mostly unmarried girls from the country—were required to live in company-owned boardinghouses under the eye of a "keeper," usually a respectable widow, who enforced a strict code and submitted regular reports to the factory supervisors. Neglect of the Sabbath, intemperance, profanity, and even "habitual light behavior and conversation" could be grounds for "dishonorable discharge" and blacklisting. In a work published in 1846, a Lowell minister praised this "strict system of moral police" and offered evidence that in the hermetic atmosphere of the company town, older modes of social control, reinforced by company rules, could still be effective.

> A girl *suspected* of immoralities, or serious impropriety of conduct, at once loses caste. Her fellow-boarders will at once leave the house if the keeper does not dismiss the offender . . . Nor will her former companions walk with, or work with her; till at length, finding herself everywhere talked about, and pointed at, and shunned, she is obliged to relieve her fellow operatives of a presence which they feel brings disgrace. From this power of opinion, there is no appeal . . . [I]t is one of the most active and effective safeguards of character.[38]

Within its limited compass, the system worked for a time. "Lowell is not amusing," wrote a French visitor in 1836, "but Lowell is clean and decent, peaceful and sober." But such a comprehensive moral control in an urban-industrial setting was never more than an isolated anomaly. Even in company towns it was not always attempted. In the mill town of Holyoke, Massachusetts, the absentee owners displayed little interest in their operatives' off-hours behavior, and in Lowell itself the system broke down in the 1850s, when Irish immigrants replaced Yankee farm girls in the mills.[39]

Occasionally, employers in more heterogeneous urban centers attempted a comparable moral supervision. In New York City, for example, the Tappan brothers insisted that their young unmarried employees live in designated boardinghouses where religious observances and strict rules were part of a daily regimen Lewis Tappan's biographer calls "monastic" in its rigidity.[40] But such direct control was usually out of the question in an urban setting. The dispersion of the workers after hours, the ease with which an individual could change jobs, the anonymity of urban life—all undermined its effectiveness.

This mid-century era of deepening urban concern, then, also brought numerous reminders that neither the law nor older modes of oversight could be counted upon to deal with the moral challenge of the city. One result was a renewed interest in bringing the force of evangelical voluntarism to bear on the cities. Despite earlier discouragements, for example, fresh efforts were made in this period to promote urban revivals. Evangelists who had earlier given up on the cities resumed their urban campaigns in the 1850s, enjoying some success in the newer centers of the West.[41]

In the so-called Great Revival of 1858 even New York City was profoundly affected, though the whole phenomenon appears to have been primarily an expression of middle-class longings for emotional closeness and social cohesion; the same longings that had helped draw thousands of volunteers into tract and Sunday school work. This revival originated in the fall of 1857 (after a summer of business depression and street violence) when great numbers of middle-class New Yorkers—merchants, clerks, book-keepers, and bankers, together with their wives and daughters—seemingly drawn by a common impulse, began to gather in small groups at noontime, in houses and public halls as well as in churches, for prayer and spontaneous testimonies "interspersed . . . with hymns and tunes . . . sung from childhood." These gatherings attracted thousands of the "busiest men of the age," wrote one observer, many of whom had "never looked into each other's faces before." To such harried men of affairs, the simplicity and warmth of these informal assemblies supplied a deep need. They enabled the participants to feel part of close-knit if ephemeral little "communities" that came together, separated, and then re-formed on a daily basis. Their great value, noted another observer, was in counteracting the "centrifugal tendency" of city life.[42]

But this ambiguous "revival" did not penetrate beyond the middle class. In the slums, the principal modes of evangelical outreach continued to be the city missions and the voluntarist approaches examined in Part One. By 1865, seventy-six missions were operating in New York City alone, including the famous Old Brewery mission established in Five Points in 1850 by the Ladies' Home Missionary Society, a Methodist group. In nearby Brooklyn, Henry Ward Beecher's Plymouth Church opened several water-front missions in the 1840s.[43]

As for the Bible, tract, and Sunday school societies, they increasingly turned their attention cityward in these years. The American Bible Society urged more attention to the slums where "man is transformed into the brute . . . , crimes against society are plotted, and the most savage passions stimulated to action."[44] The ASSU in 1856 described the urban challenge in similarly lurid terms: "The refuse population of Europe . . . congregate in our great cities and send forth . . . wretched progeny, degraded in the deep degradation of their parents—to be the scavengers, physical and moral, of our streets. Mingled with these are also the offcast children of American debauchery, drunkenness, and vice. A class more dangerous to the community . . . can hardly be imagined."[45]

Nor was this heightened urban concern merely a matter of rhetorical hand wringing. Countless thousands of Bibles and tracts continued to pour into the cities in these years, and by 1850 the ASSU was concentrating its major organizing effort on the urbanizing East. In 1857 the Sunday school associations of the major eastern cities developed a concerted campaign to enroll more city children, especially in the slums. In New York, 2,000 volunteers covered the city on a block-by-block basis. The tract and Sunday school societies made equally determined efforts in the emerging cities of the West. In Detroit, for example, Sunday school enthusiasts had established forty-four schools by the 1860s, enrolling about 30 percent of the city's children.[46]

In terms of effort expended, the mid-century response of American Protestantism to the urban challenge justified Robert Baird's praise in his Religion in America (1856) for the "vast versatility" of the "voluntary principle" in adapting itself "wherever the Gospel is to be preached, wherever vice is to be attacked, wherever suffering humanity is to be relieved." But despite such brave declarations, the urban pronouncements of these societies and movements were increasingly tinged by pessimism. This may have been the high noon of what Robert T. Handy calls "the Protestant Era," but triumphant Protestantism seemed frustratingly unable to master the city. The ministers of New York, charged Charles Loring Brace in 1853, "know scarcely anything about the masses."[47] Even the middle-class church members who threw themselves into the city mission movement often had difficulty sustaining their commitment, either abandoning the effort or shifting to more promising neighborhoods. A recent multivolume history of Methodist missions is revealing precisely because of the almost complete absence of cities from the pages dealing with the antebellum period. Commenting on the two slum missions founded by Henry Ward Beecher's Brooklyn congregation, the church's historian conceded in 1873 that over the years both had "removed farther and farther away from the locations in which they were originally established, until they are now situated in very respectable neighborhoods, while the vicinities which they were originally intended to enlighten are still wallowing in darkness." Those who did persevere often had little to show for their efforts. A Boston city missionary summed up his frustrations in 1851. "The character of the population among whom I minister is very fluctuating. [They are] continually shifting their places of abode. The Missionary's word just begins to find a lodgement when the door abruptly closes; the chain of communion is broken."[48]

A similar uneasiness, intensified by a nagging sense of anachronism, infected the tract societies as well. As preurban memories faded, notes one historian, "the words of the old tracts sounded petulant rather than powerful." The Boston Young Men's Christian Association, arguing in 1875 for the superiority of its approach, observed patronizingly that "the good tract distributor might as well attempt to stem the mighty torrent of a Niagara" as to expect mere tracts to stand up against the "vice and iniquity" of a great city.[49]

Nor did the Sunday school prove the urban panacea its early backers had envisioned. The failure of evangelical efforts to found a Sunday school among the immigrant mill workers of Chicopee, Massachusetts, in the 1850s was typical of many such setbacks in these decades. As the discouraging reports mounted, enthusiasm waned. The Reverend John Todd concluded as early as 1841 that Sunday schools would probably have "little influence" in "saving our great cities"; Charles Loring Brace dismissed city Sunday schools as no better than "pouring water through a sieve"; and even the American Sunday School Union in 1847 reluctantly endorsed a Scottish Sunday school leader's gloomy observation that "Our object has always been to reach the masses, but we cannot get to them."[50]

Especially galling to the ASSU idealogues was the failure of many schools to achieve the order and discipline so central to Sunday school strategy. "After the lapse of a quarter of a century," the ASSU observed caustically in 1849, "we might expect to find that some general principles of organizing and instructing Sunday-schools would have been established; but . . . we are quite as far from any such attainment as we were twenty years ago." Every Sunday school, it concluded, seemed to be "a pattern to itself."[51]

A particularly blatant example here was the Sunday school conducted in Chicago in the 1850s by the young Dwight L. Moody. Ostensibly, it was a great success: as many as 1,500 children attended, and Abraham Lincoln himself visited it en route to Washington in 1861. But measured by the earlier image of the Sunday school as a model of order and routine, Moody's freewheeling approach was a travesty. "We had to keep things going to keep up the children's interest," one worker later recalled, describing how Moody would "read a passage of scripture, sing a hymn, tell an anecdote—anything to fill up the time." As for impressing the scholars with the importance of deference: "The rule of the school was that transfer of membership from one class to another could always be made by simply notifying the superintendent of the desired change, which inevitably resulted in the survival of the fittest among the teachers, as the effect of the children's liberty of choice." A favorable 1867 account of Moody's Sunday school in a Chicago religious paper acknowledged that there was "not much attention paid to order and system."[52] The very social disintegration the Sunday school was to have remedied had infected the movement itself!

The vision of the city Sunday school as a place of harmonious and mutually beneficial cross-class encounters proved equally chimerical. By the Civil War, most Sunday schools had become simply adjuncts of established middle-class congregations. With a few exceptions (such as Moody's ambiguous success in Chicago), the long effort to establish a Sunday school outpost in the urban slums and working-class districts had essentially failed. The achievements of the 1850s, impressive as they seem in isolation, were really efforts to stave off recognition of that failure. In 1859, reporting that Philadelphia's poor children were abandoning the Sunday schools in droves, a local leader of the movement offered a revealing explanation. "They contrast their personal appearance with the well dressed children around them, and through pride will not attend."[53] The urban Sunday school, once welcomed as a means of re-creating the moral and social ambience of the village, was foundering on the deepening class divisions of the industrial city.

To be sure, the proponents of city missions, Sunday schools, and tract and Bible societies continued their efforts in these years —sheer inertia would have assured that—but in contrast to the enthusiasm of the 1820s and 1830s, the mood was now distinctly subdued. The confidence that here was the answer to the moral challenge of the city drained away, and the urban social-control initiative shifted elsewhere. There were important continuities of ideology and personnel between the tract and Sunday school movements and the new moral-control organizations which emerged in the later antebellum period, but the older movements now receded to a subordinate, background position. The long shadow of Lyman Beecher was at last beginning to fade.

Symptomatic of the frustrations of urban moral reform in the 1840s and 1850s were the bursts of moral vigilantism that punctuated the urban scene in these years. As early as 1816 a pious Cincinnatian who stole the curtain of the city's new theater announced in an anonymous newspaper letter that he had done it "for a moral purpose," and as time wore on such do-it-yourself moral reformism became both more frequent and more serious.[54] In 1841 the Detroit city marshall and "a posse of helpers," acting on the slim legal authority of a city-council vote, met secretly late one night and systematically demolished a row of brothels. Eight years later a Philadelphia mob destroyed a well-known brothel and murdered the black proprietor. Similar rampages against houses of prostitution occurred in Boston and Saint Louis, and when several Detroit brothels were again demolished by fire in 1857—this time without city council authorization—the assumption was that the arson had its roots in outraged morality. And matches could be lit by the evil as well as the virtuous. In 1860, a Congregational church in Minneapolis whose minister was organizing various direct-action campaigns against local saloons mysteriously burned to the ground.[55] The frustrated moral-control impulse was itself contributing to the very disorder that many found so alarming in the city!

This thwarted impulse found expression, too, in a renewed interest in the type of single-issue reform characteristic of John R. McDowall's ill-fated antiprostitution crusade of the 1830s. In New York in 1850 a group of ministers, businessmen, and editors founded an Association for the Suppression of Gambling, with the prominent merchant Richard N. Havens as its first president. A Boston branch was set up as well. The plan was to combat gambling through a complex Intelligence Agency that would maintain a record of everyone entering any of the city's gambling establishments. If the offender ignored a confidential "admonition," his name would be turned over to the association's "subscribers" as well as to his employer and any prospective employers. Such drastic action was necessary, contended the association, to maintain surveillance over the rootless young men of the city who, released from "those restraints which once reached out and held them," readily succumbed to their "natural affinities of temper and depravity."[56]

But the Association for the Suppression of Gambling soon came to realize what McDowall and the Female Moral Reform Society had learned twenty years before: the impossibility of translating into an urban context the subtle moral oversight of the village. The founding of the association aroused a storm of protest, and its Intelligence Agency was denounced as a "spy system." Richard Havens, denying this allegation, employed a line of reasoning that would become a standard one for proponents of extra-legal moral-control efforts. "What is right in itself, a man may employ another to do for him . . . So also, what is right for each of a hundred to do personally . . . is right for the hundred to do collectively. If this line of argument be correct, where is the wrong in any body of men associating for their mutual protection against the frauds, the vices, or the crimes of others?"[57] Havens's argument was logically impeccable, but his organization's scheme for monitoring the behavior of others offended something deep in the urban spirit. Criticism continued, and the Association for the Suppression of Gambling, launched on a wave of moral-reform enthusiasm, expired after one year.

By mid-century, one long cycle of urban moral reform effort was ending in uneasiness and frustration. Old approaches were proving only partially effective at best. New strategies, new ideas, new leadership were needed.

6

Narrowing the Problem

SLUM DWELLERS AND
STREET URCHINS

In 1830, a tourist in New York City wishing to visit its most important moral-uplift agencies would probably have started his tour with the offices of the Bible society, the tract society, the city mission association, and the local Sunday school union. By 1860, his most likely first stop would have been Astor Place on Fourth Avenue. Here he would have found within a few doors of each other the headquarters of three organizations unknown in 1830: the Association for Improving the Condition of the Poor, the Children's Aid Society, and the Young Men's Christian Association. At the AICP, he would have encountered Robert M. Hartley, busily organizing the reports on hundreds of slum families filed by his ward committees; at the CAS, Charles Loring Brace, drawing up plans for transporting another company of street urchins to the West; and at the YMCA, Robert R. McBurney welcoming some raw village youth, newly arrived in the city, into the circle of "Y" fellowship. These agencies, with their counterparts in other cities, represented the cutting edge of urban moral-uplift effort at mid-century.

Though very different from each other, these three movements possessed certain common characteristics distinguishing them from earlier efforts. The evangelical ethos remained an important shaping influence, but these three groups were distinctly more secular in their leadership and aims. With the immigrant population becoming increasingly Roman Catholic, the sectarian coloration of the Sunday school, tract, and city mission movements came to be seen as a liability, and it was played down by the new generation of urban reformers.

Furthermore, all three focused their efforts exclusively on America's cities. Urban concerns had been central to the earlier evangelical undertakings, but so had other goals: winning the West for Christ, even evangelizing the entire globe. The new organizations were geared to a single purpose: urban moral and social control.

One finds differences, too, in their leadership and organizational structure. The urban uplift effort of the 1820s and 1830s, with its massive tract distributions and elaborately staffed Sunday schools, had depended upon the efforts of thousands of part-time volunteers. Now, full-time salaried staffs became the rule. The long process by which the city engendered a new profession—social work—was accelerating.

Again, in contrast to those earlier efforts that had (rhetorically at any rate) included the entire city within their sphere of concern, these mid-century organizations were much more specific in identifying their target groups. As the urban population became more distinctly stratified, so did the urban social-control effort.

Finally, these organizations tried with considerable ingenuity to adapt their techniques and goals to urban realities. The Jacksonian tract and Sunday school societies had sought quite literally, and perhaps naively, to re-create in the city the moral ambience of the village. These mid-century movements, by contrast, while equally concerned with creating a cohesive moral order, pursued that goal more fully on the city's own terms. They worked to develop alternatives to the vanished order more attuned to the dynamic of urban existence and the structure of urban society. Among this second generation of urban reformers, the lure of the village was decidedly diminished.

Robert Hartley and the Association for Improving the Condition of the Poor

By the early 1840s, as the ragged battalions poured off the immigrant boats and preoccupation with the "wicked city" intensified, a hitherto rather generalized concern over the city's moral dangers focused increasingly on those at the bottom. Somewhat illogically, the urban poor were singled out as both cause and victim of a frightening array of moral and social evils. The moral problem of the slum posed itself with increasing urgency, and among those who responded was Robert Milham Hartley, founder in 1843 of the New York Association for Improving the Condition

of the Poor. Direct ancestor of the New York Community Service
Society of a later day, the AICP was the prototype for similar
organizations that soon emerged in Brooklyn, Albany, Boston,
Baltimore, and other cities.

The AICP movement brought to culmination an approach to
moral uplift in the slums that had long been maturing. Relief societies with strong moral-reform overtones had sprung up in several cities as early as the 1790s, and the years surrounding the
Panic of 1819 saw the emergence in Baltimore, Philadelphia, and
New York of merchant-led "antipauperism" societies whose purpose was less material relief than greater social control of the
destitute. Dividing their cities into districts, these societies proposed to hire agents who would not only aid the legitimately
needy but also gather detailed information on the prostitution,
gambling, intemperance, profligacy, and economic irresponsibility
that were presumed to underlie most poverty. Armed with these
findings, so they hoped, the antipauperism leaders would be in a
position to demand stricter legal control of demoralizing behavior; mobilize public support for savings banks and other instruments of moral betterment in the slums; and in the long run reduce the relief rolls, cut the almshouse population, and diminish
the number of beggars, including the "downright and detestable
imposters" thought to be infesting the depressed coastal cities.[1]

In the same vein, Boston city missionary Joseph Tuckerman in
1833 organized a Society for the Prevention of Pauperism to systematize the work of the city's benevolent agencies, and five
years later, influenced by Tuckerman's example, a Congregationalist minister in Cincinnati, Thomas Handasyd Perkins, tried to
establish a Relief Union and a Charitable Intelligence Office in
that expanding river city. Dismayed by Cincinnati's rampant
"Pauperism, Poverty, Infidelity, Vice [and] Crime," and convinced that only organized intervention by "men of talent, knowledge, wisdom, genius and goodness" could keep the city from
"putrefying," Perkins urged systematic investigation and oversight of the poor as a way of combining "immediate physical relief
with continued moral relief." Perkins's long-range goal was to
move beyond what he called "chance visiting, a little here and a
little there," toward organized programs to help the poor overcome the vices that had brought them down.[2]

But the times were not yet ripe for this approach. The great
voluntarist programs of Jacksonian evangelicalism—tracts, Sunday schools, missions—were still in their confident, expansive
stage and seemed to offer a more promising means of combating
urban moral breakdown and incipient disorder. The antipauperism societies spawned by the Panic of 1819, beset from the first
by official coolness and the hostility of saloon keepers and other

economic interests threatened by their proposed moral surveillance, quickly faded as prosperity returned. Joseph Tuckerman's efforts in Boston and those of Thomas Perkins in Cincinnati were similarly short-lived.³

It was the Panic of 1837 and its aftermath of unemployment and unrest that revived interest in this new approach to urban moral oversight, both by reducing sharply the income of the Sunday school and tract societies, and by convincing many businessmen and others of the urgent need for more activist and forceful programs of slum uplift and control. In the early 1840s, then, drawing on strategies already developed in the earlier efforts just described, "a number of gentlemen" in New York City began to plan what emerged in 1843 as the New York Association for Improving the Condition of the Poor.

In selecting Robert Hartley as its head, the founders chose an individual whose background and outlook closely matched their own. English by birth, Hartley had been brought to America as a baby in 1799. Passing his boyhood in upstate New York, where his father combined farming with small-scale woolen manufacturing, his earliest memories were of gathering wild strawberries with his mother and of a rural village dominated by "well-to-do farmers of high moral tone," a few leading families of "culture and refinement," and a "Presbyterian meetinghouse so conspicuously 'set on a hill' that it could not be hid." But when he was ten his mother died, a stepmother came into the household, and a series of disruptive moves followed. At seventeen he left home to work in a mill some miles away, suffering acutely from the loss of friends and "the sacred influences of domestic life." Anticipating his later vocation, he was soon conducting meetings among his co-workers "in defense of Bible piety and morality."⁴

Despite the pangs of separation from home and village, Hartley rarely returned, and in 1822 he joined the throngs of young men pouring into New York City. Beginning as a dry-goods clerk, he in 1824 married the daughter of a wealthy manufacturer and soon established his own mercantile business. A devout Presbyterian, Hartley shared with the Tappans and other rising young men of similar background a deep concern about the moral welfare of the city. He became a tract society volunteer, and from 1833 to 1842 he was general agent of the New York City Temperance Society. But, again like many of his generation, he found these avenues of urban moral reform ultimately ineffective and by 1843 was ready to accept the directorship of the newly founded AICP—a position he would hold for the next thirty-three years.⁵

Like the founders of the antipauperism societies, the AICP leadership was drawn from the city's business and professional ranks. Of seventy-three early leaders whose lives have been traced, more than 60 percent were merchants, retailers, artisans, and professional men. Among them were some of the greatest bankers and merchant princes of the day: men like James Brown, James Lenox, Robert Minturn, and Apollos Wetmore.[6] Although the association's religious coloration was deeply Protestant (especially Presbyterian), the AICP was officially nonsectarian, and few ministers were among the leaders. Organizationally, the AICP, like the Sunday school, was elaborately hierarchical, in exemplary contrast to the disarray prevailing among those it proposed to assist. With Hartley as secretary and general agent, the administrative structure included a figurehead president and vice-president, a 100-member board of managers, district supervisors and advisory committees composed of "men of ability and integrity," and a cadre of paid male visitors.[7]

The impetus behind this elaborate effort was not sentimentality toward the poor (for whom Hartley in fact felt considerable distaste) or even distress over their physical sufferings but rather the dual convictions, which would continue to shape urban charitable work for decades, that urban poverty was (1) a massive threat to social stability and (2) the direct consequence of individual moral depravity.

As slums oozed like lava over the urban landscape at mid-century, swallowing up old neighborhoods and familiar landmarks, a fearful middle class became increasingly concerned about the danger such slums posed to the larger society. Sometimes the threat was described in terms of revolutionary violence —a possibility underscored by the riots, gang wars, and turbulent street brawls of the period.[8] More often, observers dwelt on the equally disturbing possibility that the slum's miasmic evils would infect the larger society by more insidious means. "The infection of moral evil is as perilous as that of the plague," declared William Ellery Channing in 1841; to ignore such a menace, he added, would be as irresponsible as to ignore a raging epidemic in the city. So pervasive were such fears that even the Reverend Edwin H. Chapin, in his generally balanced and non-alarmist 1853 book on the moral aspects of city life could describe the urban "Lower Depths" only in terms of a "swimming mist of hideous transactions and hideous faces," "pools dark with undistinguishable horrors," and masses of people "matted together in the very offal of debasement." From this foul chasm, he warned, emanated "surges of moral death" that threatened the entire city.[9]

But there remained a further, somewhat paradoxical danger: that the slums would not explode, that the urban poor would accept their lot and cut themselves off from the larger urban world. "The 'outcasts of society' " were beginning to "form societies of their own," warned Dr. John H. Griscom, a New York physician and public-health reformer in 1843, thereby debasing "the character of the community of which they are a part." "They love to clan together . . . in filth and disorder," agreed Robert Hartley in 1851, "provided they can drink, and smoke, and gossip, and enjoy their balls, and wakes, and frolics, without molestation."[10] For Hartley, these evidences of a developing sense of community in the slums suggested the emergence of a debased urban lower class not only surviving but flourishing as an encysted lump in the heart of the city, forever mocking its moral pretensions.

As for the second assumption underlying the AICP's efforts, it was a matter of firm conviction among the middle class in this period that in the overwhelming majority of cases, poverty was caused by defects of character. Of the nine causes of destitution set down as early as 1818 by a leader of the New York Society for the Prevention of Pauperism, no fewer than six (idleness, intemperance, gambling, extravagance, early and imprudent marriage, and consorting with prostitutes) focused on such individual failings. (The other three were lack of education, pawnshops, and indiscriminate almsgiving.) "The chief evils of poverty," agreed William Ellery Channing in 1834, "are moral in their origin and character." While sympathizing with the destitute, he warned, one must never overlook "the great inward sources of their misery."[11] As the slum threat loomed larger in the 1840s and 1850s, such sentiments were repeated with almost formulaic insistence. It was recognized, of course, that in some instances, such as illness, physical disability, or the injury or death of a breadwinner, the individual could hardly be blamed, but these were seen as easily identifiable exceptions to the general rule of personal responsibility.

For the AICP, as it set out in the early 1840s, the challenge was to awaken the poor to the flaws of character that underlay their degradation and lead them to change their ways. Since the causes of poverty were "chiefly moral," Hartley insisted, echoing Channing, "they admit only moral remedies."[12] Here the AICP visitor played the crucial role. In part, his task was to identify the unavoidably destitute and provide temporary relief drawn from AICP funds. But this was secondary; the central aim, as Hartley put it in 1844, was "not merely to alleviate wretchedness, but to reform character." The visitor's principal function was systematically to canvass his territory, regularly visit the poor in their tenement hovels, probe their habits of life for flaws and weaknesses, point out to them "the true origins of their suffering," offer "encouragement and counsel along the path to rehabilitation," and, finally, to file a report with the AICP central office to prevent their obtaining charitable relief elsewhere under false pretenses. As in the Sunday school, the idea was not to impose the new moral standard through external coercion but rather, through persistent and subtle pressure, to "make the poor a party to their own improvement." The visitor who wished to be an "instrument of good," advised the Baltimore AICP, should help the poor "obtain this good from sources within themselves."[13]

This strategy had its roots in earlier moral-uplift efforts. Recommended (if not actually implemented) by the antipauperism societies of the 1817–1825 period, it was introduced on at least a limited scale in Cincinnati and Philadelphia in the 1830s. Furthermore, it was from the first considered a part of the overall Sunday school strategy. In 1826 an ASSU writer urged teachers to investigate "the circumstances and conditions" of their pupils' families, and three years later the Sunday school organization asked: "Has not the time come to organize a more efficient instrumentality, that will bear upon every family and reach every child . . . within the limits of the city?" (Such a system, it added characteristically, "should resemble . . . Ezekiel's vision—every wheel should move in harmony with the rest.") Soon after, the ASSU renewed its call for a program of "systematic visitation" in which the Sunday school volunteer would compile "a moral map of the space assigned," reprove "open vice," and work to "inculcate habits of industry, and cleanliness."[14]

From the beginning, too, home visitation was a part of the urban tract societies' strategy. Indeed, Robert Hartley began his reform career as a tract volunteer, and when he became head of the AICP he recruited tract distributors as AICP visitors, noting that "their new engagement would be within their present field of labor, and among the same class with whom they are now in habits of frequent confidential intercourse." A number of New York City Tract Society agents signed up as AICP visitors, continuing quite happily in this dual capacity. "Before the formation of the [AICP]," wrote one of them in 1845, "my usefulness was greatly curtailed from the impossibility of ministering to the physical wants of the poor; now it is otherwise, thanks to the noble men comprising that society."[15] This is an illustration of a process we shall encounter frequently, whereby the urban social-control innovations of one generation, while ostensibly representing a dramatic new departure, and often even involving a repudiation of earlier efforts, in fact displayed a quite direct continuity, both in personnel and underlying objectives, with the approach of the preceding generation.

In the tract and Sunday school efforts, however, visitation had been subordinate to other purposes; with the AICP, what had been peripheral became central. The AICP represented an institutional mechanism for transmitting the values of the city's middle and upper strata downward into the ranks of the poor. In a series of addresses delivered between 1835 and 1841, William Ellery Channing not only had anticipated this strategy but had developed the justification for it as persuasively as anyone in his generation. Every social group, Channing insisted, had a solemn obligation to "watch over the moral health of its members." In cities this meant that the more privileged had a duty to awaken the "poorer and more exposed classes" to a "consciousness of their moral powers." The "happy community" was one whose members "care for one another, and in which there is . . . an interest in the intellectual and moral improvement of all." But Channing recognized that this oversight was no longer occurring naturally in the class-ridden city; planning and organization were required. "Many can devote but little personal care to this work," he declared, "but what they cannot do themselves, they can do by others . . . If we cannot often visit the poor ourselves, we may send those who are qualified to serve them better."[16] It was this impulse the AICP sought to institutionalize.

In an 1844 address to Boston's Society for the Prevention of Pauperism (recently resurrected along AICP lines), the Reverend Robert C. Waterston further illuminated the thinking that underlay the AICP approach. Waterston began by invoking the wicked-city stereotype: cities were places of "sickening obscenity and heart-withering skepticism"; urban vice was "rotting the very foundation of society, and eating like vitriol into the very core of the Republic." Nor was Boston immune; though "comparatively pure and orderly," the vaunted "City of Good Morals" had its open wickedness and "secret profligacy." What was the answer? Was a "malignant fatality" irreversibly dragging America's cities downward?[17]

Though finding little hope in elegant churches, legislative remedies, or "economic theories," Waterston saw one promising avenue: the downward plunge could be reversed if the virtuous in the cities would voluntarily band together to form "one vast machinery of moral forces" aimed at "the regeneration of the bad." In such an effort, the special responsibility of organizations like the AICP would be to the city's debased poor. Echoing Robert Hartley, he insisted that the aim was not so much to "aid persons in poverty, as to remove them out of it" by helping them overcome the vices that underlay their condition. If the moral forces of the city would apply patient and systematic effort to "inculcating temperance, frugality, and industry" among the poor, those unfortunates could be lifted from the "idleness and sensuality" of their "low and groveling life" and guided toward "higher hopes and nobler principles." Only through such means, Waterston concluded, would the city ever become "an abode of virtue and peace."[18]

It is important to note, however, that the AICP's preoccupation with the "great inward sources" of poverty had certain significant environmental implications. The connection between the morally debased individual and the physically debased environment was a complex and reciprocal one. If personal failings initially dragged a person downward into the slums, the physical conditions he encountered there deepened his moral degradation and transmitted it to his innocent progeny. "Physical evils produce moral evils," declared Robert Hartley in his usual oracular way in 1853. "Degrade men to the condition of brutes, and they will have brutal propensities and passions."[19]

Here again, the AICP leader was simply reflecting the prevailing current of social thought. All the major commentators on the urban moral problem in these years—Channing, Chapin, Griscom, and others—agreed (as Chapin put it) that before the slum dwellers could be elevated morally, "a thick crust of physical misery must be removed."[20]

Acting on this conviction, the AICP pioneered a variety of "environmental" reforms usually associated with the Progressives of half a century later: pure-milk campaigns, medical dispensaries, public baths, improved housing. Extending its focus beyond individual families, the New York AICP in 1853 undertook a monumental six-month "social, moral, and statistical census" of an entire slum ward that when completed took up 410 closely written folio pages.[21]

But these environmentalist concerns were rooted in the movement's fundamental moral purpose. Indeed, a distinction between "moral" and "environmental" reform would have been puzzling to Robert Hartley and others of the AICP movement. For them, the slum's physical, social, and moral aspects were so intertwined that whichever strand one touched, all the others were inevitably affected as well.

For a time in the mid-nineteenth century, the Association for Improving the Condition of the Poor represented the single most dynamic force in the urban social-control movement. By 1860, with annual contributions of about thirty thousand dollars, the New York AICP had divided the entire city, from the Battery to Eighty-sixth Street, into 337 sections with visitors assigned to each.[22] The AICP's of other cities (and related societies bearing different names) carried on extensive programs as well. In Philadelphia in the early 1850s, for example, the Union Benevolent Association deployed some 5,000 volunteers for a comprehensive district-by-district visitation and census of every poor family.[23]

After its heyday in the late antebellum period, however, the AICP movement entered a long period of decline. Robert Hartley had been the dominant spirit, and as he grew older his movement lost vitality as well. By the 1870s Hartley was complaining that the New York AICP had become simply another almsgiving body, with its larger vision of systematic visitation, detailed record keeping, and an unflagging commitment to moral uplift a thing of the past.[24] By the late nineteenth century the Baltimore AICP, according to its historian, was carrying on no more than a "paper program."[25] Under these circumstances, a younger generation of urban moral-reform enthusiasts who might have revitalized the AICP turned to other channels instead. But the eventual demise of the AICP movement ought not obscure the vigor of its early years or the crucial link it provided between the urban social-control movements of the early nineteenth-century era and those of the Gilded Age.

Charles Loring Brace and the
Children's Aid Society

On anyone's list of dominant figures in the history of moral control in urban America, a place near the top would certainly go to the man who, in 1853, founded the New York Children's Aid Society; Charles Loring Brace was not only the leader of an important organization, he was also an incisive, original social thinker who contributed to the relatively small number of fundamental strategies that emerged over the years.

To understand Brace's thought and career, we must first look briefly at that Jacksonian social innovation which aroused him to creative opposition: the asylum. While the AICP was developing its approach to urban moral control, a quite different strategy was also gaining ground: those individuals who seemed especially vulnerable to the city's baneful influences could simply be *removed* from the urban mass and placed for a time in highly disciplined sheltering institutions, preferably in rural areas, where their character might be shaped and strengthened.[26]

Though paupers, prostitutes, convicts, and the insane all aroused the benevolent interest of the asylum founders, the neglected children of the urban poor attracted their special notice. Introduced in the early 1820s in New York and Philadelphia, the juvenile-asylum movement waned somewhat in the 1830s, as other urban reform approaches gained favor, but it revived in the forties and fifties, as one city after another established its House of Refuge.[27] Although many of these children's asylums eventually became public or semipublic institutions, most were initially the creation of private, voluntary effort.[28] In numerous

The terrifying and ominous New York City draft riots of July 1863.

Marketing the "Wicked City": George Ellington's *The Women of New York*.

As late as 1878, as this illustration from a dime novel of that year shows,
the 1836 murder of the beautiful New York prostitute Helen Jewett could
still make sensational reading.

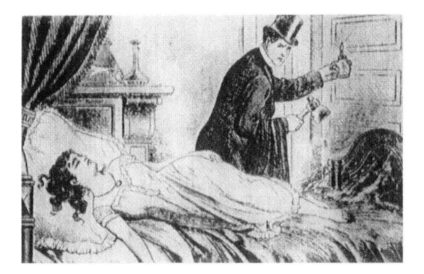

Robert M. Hartley, founder and long-
time director of the New York Association for Improving the Condition
of the Poor.

Outraged morality—and racism—as sources of urban social disorder. An
1849 Philadelphia riot directed against the California House, a tavern and
brothel run by a black man married to a white woman.

Charles Loring Brace at the age of twenty-nine, two years after he founded the New York Children's Aid Society.

Chicago's John V. Farwell, one of thousands of "young men from the country" who poured into the cities in the antebellum years.

Reminders of loved ones left behind. Young men perusing home-town newspapers in the reading room of the Chicago YMCA.

A protecting hand extended to the aspiring newcomer. A *Chicago Tribune* editorial cartoon marking the fiftieth anniversary of the Chicago YMCA.

annual reports and other publications, the founders gave expression to their hope that in the bracing moral atmosphere of the asylum, orphaned or neglected slum children could be taught a trade; armored against the city's temptations; and released as sober, orderly, industrious youths.[29]

As David J. Rothman has documented in his history of the asylum movement, the hallmark of all these institutions was uniformity, strict routine, and exacting discipline. The children were classified and ranked, clothed in standardized uniforms, and subjected to a strict schedule enforced by bells and whistles. ("It was 'beautiful to see them pray,'" Lydia Maria Child was told by the managers of an orphan asylum near New York, "for at the first tip of the whistle they all dropped on their knees."[30] As in the Sunday school, the ostensible activity—training in a craft, overt moral instruction—was probably less important than this pervasive routine and discipline. Indeed, in many respects, the Houses of Refuge simply carried the logic of the Sunday school a step further. If an hour or two a week in a disciplined and hierarchical environment could improve character, then surely the benefits would be multiplied if the impressionable childhood years were spent full-time under such a regimen!

As in the Sunday school, too, shame was a primary disciplinary device. The goal was to make the child feel contrite over his failings, eager to reform, and convinced (as the New York House of Refuge put it) that "his keepers were his best friends." To achieve this, conformity was rewarded, not by red and blue tickets, but by colored badges worn on the uniform. Of course, the greater power these institutions held over their inmates gave them a more potent array of incentives. The children who adapted to the institution's norms were released more rapidly and recommended for the more desirable apprenticeships; the recalcitrant were held longer and, in some extreme instances, bound over to a ship's captain and sent to sea.[31]

Finally, like the Sunday schools, these institutions gradually came to be thought of by their supporters as embodying all the virtues of an ideal family life—without the drawbacks of the actual families from which the children came. For example, the New York Juvenile Asylum described its approach as "strictly parental" and added: "The prominent object has been . . . to clothe the Institution as far as possible with those hallowed associations which usually cluster about home."[32]

Acting upon this broad view of their social role, the Houses of Refuge cast a wide net in drawing children within their sheltering walls. In 1839 a writer described them as designed for poor, idle, and "vagabond" children, even though they "may not have been convicted of any specific crimes." In 1851 the Boston Children's

Friend Society urged the confinement of any child whose family situation might "tend" to make him an eventual social problem.[33] In the heyday of the asylum, the mere prospect of future social disruptiveness or deviancy was sufficient to justify transferring a city child from his own family to a benevolent institution where a truer, finer "family life" might be experienced.

From the 1850s on, the asylum movement had no more outspoken and influential critic than Charles Loring Brace. While agreeing that the key to combating incipient urban disorder lay with the children, he repudiated the asylum (and Sunday school) obsession with discipline, conformity, and hierarchical authority. The "drilled and machine-like" institutional child, Brace contended, became "monastic, indolent, [and] unused to struggle," possessing little of the "independence and manly vigor" necessary for "practical life." In one annual report after another, Brace hammered away at this theme, insisting on the superiority of the Children's Aid Society approach to that of the asylum.[34]

Brace's hatred of the asylum was rooted in his larger view of urbanization and its social consequences. In the opening sentence of his first annual report (1854), he placed the new movement in the broadest possible context: the founding of the Children's Aid Society reflected "the increasing sense among our citizens of the evils of the city." And what were these evils? Brace's answer at first seemed the by now hackneyed one: because of immigration, a "thriftless, beggared, dissolute population" was settling and stagnating in the great cities, creating an "ignorant, debased, permanently poor class"—a group as cut off from the urban well-to-do "as if they were different cities." The neglected children of this class—the "ragged outcasts" of the streets—Brace went on, constituted a particular menace. He cited an 1849 report by New York Police Chief George Matsell that had portrayed the city's 10,000 "idle and vicious children" as a "corrupt and festering fountain" endlessly flowing into the brothels and prisons.[35]

But at this point, Brace's view diverged from the more generalized laments of the wicked-city hand wringers. Throughout the literature of the CAS, one finds comparatively few references to the wickedness, intemperance, profanity, or wildness of individual slum urchins. Rather, the danger Brace emphasized was their potential for destructive *collective* action. "Herding together," he wrote of the origins of street gangs, they soon "form an unconscious society"—and then trouble begins. Allowed to coalesce as a social force in the city, these urchins, grown to maturity, would "come to know their power and use it!"—perhaps at the ballot box, perhaps in the streets: "If the opportunity offered," Brace wrote in 1872, recalling the terrible Civil War draft riots, "we should see an explosion from this class which might leave this city in ashes and flood."[36]

Viewed as individuals, however, rather than collectively as an incipient urban proletariat, the street urchins possessed many traits that Brace clearly esteemed. "I have sometimes stopped, admiringly, to watch the skill and cunning with which the little rascals, some not more than ten years old, would diminish a load of wood left on the docks . . . If the woodman's attention was called to his loss, they were off like a swarm of cockroaches."[37] Only "the streets of New York," he wrote, in a proto–Al Smith vein, could have produced "as bright, sharp, bold, [and] racy a crowd of little fellows." Far from being degenerate human specimens, the newsboys, bootblacks, match sellers, and even petty thieves who swarmed Manhattan's thoroughfares were "quick to understand and quick to act, generous and impulsive, with an air of being well used 'to steer their own canoe.'" The "executive faculties mature early," he wrote, in these "little traders of the city . . . battling for a hard living in the snow and mud of the street." Clearly something in Brace responded very deeply to this "happy race of little heathens and barbarians," and even in his sternest condemnations of them as "'street rats' who gnawed away at the foundations of society, and scampered away when the light was brought near them," the admiration was never wholly missing.[38]

Brace's positive attitude toward the street arab played an important role in shaping popular perceptions of this group. In Elizabeth Oakes Smith's *The Newsboy* (1854), a shivering, barefoot lad responds to a sympathetic query as to whether his feet are cold by snapping: "What in hell is that to you?" Horatio Alger's *Ragged Dick* (1867), based on his observations as a resident in the Newsboys' Lodging House conducted by the CAS, offered the first of many spunky, streetwise Alger heroes. Jacob Riis was invoking a well-established stereotype when he wrote in 1890 of the "Street Arab . . . acknowledging no authority and owning no allegience to anybody or anything, with his grimy fist raised against society whenever it tries to coerce him."[39]

The CAS program reflected its founder's views. The aim, as Brace saw it, was not to turn slum urchins and street wanderers into meek conformists but to direct their tough individualism and resourcefulness into acceptable channels; to "break up their service in the army of vagrancy" without weakening their "free, natural habits" or "sturdy independence." He pursued this goal in two ways. The first was to establish dormitories, reading rooms, and "industrial schools" (really workrooms where cobbling and other skills were taught) to which youthful news vendors and other street boys could repair for brief intervals while continuing their independent life. (This aspect of the program was soon extended to girls as well.) The second and (according to Brace) more "permanent and useful" aspect of the CAS program was to transfer street urchins to towns and settlements in the West, placing them with local residents who would provide for them in return for work.[40]

As head of the CAS, Brace pushed both these lines of endeavor with enormous energy and substantial results. By the mid-1890s, the CAS had transported some 90,000 boys to new lives in the West, and was conducting twenty-one industrial schools, thirteen night schools, and six lodging houses in New York City. In addition, Children's Aid Societies were operating in Baltimore, Boston, Philadelphia, Washington, Chicago, Saint Louis, Cleveland, San Francisco, and Brooklyn.[41]

Reflecting Brace's high regard for the individualism and autonomy of the street urchin, the CAS dormitories and workrooms were wholly voluntary, with the boy free to come and go at will. "No restraint of any sort is put on his independence," wrote Jacob Riis admiringly in 1890. A small fee was charged, to avoid the debilitating effects of charity and to underscore the voluntary nature of the arrangement. Even for Brace, of course, laissez faire had its limits. Rules were enforced in the lodging houses and industrial schools, and without question Brace sought through exhortation and example to inculcate his own rather simple and practical code. This he once summed up as a commitment to "economy, good order, cleanliness . . . , morality . . . , the 'sense of property,' and the desire of accumulation, which, economists tell us, is the base of all civilization." Above all, Brace believed in hard work. "I have been educated in the severe Puritanic, Saxon idea of work," he wrote. "It stands for duty, responsibility, almost religion, with us. I should wish to labor if my body were dropping away piecemeal."[42]

Though he was fully committed to these values, the general thrust of Brace's approach was against either social or moral conformism. Contemporary visitors to CAS lodging houses invariably commented on the prevailing high spirits, the street slang, and the boisterous shouts of tough little gamins totally unintimidated by the surroundings of a benevolent institution. In his own lodging house talks, Brace favored a forceful, informal, and practical-minded approach, and he reveled in the discomfiture of guest speakers who were hooted down when they became excessively moralistic or sentimental.[43]

As for the other prong of the CAS program, the sending of street urchins to the West, the idea hardly originated with Brace. Rooted in the colonial "placing out" system, it was very much in the air when Brace picked it up in 1853. Robert Hartley of the

AICP urged in 1850 that the urban poor be encouraged, "if necessary by rigorous measures" to migrate to the interior "where . . . they may . . . become blessings instead of burdens to the country." A New York minister of the period agreed that it would be "a great triumph of philanthropy" if the cities could be "swept clean" by the mass removal of the poor to the interior. Acting on such advice, organizations in a number of cities tried to persuade immigrant newcomers to move on.[44]

As well as appearing rather derivative, the western migration idea seems at first glance to contradict some of Brace's central ideas. If the street urchins were so adaptable and resourceful, why labor so diligently to transfer them to the West? And if the absence of social oversight and control was what had forced them to develop these qualities, why the eagerness to subject them to family constraints?

In fact, Brace's contribution was more original and less contradictory than the foregoing might suggest. In the first place, he made a crucial shift in the age group at which the effort was aimed. Others had set out to persuade the *adult* poor to pull up stakes, and most soon confessed failure, often berating the poor for their perverse attachment to an urban life that seemed so futile. By the end of the 1850s, the AICP, for one, had abandoned this aspect of its work. Brace, by contrast, focused on young adolescents—the one group among the poor who could most easily be induced to accept such a major upheaval in their lives. "All seemed as careless at leaving home forever, as if they were on a[n] . . . excursion to Hoboken," he wrote of one early party leaving New York for the West.[45] The impressive statistics on the numbers of young migrants transported West by the CAS bear witness to the importance of this shift.

And although western migration was by 1852 a familiar idea in urban moral-reform circles, Brace's version of it grew out of his distinctive social vision. He did not see migration as a plan for ridding the city of undesirables; he did not entertain romantic notions about the moral superiority of the country or nostalgia for a social order based on the scrutiny of family and close-knit community; and he had no desire to restrain the freewheeling autonomy that he so admired in children of the urban poor. Rather, he sought to give it a wider and more secure social arena in which to operate.

As we have seen, Brace was concerned lest children subjected to the hard life of the streets band together and express their discontents through revolutionary violence. He deplored even the most rudimentary gropings toward proletarian class consciousness or collective action (such as the so-called "Shoe-Black Brigades" formed to keep prices up), because "such movements tend to keep the street-children in the city." But spread over a vast continent, these same youths, with their individualism, shrewd opportunism, and contempt for conventional restraints, could represent a major social resource. "Scatter them broadcast over the land" was his prescription; give "their ambition . . . scope for exercise."[46]

It was not the quiet stability of the farm or provincial town that excited Brace's imagination, but the supposed openness and mobility of the raw, developing regions. Significantly, the destinations to which he sent his trainloads of urchins moved steadily westward with the advancing line of settlement, "towards the newer and more distant states." Out there, he believed, the "rough, thieving New York vagrant" would be transformed into the "honest, hardworking Western pioneer"—less by a change in character traits than in the social context against which those traits were played out.[47]

Brace showed little interest in determining whether the boys he sent West actually became settled members of communities; it was enough that they were being "absorbed into that active, busy population." He cheerfully acknowledged that little was known of the fate of the CAS boys who annually disappeared into the interior. Sharing "the national characteristic of love-of-change," these "youthful wanderers" often "change[d] their places and [were] heard of no more"; "left one place for another, merely for fancy or variety"; or "disappeared, and then, after a few years" turned up again elsewhere. Perhaps the quintessential CAS hero was "Little Butch," a lad whose adventures were admiringly recounted in the 1858 annual report. Transported to Michigan early in 1857, he bummed freights from Kalamazoo to Alton to Saint Louis to Chicago to Buffalo, sleeping in post offices and selling newspapers to survive. Hearing of the riots in New York that summer he came back to see what was going on, paid a boasting visit to the Newsboys' Lodging House, and then disappeared again—back to Kalamazoo, he said.[48]

In taking in a CAS boy, the western family made no legal commitments, and the whole arrangement was exceedingly casual. The lads could leave at will (and often did) or be "dismissed" if their work failed to satisfy. This totally voluntary relationship, Brace noted proudly, "is much more free, and . . . of better effect to both parties."[49]

Brace's off-hand attitude toward such matters was not simply the unwillingness of a busy administrator to be bothered by details. It reflected a deep-seated suspicion of all confining social institutions, including the family. In an era when florid tributes to the sacredness of the home were required of anyone seeking a hearing on social topics, Brace made his share. But there is much in his letters, annual reports, and other writings to suggest that his essential attitude fell somewhere between cool skepticism and outright hostility. The family had a powerful role in character formation, to be sure, but for Brace this was a morally neutral fact, since that influence might as easily be bad as good. Time and again, his admiration for the "bright" and "sharp" street urchins is balanced by denunciation of the "stupidity and ignorance" of their debased and "vicious" parents. "It is cheering," he wrote in 1855, "that the children are so much superior to the parents . . . God has given every fresh human soul something, which rises above its surroundings, and which even Want and Vice do not at once wear away."[50] Even his favorable words for the western families with whom CAS children were placed consisted mainly of pointing out that they were preferable to that even more confining social institution, the asylum.

In an era of rapid change, Brace argued, the family could be a regressive social force, holding back the able individual from a creative response to new circumstances. For this reason, in a significant inversion of the conventional approach, he welcomed urbanization not despite but because of its destructive effect on family cohesiveness. Villages, he contended, offered more instances of "inherited and concentrated wickedness and idleness" than cities, because in the "stable and conservative" village environment, the "wicked or idle family" becomes a "morally tabood" pariah, and each successive generation, inheriting the taint, perpetuates its evil ways. In the anonymous city, by contrast, children can more easily "break off from the vicious career of their parents, and grow up as honest and industrious persons." The disruptions of urban family life were thus for Brace a reason for hope. "In New York the families are constantly broken up; some members improve, some die out, but they do not transmit a progeny of crime." This, he believed, "gives most happy promise of the future for the lowest class in the city."[51]

With this background, one can better understand Brace's attitude toward the children who roamed the streets of New York and other cities in the mid-nineteenth century. They were not pathetic victims of a cruel and unheeding metropolis, but exceptional individuals who, under the city's cloak of anonymity and unconcern, had managed to shake off a debased and stultifying family environment. The duty of the reformers was not to try to reconstitute that shattered family, or to subject the child to the ersatz family structure of an asylum, but to complete the break to freedom the child had already begun.

Brace plunged with enormous zest into this campaign to release the slum family's grip upon its ablest members. He recorded few second thoughts about spiriting away from the city many children who "could not easily, on any legal grounds," have been committed to a public institution. Of the 3,000-odd children transported West by the CAS in a typical year—1873—some 40 percent had one or both parents living, and the parental status of an additional 13 percent was recorded as "unknown." On the very day in September 1854 when the first party of boys was being readied for departure, CAS agents were still scouring the streets, rounding up last-minute recruits. One twelve-year-old was added simply on his own assertion that he had no home. Another was taken on "a few hours before we left," and still another during a change of trains in Albany. Over the rails to Michigan, then, went this motley assortment of city boys, "and before Saturday they were all gone."[52]

Were the CAS allowed "full scope," Brace wrote, it "could easily 'locate' 5,000 children per annum." The "great obstacle," however, was the "superstitious opposition" of parents whose "attachment to the city, ignorance or bigotry, and . . . affection for their children" prevented them from "making use of such a benefaction to any large degree." With bemused puzzlement he described the tearful scenes in which a slum parent (usually "drunken," to be sure) had tried to retrieve a child from a departing company of CAS "emigrants." With greater asperity he reported the anti-CAS gossip circulated in the slums (he believed) by Catholic priests. "All sorts of stories were spread among the most ignorant," he wrote, "such as that the children were sold as slaves" or that they were given new names in the West so that "even brothers and sisters might meet and perhaps marry!" (Brace was quite ready to play upon such fears when it suited his purposes. Troubled by vandalism at one of his industrial schools, he "induced" several of the ringleaders to migrate to the West with a CAS party, until a "dark suspicion spread" that he "had the power of spiriting away bad boys by some mysterious means.")[53] What one misses in all this is any recognition on Brace's part of the well-founded parental fears that underlay such rumors and suspicions: fears of an urban order in which the frayed bonds of family, community, and church could be severed with a single stroke by a charitable organization determined to release slum children from the few social strands still holding them, thus granting them the ambiguous gift of total freedom.

Clearly, in Charles Loring Brace we confront an original and innovative force in urban moral reform. Other nineteenth-century efforts—the tract societies, the Sunday schools, the asylums, the AICP, and (as we shall see) the YMCA and the charity organization movement—tried in some fashion to re-create or find substitutes for the moral atmosphere of a traditional social order revolving around family, church, and close-knit community. Their aim was to produce an orderly, disciplined, deferential urban type adhering to a clear-cut code of personal morality. Brace, by contrast, *welcomed* the social upheaval wrought by urbanization. The city, with its anonymity, deracination, and weakened communal ties, was the crucible from which would emerge a stronger and better human type: flexible, self-reliant, autonomous, free of unmanly dependence on others. Through intelligent social engineering, the potentially dangerous concentration of such types in the cities could be prevented, and their energies channeled into the development of the vast interior. Such was Brace's vision, and if it remained a minority view in his day, it was nevertheless influential and portentous.

Though Brace was by training a minister, his approach was almost completely secular. He delivered "sermons" to the boys in the CAS lodging houses, but as he emphasized in *Short Sermons to Newsboys* (1866), his interest was not in winning converts or expounding Christian doctrine, but in calling attention to the "illustrations of truth" in the Bible—truths that had to do with the traits of character he prized. In recruiting his staff he imposed no "dogmatic limitation," even welcoming those of "no defined religious belief." The CAS's encouragement of juvenile independence and autonomy, he wrote, was "of far more importance to a certain class of vagrant children than any possible influence of Sunday-schools or Chapels." Repelled by all institutional rigidities, he adopted the same pragmatic flexibility in his programs that he admired in New York's street wanderers. "We were forced at every step, to test our means by the practical results on the children," he later wrote. "If one method failed, we attempted another."[54]

Yet for all the New Dealish, try-anything tone of such comments, Brace adhered firmly to one central principle: his individualistic social philosophy. The CAS was founded three years after the publication of Herbert Spencer's *Social Statics* (1850), and Brace fully shared the British philosopher's conviction that competitive laissez faire individualism offered the most favorable social environment for human progress. He read Darwin's *Origin of Species* thirteen times and praised the theory of natural selection as "one of the great intellectual events" of the age and one that would prove profoundly relevant to "the moral history of mankind, as well as the physical."[55]

The more intense the struggle, the higher the quality of the survivors. From this assumption followed Brace's notion that the street urchins of the very worst slum areas, such as Five Points, were superior to those in the more prosperous districts.

"Possibly by a process of 'Natural Selection,' " he wrote in 1872, "only the sharpest and brightest lads get through the intense 'struggle for existence' which belongs to the most crowded portions of the city, while the duller are driven to the up-town wards." What happened to those who went under in the struggle was not a question of much interest to Brace; his concern was for the victors. Once they had been identified and "scattered over the whole country" where "the great natural laws of society" could aid them, Brace wrote, they generally succeeded. "Their shrewdness and quickness, with the self-reliance they had acquired in their rough life, made them very efficient in whatever they undertook."[56]

In founding the Children's Aid Society and giving its program his distinctive stamp, Charles Loring Brace not only brought a fresh ideological orientation to the urban morality movement, but he also resolved certain personal problems and career difficulties of his own. If the Tappan brothers exemplify the evangelical urban reformer of the Jacksonian era, Brace was representative of the generation of reformers that dominated the middle decades of the century.

He was born in Litchfield, Connecticut, in 1826—the year Lyman Beecher left to take up a pastorate in Boston. When he was seven, the family moved to Hartford, where his father became principal of a female seminary and, later, editor of the *Hartford Courant*. At fourteen, his mother died. In 1848, after graduating from Yale College and studying for a time at Yale Divinity School, Brace enrolled at New York's Union Theological Seminary. His initial reaction to the city was one of youthful exuberance at its overwhelming variety. He loved to stroll on Broadway and watch "the perfect *flood* of humanity." "Faces and coats of all patterns, bright eyes, whiskers, spectacles, hats, bonnets, caps, all hurrying along in the most apparently inextricable confusion. One would think it a grand gala-day. And it's rather overpowering to think of that rush and whirl being their regular every-day life."[57]

Brace would never wholly lose that initial zest for urban life, but it was soon overlaid with more complex and less enthusiastic emotions. Living in a boardinghouse, he made few friends and corresponded actively with college classmates lest he lose those he already had. "Do you not feel afraid [he wrote one of them] of this crowding of life's business in wearing off some of our best *human* feelings . . . ? God thus far has given me nothing better than my friends. Can't I keep them?" And, like the Tappan brothers, he learned that not only old friendships but even family ties were difficult to maintain in the metropolis. "How stiflingly in odd places memories do come over me," he wrote after the death of a beloved sister in 1850. "The thought of the old home, and how it's all broken up, and how we can't meet again, and if the rest of us do, it will not be the same."[58]

Compounding these concerns were serious career uncertainties. He seemed adrift, acutely conscious that he was but one of thousands of young men trying to forge ahead in the city. His theological degree did not lead to a ministerial appointment, and his father's journalistic position in Hartford counted for little in New York circles. "It is certainly unfortunate," he wrote two Yale friends, the brothers Frederick and John Olmsted, in 1851, a wry tone masking genuine frustration, "that none of us ever gained the position in [New York] society . . . that we had in New Haven or Hartford."[59] A winter of study in Germany in 1850–51 (including brief imprisonment in Austria for remarks sympathetic to the Hungarian nationalist Kossuth) produced two travel books, but they attracted little notice.

Like many other native-born urban newcomers of the middle class, Brace found in religious and moral-reform work both an anodyne to loneliness and a means of dealing with his career problems. He assisted the Reverend Lewis Morris Pease in mission work in Five Points, preached to the prostitutes in the charity hospital on Blackwell's Island, and joined with several other young men to organize "boys' meetings" in the slums. (These, in fact, were the direct forerunner of the CAS.) In these contacts with the city's underside, he saw distorted but recognizable reflections of his own situation. "No one can realize, who is not familiar with this class," he later wrote, "the entire solitude and desertion into which a human being can come in a large city." He might have been describing himself when he wrote of the young people "drifting about our streets, with hardly any assignable home or occupation."[60] Through a somewhat sentimental haze, he saw in the prostitutes the same sense of loneliness and loss that he was experiencing. Of one, whom he described carefully as "voluptuous, but really with a very fine expression," he wrote: "She had seen better days, I suspect, than most of them, and seemed to look on almost proudly as we spoke. But as we—no I —alluded to old friends, and the home and the love which they had had once . . . and then told them in the simplest, most untechnical words I could use, of the Friendship they might have in Jesus, and of his love to them, she could not restrain her tears, as I hardly could mine."[61]

Despite such emotionally rewarding moments, Brace soon became convinced (as he later wrote) that the "neglected and ruffian class" was not to be reached by "distributing tracts, and holding prayer meetings, and scattering Bibles." It was thus, in 1853, at twenty-seven, with no clear vocation and no established position in the city, that Brace founded the CAS. Almost at once, it seemed, his life fell into place. He married the next year and went on to rear a family of four. And although he later indulged the conceit that in turning to philanthropy he had "cast aside whatever chance he may have had for the prizes and honors of life," it was precisely through this decision that he achieved the recognition and status he clearly craved. From the first, the CAS attracted support from the socially prominent, and soon Brace was moving in the orbit of people like Mrs. William Astor and yachtsman George Schuyler, at whose estate he was introduced to Washington Irving and Alexander Hamilton's son. "It was mainly because of the Children's Aid Society," he candidly wrote his father after this particular social triumph.[62]

His fourteen-member board of trustees included merchants, bankers, and lawyers. (But no ministers; the CAS, like the AICP, reflected the increasing secularization of the urban social-control movement.) Among them were several young men who later rose to prominence, including paper merchant Cyrus W. Field of Atlantic-cable fame, and iron manufacturer Abraham S. Hewitt, future mayor of New York and national chairman of the Democratic party.[63]

Brace's newfound prominence also gave a fillip to his journalistic and literary ambitions. He wrote extensively not only on charity topics but on various public issues for a number of newspapers and magazines, and from the 1860s on, published a stream of books on varied themes, culminating in his *History of Human Progress under Christianity*, which went through four editions in the 1880s.

In 1872, the year of the publication of his history of the CAS, *The Dangerous Classes of New York and Twenty Years Work among Them*, Brace made a trip to England that amounted to a triumphal tour. "Only two commoners [were] present besides myself," he wrote of one of the many elegant dinners that marked his progress; "all the family had read enough of my book to be able to talk of it." Among his hosts were Gladstone's education minister, William Forster, and his wife, a daughter of Thomas Arnold. Fittingly, the tour culminated with an invitation from the man most responsible for shaping his intellectual world, Charles Darwin.[64]

In building a career upon the lives of street urchins cast up by the family wreckage of the slums, Brace was also dealing with certain unresolved aspects of his own experience. His initial encounter with the city had left him with ambivalent feelings about its meaning, and yet from his forum as head of the CAS, he assured his generation that urbanization was producing a new and valuable human type: less bound to family, home, and traditional ideas; shrewdly responsive to the kaleidoscopic opportunities of a changing order; free. Without guilt or remorse, the urchins with whom he dealt had adapted to the demands of their environment —an adjustment that Brace himself had found so wrenching. Here, at the deepest level, was the source of his admiration. "You must not think of me as tending delicate, fatherless children, or anything of that sort," he wrote a' friend at the end of his first year with the CAS; "I have to do mostly with rough, hearty, poor boys, and with friendless children who have learned how to take care of themselves—such as I do love or like. I think there is nothing in the world so interesting as a healthy, manly boy, and the attempt to help these fellows to help themselves is the most pleasant to me possible."[65]

This emotional and institutional identification with the children of the slums gave Brace a secure niche in New York society and helped him accept the psychological demands of urban existence. Significantly, when he sought in his old age to reach across the years and renew his link with the past, it was not, like the Tappans in 1848, by returning to his boyhood haunts. As he had long ago realized, those ties, once severed, were not to be revived. Instead, in 1889 he revisited the lake in the Adirondacks where he had vacationed years before, and in this sylvan retreat far from the city he achieved at least an aesthetic continuity with a vanished world. "This revisiting the old scenes of my exuberant youth and manhood is very interesting to me," he wrote. "I am now a father in Israel to the Adirondackers. It is lovely, solitary, dreamy as ever. A lifetime has hardly touched this lake." But even here, one could not escape the forces of change: "The desolater, the lumber-man, has not reached here, but next year he will come, and all will be ruin. (I have written to the 'Times'!)."[66] By the following summer, Charles Loring Brace was dead.

There remains an ironic postscript. Brace was succeeded as head of the Children's Aid Society by his son and namesake, who continued in that position for another forty years. Thus at the very end of his life, Brace had a satisfaction denied to most of the fathers he had dealt with over the years: the knowledge that a son was following in his footsteps.

7

Young Men and the City

THE EMERGENCE OF
THE YMCA

Robert Hartley and Charles Loring Brace were but two of thousands of young men who poured into the city from the hinterlands in these antebellum decades, eager for the rewards it dangled so tantalizingly before their eyes. Clinging precariously to the bottom rungs of the middle class, these clerks, salesmen, bookkeepers, and bank tellers were in constant danger of slipping into the lower depths, lost forever to morality, to religion, and to settled society.

Thus, while the immigrant slums received massive attention from moralists in these years, the plight of these "young men in the city" aroused deepening concern as well. As the objects of moral-control effort, however, they posed a special challenge, for they were not as manipulable as those at the very bottom. They were not impoverished slum dwellers to be controlled through AICP-type schemes of moral uplift. Nor were they street arabs who could be enrolled in a Sunday school, sent to an asylum, or transported West by the Children's Aid Society. Of the organizations that emerged to deal with this perplexing situation, none was more seminal in its influence than the Young Men's Christian Association. Although the "Y" has long since subsided to a comfortably prosaic urban role, inspiring neither deep commitment from those who utilize its facilities nor close scrutiny from social thinkers and urbanologists, it was once—like the Sunday school before it—perceived as a highly promising new social-control instrument. By exploring its background, ideology, and early strategies, we view from yet another vantage point America's response to the moral challenge of the city.

Young Men in the City: Diagnosing the Risks, Searching for the Remedy

In numerical terms, the mid-nineteenth-century apprehensions about young men in the city were well founded, for most urban centers in these years did harbor a high proportion of recently arrived, unmarried young men. "I have no recollection of ever having seen a man over fifty years of age," wrote one such newcomer in Chicago in 1836; "Most of us are under thirty. I seldom see a child." Demographic data bear out his impression. By 1850, 94 percent of Chicago's male population was under fifty and 67 percent was under thirty, with about half the latter group young men in the fifteen to twenty-nine age range. New York, Boston, Philadelphia, and other big cities presented a similar picture.[1]

When reformers and moralists tried to articulate what they found so alarming in the situation of these thousands of youths of ill-defined status and uncertain future, they usually visualized a stereotyped set of interconnected vices any one of which, once yielded to, would quickly bring all the others in its train. The gambler would drown the shock of his losses in alcohol; the theatergoer ("his feelings excited, and his passions fired, until he is maddened") would inevitably seek out the brothel; even the Sabbath breaker risked a general moral collapse. After "the first advance of vice," wrote one moralist in 1845, "the descent is swift, like the swollen and headlong torrent, sweeping every landmark away."[2]

The green provincial youth confronted these urban hazards with particular vulnerability. At life's most treacherous stage— no longer a child, not yet a man—he had left behind the influences by which his still unformed character might have been molded, cutting himself off "from the eye and conscious watchcare and restraint of parents, friends, and neighbors."[3] Indeed, one observer suggested in 1857, a rural upbringing *increased* the likelihood that a young man would succumb morally in the city. Whereas the urban native early acquired an armor of self-sufficiency, the new arrival lacked such a protective shell. The social affections he had once innocently expended upon family and friends remained "awake, clamorous, [and] vehement," yet now without a natural outlet, posing the obvious possibility that they would "rush on, turbid and defiled, over the wild precipice of forbidden indulgence." Most young men did not come to the city *seeking* "vicious indulgence" and "bacchanalian entertainments," agreed another, but the isolation of their new situation soon generated a need for "variety and entertainment" that made the city's temptations irresistible.[4]

In an 1864 address to the New York YMCA, the physician Verranus Morse offered a comprehensive statement of these concerns. In the village, Morse suggested, echoing hundreds of tracts, moral distinctions were clear-cut. Vice, "seen in its natural loathsomeness," could be easily recognized and avoided. What boy could be drawn to "the dingy grog shop, with its few ragged, bloated patrons"? This fact, coupled with the "general knowledge of each other's affairs and neighborly supervision of each other's habits," meant that most rural youths, "if not moral from principle," were "at least passively moral."[5]

How different in the city! Here, Morse went on, "inexperienced and unaided" newcomers not only found saloons "fitted up like royal palaces," but they could join the crowds at such haunts "with as little seeming individuality to the unpracticed eye as the particles of vapor that go up before the morning sun." Far from "mothers' watchful eyes, fathers' warning voices, and neighbors' tell-tale tongues," they were free to indulge "every degree of wickedness, from the slightest excesses to the foulest villainies."[6]

Dr. Morse knew whereof he spoke. Born and reared in a New Hampshire village, he had come as a stranger to New York in 1845 to begin medical studies. He was doubtless drawing on personal memories in later describing the boardinghouses that catered to young bachelors as not only "cold, dimly lighted, scantily furnished, and badly cared for, [with] two or three or more beds" per room, but also as a kind of treacherous pseudo-home, supplying some of the emotional support of family life, but none of its moral oversight. In the boardinghouse, "young men brought up in comfort and refinement are compelled to lodge with those whose systems are saturated with whiskey, tobacco juice and foul diseases, and whose minds are still more impure . . . A few weeks of such intercourse is sufficient to benumb the moral sensibilities and prepare young men of no thoroughly fixed principles to accept invitations to the theater, the concert saloon, and other places of low amusement, where they may be induced to take their first step in vice."[7]

What was to be done? Convincing themselves that the situation of young men in the city was highly precarious, antebellum reformers experimented with a variety of strategies, some of which we have already explored. Numerous books and tracts such as the Reverend George Burnap's *Lectures to Young Men* (1840) were directed specifically to young urban males in these years, and many were recruited as Sunday school teachers and tract society volunteers.[8] But as we have seen, the printed word was a pallid substitute for the moral support of an actual social institution—a fragile bulwark against what temperance writer T. S. Arthur in 1848 called the "host of ungovernable impulses" assailing the isolated young man of the city, "overmastering him in every feeble effort he makes to subdue them."[9] And by the 1850s, the Sunday school and tract movements were undergoing changes that made them less effective than formerly in providing support and moral oversight to the young volunteer.

The challenge, then, was to discover a viable urban alternative for the web of supportive moral institutions the young man had left behind. The most basic of these, most moralists were convinced (despite the reservations of Charles Loring Brace), was the family itself. "How early do these silken cords bind the heart!" exclaimed John Todd in discussing the family's role in moral development; "no human institution can bear any comparison with this." Accordingly, much lip service was paid in these years to the desirability of drawing the unmarried young men of the city within the domestic fold. Pious, settled urban families were urged to take in newcomers, thereby throwing around them the protective mantle of familial oversight and maternal influence. Employers were exhorted to take a fatherly interest in their young employees. "Every merchant should know where his clerks live and how they spend their time," declared Verranus Morse in 1866; "They should be treated as branches of his own family."[10]

But as Morse himself acknowledged, urban class realities made such an ideal difficult to achieve. A merchant's employees might be ill fitted "to associate with virtuous and refined families," or "so numerous that his family would be discommoded if they were permitted to call at their own convenience." Pondering these problems, Morse could only suggest that the merchant "set apart an evening every month, or oftener" when he and his family would be at home for his workers, to give them at least an occasional exposure to domesticity.[11]

What of the churches? As early as 1828 the American Sunday School Union had charged that single young men were being ill served by the urban churches ("Many . . . do not attend because they are not made welcome . . . [F]requently, they are regarded as intruders"), and a generation later, despite such efforts as Lyman Beecher's Association of Young Men in Boston, Verranus Morse reiterated this harsh judgment, again speaking in a clearly autobiographical vein:

Young men, fresh from the homes and the churches of their childhood, nowhere feel such utter loneliness, such complete isolation, as in the midst of a city congregation; . . .

nowhere does it require stronger efforts to keep tears of sadness from their eyes than in a city church. Week after week they go in and out, and no one greets them, no one notices them. Sad and discouraged, they try others with similar results, until at last they desert the sanctuary altogether or fall into a vagabondizing way, wandering about from one church to another.[12]

Symptomatic of the emotional isolation Morse described were the scores of young men's associations and societies that sprang up in many cities from the 1820s on. Self-education was often their ostensible object, and many boasted a library and reading room as their central features. This is especially true of the mercantile library movement that originated in New York City and soon spread to Boston, Pittsburgh, Cincinnati, and elsewhere.[13]

Some of these societies appear to have been the spontaneous creations of young men. The New York Mercantile Library Association, for example, began in 1820 when a few young clerks rented a room and pooled their personal books. And in 1857, when the notorious Franklin volunteer fire company of Saint Louis disbanded under strong civic pressure, the members bought a stock of books and established the Franklin Library as a rendezvous for former members. But moral reformers at once recognized the potential of this movement and lent strong support. A prominent backer of the New York City Mercantile Library Association, for example, was William E. Dodge, whom we have encountered as a Sunday school and tract society supporter.[14]

Under the aegis of such figures, the mercantile libraries and similar endeavors dedicated themselves to shielding young men from "the society of the vicious and profane" and furthering their "*moral cultivation.*" Such goals would not be achieved through coercive rules of behavior, insisted the leaders and backers, but by offering companionship and mutual help as alternatives to isolation and dissipation. In relieving the "aching sense of loneliness and desolation" that went with city life, the mercantile library would provide an anchor against "moral shipwreck on the lee shore of the brothel and grog shop."[15] As another supporter, Philip Hone, put it in 1843, it would offer the benefits of "association" to young men who might otherwise be "swept away, and lost in the undiscriminating ocean."[16]

Enter the YMCA

It was in the 1850s that these impulses at last found full-fledged institutional expression in the Young Men's Christian Association. The movement originated in England in 1841 with a twenty-year-old dry-goods clerk, George Williams. A farm boy, Williams had migrated to London as a youth and become one of the 140-odd clerks employed by a large dry-goods firm, Hitchcock and Rogers, and housed in a large and cheerless dormitory above the store. Disturbed by the loneliness and moral hazards of this existence, he opened a reading room where he and his friends might spend their evenings in more sociable and elevating surroundings. A Young Men's Christian Association was formed to support this effort, and from these small beginnings a great world movement grew.[17]

The idea was brought to America in 1851 by George M. Van Derlip, a divinity student, and George H. Petrie, a fledgling New York City merchant. While in London for the Crystal Palace Exposition, these two young Americans visited the rooms of the YMCA and returned as converts to the idea. Van Derlip expressed his enthusiasm in a letter to a Baptist paper in Boston, the *Christian Watchman and Reflector*, and soon YMCA's were founded in Boston, Montreal, and New York City. The first convention was held in Buffalo in 1854, and a national confederation was formed a year later. With remarkable rapidity the movement spread to every major urban center (and many lesser ones) from the Atlantic to the Mississippi, and by 1860 over 200 local YMCA's were serving some 25,000 members. When a city attained a certain size, a YMCA inevitably emerged. In Los Angeles, for example, this point was reached in 1882, in the midst of a boom triggered by the arrival of the railroad in 1876. By the end of the century, the YMCA was a familiar urban feature from coast to coast, with more than a quarter of a million members in about 1,500 local associations.[18]

A glance at the early proponents of the American YMCA underscores the emergence of a new generation of secular leaders in the urban social-control movement. Although aging revivalists, Sunday school pioneers and tract society stalwarts lent their blessing (the venerable Lyman Beecher delivered the dedicatory sermon at the opening of the Boston YMCA in 1852), the first trustees and officers were not ministers, but merchants, manufacturers, and bankers. They were men like Philip Moen in Worcester, Massachusetts; Samuel Dexter Ward and John V. Farwell in Chicago; William E. Dodge, Jr., Morris K. Jesup, and J. P. Morgan in New York. Although a striking number of them later achieved fame and power in the commercial world, in the 1850s most were, like young George Petrie himself, still in their twenties or early thirties and still on the thresholds of their careers. Samuel Dexter Ward, for example, later prominent in hardware and insurance, was just thirty-one and a newcomer in Chicago business when he became first president of that city's YMCA in 1853.[19]

And although some, notably Morgan and Dodge, belonged to

established and prospering mercantile families, many had themselves recently been "young men from the country." Morris Jesup, for example, was brought from Connecticut to New York City by his mother after his father's bankruptcy and early death in the 1830s. Here, in the mid-1840s, still hardly more than a boy, he began a business career that would make him an extremely wealthy merchant, banker, and railroad financier in the years after the Civil War. Similarly, Philip Moen, a founder of the Worcester YMCA in 1852, was a small-town youth who had recently married a Worcester girl and joined her father, Ichabod Washburn, in the wire business. (Incorporated for $1 million in 1868, the firm of Washburn and Moen eventually became the world leader in its field.)[20]

No one better illustrates this pattern than John V. Farwell, a dry-goods wholesaler who became one of Chicago's great merchant princes in the Gilded Age. Migrating with his family by covered wagon from New York State to Illinois in the 1830s, Farwell grew up in a pious, close-knit farm family and was converted at an early age at a nearby camp meeting. "My own father led me to the altar," he later recalled, "after I had heard my sainted mother praying for me before retiring for the night."[21]

At nineteen, Farwell made the big move to Chicago. Working as a court stenographer and dry-goods clerk, he lived in boardinghouses until his marriage in 1849, and again after his wife's death in childbirth two years later.

Though he found companionship in occasional visits home, in a volunteer fire company, and as a Sunday school teacher, his diary vividly conveys the loneliness and uncertainty of his life in this period. "Our friends separated from us by distance come up before the mind's eye," he wrote in 1849, "and we long to smother and while away the lonely hours in having an agreeable chat with them."[22] For Farwell, the YMCA was a lifeline in a stormy sea, and from the beginning he was a dedicated and generous supporter.[23] His preurban roots and sharply etched memories of a newcomer's encounter with the city made him typical of many rising young businessmen who rallied to the infant enterprise in the 1850s.

Predictably, with such men shaping YMCA policy, the emphasis on newcomers was central. Nor was this emphasis merely rhetorical: of the 200 young men who turned out for the founding of the Boston YMCA in 1852, only about a dozen raised their hands when a speaker asked how many were natives of the city.[24]

Day-to-day management of each local association was in the hands of a resident director first called "librarian" and later "secretary." These were usually young men recruited from the lower rungs of commerce: twenty-one-year-old Levi Rowland in Boston; twenty-eight-year-old shoe salesman (and Sunday school teacher) Dwight Moody in Chicago; a young clerk named John Wanamaker in Philadelphia; and, in New York, Robert R. McBurney, a hat salesman who emigrated from Ireland in 1854.[25]

Many of these early YMCA secretaries knew firsthand what it meant to be alone in the city. Moody, for example, migrated from the village of Northfield, Massachusetts, to the manufacturing center of Worcester in 1854, at seventeen, only to find himself jobless and friendless. "I walked the streets, day after day, trying to find work," he recalled on a later visit. "If only I had succeeded I might have been a citizen here . . . , but Worcester didn't want me. I couldn't get hold, I couldn't get in." He went next to Boston, where he discovered the YMCA. "I am going to join . . . to-morrow night," he wrote his family, "then I shall have a place to go to when I want to go away anywhere." Moving on to Chicago in 1856, Moody quickly sought out the YMCA, and after the Civil War he became its secretary.[26]

Although in theory the movement was aimed at all young men, in practice the early YMCA labored almost exclusively among native-born Protestants of vaguely middle-class standing. To be sure, efforts were made from the beginning to broaden the class base. In Baltimore a branch was established in the 1850s "to reach the young men who now compose the numerous rowdy clubs which have been so notorious . . . , viz., Plug Uglies, &c." A branch was opened in a New York slum district shortly after the Civil War, and in Worcester the YMCA contemplated "outposts" in poor neighborhoods where the poor youth would "feel at perfect liberty to go without the preliminaries of a complete change of garb." For a time in the late nineteenth century, various railroad companies subsidized YMCA branches in areas where railroad workers congregated; indeed, in 1887 Cornelius Vanderbilt contributed nearly a quarter million dollars for such a "railroad branch" near New York's Grand Central station.[27]

But the effort to attract working-class membership was rarely successful in this early period. The slum "outposts" languished, and the "railroad branches," as symbols of paternalistic capitalism, became the targets of worker hostility in times of labor unrest. The typical YMCA member in the nineteenth century might be a clerk, student, or skilled craftsman, but rarely was he a common laborer or a factory worker. As C. Howard Hopkins notes, the movement began within the middle class and it "remained with few exceptions the creature . . . of that economic class."[28] More precisely, the original impetus and financing came from the upper stratum of the business and professional class; the clientele, from the lower ranks of urban commercial life, including many newcomers whose class standing was largely still a matter of aspiration.

By the end of the century, the class orientation of the YMCA was firmly established. When the Chicago "Y" showed off its new building on New Year's Day, 1894, "carriages lined up as if for a great society event," the wives of prominent Chicagoans served as hostesses, "congenial" young YMCA members greeted visitors at the door, an orchestra played popular airs, and guests sipped "a white frappe from red cups"—all in all, as a reporter noted, an "eminently proper occasion."[29]

But if the YMCA's class horizons were limited, its aspirations in other respects were not. The goal was no less than to guide the moral development of young newcomers to the city: to erect a "wall of iron" (as Verranus Morse put it) between them and the city's evil underside. At first glance, the specific means seem confusing and lacking in focus. Common to all the early YMCA's was a reading room (a legacy from the mercantile-library movement), but beyond that, programs diverged widely. Some inaugurated lecture series and Bible study programs; others stressed evangelism, street meetings, and similar religious work; still others devised schemes of charitable relief in the slums; and some concentrated on finding housing and employment for newcomers. And it was not long before the evening classes, exercise rooms, and swimming pools that would ultimately dominate the YMCA program made their appearance. Reminiscing in his later years, Boston's Levi Rowland described the rather hectic routine of the early YMCA secretary: though still only in his early twenties, Rowland "had charge of the Library, and rooms—met strangers, . . . called upon young men in stores & offices & shops, [encouraged those] who were Christians or converted. Introduced them into some church connection, . . . wrote letters to parents in the country."[30]

But in all this diversity, one unifying characteristic shines through: association itself, the determination to draw the city's anonymous young men out of their isolation and into a sheltering institutional fold. "We shall meet the young stranger as he enters our city," pledged the Boston "Y," "take him by the hand . . . , and in every way throw around him good influences so that he may not feel that he is a stranger."[31] In a period when moralists and imaginative writers alike were obsessed by the city's power to dissolve the social bond, the YMCA set out to restore it.

Addressing the Worcester YMCA, the Reverend A. J. Gordon of Boston summed up the organization's mission by describing the tragedy that had befallen a young Boston physician on an Alpine climb. The climbers

all were linked together, but the young man grew tired of the restraint and begged that he might be loosed from his bonds . . . His request was granted. The instant he was free, he slipped, fell over the precipice, and was dashed to pieces on the icy rocks in the chasm below, because he had been loosed from the bonds which held him to the others. It is worth everything to have a great association which links hearts to heart, and man to man, each doing something to keep the other from slipping; for as it was in the Alps, so it is in the city, when the young man is loosed from the restraint of family, friends and the church.[32]

The association ideal was expressed in many ways. Some YMCA's pursued it literally by establishing residential facilities, but this idea was not initially popular, since many feared that the evils of the morally dubious boardinghouses would simply be replicated in YMCA dormitories. (Young men needed "the ennobling and refining presence of woman," noted one YMCA spokesman, and "of this there can be nothing in . . . association dormitories.") Others, notably in Chicago, tried for a time actually to place their members in families.[33]

More often, however, the emphasis was less on actual living arrangements than on helping the YMCA recruit "keep up the home *feeling* associated in his mind with the sweetest recollections." Again, the specific techniques were as varied as the imaginations of local YMCA secretaries. In some cities, members pledged to visit each other when sick or in need. Elsewhere, Thanksgiving dinners and other evocative traditional observances were held. In Boston, the "Y" reading room displayed over forty small-town New England newspapers so every member could find "a paper familiar to him and associated with the social remembrances of his early home and friends." Philadelphia's John Wanamaker wrote every minister within a fifty-mile radius requesting the names of all young men migrating to the city and then tracked down the newcomers and invited them to join. In Chicago, Dwight Moody organized a YMCA group called the "Yokefellows" whose members visited saloons and gambling halls in teams, urging young men to enter the circle of YMCA fellowship.[34]

It was essential to the YMCA approach that the decision to enter into association be voluntary and unpressured. The new member freely accepted the moral restraint his step implied; he willingly joined an organization collectively possessing (in Verranus Morse's words) "more eyes than Argus to watch the footsteps of the unwary."[35] And he did so not out of fear of the law or in hope of immediate material benefit (no AICP-type charity available here!) but from a perhaps even stronger motive: loneliness.

Keen practical psychologists, the early YMCA leaders knew how isolated a country boy like Dwight Moody or John Farwell could feel in the city and how strongly "social want" could motivate his behavior. Accordingly, they offered the newcomer an implicit bargain: instead of lonely streets, drawn shutters, and impersonal churches, he would be welcomed into *association*. Real comradeship would replace the saloon, gambling den, or brothel where the alleviation of loneliness was reduced to a fleeting economic transaction. A cheerful building "warmed and lighted during the long winter evenings" would provide an alternative to dreary hours in one's "cold, dimly lighted" boardinghouse. Here at last was the promise of genuine "social intercourse," "moral and intellectual culture," and, above all, the "sympathy and counsel of true friends."[36]

Of course, there was a quid pro quo. In joining the YMCA the young man gave up a degree of autonomy, sharply limited his freedom to sample the city's vices with impunity, and once again subjected himself to a replica of the institutionalized moral oversight he had escaped in coming to the city. But he did so of his own free will, out of the desire to be part of a social group whose esteem he prized and whose companionship he craved.

In a sense, this process simply represented a refinement of already well-established moral-control techniques. The Sunday school and tract societies, as we have seen, subjected their volunteers to considerable moral oversight while offering friendship and emotional warmth in return. This was a feature, too, of the mercantile-library associations and indeed of many labor, reform, and fraternal organizations of the period. The constitution of the New York Society of Journeymen House Carpenters, established in 1833, provided for the expulsion of any member "spending his time in brothels or gambling," and the leader of the Sons of Temperance noted in 1848 that the organization's halls were not only outposts in the temperance battle, but also "pleasant places of resort and social intercourse."[37]

One can discern this pattern, too, in a quite different part of the antebellum social landscape: the communitarian movement. A small but significant number of Americans in the 1830s and 1840s were sufficiently disoriented by the social transformations of the period to cast their lot with a variety of utopian ventures that not only provided a patterned routine for disordered lives but also the emotional support of a close-knit communal environment. Indeed, the very word "association" in the YMCA's name had powerful resonances in the 1850s, for in *The Social Destiny of Man* (1840), Albert Brisbane, an American disciple of the French utopian socialist Charles Fourier, had announced that "association" would be the principle underlying the social order of the future, and it was under this banner that a number of Fourierist communities, called phalansteries, were established in the 1840s.[38]

But if the YMCA was only one of many similar institutional responses to the social disruptions of urbanization, it was unique in the flexibility with which its early leaders pursued their objectives. Unlike the Sunday school and tract societies, they did not confine their membership to volunteers willing to engage in a specific uplift activity. Unlike the temperance groups, they avoided focusing narrowly on a single reform goal. And, though a decision to join the "Y" was a more serious step in the early years than it would later become, it never required, even in the 1850s, anything like the renunciation of personal autonomy and ambition earlier imposed upon anyone joining a Fourierist phalanstery or other communitarian venture. If YMCA membership was a vastly diluted form of association, it was also a considerably more palatable one. Thanks to the YMCA, the ambitious young man of the city could continue to swim outward through the treacherous urban currents and yet remain linked, by a single thin lifeline, to the familiar, receding shore.

From the beginning, however, the rather passive ideal of association was balanced by a militant aggressiveness when the YMCA turned outward. The program was flexible, to be sure, but once a newcomer had been drawn into the fold, he was expected to participate actively in *some* "Y" endeavor directed to urban moral betterment. One reason, of course, was to cement his commitment to the organization and its values—to make him more resolute in moral purpose, more conscious of his "solemn responsibilities" as a member of a select group, and more aware that the YMCA occupied an "important and dignified" place in the life of the city.[39]

But these moral-uplift activities were also a means by which the YMCA's influence might reach the lower strata of the urban population, not by the lure of association, but through more overt social-control techniques. Addressing the New York YMCA in 1854, the Reverend George W. Bethune likened the social threat of the city's "lowest order" to that of an armed uprising and cast the young men of the YMCA in the role of defending soldiers, "calm, resolute, armed, drilled, and prepared for the fight, taking their positions as the guardians of the city." As YMCA influence percolated downward to all levels of the city population, agreed Verranus Morse, the whole of urban society would be "purified and lifted up."[40]

The more militant side of the YMCA ideology was reinforced during the Civil War years when the organization, having transformed itself into the Christian Commission, maintained agents in northern cities, in military hospitals, and even at the front, to look after the spiritual and moral well-being of the soldiers. A year after Appomattox, Verranus Morse sought to sustain the wartime mood. It was the duty of YMCA members, he declared, "to stand together like the Roman phalanx, protecting each other with their overlapping shields, not simply that we may be at rest, safe from every assaulting missile, but that we may move forward, unyielding and resistless." The centurions clanking out of YMCA reading rooms across the nation, Morse went on, would collectively strike down the "trees of evil fruitage" that flourished in the cities, including the gambling halls, saloons, brothels, "and all similar demoralizing agencies."[41]

Morse's coercive vision was not entirely hyperbole. Even as he spoke, the YMCA leadership was organizing "moral surveys" of the major American cities and planning state and local conventions to awaken the public to their "moral destitution." Armed with a survey that revealed the existence of 8,000 saloons, 700 brothels, 4,000 prostitutes, and numerous outlets for indecent books in New York City alone, YMCA lobbyists in Albany secured the enactment of more stringent laws regulating the liquor traffic and the flow of obscene publications.[42]

Pursuing this vendetta against urban immorality, the New York City YMCA in 1872 placed young Anthony Comstock, a dry-goods clerk who had served in Florida with the wartime Christian Commission, in charge of its newly established Committee for the Suppression of Vice. Two years later, this committee began an independent career as the New York Society for the Suppression of Vice, and Comstock was launched on a forty-year battle against the urban gamblers, swindlers, abortionists, birth-control advocates, lottery operators, and obscenity purveyors who were gnawing away at the moral order. Under Comstock's aegis the New England Watch and Ward Society was established in Boston in 1873, and similar antivice organizations sprang up in Saint Louis, Chicago, Louisville, Cincinnati, and San Francisco.[43] In these same years, many YMCA's organized poor-relief programs that, like those of the AICP, stressed moral surveillance as much as material assistance.[44]

Launched at the midpoint of the nineteenth century, the Young Men's Christian Association not only absorbed and extended earlier urban social-control strategies, but it also anticipated and helped shape those that followed. Indeed, no organization better epitomizes the Janus-faced quality of the entire effort. On the one hand, it sought gently to draw the vulnerable newcomer into the circle of its fellowship, where he would be unconsciously molded by its moral ambience while enjoying the emotional gratifications of association. But, on the other hand, the YMCA also dreamed of welding these same young innocents into a powerful force for imposing moral uniformity upon the larger society by more forcible techniques. Both approaches—the subtly manipulative and the openly coercive—are familiar to us from our examination of the Jacksonian era, and both will recur in the chapters to come.

PART

Three

The Gilded Age

URBAN MORAL CONTROL
IN A TURBULENT TIME

In 1933, selecting a title for his soon-to-be-published social history of the United States in the late nineteenth century, Arthur M. Schlesinger came up with a choice that, in retrospect, seems not only apt but inevitable: *The Rise of the City*. It was in the Gilded Age that urbanization, long a shaping force in American life, became the controlling reality. As Dixon Ryan Fox wrote in his foreword to Schlesinger's volume: "The United States in the eighties and nineties was trembling between two worlds, one rural and agricultural, the other urban and industrial. In this span of years the fateful decision was made."[1]

Fueled as before by massive foreign immigration and a continuing influx of migrants from the hinterlands, the urban growth of this period widened the already vast chasm between the lower class crowded into downtown slums and the middle and upper classes who were fleeing to new suburbs on the outskirts. From these outlying enclaves the more well-to-do city dwellers, together with millions of Americans still living in rural regions, watched in fear and anxiety as storms of urban-industrial violence—more alarming in their way than the brawls and disorders of earlier years—broke over the city.

Responding to these developments, American Protestantism intensified its long-standing effort to develop institutional modes that would enable it to exert moral influence, if not ecclesiastical authority, over the increasingly non-Protestant urban masses.

Significantly, however, the most comprehensive and important urban social-control innovation of the period—the charity organization movement—arose outside the framework of the churches.

In their heyday from the 1870s to the 1890s, charity organization societies across the land worked to transform the urban immigrant masses into models of middle-class respectability and moral probity. Like the Sunday school teachers of an earlier generation, thousands of charity organization volunteers—somewhat poignantly called "friendly visitors"—offered themselves as living models upon which the urban poor could pattern their lives. In sprawling, class-ridden industrial cities, they sought to foster between the poor and themselves a "neighborly" relationship derived from an idealized image of the village social order.

At the end of the century, during the Depression-ridden 1890s, a powerful if ill-defined "moral awakening" stirred the urban middle class, generating new reform energies and strategies that would decisively influence the crescendo of urban social-control activity that came in the Progressive era.

8

"The Ragged Edge of Anarchy"

THE EMOTIONAL CONTEXT OF
URBAN SOCIAL CONTROL IN
THE GILDED AGE

One could document with interminable statistics the accelerating pace of urban growth in the Gilded Age, but the essential pattern is so clear as to need little demonstration. Not only did the established centers continue to expand, but through vast regions of the country new cities emerged in the interstices of the familiar network. In regions long considered "rural" despite the presence of one or two big urban centers, the burgeoning of these "second-tier" cities forced a fundamental reorientation of perceptions. In Pennsylvania, for example, where antebellum urbanization had been largely confined to Philadelphia and Pittsburgh, the post–Civil War decades brought the emergence of such rail, mining, and lumber centers as Scranton, Altoona, and Williamsport. At mid-century, America had been a rural society with a number of important cities; by 1900, it was an urban-industrial nation with a strong agricultural component. The 1900 population of New York City alone—3.4 million—was almost precisely the same as the total urban population of 1850![1]

As in the pre–Civil War years, urbanization continued to be directly linked to the influx of foreigners. Over 11 million immigrants arrived from 1870 to the end of the century, and the great majority of them settled in the cities. By 1900, 60 percent of the residents of the nation's twelve largest urban centers were either foreign-born or of foreign parentage, and in many cities—Saint Louis, Cleveland, Detroit, Milwaukee, Chicago, New York—the

figure approached and sometimes exceeded 80 percent. More-
over, as textbook writers never tire of reiterating, these newcomers, especially after 1890, were often more alien-seeming—in
dress, religion, and mores—than those of the antebellum period:
Catholic peasants from Italy, Poland, Austria-Hungary, and the
Balkans; Orthodox Jews from the ghettos of Eastern Europe. Simultaneously, waves of native-born Americans continued to pour
into the cities, producing, in John Garraty's words, "the same
kind of swirling confusion that occurs in the mouth of a harbor
when a river discharges its waters against the force of a rising
ocean tide."[2]

As these newcomers arrived, the more well-to-do residents
continued to depart, aided in their flight by expanding interurban
transit systems and streetcar lines. As early as 1873 a journalist
described Chicago as "more given to suburbs than any other city
in the world," and noted that in a vast semicircle radiating outward thirty miles from the city's center, property lots were "selling nearly as fast as the transfer papers can be filed." Sam Bass
Warner's description of turn-of-the-century Boston as divided
between "an inner city of work and low-income housing, and an
outer city of middle- and upper-income residences" could with
equal accuracy be applied to many cities of the period.[3]

Abandoned by the wealthier classes, the old urban centers increasingly became the domain of newcomers divided by language,
religion, and tradition, but often united in poverty and a pitiful
lack of preparation for urban existence. Settling "in any old, decaying street that was not being seized by business," they were
often denied even the comfort of the neighborhood enclaves
which had once served as "way stations between urban and rural
living," but which now disintegrated under the steady battering
of population growth.[4]

Politically, the demographic changes of these years, coupled
with the structural inadequacies of most city governments,
brought the boss system to full flower. In city after city, power
flowed to tough, colorful, and resourceful men whose dominance
rested on patronage, immigrant voter loyalty, complex alliances
among local ward chieftans (often saloon keepers), the payoffs
they received from companies seeking contracts and franchises,
and their ability, somehow, to get things done. The Irish, first on
the scene, were in many cities the first to seize political power:
Irish mayors were elected in Scranton in 1878, New York in 1880,
and Boston in 1884.[5]

This period also witnessed a continued deterioration in the
physical condition of the slums. As newcomers jammed into already crowded tenements, the decay of urban housing and of
essential municipal services deepened and spread. With police

protection still lagging behind population growth, crime represented a constant and, in some instances, a growing menace. In Boston, for example, arrest rates for burglary, robbery, larceny, assault, and murder rose to an all-time high in the later 1870s.[6]

Violence and disorder continued to plague many cities in these years. New York was the scene of periodic battles between Protestant and Catholic Irish immigrants, particularly around Saint Patrick's Day and July 12, when Ulstermen commemorated the defeat of James II at the battle of the Boyne. (On the latter date in 1871, panicky militiamen fired into a crowd, killing thirty-one.) In 1884, a Cincinnati law-and-order mob, enraged by the acquittal of several accused murderers, put a torch to the county courthouse. The state militia at last restored order, at a cost of fifty-four lives. In New Orleans a "general atmosphere of lawlessness" caused by political corruption, official protection of prostitution and gambling, and the depredations of powerful street gangs like the "Spiders" and the "Yellow Harry mob" culminated in 1890 with the assassination of the chief of police by gangsters. When the accused were acquitted amid charges of jury tampering, vigilantes raided the jail and lynched eleven of them.[7]

Urban disorder was familiar enough from the antebellum period, but in the Gilded Age it took on a more menacing aura as a direct expression of labor unrest. The first ominous portent came in the summer of 1877, during a period of severe business depression, when a wildcat railroad strike led to tense confrontations, violent outbreaks, and scores of deaths in Pittsburgh, Chicago, and many other rail centers. The tempo of working-class discontent picked up in the 1880s and culminated in 1886 when a massive wave of strikes, armed encounters, and (in some instances) strike-related deaths hit Saint Louis, Milwaukee, New York, Cincinnati, Chicago, and other cities. On the evening of May 4, 1886, in Chicago's Haymarket Square, an unknown person threw a bomb at police attempting to break up a peaceful, anarchist-sponsored strike rally. One policeman was killed by the bomb and seventy injured; four demonstrators were shot dead, and many wounded, when the enraged police retaliated with gun and club.[8]

In the parlors of middle-class America, these developments were the source of profound uneasiness—an uneasiness that assumed almost hysterical proportions during periods of labor violence and armed confrontation. In the midst of the upheaval of 1877 a New York labor newspaper printed the terrifying headline "War!!! Plundered Labor in Arms," and the *Independent*, an influential New York religious weekly (perhaps recalling the bloody repression of the Paris Commune only six years before) burst out: "If the club of the policeman, knocking out the brains of the rioter, will answer, then well and good; but if it does not . . . , then bullets and bayonets, canister and grape . . . constitute the one remedy . . . Napoleon was right when he said that the way to deal with a mob was to exterminate it."[9] The trauma of 1877 is evoked, too, in John Hay's 1883 novel *The Bread-Winners*, with its portrayal of the urban proletariat as "a vast mass of inflammable material" dangerously vulnerable to demagogues preaching "riot and plunder."[10]

The disorders of 1886, and especially Haymarket, sent even more massive shock waves through the middle class. On that May evening in Chicago, the triple menace of class warfare, alien radicalism, and urban mass violence came together in one terrifying outburst. Here seemed to be the opening scene of that long-feared urban *Götterdämmerung*. What city would explode next? "Some of these beasts are now prowling around Cincinnati," warned the *Cincinnati Times-Star* the next day, "intent upon instigating wild spirits among the strikers to riotous demonstrations." The *Independent* reiterated its grim 1877 formula for dealing with mobs, and the *Congregationalist* agreed: "When anarchy gathers its deluded disciples into a mob, as at Chicago, a Gatling gun or two . . . offers, on the whole, the most merciful as well as effectual remedy." The "masses of ignorant foreigners congregated in many cities," declared the *New York Tribune*, were "the magazines of explosives to which these fiends continually try to apply the match." Vigilante-type law-and-order leagues were formed in a number of cities to deal with the anticipated revolutionary outbreak, and when several Chicago anarchist leaders were tried and hanged for alleged complicity in the Haymarket bombing, editorial approval was practically unanimous.[11]

The 1890s brought no relief. In 1892, the bloody clash of strikers and Pinkerton agents at Andrew Carnegie's Homestead steel works near Pittsburgh was followed by an assassination attempt against Carnegie's lieutenant Henry Clay Frick in his Pittsburgh office. In 1894, an American Railway Union strike in support of a Pullman walkout led to violent confrontations in Chicago, Los Angeles, Hammond, Indiana, and other rail centers. In Chicago, where more than 14,000 federal troops, deputies, and police patrolled the troubled areas, at least thirteen persons were killed and substantial amounts of railway property destroyed.[12]

The Depression of 1893–1897, when jobless men thronged the streets, further exacerbated urban tensions in this unhappy decade. All the indexes told the same grim story: production and wages declined alarmingly, 156 railroads went into receivership, more than 800 banks failed, business bankruptcies soared, and unemployment ranged as high as 20 percent. (One of the few sectors of the economy that flourished in these years was street-railway construction: the middle-class flight to the suburbs was continuing.)[13]

The intensification of urban-industrial violence, coupled with Depression-related anxieties, quickened the flow of grim pronouncements by editors and public figures. During the Pullman strike, Attorney General Richard Olney pronounced the nation at "the ragged edge of anarchy," and when violence did erupt in Chicago, newspapers across the country broke out in grim head-lines reminiscent of 1877 and 1886.[14]

Sensational newspaper coverage of labor violence was not the only means by which the urban menace was underscored in the Gilded Age. In 1868 a popular magazine of the day featured an article entitled "The Wickedest Man in New York" about the proprietor of a Five Points brothel, and the success of this venture in moral muckraking soon inspired numerous imitations. Anthony Comstock contributed *Traps for the Young* (1883), a potpourri of stories about the city's "gambling saloons, . . . pool-rooms, low theatres, and rumholes," and the 1887 autobiography of a retired New York police chief offered a vivid picture of the city's seamier side. "Let the reader who has never visited this illuminated den go with me in imagination," he invited at one point, "and see the wicked character of the place pictured as well as I am able to paint it."[15]

This genre took on a new dimension in the 1880s when advances in flash photography made it possible actually to show such scenes. Books like Jacob Riis's *How the Other Half Lives* (1890), with its arresting photographs of the New York slums, and Helen Campbell's *Darkness and Daylight; or, Lights and Shadows of New York Life* (1892), featuring scenes of tenements, opium dens, and all-night dives, produced an effect comparable to Jacques Cousteau's photographs, in our day, of eerie life forms in the ocean depths. "We have a new literature of exploration," the Reverend Walter Rauschenbusch was to write in a few years. "Darkest Africa and the polar regions are becoming familiar; but we now have intrepid men and women who plunge for a time into the life of the lower classes and return to write books about this unknown race."[16]

And to Anthony Comstock's endless discomfiture, the popular image of the city continued to be powerfully influenced by sensational newspapers, crime magazines, and dime novels. If such literature did not lie on many reformers' bedside reading tables, it did contribute to the cultural climate in which they pursued their endeavors. While frontier outlawry remained a stock theme in the pulp fiction of the period, melodramatic tales of urban crime became increasingly popular after about 1880. The opening of an 1881 potboiler is typical in portraying cities as reeking of blood and violence: "New Haven, the beautiful City of Elms, was startled from its propriety and awakened to a sense of horror by a terrible announcement . . . on the morning of the 6th of August, 1881. Jennie E. Cramer, a comely young girl, was discovered in the water, face downward, DEAD!"[17]

The images of urban menace pouring in from so many sources in the late nineteenth century were all the more potent because the actual, tangible city was increasingly a terra incognita for many Americans—not only country folk, but the urban middle and upper classes, too, as they moved to the suburbs or withdrew into sharply demarcated urban enclaves to form what Theodore Dreiser called "little islands of propriety." As the well-to-do drew apart from the city, they viewed the urban masses in increasingly menacing terms. From the vantage point of Boston's newer suburbs in these years, writes Sam Bass Warner, the city loomed as "an unknown and uncontrolled land" of slums, sweatshops, and sordid immigrant politics where "vice and drunkenness flourished out of reach of middle-class supervision." In a tight little middle-class enclave like the one around Union Park in Chicago, agrees Richard Sennett, the sprawling immigrant wards assumed an abstractly sinister quality as the domain of degenerates, anarchists, and an ill-defined but fearsome rabble.[18]

Since these new middle-class districts were essentially real-estate developments determined mainly by patterns of streetcar-line expansion, their inhabitants were uneasily aware of their own lack of community cohesiveness, and this exacerbated the fears of social collapse they projected outward upon the poor. Under such volatile conditions, as Sennett notes, a riot, a particularly shocking crime, or a scary event like Haymarket could assume enormous symbolic significance as the "harbinger of an unnameable threat coming from a generalized enemy."[19]

Antonio Gramsci once commented on the tendency of all social elites to find "something barbaric and pathological" in those below them on the scale, and this process was clearly at work in late-nineteenth-century America. An 1879 outburst by a New Jersey educator expressed in only somewhat exaggerated terms convictions that were widespread in middle-class circles: the urban masses were not only ignorant and irreligious, he declared, but for the most part they knew "little, or positively nothing . . . of moral duties, or of any higher pleasures than beer-drinking and spirit-drinking, and the grossest sensual indulgence . . . [T]hey eat, drink, breed, work, and die."[20]

The revulsion pervading this passage recurs with monotonous regularity in the Gilded Age. Even the reformer Henry George believed that city life was "not the natural life of man" and that any urban population would inevitably "deteriorate, physically, mentally, morally." Great cities, agreed a writer in the *North American Review* (echoing William Ellery Channing), were "plague-spots of the nation" whose evil influence spread to every corner of the country.[21]

Even the few who rejected such ideas acknowledged their potency. The author of an 1897 article on rural poverty and degeneracy in the *American Journal of Sociology* conceded the power of the "popular belief" that "large cities are the great centers of social corruption and . . . degeneration, while rural districts and country towns are quite free from immoral influences." Similarly, the author of an 1899 statistical study of city growth, clearly an urban partisan, somewhat peevishly complained that urban "viciousness and criminality" were much exaggerated in the public mind. (Rural America had no right to flaunt its moral superiority, he suggested, citing as evidence a recent brutal murder in bucolic Shelburne Falls, Massachusetts.)[22]

Sometimes the insistence on the city's wickedness and degradation took the form of sympathy for the urban poor who were its victims, as in the famous opening chapter of Henry George's *Progress and Poverty* (1879) or the "nightmare" chapter in Edward Bellamy's *Looking Backward* (1888), in which Julian West, having awakened in the year 2000, returns in a dream to a Boston slum of the 1880s and finds it horrifyingly repellent.

> From the black doorways and windows of the rookeries on every side came gusts of fetid air. The streets and alleys reeked with the effluvia of a slave ship's between-decks. As I passed I had glimpses within of pale babies gasping out their lives amid sultry stenches, of hopeless-faced women deformed by hardship . . . Like the starving bands of mongrel curs that infest the streets of Moslem towns, swarms of half-clad brutalized children filled the air with shrieks and curses as they fought and tumbled among the garbage.[23]

But once again, it mattered little whether such descriptions were penned in sympathy or hostility: either way, they contributed to the image of the city as a moral blight and social menace.

As this conviction gripped the middle-class consciousness more firmly, the sense of the precise nature of the menace shifted in a subtle but significant way. In the antebellum period, as we have seen, concern over urbanization usually focused on its effect upon individual city dwellers: the hardening of conscience, the physical toll of sensual indulgence, the degradation and ruin of the person who yielded to its temptations. This concern did not disappear in the Gilded Age, but it was increasingly expressed in conventionalized formulas lacking the old intensity. As early as 1872, in a novel by John Ferguson Hume, a hayseed's uneasiness over a young bumpkin's move to the city is treated humorously, like a familiar stage routine. "I warned him agin it—told him there wus more'n enough people there already—that a good share of them, men and women, wusn't fit fur no young man of good morals to sociate with." In 1886 a New England agricultural journal produced this bit of doggerel:

> The city has many attractions,
> But think of the vices and sins,
> When once in the vortex of fashion,
> How soon the course downward begins.

To be sure, conventional wisdom still insisted, as an Illinois educator put it in 1896, that it was "*better . . . to be a country boy than . . . a nursling of a palace in a great city,*" but the hackneyed rhetoric was growing decidedly threadbare.[24]

In contrast to such formulaic cluck-clucking over the city as a menace to personal virtue, one finds in these years an authentic, intense, and growing fear of the threat urbanization posed to society itself. The stakes had become immeasurably higher. A generation or two earlier, reformers like Eleazer Lord, Arthur Tappan, William E. Dodge, or even Robert Hartley could still see themselves as representatives of the great and stable mass of the American people as they set out to deal with a serious but nevertheless limited and manageable problem of urban vice and disorder. As late as 1872, in raising the specter of revolutionary violence in the cities, Charles Loring Brace was clearly still thinking of some future possibility that could be forestalled if sufficient support were given to organizations like his Children's Aid Society.

That comfortable assumption of dominance and mastery faded as middle-class social observers spoke ever more somberly of the "urban menace." The threat which a few antebellum observers had perceived on the horizon now loomed in its full magnitude and immediacy: not just the moral fate of individuals but the very survival of the social order—by any definition of "social order" that would have been tolerable or even comprehensible to the middle class—was riding on what happened in the great industrial cities. The slum population was no longer simply a submerged and morally endangered group of individuals but a vast human sea threatening at any moment (in Jacob Riis's words) to become a "resistless flood . . . , sweeping all before it."[25]

The quintessential expression of such fears was that famous 1885 work of social exploration and warning, the Reverend Josiah Strong's bestseller *Our Country*. Secretary of the American Home Missionary Society (and the product of a rural Midwestern upbringing), Strong devoted a substantial part of his book to anxious speculation about America's cities. These "tainted spots in the body-politic" filled him with a profound sense of foreboding and crisis. Not only was the city "multiplying and focalizing the elements of anarchy and destruction," but elevators and skyscrapers now made it possible to "build "ǫne city above another"! *Our Country* ends with a horrifying vision of urban cataclysm. Citing Tocqueville's warnings about urban growth, Strong insisted that what the French visitor had discerned as a distant danger in the 1830s was now at hand. When, in the near future, "our Cincinnatis have become Chicagos, our Chicagos New York, and our New Yorks Londons"—when the "ignorant and vicious power" of urban American had "fully found itself"—then would "the volcanic fires of deep discontent" explode with terrible force.[26] The bombs and bullets of Haymarket, coming just a few months after *Our Country* appeared, provided a grim coda to Strong's message.

Though Strong's work is the best known, his conclusions were echoed endlessly in the sermons, political oratory, periodical articles, and imaginative literature of these years. In 1886, the year of Haymarket, nature poet Joaquin Miller published a perfervid novel, *The Destruction of Gotham*, portraying the burning of New York City by a mob in lurid, almost erotic, terms: "The great city lies trembling, panting, quivering in her wild, white heat of intoxication, excitement [and] madness." Five years later appeared Ignatius Donnelly's *Caesar's Column*, another nightmare of urban holocaust. In earlier works this Minnesota visionary and unsuccessful politician had speculated about the destruction of Atlantis and other legendary convulsions of the prehistoric era, and in *Caesar's Column* he shifted these violent obsessions from the past to the future. The story is set in New York City, which Donnelly (like George Lippard) described as "a gorgeous shell . . . outwardly beautiful and lovely, but inwardly full of dead men's bones and all uncleanliness." In Donnelly's fantasy, this corrupt and repulsive metropolis is reduced to rubble in an Armageddon-like struggle between its capitalist rulers and its brutalized poor. Calling to some deep level of the nation's consciousness, *Caesar's Column* was an immediate success: by 1906, it had sold more than a quarter of a million copies.[27]

This heightened sense of urban menace, expressed at its most extreme in visions of revolutionary chaos and mass carnage, formed the psychic substratum of the urban social control efforts to which we now turn. In these unsettled and unsettling years, all such efforts took on a sharp new urgency. The challenge now (so it appeared to many middle-class reformers) was not simply to fish out individuals floundering in the urban maelstrom but to keep society itself from crumbling into the swirling waters.

9

American Protestantism and the Moral Challenge of the Industrial City

From the days of Lyman Beecher and Charles G. Finney, Protestant leaders had regarded the nation's cities with an anxious eye, and these apprehensions deepened immeasurably in the late nineteenth century. The dramatic overall increase in Protestant church membership in these years—from 4.5 million in 1860 to 12.5 million in 1890, according to one informed estimate—only threw into sharper relief the church's failure in the crucial urban arena. As early as 1862, a Congregationalist leader warned that 60 percent of New York City's population was unreached by Protestant churches and that things were just as bad in other cities. Furthermore, he warned, the gap was increasing yearly.[1]

In her novel *We and Our Neighbors* (1873), Harriet Beecher Stowe—always a sensitive barometer of middle-class Protestant concerns—sends her well-to-do heroine on an all-night search through New York's slums for the wayward daughter of her Irish maid. "Can it be," Mrs. Stowe exclaims through this character, after describing the city's dance halls, brothels, and cellar "bucket shops" where cheap beer was sold by the pail to the poor, "that in a city full of churches and Christians such dreadful things . . . are going on every night?" Impressing upon her readers the "paganism" of contemporary city life, she posed the central question "perplexing modern society": How could the church once more influence behavior and "regulate society" in urban America?[2]

Josiah Strong's *Our Country* made clear that, as of 1885, the answer to Mrs. Stowe's question had yet to be found. The ratio of churches to population in Chicago, Strong reported, had plummeted from one for every 747 persons in 1840 to one for every 2,081 in 1880. In many big cities, he went on, vast districts were utterly destitute of the gospel. The same point was often made by the Evangelical Alliance, an association of Protestant leaders with affiliates in New York and some forty other cities; it is the central theme of Samuel Lane Loomis's *Modern Cities and Their Religious Problems* (1887); and it was heavily underscored by the Reverend William S. Rainsford, an Episcopal churchman and reformer, in 1891. "The whole aspect of the modern Protestant churches, in our large cities at least," Rainsford wrote in *The Forum*, "is repellent to the poor man."[3]

133
American
Protestantism
and the Moral
Challenge
of the
Industrial
City

Statistics on the soaring Catholic and Jewish populations in the cities were often cited by such spokesmen as a further reason for alarm. In retrospect, of course, it is plain that these "alien" faiths were themselves powerful forces for stability in immigrant communities and that their leaders were as concerned as any Protestant churchman about the moral impact of urbanization. Indeed, some Protestant moralists recognized this at the time. Samuel Lane Loomis, for example, conceded that the influence of Roman Catholicism was "doubtless conservative" and that as religions went it was "far better than none."[4] More typically, however, Protestant churchmen of the Gilded Age saw their creed not just in theological or ecclesiastical terms but as the foundation stone of the American social order. For them, the urban decline of Protestantism was not just frustrating, it involved moral and social ramifications of the gravest kind. They would not, if they could help it, watch from the sidelines as the moral destiny of the city was decided.

Accordingly, Protestant leaders in these years made determined efforts to revitalize the urban techniques with which we are already familiar. The tract societies issued an array of updated tracts aimed at a new generation of readers, and the Sunday school movement, despite past discouragements and the shift to a predominantly middle-class base, renewed its concern for the urban poor. By 1899 Chicago Protestants were maintaining some 120 Sunday schools in the slums, and in a survey conducted that year the superintendents unanimously agreed that they were a "great social force" among the poor.[5]

Another familiar Protestant technique whose urban relevance was again tested in the Gilded Age was the revival. Dwight L. Moody, already locally celebrated for his Sunday school and YMCA work in Chicago, conducted a successful evangelistic tour of the British Isles in 1874–75 and upon his return led highly publicized revivals in Brooklyn, Philadelphia, New York, Chicago, and other cities. Moody insisted that these urban crusades be carefully planned and amply financed—a requirement gladly met by sympathetic men of wealth like John Wanamaker, John V. Farwell, and the indefatigable William E. Dodge. (A Moody revival, wrote a New York journalist, was "a vast business enterprise, organized and conducted by businessmen, who have put money into it on business principles, for the purpose of saving men.") Such attention to detail, coupled with the evangelist's unaffected vernacular preaching and the rich baritone voice of his song leader Ira D. Sankey, brought large crowds to Moody's urban campaigns in the 1870s and to a lesser extent thereafter.[6] Here, at least, the church seemed to be exerting its rightful moral influence in the cities.

Less colorful, but equally ambitious in their urban objectives, were the many city missions established in these years. One of the few bright spots in We and Our Neighbors is Mrs. Stowe's account of a Methodist mission and home for prostitutes situated in "the very center of [the] worst district of New York." The middle-class heroine is deeply affected by the discovery of "so peaceful a home in the midst of this dreadful neighborhood." Of the reformed prostitutes who have joined the "mission family," she observes, in a flight of blatant authorial wishful thinking: "When I looked at them setting the tables, or busy about their cooking, they seemed so cheerful and respectable, I could scarcely believe that they had been so degraded."[7]

The American Home Missionary Society, a Congregationalist agency, in 1883 allocated a major share of its budget to mission work among urban immigrants. In a parallel move, the Congregationalists launched a $200,000 fund drive for the construction of city missions and churches. But the city mission impulse was not confined to any one denomination. No single body could "claim distinct precedence in originating this work," observed the movement's historian in 1903. "The alarm was sudden and the response simultaneous." Scores of Methodist missions were founded in the poorer sections of many cities in these years, and various Pentecostal and holiness sects established city missions aimed at urban newcomers. The Baptist Home Mission Society concentrated on recruiting immigrant converts to serve as missionaries to their own ethnic groups in the cities. In 1888, for example, Joseph Antoshevski, a Polish Catholic convert, began missionary work among Detroit's Polish immigrants.[8]

In an interesting extension of the city mission idea, the major railroads donated land to various missionary societies for the construction of churches in the cities they expected to spring up along their rail lines in the West. In 1884 the Baptist Home Mission Society explained the importance of this form of anticipatory urban moral effort. "If a community starts under the auspices of the saloon, the gambling table, the brothel, the tendency is downward, and these influences are hard to eradicate. What the Northwest needs is a systematic seizure of all available points for Christ. The Church ought to precede rather than follow the tide of immigrants pouring over the mountains. It is far easier to keep in advance than to overtake."[9] Perhaps by getting in on the ground floor, the church could prevent in the West the moral and social degeneracy which so menaced the older cities of the East!

135
American
Protestantism
and the Moral
Challenge
of the
Industrial
City

Some of the best known of the late-nineteenth-century city missions had only tenuous denominational ties, reflecting mainly the dedication of particular individuals: John C. Collins's Union Gospel Mission in New Haven; Walter Swaffield's Bethel Mission in Boston's North End; and, in Chicago, George Clarke's Pacific Garden Mission (founded in 1877) and Martin Van Arsdale's "Newsboys' and Bootblacks' Mission," where free meals and magic-lantern shows drew crowds of city youths.[10]

The most famous of these nondenominational missions was established in 1872 on New York's Water Street by a former alcoholic and Sing Sing veteran named Jerry McAuley. Until his death from tuberculosis in 1884, McAuley conducted his mission along time-tested lines: lively preaching, lots of singing, spontaneous testimonies by reformed drunkards and tramps, and no-nonsense charity: soup, baths, and beds. His funeral attracted great crowds, a memorial fountain was erected in Greeley Square (Broadway and Thirty-second Street), and for years his efforts were cited as evidence that Protestantism was still a viable force in the immigrant city.[11]

Like the revival crusades of Dwight L. Moody, these free-lance city missions often attracted heavy business support. Among McAuley's major backers were William E. Dodge, nearing the end of a lifetime devoted equally to money making and urban uplift, and the financier and New York Stock Exchange president Alfred S. Hatch. The Armour Mission in Chicago, drawing upon a $100,000 endowment created by meatpacker Joseph F. Armour and supplemented by his brother Philip D. Armour, opened in December 1886—seven months after Haymarket. One channel through which Chicago wealth flowed into the mission effort was the City Missionary Society, which from 1883 to 1903 received an astounding $7 million in contributions![12]

With backing like this, the Protestant city mission movement exuded at least a superficial glow of health. Its confident aspirations were demonstrated in 1886 when leaders from all over the country gathered in Chicago (the year and the city are again significant) for a great Convention of Christian Workers. A magazine and a permanent organization were established that in succeeding years provided an important focus for the movement. By the 1920s, nearly 3,000 city missions from coast to coast were addressing themselves to the salvation and moral uplift of urban America.[13]

These seemingly substantial achievements, however, did little to mute the frustration expressed by Gilded Age Protestant leaders when confronting the city. The reports of the Bible, tract, and Sunday school societies, even as they told of expanded urban effort, often concluded on a note of caution or outright pessimism: much was being done, the message went, but the pace of city growth, and the unresponsiveness of the masses, continually threatened to overwhelm the most determined effort.

Dwight L. Moody was dogged by charges that his city revivals reached mainly middle-class churchgoers, and the evidence bears out the charge. The pro-Moody *New York Tribune* reported that a large part of the audience at his Brooklyn revival of 1875 were already professed Christians. A reporter mingling with the throng outside the Hippodrome Auditorium during a New York City revival characterized it as "a well-dressed, good-humored crowd, that stamps its feet and chats pleasantly." (He did observe one lady approach "several rough-looking young fellows, apparently inviting them to the meeting, but without success.")[14]

Moody himself implicitly acknowledged the limited class base of his following when night after night, echoing his predecessor Charles G. Finney, he chided his comfortable, churchgoing audiences for occupying seats that otherwise (so he hoped) might be filled by the immigrant poor. But the immigrants never came, and Moody grew discouraged. After the 1870s he generally avoided the largest cities, first by confining himself to the smaller interior cities (still predominantly native-born and Protestant) and then by gradually withdrawing from evangelistic work almost entirely to concentrate on the Bible schools he had founded in Chicago and in his native Northfield, Massachusetts. "We cannot get the people we are after," he lamented, when urged to resume urban revivalism. "The city is no place for me," he wrote his family in 1896 on a rare visit to New York. "If it was not for the work I am called to do, I would never show my head in this city or any other again."[15]

To be sure, as Bernard Weisberger notes, Moody's Biblical sermons, with their evocations of home, family, and mother, together with Sankey's singing, did enable small-town Americans transplanted to the cities to reassure themselves, at least fleetingly, that the old order still survived.[16] But providing spiritual and emotional succor to the middle class was not Moody's goal. From his days as a Sunday school worker, his mission had been among the poor. Nor was it the goal of the capitalists who financed his crusades. For them, the fundamental issue—on whose outcome, they told themselves in their more apocalyptic moments, America's survival depended—was whether the urban masses could be won. By this test, Moody (and Gilded Age revivalism generally) was a failure.

Even the city mission movement, for all its apparent accomplishments, was infected with a nagging sense of unfulfilled promise. The heart of the city—the densely packed immigrant wards —seemed impervious to even the most dedicated effort. Joseph Antoshevski (not unpredictably) enjoyed little success in transforming Detroit's Polish Catholics into Baptists. Indeed, the recent historian of Baptist work among urban immigrants has drawn a pessimistic general conclusion. Viewed statistically, he writes, "the whole operation appears as a failure." And despite the large number of Methodist city missions founded in these years, the denomination's historian notes that many were struggling enterprises chronically "near cessation." The author of an 1894 *Methodist Review* article on urban religious work noted "one great and grave fact": "The larger the city . . . the more pronounced . . . the diminishment of evangelical forces."[17]

137
*American
Protestantism
and the Moral
Challenge
of the
Industrial
City*

A 1903 appraisal by an official of the American Home Missionary Society was similarly bleak. The immigrant city, he wrote, "has not as yet been adequately touched." Like many other frustrated urban moral reformers, he concluded his chronicle of failure with an aggressive outburst: "The wise general masses his army where the enemy is densest. The hostile forces that threaten the future of America . . . camp to-day in solid city wards; they are intrenched behind miles of tenement blocks. The enemy has shifted his ground. What is the home-missionary army for but to follow on and train and mass its guns against this new attack?"[18]

Among the sharpest critics of the city mission movement were those who shared its goals but believed they had discovered a more effective strategy for achieving them. The Reverend William S. Rainsford, a leader in the Gilded Age "institutional church" movement, had little good to say of city missions in his 1922 autobiography. They represented, he charged, a feeble rearguard action by a dispirited and retreating Protestantism. How could the "ugly little mission chapel service" hope to win "the very people that the strong preacher and beautiful service had failed to draw?" Rainsford's conclusion was harsh: "The small mission church, struggling to live, equipped with second-rate machinery, human and material, can never succeed and is a waste of energy."[19]

In the face of such discouraging assessments, city mission enthusiasts simply urged redoubled effort. "Proselytizing is not the terrible sin which some would have us believe," declared a Baptist periodical in 1897. "Let us have even more of it."[20] They pointed to the occasional Joseph Antoshevski or Jerry McAuley (an Irish Catholic converted to Protestantism in Sing Sing) as forerunners of a vast tide of immigrant converts. But giving the lie to such wishful thinking was the hard fact that Catholic and Jewish immigrants were overwhelmingly impervious to Protestant proselytizing effort.

What was to be done? One strategy favored by some liberal churchmen was to deemphasize the doctrinal elements that rendered Protestantism unacceptable to the newcomers, as the price of remaining a force for moral order in the city. From such thinking grew the institutional church movement. While many urban churches followed their members to the suburbs, some (especially those with heavy investments in their downtown sites) opted to remain and offer a variety of secular activities and programs geared to the interests and needs of the surrounding immigrants.

The best known of the institutional churches was Saint George's Episcopal Church in New York, a once flourishing parish on the Lower East Side that by the 1880s found itself with a dwindling membership, a $35,000 debt, and immigrants on all sides. Efforts to sell to the Catholics were unsuccessful, and in 1882, more in a mood of despair than of innovation, Saint George's named as its rector the thirty-two-year-old William S. Rainsford. A native of Dublin, Rainsford had been identified with his denomination's urban ministry since the mid-1870s, when he led tent crusades in New York, Baltimore, and other eastern cities. Concluding that a move uptown would be "retreat in the face of the enemy," Rainsford convinced his vestrymen (including senior warden J. P. Morgan) that Saint George's must respond to "the social needs and aspirations of the masses of the people." Introducing a boys' club, recreational facilities, and an industrial training program and spicing up the church's religious ministry with a Sunday school, congregational singing, and his own vigorous preaching, Rainsford by 1890 had attracted some 7,000 Lower East Siders to one aspect or other of Saint George's program. Together with Jerry McAuley, at the other end of the social scale, he became a hero to many who were alarmed over Protestantism's diminished urban influence. Emulating Saint George's, a number of other big-city churches "institutionalized" themselves, leading the newly formed Institutional Church League to conclude hopefully in 1894 that "the burning question, 'How to reach the masses'" was "practically solved."[21]

Not surprisingly, the institutional church has figured prominently in most accounts of Protestantism's response to the city. In fact, however, few churches went very far in this direction. According to one turn-of-the-century survey, only about 15 percent of the churches of New York City, where the idea originated, were engaged in community programs, and the percentage was still lower in other cities. Of the 751 Chicago clergymen polled, 54 reported that their churches had "literary and religious societies," a handful mentioned sports programs and gymns, 17 said they "hoped to enter social work" and 500 ignored the questionnaire altogether! This decidedly mixed picture is illustrated by the situation in Minneapolis, where only one of the three major Congregational churches seriously attempted to attract the Scandinavian immigrants in their vicinity. The second made some feeble attempts in this direction before turning to a more congenial affiliation with the University of Minnesota, and the third moved repeatedly in a headlong flight from the oncoming Nordic tide.[22]

139
American
Protestantism
and the Moral
Challenge
of the
Industrial
City

The cool reception given the institutional church idea in many quarters reflected a developing strategic schism within the larger urban moral-control movement. Those who were beginning to see the problem in environmentalist terms generally welcomed the institutional church as an ally in the struggle to upgrade' and enrich the physical and social conditions of slum life. On the other hand, those who were tending toward the more coercive strategies that would culminate in the prohibition and anti-prostitution crusades of the Progressive era felt little enthusiasm for the institutional church. "It is very difficult, if not impossible, to carry on a church and a club-house under the same management," noted one church journal sarcastically in 1898.[23] Undoubtedly, a Rainsford could attract crowds of slum dwellers by installing gymns and public baths and organizing evening classes and amateur theatricals—but were those who responded to such lures being fundamentally transformed? Were the "moral defects" that underlay their debased condition being confronted? Were the "festering centers" of "urban corruption" being attacked?

One outspoken critic of the institutional church was the Baptist minister and fundamentalist leader William Bell Riley. From the 1890s on, Riley made his First Baptist Church in Minneapolis a bastion of evangelical Protestantism and a rallying place for city dwellers who longed for a reaffirmation of threatened beliefs and values. Denouncing secularism and Protestantism's liberal drift and upholding a strict code of personal morality, Riley built a congregation of 3,500 members and became a major religious spokesman of his day. On the subject of the church's urban role, Riley minced no words.

There is an institutional church that dotes upon ice-cream suppers, full-dress receptions, popular lectures, chess boards, bowling-alleys, the social settlement, not to speak of the occasional dance and amateur theatricals; And there is the institutional church that expresses itself in the organization of prayer meetings, mission circles, Bible study classes, evangelistic corps, and multiplied mission stations.[24]

Some Protestants reacted with hostility to the compromises of the institutional church; others sought to match its social awareness while remaining faithful to the Bible-based theology, missionary zeal, and strict moralism characteristic of evangelical Protestantism. Of the groups that attempted this difficult feat, none was more successful than the Salvation Army, "the Church of the Poor." Founded in England in 1865 by Methodist minister William Booth, the Salvation Army crossed the Atlantic in 1880 when a company of volunteers under George S. Railton arrived in New York—and promptly held a prayer meeting on the dock. The Army's street meetings, rousing music, and quasi-military uniforms and organization initially met suspicion and ridicule. But this soon faded. By the late 1880s the Salvation Army had won a secure place, and many well-to-do Americans were wearing the lapel pin that symbolized their support. By 1900 the Salvation Army had established 700 corps (congregations) in cities throughout the United States, staffed by 3,000 officers.[25]

Ostensibly, the Salvation Army followed a complex strategy elaborated by William Booth in his 1890 work *In Darkest England*. Booth's "Social Scheme" was, first, to attract the lowest stratum of the urban population by any means necessary—food, shelter, music, the lure of the uniform—and then to provide temporary employment (in a Salvation Army salvage store, for example) and a stable institutional environment during an initial period of rehabilitation. After a time they would then be transferred to rural colonies far from the city's temptations for training in habits of regular work, sobriety, and moral responsibility. Any who proved incorrigible—the "moral idiots"—would be held permanently in these remote camps, so as not to "infect their fellows, prey upon society, and multiply their kind," but most would be sent to overseas colonies or settled as farmers on land to be provided by the government.[26]

Though Booth's scheme was designed for England (the provision for sending the destitute to overseas colonies, for example), the American leadership—including the founder's son Ballington Booth and his son-in-law Frederick Booth-Tucker—did make some efforts to put it into effect in the United States. In the later 1890s, extensive if short-lived farm colonies were established in Ohio, Colorado, and California.[27]

Although William Booth's ideas were an influence, the most

striking characteristic of the Salvation Army's American program was, in fact, its flexibility and lack of dependence on any single strategy. "The Salvation Army is adaptive," noted its journal, the *War Cry*, in 1895, "and therein lies one of the secrets of its success. Rules for the conducting of its operations remain only hard and fast as long as they are successful; when a change is thought beneficial, said change is tested and tried." So long as the "grotesque or unseemly" were avoided, this editorial concluded, "fresh and attractive" new features were always welcome.[28]

Faithful to this philosophy, the Salvation Army supplemented its street meetings and soup kitchens with day nurseries; a junior corps for children; homes for prostitutes; secondhand stores where the destitute could find employment and needed provisions; and "slum brigades" that carried the Army's message into tenements, saloons, brothels, and dance halls. With its single-minded concentration on the urban masses and its protean capacity for incorporating the strongest features of earlier urban moral-reform strategies—including the orderly hierarchy and emotional support of the Jacksonian Sunday schools and tract societies, the clear-cut moralism of the AICP, and the zealousness of reformers ranging from John R. McDowall to Jerry McAuley— the Salvation Army did more than any other religious group to adapt the moral outlook and social values of Protestant America to the immigrant cities of the late nineteenth century.

141
American
Protestantism
and the Moral
Challenge
of the
Industrial
City

Yet this comparative success only highlights the general retreat of the Protestant churches before the rising immigrant tide in these years. For all the effort expended, writes Aaron I. Abell, the church by 1900 had reached "only a relatively small portion of the immigrant working population."[29] The "urban problem" remained. Some—like the Boston reformer Benjamin O. Flower —blamed this on the "cowardice" or "lethargy" of the Protestant clergy itself, but the problem went beyond the shortcomings of individuals.[30] The fundamental difficulty, as Samuel Lane Loomis recognized in 1887, was that the various components of the urban population were each year becoming "more widely separated from one another." Not only were the two major urban groups— the one native-born, Protestant, and comparatively well-to-do; the other poor, foreign-born, and usually Catholic or Jewish— taking on "the characteristics of two nations," but each was in turn riven by innumerable internal fissures and divisions reflecting ethnic, religious, cultural, and economic differences. What Rowland Berthoff has written of the anthracite towns of Pennsylvania in this period might with equal aptness be applied to many larger cities. The most striking fact about the complex class, religious, and ethnic alignments in places like Wilkes-Barre and

Scranton, he concludes, was not that they were openly hostile but rather "so equivocally related as to be mutually unintelligible and quite heedless of each other."[31]

Social distance was increasing not only between the middle class and the poor but between the middle class and the urban elite as well, and this further complicated Protestantism's response to the city. Although some of the newly rich capitalists of the Gilded Age—an occasional Wanamaker or Farwell—emulated their antebellum counterparts in supporting urban religious effort, many others remained aloof—some because they were committed to other reform approaches, others simply because they were preoccupied with their own economic or social advancement.

In earlier days, Protestant churchmen confronting the city had been sustained by the sense that between themselves and all levels of the city population—from the wealthiest to the poorest—existed a bond of shared religious loyalties and institutional ties rooted in the preurban era. Antebellum churchmen had invoked these loyalties both in appealing to the wealthy for support and in calling wanderers back to the fold. The evaporation of this confidence in the late nineteenth century underlay the uncertain and sometimes almost panicky efforts of American Protestantism to develop new urban strategies in these years. By no coincidence, the most important urban social-control effort of this era, the charity organization movement, not only arose outside the church but took pains to remove itself from the church's shadow. As a seedbed of values, and a generator of reform zeal, Protestantism would remain a potent force in the urban moral-control movement; as a formal institutional factor, its day had passed.

10

Building Character Among the Urban Poor

THE CHARITY ORGANIZATION MOVEMENT

Josephine Shaw was a pretty and vivacious young woman of Boston, the daughter of a prominent old family, when the Civil War began. But when her beloved brother Robert Gould Shaw and her husband of a year, Charles Russell Lowell, were killed in battle, a great gash was torn across the familiar contours of her life, leaving it permanently altered. Donning the black mourning garb she would wear for the rest of her life, the twenty-year-old widow and new mother plunged into a round of charitable activity that led eventually to the directorship of the New York Charity Organization Society.[1]

What was "charity organization"? Why did it so appeal to Mrs. Lowell and others of her generation? And why does it merit a chapter in a study of social control in the American city?

While some urban moral reformers of the Gilded Age tried to work through the church, many others operated outside ecclesiastical channels. These ostensibly secular efforts took many forms and were aimed at many targets. "Social purity" organizations in a number of cities directed their fire against those who advocated municipal toleration of prostitution. (When the Saint Louis City Council began an experiment with regulated prostitution in the city in 1870, alarm bells rang in moral-reform circles all over the country.) Anthony Comstock's vice society and its counterparts focused on the urban purveyors of obscene literature, gambl ng schemes, and contraceptives. Elbridge Gerry's Society for the Prevention of Cruelty to Children (founded in 1875 in New York, and later extended to other cities) combated not only the physical abuse of the young but their moral degradation as well.[2]

And, like the antebellum mill owners of Lowell, a few Gilded Age industrialists tried to supervise the moral lives of their employees. The best known of these was George Pullman, builder of railroad sleeping cars, who in 1880 founded the town of Pullman on the outskirts of Chicago to house his workers and their families. As both employer and landlord (houses were rented, never sold), Pullman made his company town a controlled environment reflecting his own moral standards. Brothels, dance halls, and gambling establishments were banished, and liquor was available only in a hotel patronized by visitors rather than the resident workers. To fill the vacuum created by the absence of alcohol, he developed a variety of positive alternatives, as he explained in an 1882 interview: "We have provided a theatre [limited to plays of the "utmost propriety"], a reading room, billiard room, and all sorts of outdoor sports, and by this means our people soon forget all about drink, . . . and we have an assurance of our work being done with greater accuracy and skill."[3]

But single-issue societies and paternalistic efforts like Pullman's did not represent the major innovative thrust of Gilded Age urban moral reformism. In these years, increasing numbers of middle-class Americans became persuaded that only a comprehensive, systematic, and orchestrated effort could stave off moral decay and social disintegration among the urban masses. Out of this conviction grew the charity organization movement, which for a few heady decades seemed to hold out the promise that the chronic moral and social concerns associated with the slums were at last on the road to solution.

Reduced to essentials, the charity organization movement rested on three simple but sweeping assumptions: first, the roots of urban poverty lay in the moral deficiencies and character flaws of the poor; second, the eradication of the slum evil depended upon bringing the poor to recognize and correct these deficiencies; and third, the realization of this goal would require a greater degree of cooperation among the diverse, often overlapping charitable societies of the typical large city. These were the ideas that struck the generation of the 1870s and 1880s with such revelatory force and drew thousands of middle-class volunteers into charity organization work.

Developments in England provided the immediate inspiration. In 1864 a well-to-do London woman named Octavia Hill had begun to buy and renovate tenements and rent them to poor families whom she then visited regularly, not only as landlady but as moral guardian. Soon Hill was managing over 400 rooms, and sympathetic observers were marveling at the "social and moral reformation" as she "gradually fashioned each tenement into a 'home.' "[4]

What Octavia Hill attempted individually, the London Society for Organizing Charitable Relief and Repressing Mendicity (1869) tried to achieve institutionally. Influenced by the earlier work of the Reverend Thomas Chalmers in Edinburgh and guided by the able Charles Stewart Loch, general secretary from 1875 to 1913, this organization worked to expose professional beggars, eliminate indiscriminate almsgiving, and bring about the moral rehabilitation of the poor.[5]

It was a onetime volunteer in London charitable work, the Anglican clergyman S. Humphreys Gurteen, who founded the first American charity organization society, in Buffalo, in 1877. Having witnessed the New York draft riots of 1863, Gurteen could never forget the "revolting spectacle."

> 5,000 men, women and children sweeping down the leading avenue of the city in the darkness of night, the lurid flames of a hundred torches disclosing a scene of wild license scarcely surpassed by any single incident of the French Revolution; women, and mothers at that, with their bare breasts exposed to the winds of heaven, brandishing deadly weapons and uttering foul and loathsome language; . . . while the very air as they passed was polluted by their drunken breath.[6]

The rail and shipping center of Buffalo, where Gurteen was associate rector of Saint Paul's Episcopal Cathedral, had suffered severely in the Depression of the mid-1870s, and in the turbulent year 1877 it seemed that the scenes of 1863 might soon be reenacted. Such grim forebodings form the backdrop of Gurteen's appeals on behalf of the charity organization idea. "*We shall have ourselves alone to blame,*" he wrote, "*if the poor, craving for human sympathy, yet feeling their moral deformity, should some fine day wreak their vengeance upon society at large.*"[7]

For all the urgency of his rhetoric, Gurteen's proposed remedy was hardly new in 1877. In addition to the English precedents, a number of Americans—Boston's Joseph Tuckerman, Cincinnati's Thomas H. Perkins, New York's Robert Hartley, and others—had earlier urged comprehensive moral-control strategies almost identical to those of the charity organization enthusiasts: the division of the city into districts; the compilation of dossiers on everyone requesting relief; and the use of middle-class visitors to approach the uplift task on a family-by-family basis.[8]

What happened in 1877 was not that a new approach to urban moral control was discovered but that the moment was ripe for one that had been around for years. Labor violence had raged in many cities that summer; the urban moral challenge seemed beyond the capacity of existing organizations; and the non-Protestant character of the new immigrants sharply limited the effectiveness of traditional church-based approaches. So it was that from its beginnings in Buffalo, "charity organization" spread like wildfire in the later 1870s and the 1880s, quickly becoming, as one historian has noted, almost a fad. By the 1890s over 100 cities had charity organization societies; the movement had attracted an impressive array of able leaders; journals like *Lend-a-Hand* (Boston), *Charities Review* (New York), and *Charities Record* (Baltimore) were providing publicity and a forum for ideas; and the annual National Conference of Charities and Corrections (NCCC) had emerged to give the leadership an opportunity to formulate policy and discuss issues of common concern.[9]

Like the supporters of the AICP in an earlier day, the men and women who rallied to the charity organization movement believed implicitly that urban poverty was mainly the result not of economic or structural maladjustments in society, but of the individual failings of the poor themselves. Indeed, the judgmental moralism that had from the beginning shaped American responses to the slum found its fullest expression in the charity organization movement.

The conviction that the able-bodied poor were *personally responsible* for their condition saturates the handbooks, journals, speeches, and even private correspondence of the early charity organization leaders. These were not callous people. They could write feelingly of the physical circumstances of slum life—the overcrowding, the epidemics, the infant mortality, the poor nutrition, the family disruption—but like William Ellery Channing a generation before, they always probed for the moral flaws that underlay such conditions. "Misery and suffering," declared one handbook, "are the inevitable results of idleness, filth, and vice." In most instances, agreed a Boston leader, poverty's roots lay in "the characters of the poor themselves." S. Humphreys Gurteen left no doubts on this score in his influential *Handbook of Charity Organization* (1882). It was "self-indulgence" and other personal failings, he asserted, that produced urban poverty, turned the tenement household into a "sickening and ghastly caricature of a 'home,' " and made the "moral atmosphere" of the slum "as pestilential as the physical."[10] (Influenced by advances in germ theory and epidemiology, the early charity organization spokesmen often employed public-health analogies, speaking freely of moral "infections," "contagions," and "plague spots.")

The task, then, was what Gurteen called "the moral elevation of the poor," or, in Mrs. Lowell's more poetic phrase, "moral oversight for the soul." Others spoke of the need to "diffuse character" among the poor and to "lead these cramped and fettered lives into the knowledge and practice of something better than they have yet known."[11] It is impossible to understand the charity organization movement without grasping the intensity of this underlying concern. Eradication of that "immoral taint" festering at the core of every slum was the central, compelling goal.

The career of Josephine Shaw Lowell offers a revealing insight into the kinds of experiences that could engender such a powerful reform commitment. Although of old Boston stock, Josephine grew up on Staten Island, where her family had established residence to be near the New York eye specialist treating her mother. The coming of the Civil War initially produced in her a mood of spiritual exaltation. "These are extraordinary times and splendid," she wrote in her diary in August 1861. "This war will purify the country of some of its extravagance and selfishness . . . It can't help doing us good; it has begun to do us good already. It will make us young ones much more thoughtful and earnest, and so improve the country. I suppose we need something every few years to teach us that riches, luxury and comfort are not the great end of life." She soon realized, though, that in nearby Manhattan, especially in the slums, lived many who did not share her mood. Attending the theater in October 1862, she was shocked when an antiwar scene was enthusiastically applauded, and noted particularly that the cowardly display had been confined to the cheaper upper-gallery seats.[12] Then in July 1863 came the terrible antidraft riots and, a few days later, word that her brother Robert had been cut down in South Carolina under heroic circumstances. The war touched her even more deeply, as we have seen, when in October 1864 her husband was killed in action. Six weeks later she bore their child, a daughter.

Her role as a passive if passionate social onlooker was at an end. She plunged into work for the Freedmen's Bureau, investigated conditions in Staten Island's jail and almshouse, and in 1876 was appointed to the New York State Board of Charities. When the charity organization movement began soon after, she was at once drawn to it. A founder of the New York City Charity Organization Society in 1882, she was for twenty-five years its guiding spirit. Through speeches, articles, and the book *Public Relief and Private Charity* (1884) she became one of the movement's best known national leaders.

Though Mrs. Lowell's career was involved with urban immigrants, she viewed them with an unsentimental and sometimes even hostile eye. "Often it is brains more than anything else that is lacking to the poor," she once observed. And while her outlook eventually shifted somewhat, in the 1870s and 1880s she staunchly insisted that the charity organization movement's central aim was not the amelioration of physical hardship ("We exaggerate the importance of physical suffering," she believed), but rather the moral oversight of the poor, even if the process proved "as painful as plucking out an eye or cutting off a limb." As for relief of the needy, her position was equally tough-minded: society should "refuse to support any except those whom it can control."[13]

In committing herself to the charity organization movement, Josephine Shaw Lowell found a career that enabled her not only to sublimate her bitterness and perhaps even hatred toward the urban poor who had behaved so ignobly during her own and the nation's great ordeal but to instill into them something of the moral strength and sense of purpose that her martyred brother and husband had displayed on the battlefield.

The visionary and sometimes vague rhetoric with which Mrs. Lowell and her cohorts espoused their moral goals did not prevent them from developing a detailed and clear-eyed strategy for achieving those goals. Indeed, they dismissed most urban charitable effort as naive and misdirected. Random and sentimental almsgiving, they contended, was not only inefficient but downright injurious in failing to discriminate between the few whose destitution was the result of external circumstance (such as the death or injury of a breadwinner) and the vast majority for whom it was simply the outward badge of inner moral deficiency. Providing alms to persons of the latter type could do "fatal moral injury," argued Mrs. Lowell, for their "salvation" became nearly impossible if they grew to believe that society would cushion them from the consequences of their failings. This was particularly true of individuals in whom higher and lower impulses were at war: the normally hardworking laborer, for example, who periodically went on a spree. The aim, obviously, was not to coddle such waverers with handouts, but to stiffen their powers of resistance; not just to apply external balm to their moral illness, but to "cure it internally."[14]

They rejected, too, the church-related approaches dominant a generation before and still prevalent in the Gilded Age. The moral regeneration of the slums, declared Gurteen (himself a clergyman!), would never be achieved by "pulpit or platform oratory . . . , the distribution of tracts and pledges . . . , street preaching or the occasional visit of clergy or city missionary." Charity organization "should never be in the hands of the clergy," he warned, and no one connected with it should "use his or her position for the purposes of proselytism or spiritual instruction." Church-sponsored relief work, charged Mary Richmond of the Baltimore

COS, was usually a covert form of bribery for church attendance. The basic support for charity organization, asserted Gurteen bluntly, must come from "business and professional men" and "noble-hearted women of the wealthier class," not from "missionaries . . . , prayer meetings and Bible classes."[15] The church had had its chance at urban moral control; now it was time for others! With the urban masses overwhelmingly non-Protestant, the architects of the new movement were determined to avoid sectarian taint.

Underlying the charity organization strategy was the assumption that the urban poor had degenerated morally because the circumstances of city life had cut them off from the elevating influence of their moral betters. This notion crops up repeatedly in the literature of the movement. In small-town society, observed a charity organization speaker at the NCCC in 1884, one individual of "lofty character and high purpose" could influence hundreds of his neighbors and fellow townsmen; in the city, such influence was "practically impossible."[16] In the village, agreed charity organization leader Charles D. Kellogg in 1887, neighbors of many years' standing could easily exchange "counsel [and] admonition," and "speak of each other's affairs with fuller knowledge and discernment." In cities, by contrast, "the classes which wealth and poverty and occupation make have drifted apart, and are more monotonously uniform . . . [S]urface and rapid transit . . . distributes population according to wealth; and the poorer stratum is in one district, the middle classes in another, and the rich upon some Beacon or Murray Hill. There is no solvent of social ties like urban life."[17] The urgent task, then, was to restore the social ties that urbanization had severed—to re-create between the classes the "natural relations . . . of which life in a city has robbed them," and establish "neighborliness . . . as a feature of civic life." Such a "reunion between the classes," insisted S. Humphreys Gurteen, could not fail to have a "civilizing and healing influence."[18]

But how? The somewhat paradoxical answer, in the words of one COS leader, was to devise some "machine," some "artifice," for re-creating in the city those "natural" social relations essential to the development of character among the poor.[19] Not surprisingly, that "artifice" was the charity organization movement itself.

The first step in reopening the moral conduits between the classes was simply to learn more about the lives of the poor. In simpler days, such knowledge came naturally through numerous informal channels; now a mechanism was needed to penetrate the slums. The "fundamental law" of charity organization, wrote Gurteen, "is expressed in one word. INVESTIGATE." The nerve center of every charity organization society was the central file where information on the city's poor was systematically accumulated, arranged, and stored. By the mid-1890s, the New York City COS held data on 170,000 families or individuals, and could supply information by return mail to anyone "charitably interested" in a particular family. Thanks to its records system, boasted an early historian of the movement, charity organization was the first moral-welfare movement "to apply scientific methods to human relationships."[20]

The procedures may have been "scientific," but the data itself reflected the movement's moralistic preoccupations, focusing on character and behavior as well as on the family's history and economic situation. Is the applicant "well conducted and industrious"? ask the model questionnaires included in Gurteen's *Handbook of Charity Organization*. Is he "temperate and steady"? What is the family's general moral condition?[21] Endlessly the probing went on, seeking to pinpoint the character flaws that were surely somewhere present.

The investigative feature of the undertaking was profoundly appealing to the middle-class COS volunteers, perhaps because the sheer mass of dossiers offered deceptively tangible assurance that the complex and disturbing human reality they documented had somehow been subdued and rendered manageable. A charity organization society, declared a Boston leader, was a "clearinghouse" that could help reestablish "orderly and effective relations" among the city's varied elements. When each of the "individual units" of the urban mass had been "located, guided, helped, and controlled," declared another speaker rather grandly in 1891, "we shall have a model state of society."[22]

The Friendly Visitor

But the accumulation of information was only a first step. Once the needy family had been investigated, its moral flaws diagnosed, and a COS file established, the harder task remained: actually to effect the needed transformation. The crucial factor at this stage—and indeed the keystone in the entire charity organization structure—was the "friendly visitor." This was a middle-class or upper-class volunteer—usually female—who each week visited a limited number of slum families to which she had been assigned by the COS district supervisor. By the early 1890s some 4,000 friendly visitors were regularly knocking on tenement doors in Boston, New York, Brooklyn, Baltimore, and other major cities from coast to coast.[23]

It is difficult today to recapture the excitement that this aspect of charity organization generated. Here at last was the key to ur-

Chicago World's Fair, 1893. Many contemporary observers perceived a clear and significant connection between the orderly and harmonious arrangement of the Fair's imposing buildings and the remarkable discipline that prevailed among the throngs of visitors.

Pittsburgh, 1909. It was amid scenes like this that middle-class Charity Organization volunteers sought the moral uplift of their slum "neighbors" in the late nineteenth century.

Charity Organization Society.

VISITOR'S REPORT TO DISTRICT OFFICE No. ....

Record No. ....

Name, ...

Address, ...

REPORT.

N. B.—Here insert remarks upon (1) the social and moral condition of the family; (2) the sanitary condition of the dwelling; (3) character of surroundings; (4) what the Visitor considers necessary for the further improvement of the family.

....

....

....

....

Signed ....

Visitor.

Received at District Office, ...

In this way, the District Committee is kept informed of all relief that is daily being given to the poor of the District; the office books can be written up day by day, and will at all times be of use for immediate reference. So much for the individual District.

The other side of "Friendly Visiting." In this model form drawn up by Charity Organization Society pioneer S. Humphreys Gurteen, the visitor was asked to assess the slum family's "social and moral condition" and indicate (in four lines) what was necessary for its "further improvement."

The railroad strike of 1877. Massive scenes of urban violence associated with labor unrest added a new and frightening dimension to concern about urban social disorder in the Gilded Age.

Mastering the slums through organization. This sketch prepared by Cleveland's Charity Organization Society illustrates one of the movement's aims: to systematize and make more accessible the mass of data about the urban poor accumulated by overlapping and often competing benevolent agencies.

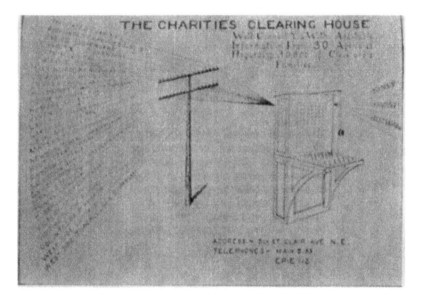

ban America's redemption. "Charity Organization perfectly carried out would produce a state of society nearer the Christian ideal than has ever yet been known," exclaimed one leader in 1884. Three years later Charles D. Kellogg described friendly visiting somewhat more militantly (Haymarket had intervened) as the movement's "right arm of aggressive work." He envisioned an army of 100,000 friendly visitors sweeping "like a tidal wave" over urban America, "flooding every part" with "sweetness and order and light."[24]

How would the friendly visitor achieve such wonders where so many others had failed? The first step—as the Reverend Ward Stafford had urged as long ago as 1817—was simply to establish a human tie across the barriers of class, religion, and nationality. The central object of the entire scheme, wrote Gurteen, was to promote "the *personal* intercourse of the wealthier citizens with the poor at their homes" and thereby bring together "the extremes of society in a spirit of honest friendship." Once class divisions had been overcome, and the friendly visitors had begun to "think of the poor as husbands, wives, sons and daughters, members of households as we are ourselves instead of contemplating them as a class different from ourselves," they could start to "impart to the cheerless tenement or the wretched hovel, a little of their own happiness."[25]

However, if mere camaraderie or a temporary lift in spirits were the only result, the encounter could be worse than useless. "It is a mistake to believe that any letting of ourselves down will ever lift them up," friendly visitors were advised. "The 'hail fellow, well met' air which we sometimes see in those who would avoid condescension, often leads to rash relations with those we would benefit, and consequent disappointment."[26]

The friendly visitor's profoundly serious purpose was to use "*the moral support of true friendship*" to bring about transformations of character: to embed in the poor a "new desire to live rightly" and to marshal more effectively their own resources of "energy and self-control."[27] In Boston, friendly visitors were given explicit instructions on this point: "Your duty to the family requires you to consider their moral good, and not the gratification of your own emotions . . . You who are strong, give some of your strength to those who are weak . . . You who love industry, teach it to the idle. You in your strength of character, steady the stumbling."[28]

For all their pride in being nonsectarian and scientific, charity organization leaders easily lapsed into the rhetoric of earlier evangelical urban-reform crusaders in urging the friendly visitors to persevere in their vital mission: "We must keep at work continually, season after season, pulling up the weeds of degradation and destitution, cultivating the thrift, self-dependence, industry, virtue, [and] health, as well as the intellectual and social natures of our poor friends."[29] In trying to define the changes they envisioned, they typically fell back on the familiar litany of middle-class virtues: honesty, thrift, sobriety, self-dependence, and respect for "the dignity of honest work."[30] In fact, however, specificity was unnecessary, for the friendly visitor understood her task implicitly: to bring the poor to share her own values and moral standards—to make them more like herself.

But—and here matters became delicate indeed—the visitor must never *appear* to be seeking such a transformation. The pose of simple friendship and "neighborliness" had to be sustained. "Avoid anything like dictation," Gurteen cautioned. "Treat even the poorest with the same delicacy of feeling and kind consideration that you would wish to have shown to yourself." The handbook for friendly visitors in Boston made the same point: "Do not announce yourself as a visitor of any charitable organization, but as a *friend* or neighbor anxious to know those among whom you live."[31] And it was reiterated by the keynote NCCC speaker in 1890: "human hearts are not like cattle—they cannot be driven ... [E]ach one of the vast multitude of the wayward or ignorant ... must be handled like an individual ... if the germs of the higher life within him are to burst the matted soil and seek the light."[32] *Handled like an individual!* The phrase not only captures the quintessential COS outlook but reveals how precarious was this effort to create, through the magic of friendly visiting, an urban social order where currents of personal moral influence might flow once again between the upper social ranks and the poor.

The "friendship" offered by the friendly visitor was thus of a rather special kind. Seemingly artless and spontaneous (when the visitor was skilled in her role), it was in fact simply the necessary first step in a larger moral-uplift process. Only by "holding on with firm grip, until at last you reach the heart-strings of someone in the family," wrote one COS leader in 1891, could the friendly visitor achieve that larger goal.[33]

With so much at stake, the friendly visitor was urged to plan her strategy with all the care of a military commander besieging an entrenched stronghold. If "her" family frittered away its meager resources on short-term pleasures and petty vices, for example, she was advised not to expound the virtue of thrift but to demonstrate it by planning some "pleasant occasion" to which the family members might "look forward from one week or month to another" and thereby gradually acquire the habit of delayed gratification. Even the "gift of a plant or picture or some other tasteful suggestive object of beauty" could play a part in this delicate process of character building.[34] Delegates to the 1895 NCCC were told of the amazing results when a friendly visitor set out to stimulate the "artistic imagination" of an "unruly" boy by taking him to the art museum: "When he went home, he could not begin again slashing up the furniture with his pocket knife, or beating his younger brother; for on every pine chair and table, as well as on his brother's jacket, arose visions of a soldiers' camp-fire at sunset, of a cardinal in his crimson robe of state, of three boats sailing out into the moonlight. He soon became a good boy."[35]

More important than any such stratagem, however, was the friendly visitor's own personality, as it gradually unfolded during her repeated visits. Almost by osmosis, the charity organization literature sometimes seems to suggest, the faithful friendly visitors would slowly "impart their own virtues" to the poor. The "life of the visitor," declared the leader of the Minneapolis COS, would be "the light that guides them to self-help, respectability, and multiplying opportunities."[36]

For all the talk of "neighborliness" and even of "guidance," what was involved here was social control of a quite explicit variety. The aim, wrote Gurteen, was to subject the poor to "the firm though loving government of heroic women." Once the friendly visitor had become a slum family's "acknowledged friend," he added, she would be "a power in that home."[37] *Power* was the issue, and in the shadowy struggle to gain moral leverage over the poor, the friendly visitor had certain important strategic advantages. Although she did not herself distribute relief, she helped compile the dossiers that were then made available not only to relief agencies but also to prospective employers, landlords, banks, "charitably interested individuals," and even the police. How ever glossed over, this 'fact could not long be concealed, and it surely added further tension to the already strained and ambiguous encounters between the needy family and its self-invited "friend." In *Democracy and Social Ethics* (1902), settlement-house leader Jane Addams offered a telling analysis of the "moral deterioration" which, she believed, frequently resulted from the relationship between slum family and charity visitor.

> When the agent or visitor appears among the poor, and they discover that under certain conditions food and rent and medical aid are dispensed from some unknown source, every man, woman, and child is quick to learn what the conditions may be, and to follow them . . . [T]o the visitor they gravely laud temperance and cleanliness and thrift and religious observance. The deception in the first instances arises from a

wondering inability to understand the ethical ideals which can require such impossible virtues, and from an innocent desire to please.[38]

By 1902, when this insightful criticism was published, the once-confident charity organization movement was beset by doubt and division. As early as 1891 an NCCC committee reported that the future of friendly visiting seemed "not altogether encouraging."[39] A year later, the Boston Associated Charities, while singling out one ethnic group, summed up a more general frustration friendly visitors were experiencing in dealing with some of their slum "neighbors."

> Until the Italians became numerous, we had at least intelligent means of communication with most of the families we knew. We not only spoke the same language, but they knew what we were talking about when we urged the advantages of temperance, industry, or economical living. Though their acquiescence in our standards might be feigned and though they might never live up to them, we seldom failed to agree in theory. [But the Italians] are truly foreigners to us. We do not speak a common language; our standards have no meaning to them, and we may well doubt whether they have any applicability.[40]

Even more dispiriting was the mounting criticism from those who should have been the movement's strongest supporters. In an 1890 symposium on poverty published in a Boston reform magazine, Benjamin O. Flower's *Arena*, one participant bitterly attacked the city's Associated Charities as a monopolistic "syndicate," and urged readers to consider the "torture" endured by needy families upon discovering that their relief application had caused "their names, history, and troubles to be spread in a written record to be coddled and gossiped over; [and] the privacy of their home to be invaded by inquisitive visitors whose unasked advice is the substitute for practical relief."[41]

The criticism increased in the mid-1890s as a devastating Depression called into question the two ideological pillars of the charity organization movement: that poverty was rooted in individual flaws, and that those flaws could be remedied through personal uplift effort. If, as the economic crisis of 1893–1897 seemed to make clear, the physical and moral dislocations of slum life were often the result of causes beyond individual control, where was the justification for the hand-crafted, family-by-family COS approach? As the Depression worsened, even so conservative an organization as the American Academy of Political and Social Science could publish an essay by a sociologist-reformer that scornfully dismissed the entire charity organization ethos: "It is said that the interests of the laborers are subserved best if the well-to-do classes do their charities for them . . . The time has passed when one class . . . will longer accept this sort of advice . . . The traditional charity . . . is a gift from success to failure, from superiority to apparent inferiority, from one who pities to one who is an object of pity."[42]

Their guiding principles confounded by events, the charity organization movement and its foot soldiers, the friendly visitors, lost their aggressive confidence and went on the defensive. "The work is developed under great discouragements in most of our large cities," acknowledged Amos G. Warner in 1894. The once path-breaking movement was subsiding into "mere officialism," agreed a Baltimore leader.[43] The familiar urban moral-control cycle, from initial enthusiasm to baffled discouragement, was playing itself out yet again.

Charity Organization and the Settlement-House Movement: Conflicts and Continuities in Urban Moral Uplift

Of all the late-nineteenth-century challenges to the assumptions of the charity organization movement, none was more pointed than that which came from the settlement houses. The history of the settlement movement—thanks in large part to Jane Addams's role in it—is comparatively well known.[44] Originating in London, the idea took root in America in 1886 with the opening of Stanton Coit's Neighborhood Guild in New York City. Three years later came the College Settlement in New York and Jane Addams's Hull House in Chicago. By the end of the century over 100 settlement houses had sprung up in the immigrant sections of most big cities, and for young college-bred volunteers, the movement had acquired much of the cachet that "charity organization" had possessed two decades earlier.[45]

From the first, relations between the upstart settlement movement and the older charity organization societies were strained, reflecting in part their differing perceptions of the urban moral situation and the duty of the middle classes toward the poor. A typical encounter occurred at the NCCC in 1896 when a charity organization speaker made the usual allusions to the failings of the urban poor and the need for "moral force" to lift them up. The next speaker, Mary McDowell of the University of Chicago Settlement, adopting the self-deprecatory yet slightly mocking tone at which settlement workers excelled, commented that she could not bring herself to criticize a filthy tenement apartment when she knew that smoke and soot were pouring into it from unregulated factories nearby. "When I try to apply some of that 'moral force' Mr. Ayres has spoken of," she concluded, "somehow I don't know how."[46]

The sarcasm flowed in both directions. At the NCCC the year before, COS leader Mary Richmond criticized the naiveté of youthful settlement-house residents who too readily abandoned their own convictions to accept uncritically the outlook of those among whom they lived. "They are bowled over," mocked Richmond, "by the first labor leader, or anarchist, or socialist" they meet.[47]

In retrospect, this quarrel appears as something of a family spat. The two movements had more in common than either liked to admit. Indeed, the early settlement houses were often viewed as extensions of the COS approach; settlement volunteers were simply "friendly visitors" who actually took up residence in the poor neighborhood, creating a model middle-class household: orderly, cultivated, temperate, and industrious. Josephine Shaw Lowell, bestowing her blessing on the settlement movement in 1895, described it as simply another means by which the privileged could "awaken nobler ambitions and create higher ideals" in the slums.[48]

For all their criticism of the COS's self-righteousness, the settlement leaders, too, fundamentally judged urban working-class life by their own solidly middle-class standards. Robert A. Woods of Boston's South End House, a staunch prohibitionist who advocated the isolation and segregation of tramps, alcoholics, paupers, and other unfit types, viewed the settlement house as the nucleus of purified slum neighborhoods that would ultimately banish rowdiness, drunkenness, and vice from their midst.[49] Even the determinedly tolerant Jane Addams eyed her Hull House neighbors from behind a barricade of moral and social preconceptions. She found much of value in immigrant life, but, as Allen Davis has noted, she also never really questioned that "the lower-class environment of saloons, dance halls, and street life needed to be . . . made more like a middle- or upper-class neighborhood." A wholly conventional morality underlay her 1913 work on prostitution, A New Conscience and an Ancient Evil, and in The Spirit of Youth and the City Streets (1909) she harshly criticized almost every aspect of urban mass culture. "Let us know the modern city in its weakness and wickedness," she wrote, "and then seek to rectify and purify it."[50]

If the moral outlook of the hundreds of now-obscure settlement volunteers who didn't write books or achieve fame could be recovered, we might find—despite Mary Richmond's charge that they were all being radicalized—a far higher degree of continuity with the conservative assumptions and strategies of the charity organization societies than the sniping between the two movements might suggest.

But this is not to say that the differences were all illusory. While the social-control impulse was present in the settlement movement, it was usually expressed in more nuanced terms, and subjected to more soul-searching scrutiny, than in the aggressively moralistic early COS pronouncements. More sensitive to the ambiguities involved in their encounters with the urban poor, chastened by the Depression of the 1890s, and determined to recognize the "admirable" qualities as well as the "failings" of their working-class neighbors, the settlement leaders generally muted their negative moral judgments or placed them within a larger framework of positive comment.

Furthermore, the young settlement workers were more responsive than the older COS leaders to the newer social thought, with its emphasis on the role of environment in shaping behavior and morals. Accordingly, their activism tended toward environmentalist rather than individualistic remedies. At times this environmentalism was rather baldly moralistic, as in their advocacy of movie censorship, dance hall regulation, and sometimes prohibition, but the settlements also supplied recruits for a wide range of reforms aimed at bettering not only the *moral* environment of the urban poor, but their *industrial* environment as well: campaigns for wage-and-hour legislation, child-labor laws, factory-safety regulations, etc.[51] While the charity organizations accumulated masses of data on individuals and families, the settlement workers—equally fascinated by statistics—chose the neighborhood, the political ward, or the industry as their unit of investigation. *Hull-House Maps and Papers* (1895), with its bristling pages of maps, graphs, charts, and statistical tables profiling Chicago's entire South Side, is a notable example of this broadened perspective.

When the settlement workers' moral-uplift efforts *were* directed at individuals, they typically involved not the inculcation of specific values or patterns of behavior, but what would later be called "consciousness raising": awakening the urban immigrants to the larger world beyond the tenement or factory, the richness of their cultural heritage, and the possibilities of community organization and cooperative effort. The most "difficult task" of any settlement house, said Mary K. Simkhovitch of New York's Greenwich House, was to assist the poor to become "a consciously effective group."[52]

If the two reforms had much in common, then, there were also important differences of emphasis. A crucial summation of those differences—and a major salvo in the running feud between the charity organizers and the settlement workers—was Jane Ad-

dams's 1902 work *Democracy and Social Ethics*. The book begins
with a fifty-seven page critique, characteristically gentle but devastating, of the charity organization movement and its substitution of "a theory of social conduct for the natural promptings of
the heart." Confronted by the "daintily clad charitable visitor"
with her air of moral superiority, wrote Addams, the poor usually
responded with a superficial complaisance masking their true
feelings: "good-natured and kindly contempt." The "scientific"

social investigation in which the charity organization societies
took such pride she compared to eighteenth-century botany,
"when flowers were tabulated in alphabetical order." In a key
passage, she simply inverted a classic charity organization formulation: the moral defects of the poor were not the *cause* of
their poverty, she suggested, but a *consequence* of "the struggle
for existence, which is so much harsher among people near the
edge of pauperism."[53] When the National Conference of Charities
and Correction, long a forum for COS pronouncements on the
moral shortcomings of slum dwellers, elected Jane Addams president in 1904—two years after *Democracy and Social Ethics*—the
symbolic import of the moment was not lost on the partisans of
either movement.

Beset by criticism, their ideology under challenge, charity organization spokesmen tried to adapt to the altered climate of the
1890s by soft-pedaling their preoccupation with the failings of
the poor and paying more attention to environmental factors.[54]
A COS spokesman in 1896 portrayed friendly visitors not only as
agents of individual moral uplift but also as instruments for marshaling public sentiment against child labor, sweatshops, and
other exploitative aspects of the industrial system.[55] At the NCCC
gathering of 1897, Edward T. Devine, the new general secretary
of the New York COS, implicitly dismissed two decades of charity organization rhetoric as he poked fun at the heavily moralistic
aura of the typical COS office: "Sometimes a caller . . . will bring
in the word 'worthy' or 'deserving,' doubtfully, as if not exactly
accustomed to use it when talking of their neighbors, but as if
thinking that no other classification would be quite in place
in a charity organization office, just as we half unconsciously
drop into the use of such semi-technical words as 'acute' and
'chronic,' when speaking to a physician, or 'believer' and 'un-
believer,' in a clergyman's presence."[56] At that same conference,
a Chicago leader, discussing "Friendly Visiting as a Social Force,"
rejected the old preoccupation with individuals and single families. Displaying a sociological map of a Chicago immigrant ward,
he described how a group of COS visitors, working as a team, had
helped establish a neighborhood employment committee, a sav-

ings bank, a women's workroom, and a forty-acre cooperative vegetable garden.[57]

The turn toward environmentalism is evident, too, in several important books produced by charity organization leaders in the 1890s. In *The Development of Thrift* (1899), Mary Willcox Brown blamed the fact that the poor were often "stunted" in spirit as well as in body on their "wretched material environment." Amos Warner in *American Charities* (1894), explicitly rejecting the view that eradication of the slums depended exclusively or even primarily on individual "moral reformation," offered a list of "objective" causes of poverty that included "Bad Industrial Conditions," "Defective Legislation," and "The Undue Power Of Class Over Class."[58]

Similarly, Mary Richmond's widely used COS manual of 1899, *Friendly Visiting among the Poor,* was marked by a positive attitude toward the poor far different from the earlier handbooks of Gurteen and others. (Her own background, as well as the shifting intellectual climate, helped determine her outlook. Orphaned at two, she passed a poverty-stricken girlhood with working-class relatives and worked for two years at starvation wages in New York City before joining the Baltimore COS in 1889.) Like the contemporary settlement-house leaders, she warned COS volunteers against rigid moralism and urged receptivity to every hint of goodness and nobility in the poor. Rather than isolating specific character traits or behavioral details, she advised, the charity visitor should try to grasp "the family life as a whole," including the "joys, sorrows, opinions, feelings, and entire outlook upon life." ("One never feels acquainted with the poor family until [one] has had a good laugh with them," she added in a later work.) Only a "benighted social reformer," she wrote acerbicly, "thinks of all who drink as drunkards, and of all places where liquor is sold as dens of vice."[59] (A charity worker with such an attitude would not long have survived in Baltimore!)

At the same time, however, these works also reveal that even in the wake of a catastrophic Depression, the charity organization leadership continued to be preoccupied with the moral sources of poverty. Along with his "objective" causes of destitution, Amos Warner drew up a lengthy list of "subjective" causes, including "Indolence," "Lubricity," "Lack of Judgment," "Unhealthy Appetites," "Shiftlessness," "Abuse of Stimulants and Narcotics," and "Disregard of Family Ties." (Indeed, one of his "objective" causes was "Evil Associations and Surroundings," revealing how easily the new "environmentalist" outlook could be accommodated to the old moralism.) Discussing the "Personal Causes of Individual Degeneration," Warner deplored the grossness of "the rougher class of day laborers" among whom "the whole undercurrent of thought . . . is thoroughly base and degrading." The "inherent uncleanness of their minds," he concluded, ruins them for positions requiring "alertness and sustained attention" and thus "prevents them from rising."[60]

Even for Mary Richmond, a heightened concern with the human realities of slum life did not override a continued belief that deficiencies of character figured prominently among the causes of poverty, and that a part of the charity worker's duty was to lead the poor to a higher moral plane. "Character is at the very center of this complicated problem" of poverty, she wrote in *Friendly Visiting among the Poor*. Neglect of "the discipline that makes character," she added in another work of this period, was a "common fault of modern philanthropy." It was on a foundation of individual industry and thrift, she argued, that "all the social virtues are built." Richmond also believed that any household that violated the strict Victorian division of sexual roles (the husband the breadwinner, the wife devoting herself exclusively to domestic duties) would quickly become "a breeding place of sin and social disorder." This, in part, was what she had in mind when she urged COS visitors to work to strengthen "true" home life among the poor and to transform "the sham home into a real one." In addition to warning children about "bad reading" and "low theatrical performances," she wrote, the friendly visitor must help the husband who had "lost his sense of responsibility toward wife and children to regain it," dissuade restless wives from seeking outside employment, and introduce messy housekeepers to "the pleasures of a cleanly, well-ordered home."[61]

In important ways, then, *Friendly Visiting among the Poor* reaffirmed the long-standing charity organization hope that the poor would "unconsciously imitate" the middle-class visitor and gradually adopt her values. Like the antebellum Sunday school ideologists, Richmond suggested that this influence could be especially effective with the young. "We should not despair of the children, if we can attach them to us and give them a new and better outlook upon life."[62]

But this was, after all, a book of 1899 and not 1879, and Richmond, acknowledging that some of her ideas might seem "old fashioned," adopted a decidedly defensive tone as she refurbished the old verities: "Some . . . question our right to go among [the poor] with the object of doing them good, regarding it as an impertinent interference with the rights of the individual. But . . . [w]e must interfere when confronted by human suffering and need. Why not interfere effectively?"[63]

The efforts to bring charity organization abreast of the shifting social and intellectual climate of the 1890s could not conceal the fact that the movement as its founders had conceived it was fad-ing with the old century itself. The early leaders were passing from the scene, taking their bold moral certitudes with them.

But despite its eventual decline, the charity organization movement for a crucial twenty-year period in the Gilded Age provided a powerful rationale and institutional outlet for the urban social-control impulses of the American middle class. In these decades when the middle class was in fact abandoning the immigrant cities and their complex problems—fleeing to the suburbs, retreating into tight neighborhood enclaves, dismissing municipal politics with ridicule, and allowing the industrial capitalism that was shaping the city to proceed unchecked and uncontrolled—charity organization had provided the illusion that in the moral realm, at least, it was still firmly at the helm.

11

The Urban Moral Awakening of the 1890s

It is autumn 1894, and New York City is in the throes of a bitterly contested election battle. The dominant figure and most tireless campaigner is not a politician at all, but a man of God: the Reverend Charles Parkhurst of Madison Square Presbyterian Church. His speeches—hardly the usual political fare—are in fact ringing jeremiads against official connivance in vice, corruption, and immorality in the city. At one rally, Parkhurst's stern recital of the Ten Commandments brings the audience to its feet in an explosion of fervent applause![1]

This moment epitomizes the wave of moral reformism and "civic-uplift" zeal that swept urban America—or at least *middle-class* urban America—in the 1890s. John Higham has noted the strenuous, activist tone of American culture in this decade, and a part of this activism flowed into an intensified urban moral-control effort.[2] This phenomenon merits examination not only for its intrinsic importance but also because it was the spawning ground for a variety of reform efforts that profoundly affected the nation's cities in the decades that followed.

At first glance, the specific expressions of the urban moral-control impulse in this turbulent and Depression-wracked decade seem frustratingly diffuse. That diffuse quality is perhaps best typified in the eclectic reform enthusiasm of an appealing trio of Kansas-born brothers—Walter, Frank, and Hiram Vrooman—and their staunch supporter Benjamin O. Flower. In 1891 Walter

Vrooman, a reporter for the *New York World* who had taken the lead in establishing a playground on New York's Lower East Side, attempted to sustain the momentum of this achievement by founding in New York a Union for Concerted Moral Effort. He went on to establish similar societies in Philadelphia and Worcester, Massachusetts, where Frank Vrooman was a minister. Hiram, meanwhile, was presiding over the birth of a Union for Doing Good in Baltimore.[3] In mid-1893, Benjamin O. Flower began to give enthusiastic publicity to these efforts in the *Arena*, the wide-ranging reform monthly he had founded in Boston a few years earlier. Under the *Arena*'s sponsorship a National Union for Practical Progress was soon established with Hiram Vrooman as secretary-treasurer and such figures as Stanford University president David Starr Jordan, federal labor commissioner Carroll D. Wright, and Frances Willard of the Woman's Christian Temperance Union on the advisory board.[4] By the summer of 1894 approximately forty local unions (some with variant names, but all loosely linked to the national movement) had been established in as many cities.[5]

In retrospect, the objectives of the National Union for Practical Progress seem impossibly diverse, and its tactics nebulous at best. "A new moral issue will be presented to the people each month," wrote Walter Vrooman in the *Arena*, including "any and every measure approved by the average disinterested conscience." Among the projects mentioned were public band concerts, playgrounds, and "magic-lantern" shows for slum children; gymns, exercise rooms, and bowling alleys in big-city churches for their fathers; model tenements; and crusades against prostitution, the saloon, and urban political corruption. These reforms would be achieved by focusing attention on them in the *Arena* and other publications, organizing local study groups and publicity campaigns, and working for "such legislation as may be necessary."[6]

Reflecting this broad-gauge reform spirit, local uplift campaigns proliferated in New York, Chicago, and numerous other cities. In New Orleans, an Anti-Lottery League led by the local Methodist bishop organized a successful campaign against the state lottery. (The Catholic archbishop cooperated by forbidding priests from blessing lottery tickets.) In Cleveland, a "purity alliance" ousted a police commissioner who favored municipal regulation of prostitution. Reformers in Los Angeles closed the city's gambling establishments in 1896.[7]

But if the urban moral-reform agenda of the nineties was vague and concrete results few, its urgency shone through with unmistakable clarity: the social and moral challenge of the city was growing more critical, approaches that had once held promise were proving inadequate. The crisis had to be confronted *now* by efforts as dedicated as any religious revival, as coordinated as any military campaign. At the 1893 convention of the Young People's Society of Christian Endeavor (an interdenominational Protestant youth organization founded in 1881), the delegates enthusiastically pledged themselves to "a bettering of civic conditions" through "the election of good men," "the enactment of good laws," and "steady opposition to the saloon, the gambling-hell, the lottery, [and] the violation of the Sabbath." At mid-decade, one reform leader compiled a list of fifty-seven organizations throughout the country dedicated to municipal uplift and a purification of the moral tone of civic life. Benjamin Flower wrote of the "heart hunger" of thousands who longed to "aid the best and discourage the worst in the city" by beating back "the waves of want, vice, and misery." A "gigantic moral upheaval" was "fast gathering," added Walter Vrooman; by joining together in a Union for Practical Progress, he promised, even a handful of "earnest men or women, without wealth or special talents" could "revolutionize" the "moral work" of their town or city.[8]

This moral intensity was spectacularly demonstrated in the urban reform crusades of William T. Stead in Chicago and Charles H. Parkhurst in New York City. Stead, born in an English country parsonage at mid-century, won his reputation as a moral-reform journalist and editor in London in the 1880s, especially through "The Maiden Tribute of Modern Babylon," an exposé of London prostitution published in his *Pall Mall Gazette* in 1885. In Chicago for the World's Fair of 1893, he called a mass meeting where he described his firsthand observations of vice in the city and offered his panacea: a "Civic Church" uniting "all who love, in the service of all who suffer." In February 1894, as an outgrowth of Stead's agitation, the Chicago Civic Federation was established with the reform-minded banker Lyman J. Gage as president, Mrs. Potter Palmer as vice-president, and a central committee of 100 prominent Chicagoans. Like the Union for Practical Progress, the Federation's initial program was eclectic, including relief for the unemployed, improved street cleaning and garbage collection, and campaigns against gambling and prostitution. Though Stead had provided the catalyst, he played no direct role in the formation of the Civic Federation; "I am very careful to keep out of everything," he wrote; "after having started them I let them go their own way."[9]

Charles H. Parkhurst, by contrast, plunged with gusto into the movement that he helped precipitate. Another reformer whose roots lay in preurban America, Parkhurst grew up in Massachusetts and served as a school principal and Congregational minister in the towns of Amherst and Lenox before coming to New York's Madison Square Presbyterian Church in 1880. Early in the

1890s, Parkhurst began to focus his sermons on Manhattan's moral condition, denouncing not only organized gambling, wide-open brothels, and saloons where liquor flowed freely on Sundays but the connivance of municipal officials in these evils. New York's "thoroughly rotten" moral climate, he charged, was simply a by-product of the "slimy, oozy soil of Tammany Hall" and its police—"the dirtiest, crookedest, and ugliest lot of men ever combined in semi-military array outside of Japan and Turkey."[10]

Parkhurst's bombast soon attracted attention beyond his church. Newspapers began to praise or denounce him, depending on their politics, and the Society for the Prevention of Crime, a rather somnolent merchant-dominated group founded in 1878, invited him to become its head. At a mass meeting in May 1892, several hundred New Yorkers rose to signal their support for Parkhurst's proposed City Vigilance League, pledging to do everything in their power to "promote the purity and honesty" of municipal government. In the ensuing months, league members secretly investigated police connivance in prostitution, gambling, and liquor-law violations. When a legislative committee headed by Republican Clarence Lexow came from Albany in 1894 to investigate corruption in New York, Parkhurst and his followers inundated it with evidence of officially tolerated vice.[11]

Parkhurst's crusade turned even more overtly political in September 1894 when the Committee of Seventy—a "nonpartisan" but mainly Yankee, Protestant, and Republican organization including J. P. Morgan, William Bayard Cutting, Morris K. Jesup, William E. Dodge, Jr., and the younger Cornelius Vanderbilt— issued a call for a political clean-up in New York City. Augmented by other reform groups and joining with the Republican organization on a fusion basis, the Committee of Seventy chose William L. Strong as its candidate in the upcoming mayoral election.[12]

As we have seen, the ensuing campaign was evocative of a religious revival. Parkhurst spoke incessantly, insisting, in a wonderfully mixed metaphor, that the election was "a chance to lift the chariot wheels [of city government] out of the muddy ruts of human villainy and filth, and set them down on the hard, ringing pavement of the mind and will of God." Riding the crest of such political sermonizing, William Strong was elected mayor. For the next three years (thanks in part to the efforts of his energetic young police commissioner Theodore Roosevelt), the statutes relating to prostitution, gambling, and Sunday liquor sales were enforced with unprecedented rigor. The Strong coalition soon fragmented. German voters disliked its Sabbatarian preoccupations, the Republican leadership wished to run its own candidates, etc., and in 1897 Tammany won as usual, installing as police chief a man James F. Richardson has called "one of the great scoundrel cops of New York history."[13] Nevertheless, the reformist energies Charles Parkhurst had unleashed in New York (and William Stead in Chicago) offered striking evidence of the gathering power of the urban moral-control impulse as the nineteenth century drew to a close.

Despite the surface diversity of these movements, the themes their leaders emphasized were remarkably similar. One finds over and over again, for example, the notion that a great reserve of reform potential lay untapped in the city, and that civic purification depended upon its release. Benjamin O. Flower wrote of the throngs of reform-minded city dwellers who "for lack of organization and a directing brain, find the days flitting by with nothing accomplished." In *The Cosmopolis City Club* (1893), an urban-reform novel by the Congregational minister and Social Gospel publicist Washington Gladden, for example, a character complains that too much of his city's "moral energy" is "packed up and stored away."[14]

Yet the mood was far from bleak, for a second major theme was that this latent moral force was at last beginning to coalesce, promising a new day for the American city. The image of an "awakening," so evocative of the revival outpourings of earlier generations, was often employed. "What New York City needs is a general waking up; something big enough and of sufficient importance to arouse the slumbering powers of the people," declared a Manhattan minister in 1891, welcoming Walter Vrooman's Union for Concerted Moral Effort as "the beginning of a new enthusiasm that will sweep away like a flood the accumulating evils of our modern cities."[15]

The challenge, then, was to transform these inchoate stirrings into effective action. "Only by union," wrote Walter Vrooman in 1894, "can the moral forces of society defend themselves against aggressive evil." The need of the hour, he declared, was to "unite all moral forces, agencies, and persons for concerted, methodical, and persistent endeavor"—to invent (once again!) a "mechanism" linking the reformers of all cities so that, "like so many myriads of hammers," they could "strike all at a given signal." Walter's brother Hiram dreamed of the day when "scientific" moral-reform unions in every American city, following a nationally coordinated program, would uproot "one evil . . . after another according to intelligent plan."[16]

The need to energize and link together the scattered moral resources of urban America obsessed the reformers of this decade. "We must have organization, the organization of the industrious and respectable people of this city," declares a character in Gladden's *Cosmopolis City Club*; "You can't do much in these days without it." In Charles M. Sheldon's famous reform novel *In His Steps* (1896), when several well-to-do citizens set out to banish vice, intemperance, and social injustice from the city of Raymond (a fictionalized version of Topeka, Kansas, where Sheldon was a Congregational minister), their first action is to form a close-knit band united by the motto "What Would Jesus Do?"[17] Only when the free-floating moral energies of a city's respectable element were pooled in this way, Sheldon suggested, would effective action become possible.

But what, precisely, would be the organizational channel through which this pooled moral force would flow, and to what specific ends would it be directed? One obvious institutional prototype was the charity organization movement; indeed, much of this talk about harnessing the cities' moral resources simply echoed two decades of COS pronouncements. But while the reformers of the 1890s had much in common with the charity organization outlook, they conceived their mission in far broader terms, dreaming not just of pulling slum dwellers up to some minimal standard of respectability, but of purifying the entire urban moral climate. Their attitude toward charity organization was not hostile, but somewhat condescending: the older movement, they felt, was a little fusty, its family-by-family approach too confining.

Toward the church, the spokesmen for the "urban awakening" of the 1890s showed ambivalence. Like the charity organization leaders, they often dismissed the churches of urban America as a hindrance to the moral transformation they envisioned. Sectarian narrowness was blamed for the collapse of Walter Vrooman's Philadelphia Union for Practical Progress (Protestant ministers refused to accept the leadership of a Jewish rabbi), and the failure of the New York Union for Concerted Moral Effort, another Vrooman project, was attributed to the same cause. "At the first mass meeting held in the Marble Collegiate Church about eighteen hundred persons crowded in to hear of the proposed reform work," one participant recalled. "But all the speakers were clergymen, and soon ill feeling arose, with petty jealousies, and not being anchored by any lay organization, the Union . . . fell to pieces."[18]

Though themselves ministers, neither Charles Sheldon nor Washington Gladden was willing to ascribe a central role to the church in his urban reform novel. In Sheldon's *In His Steps*, only a fraction of the churchgoers of Raymond rally behind the cause, and what is accomplished is the work of organized laymen, not the churches themselves. In *The Cosmopolis City Club*, one reformer warns against tying the movement to "any form of ecclesiasticism," and the clergyman whom Gladden includes in his cast of uplifters is a flighty and somewhat comic figure whose naive suggestions are invariably ignored.[19]

Clearly, Benjamin Flower's attacks on the "cowardice and lethargy" of city churches "rich in gold but poor in . . . moral energy" were authentic expressions of an important strand of urban moral-reform thought in the 1890s. But for all its flaws, the urban church still represented a resource that might yet become an instrument of moral regeneration. Hiram Vrooman envisioned a time when "the cannon of a hundred [city] pulpits" would "thunder forth at the same hour such a volley . . . that the moral enthusiasm invoked [would] be irresistible."[20] Even his brother Walter, despite his frustrations in Philadelphia and New York, remained hopeful. "The church has the money, the buildings, the membership, the latent moral enthusiasm, that are required to make a great reform movement successful . . . [I]f its huge frame can once more be made to throb with life and to respond to a high moral ideal, it will yet become the foremost power for good in the world."[21]

While hardly the vital center of the new movement, then, the church was assigned an important potential role. At best, revitalized churches might spearhead the emerging moral-reform crusade; at the least, urban congregations could provide recruits whose energies, even if expressed through other institutional channels, would be crucial to its success. Even though the moral potential of the urban churches was being "wasted as prodigally as the physical energy liberated by winds, tides, and ocean currents," observed the founder of the Boston Union for Practical Progress in 1894, if the people who had caught the vision of an urban moral awakening could carry it into the churches, "the religious Niagara" might yet be "harnessed and set to work."[22]

> Politics is the weapon. We must learn to use it
> so as to cut straight and true.
> —Jacob Riis, "The Battle With the Slums,"
> Atlantic Monthly, May 1899

Municipal politics seemed to offer a still more promising outlet for these moral-reform energies. Since the Jacksonian period, the main current of urban social-control effort had remained apart from politics. In the 1890s, however, moral reform and political reform converged, and they would remain interwoven for years.

It was in 1888 that James Bryce described city government as the "one conspicuous failure of American democracy," and for the next thirty years a host of reformers worked to refute that embarrassing charge.[23] The story of municipal political reform in these years is a familiar and much-analyzed one: the struggle against "the bosses"; the "good government" movement spearheaded by the National Municipal League and its many local affiliates; the campaigns to bring the transit and utility interests to heel; the battalions of "reform" mayors, including Hazen Pingree in Detroit, William Strong and Seth Low in New York, Charles Schieren in Brooklyn, Josiah Quincy in Boston, James Phelen in San Francisco, Samuel "Golden Rule" Jones and Brand Whitlock in Toledo, and Tom Johnson in Cleveland.

What bears emphasizing here is how thoroughly all these movements were steeped in moral-uplift preoccupations. For municipal political reformers of the late nineteenth century, the worst thing about a corrupt and thieving municipal government, or one linked to vice interests, was that it poisoned the moral atmosphere of the entire city. E. L. Godkin of the *Nation* put the matter bluntly in 1896: "The newly arrived immigrant who settles in New York gets tenfold more of his notions of American right and wrong from city politics than he gets from the city missionaries, or the schools, or the mission chapels . . . As a moral influence . . . , the clergyman and philanthropist are hopelessly distanced by the politician."[24] Washington Gladden agreed. As long as municipal political corruption survived, and elected officialdom remained the "ally and patron of lawbreakers," he declared in *Social Facts and Forces* (1897), "the task of enforcing upon the young the principles of truth and honor and integrity" would be well-nigh impossible.[25]

By the same token, the first step in urban moral betterment was to restore city hall to virtue. Throughout the later 1890s the National Municipal League and its head Clinton R. Woodruff constantly insisted that if the apparatus of city government could be wrested from those who had debased and exploited it, an almost unimaginable civic, social, and moral advance would become possible.[26]

Even the campaign for public ownership of municipal waterworks, utilities, and transit companies was often portrayed as a means to the larger moral reclamation of the city and its inhabitants. It was a battle, declared Detroit's Hazen Pingree, against "the greatest corrupters of public morals that ever blackened the pages of history." To bring to an end the political conniving and bribery of the utility and transit interests through public ownership would not only remove an influence that was debasing the moral tone of urban life, but it would symbolize the city's corporate unity and promote the emergence of a greater civic consciousness. The aim of such reforms was "primarily ethical," in Washington Gladden's view, for their ultimate goal was nothing less than "the regeneration of the municipality."[27]

These themes were interestingly developed in *Cities in the Nineteenth Century* (1899), by Adna F. Weber, a New York State labor statistician. In a section devoted to "Urban Morality," Weber deplored the "weakening of the bonds of moral cohesion" in the modern city, and suggested that one way to "unify the community" was to abandon the laissez faire economic philosophy that had allowed essential municipal services to be exploited by private speculators. As the utilities and transit companies were brought under public ownership and control, he concluded, a "social feeling" would be excited among city dwellers that would curb their self-seeking behavior and raise their ethical horizons.[28]

As we grasp this connection, we can understand how urban reformers of the 1890s could move with such ease from issues of municipal misgovernment and corporate exploitation to the familiar, garden-variety human vices: all were factors in shaping the moral climate of the city. The author of an 1895 *Arena* account of San Francisco's "Civic Awakening" proceeded with no apparent sense of discontinuity from a blistering attack on the Southern Pacific Railroad as "the great agent of corruption" to an impassioned denunciation of the city's gambling halls, saloons, and prostitutes who provided "the vilest service within human knowledge."[29] In *The Cosmopolis City Club,* Gladden similarly interwove a traditional concern about the intemperance and immorality of city dwellers with technical discussions of municipal administrative reform.

This distinctive 1890s blend of political, economic, and moral preoccupations is nowhere better illustrated than in Benjamin Flower's *Civilization's Inferno* (1893), an anthology of his *Arena* articles recounting his explorations in Boston's slums and discussing a variety of remedies—from city missions to the single tax—for urban evils. At times defiantly radical, Flower blames the capitalists for the sweatshops, starvation wages, crumbling tenements, and influx of cheap foreign labor that have created the urban "inferno," and demands "radical economic changes" to overthrow the "aristocracy of the bankers," the "gloved hand of organized capital," and the "vicious class legislation" of "a soulless plutocracy intrenched behind class laws."[30]

But then, on practically the same page, in passages that echo the evangelical moral reformers of the Jacksonian era, he unleashes strident moralistic denunciations of the vices and "degradation" of the urban poor and attacks the slum as a charnel house of "moral death" where debased creatures seek "bestial gratifications" in brothels, cheap dives, and the "low songs, oaths, [and] coarse jests" of the saloon.[31]

When reformers of this ilk turned to the ballot to destroy "the bosses," they inevitably viewed the contest as an apocalyptic, good-versus-evil struggle. In fact, of course, there was no necessary connection between machine politics and urban vice. The machine of George B. Cox in Cincinnati, as well as the twentieth-century ones of Anton Cermak in Chicago, Charles Francis Murphy in New York, Frank Hague in Jersey City, and Edward Crump in Memphis, revealed that on issues of personal morality the boss could be as strait-laced as any reformer.[32] But in the reform climate of the 1890s, such distinctions carried little weight. If the city were to experience the "moral-awakening" it so desperately needed, the immigrant political machine would have to go.

The 1894 New York City crusade that placed William Strong in the mayor's office, Theodore Roosevelt in the police superintendency, and Charles Parkhurst in the national limelight remains the classic example of the intense moralism of municipal political reform in this decade. "The foremost cause of the civic awakening was moral," wrote the secretary of Parkhurst's Vigilance League after the victory; the league had "no definite policy" or "delicately constructed theories," he insisted—only "the knowledge that New York City must be made better." Theodore Roosevelt always contended that the 1894 victory, and the reforms it made possible, had dramatically improved "the general standard of morals and behavior in the city at large."[33]

Parkhurst himself put the issue squarely. New York City, he cried in his election eve sermon, stood at "a point of moral crisis": it faced the choice between one slate standing for virtue and decency and another made up of "moral incapables that have breathed iniquity, eaten iniquity, drunk iniquity, and bartered in iniquity so long that to them iniquity is actually the normal condition of things." Parkhurst sustained this mood through the following year, and his Our Fight with Tammany (1895) is rife with fulminations against the defeated foe. Since "the slimy, oozy soil of Tammany Hall" had turned the city into an "open cesspool," he declared, the reform campaign was simply an exercise in "municipal sewerage" to "drain that political quagmire, and . . . get rid of the odor, the mire, and the fever germs."[34]

Parkhurst was also well aware that the moral stakes of his crusade were heightened by the fact that it was widely interpreted as providing a pattern for similar efforts in other cities. As Daniel Coit Gilman, the president of Johns Hopkins University, put it: "New York is an example to all this land—a colossal object lesson, . . . a sort of teachers' college where other cities may learn both what to do and what not to do."[35]

So enthusiastically did Parkhurst and his counterparts elsewhere turn every muncipal election into a moral free-for-all that Washington Gladden, while sharing their long-range goals, issued a word of caution. "The attempt to carry theological, or, perhaps I should say ethical, distinctions into party divisions often creates confusion," he warned in The Cosmopolis City Club, written at the peak of the Parkhurst crusade; "the notion that parties must needs divide on ethical grounds is a great mistake." When Gladden's fictional minister begins to plump for a "Law and Order" party, another reformer points out that this by implication turns the opposition into a "Lawless and Disorder" party, and asks: "Do you think that it would be a good thing to have . . . about half of the citizens registered as saints and the other half as sinners?" Far better, Gladden advised, for the "moral element" to remain a nonpartisan interest group wooed by both parties, thereby elevating the whole moral tone of urban politics.[36]

The politicization of the urban morality impulse in the 1890s gave the movement a far more explicit class and ethnic coloration. To be sure, all the movements examined so far in this book were led by members of the elite or middle classes, while the people they sought to influence were invariably below them on the economic scale. But a variety of factors—the voluntarist nature of earlier efforts; the rhetoric of Christian benevolence in which they were couched; the anonymity the founders, directors, and financial backers were able to maintain—had helped to obscure these class realities.

Now, however, as the effort took an openly political turn and as urban class lines and residential patterns became increasingly stratified, its class basis emerged quite openly. Much evidence supports Melvin G. Holli's contention that a central impetus behind municipal political reform in the late nineteenth and early twentieth centuries was the desire of old-stock Americans to extirpate "lower-class vices" and "impose middle class and patrician ideals upon the urban masses." The people who wrote for the *Arena* and rallied to Walter Vrooman's Union for Practical Progress were middle-class, native-born Protestants. New York's reform crusade of 1894 was dominated by old-stock patricians and businessmen. In Philadelphia, as one historian has recently noted, the political reform movement of this period was led by members of the old elite who "saw themselves as the 'moral stewards' of the community" and who "believed that honest government would restore to the entire community the moral standards to which they clung."[37]

In both *The Cosmopolis City Club* and *In His Steps*, the reformers bear such names as Spring, Thomlinson, Winslow, and Bruce, and they usually turn out to be doctors, lawyers, manufacturers, or newspaper editors. By contrast, the corrupt city councilmen in Gladden's novel are O'Halloran, Schwab, Schneider, Flynn, and Mulloy. After meeting with them at city hall, one reformer comments: "It smells to heaven. Bad tobacco, stale beer, and the incense which always arises from the assemblies of the great unwashed perfumes the air, and the moral atmosphere is not less tainted."[38]

Keenly aware of the class limitations of their "civic awakening," the urban reformers of the 1890s made determined efforts to deny it. Endlessly they insisted that their shining vision of a morally purified city must surely be shared, at some deep level, by the great mass of the urban population, however divided by creed, ethnic differences, or economic status. Was this not, after all, an uprising of the city's "moral forces" against the few who had befouled its moral atmosphere? Parkhurst's Committee of Seventy insisted that the vices it fought injured "all classes of citizens, rich and poor alike," and Walter Vrooman described his crusade as an effort to apply "the eternal truths of the universe" to the industrial city. Only "lethargy, stolidity, and sympathies utterly stifled by worldliness," he wrote, could stand in the way of civic regeneration; when these had been "melted away by the fire of enthusiasm," the entire urban populace would stand united, "thrilled by a single moral impulse, one grand social enthusiasm."[39]

Charles Sheldon and Washington Gladden made similarly valiant efforts in their novels to deal with the problem of class. When a leader of the "What Would Jesus Do?" movement in *In His Steps* addresses a group of factory workers, he has "the great good sense . . . not to recognize the men as a class distinct from himself," and says nothing "to suggest any difference between their lives and his own." In *The Cosmopolis City Club*, Gladden portrays the reform movement as a disinterested effort by the city's "natural leaders" to express the community's collective moral sentiments. Setting out to unite all "industrious and respectable people" under their banner, Gladden's white-collar reformers woo recruits from diverse backgrounds to give their campaign "dignity and influence with all classes." To this end, they somewhat improbably choose as their spokesman one Sam Hathaway, a carpenter of unpolished ways and blunt, working-class speech. Presenting the reformers' ideas at a mass meeting, Sam does so "in a manly fashion," albeit "blushingly" and "with a little tremor in his voice."[40] Except for the saloon keepers and the city hall crowd, this rally attracts a representative cross section of the city's population, including a cheerful group of blue-collar workers, pleased to see their carpenter friend on the platform with such exalted company.

Gladden takes pains to emphasize that the reform program presented at this mass meeting embodies the deepest if hitherto inchoate aspirations of the city as a whole. The affirmative vote is overwhelming, and "the noes . . . so few and feeble that the audience greet[s] their protest with an outburst of good-natured laughter."[41]

The wishful thinking underlying such a passage is itself evidence of the extent to which, for all the insistence to the contrary, this stirring of reform in urban America in the 1890s was in fact a process by which elements of the middle and upper classes were organizing for yet another determined moral-control effort directed at the urban masses. Only in the Progressive era, as that effort rose to a crescendo, would the meaning and significance of this anticipatory "awakening" become, in retrospect, fully evident.

12

The Two Faces of Urban Moral
Reform in the 1890s

When the prophets of an urban moral awakening in the 1890s
moved beyond the level of generalities, they faced some difficult
practical questions. Above all, they had to consider what new
strategies of moral control and uplift held the greatest promise
of success. Political reform—throwing out the scoundrels who
had polluted the moral springs of city life—was a first step, but
for many this only laid bare the larger challenge: how to translate civic power, once regained by the "better elements," into the
much-desired urban moral renaissance.

In answer to this challenge, two quite distinct (though ultimately complementary) strategies took shape. While some reformers drifted toward a repressive stance, urging coercive measures to uproot vice and impose a higher standard of civic virtue,
others were drawn to a subtler, less direct approach: that of
remolding the city's physical environment as a means of elevating its moral tone.

The two approaches—coercive and environmentalist—were
neither precisely defined nor sharply distinguished as yet. Each
involved a variety of modulations and permutations, and the
same individual often endorsed both—sometimes in the course
of a single book, article, or sermon. Similarly, the lurid rhetoric
in which they were discussed ran the gamut from bright optimism
to gloomy apprehension, as exalted visions of the urban future
alternated with the blackest fears.

The Coercive Approach:
The City as Menace to be Subdued

In his 1913 autobiography, with San Juan Hill and the White House behind him, Theodore Roosevelt could still recall with relish the passionate moral atmosphere of 1895–1897 when, as William Strong's police commissioner, he had waged "relentless war" against the "bestial" rulers of "commercialized vice" in "huge, polyglot, pleasure-loving" New York. His only regret was that he had not ordered them horsewhipped! TR is the best known of many urban moral crusaders in this decade who adopted a hostile and coercive tone toward the people they wanted to reform. "It is a dreary old truth," wrote Roosevelt's friend Jacob Riis, "that those who would fight *for* the poor must *fight* the poor to do it." In combating the slum menace, commented the Reverend William S. Rainsford in 1891, "we are but scraping the soil with a harrow, while it needs a steam plow."[1]

When in this coercive mood, the reformers of the 1890s tended to fall back with a vengeance upon the wicked-city stereotype. Unless countermeasures were quickly taken, declared Walter Vrooman, the rising generation of city dwellers would be transformed into "monsters." Charles Sheldon, despite his obvious desire to sympathize with the poor and unemployed, nevertheless described the urban slum as a "cesspool" full of a "vile, debauched . . . , impure, [and] besotted mass of humanity." When one of the reformers in *In His Steps* approaches a drunken prostitute with the intention of reclaiming her, she eyes the "miserable figure" with a feeling "she was afraid would grow into disgust."[2] And in *Civilization's Inferno*, Benjamin Flower warned of slum uprisings that could turn the cities into military garrisons, and conjured up a vision of Boston's moral and social corruption taking the symbolic form of a plague. "Death was everywhere present. I beheld thousands of our people fleeing . . . , but scarcely had they left the city when the wires flashed . . . the fateful news that all cities and towns were quarantined against Boston . . . The plague, impalpable but terrible, seemed omnipresent."[3]

Though often counterbalanced by more hopeful appraisals, this aggressively hostile note was seldom completely absent from this decade's urban-reform literature. Even the generally sunny Washington Gladden was touched by it. Although in *The Cosmopolis City Club* he condemned coercive law-and-order approaches to urban purification, in *Social Facts and Forces*, published two years later, he painted a picture of urban menace so grim as to justify almost any repressive response: "A horror of great darkness rests now upon our cities," he declared; a foe "more powerful and more dangerous" than any "army of invasion . . . is assaulting in overwhelming force the citadel of every one of our municipalities." The danger was "dire and imminent," he continued, and "the man who says that he is too busy to help in fighting these demons surely does not know what he is saying."[4] The stakes were high, and the risks enormous, in this struggle. In *In His Steps*, as the reformers seek to rally the "Christian forces" of their city for the "battle against sin and corruption" (by pushing through a citywide prohibition referendum), they are gripped by a "sickening dread" and even "actual terror."[5]

177
The Two
Faces of
Urban Moral
Reform in
the 1890s

No urban moralist in this decade was more militantly coercive than Charles Parkhurst. "If it is proper for us to go around cleaning up after the devil," he cried, "it is proper for us to fight the devil"—and fight he did! In this encounter with a "jungle of teeth-gnashing brutes," there was no place for compromise or procedural niceties; it was a struggle to the death. "These things do not go by arithmetic, nor by a show of hands. A man who is held in the grip of the everlasting truth and is not afraid is a young army in himself . . . The incisive edge of bare-bladed righteousness will still cut."[6]

Repressive moralism of the Parkhurst variety is not too far removed, psychologically, from the swift justice of the lynching party, and it is interesting to note that it was in 1887—the year after Haymarket—that California historian Hubert Howe Bancroft published his admiring history of the extralegal bands that had intimidated, expelled, and even hanged evildoers in San Francisco and other California boom towns a generation before. The "storms of public indignation" and "thunderbolts of justice" that had rained down upon California in the 1850s had represented "a grand triumph of the right," insisted Bancroft, contrasting orderly San Francisco of the vigilante period with the "outrages and riots" in New York and other cities.[7] In their more militant phases, the moral reformers of the 1890s seemed to perceive themselves as the latter-day inheritors of this tradition of rough-and-ready social control by an outraged citizenry.

The appeal of the coercive approach in this decade was expressed, too, in the elaborate schemes of moral surveillance and control devised by some reformers. Antiprostitution and antigambling groups had experimented with such an approach in the antebellum period, and more recently the charity organization societies had attempted close moral oversight on a family-by-family basis. Now some would-be moral wardens began to muse about controlling the entire city population. Boston's moral tone could be vastly improved, wrote Unitarian minister Edward Everett Hale in 1890, if her 500 ministers—"the moral guides of this city"—would constitute themselves a "moral police" force, each exercising "personal supervision and responsibility" for a specified area of the city.[8] Parkhurst's City Vigilance League, as we have seen, developed elaborate schemes for the secret investigation and repression of urban vice, and in *Civilization's Inferno,* Benjamin Flower exhorted all who shared his dismay over urban moral conditions to form local bands for "concerted action." Although the effort of these groups might be in part "palliative" and "uplifting," wrote Flower—planning coffeehouses and free concerts in the slums, for example—their "vastly more important" work would be to probe the sources of urban poverty and vice and devise coordinated programs for eradicating them.[9]

Common to all these schemes was the conviction that the "moral forces" of urban America must organize themselves. The City Vigilance League, wrote its secretary in 1895, intended to bring into "*coöperant relations*" that "*great company of earnest young citizens who believe in inoculating foreign-born residents with American impulses.*" Benjamin Flower insisted that his proposed urban reform bands must be tightly organized, with a clear-cut authority structure. To achieve "perfect discipline," he advised, each recruit should pledge "unquestioning obedience to the commands of the superior officers or the governing board" —a pledge "as binding as that of a military organization."[10]

In *In His Steps,* the importance of organization is discussed from a somewhat different angle. Sheldon's middle-class characters—outwardly successful yet plagued by emotional sterility and the lack of strong social ties—resolve these problems by joining the "What Would Jesus Do?" fellowship. Although less authoritarian than Flower might have recommended, this band does give its members emotional warmth and "unspoken comradeship such as they had never known." Whenever they assemble, "a spirit of fellowship . . . flows freely between them," and long-dormant emotions begin to bubble and flow. Most of their meetings end in a good cry. Stronger than the bonds of church or family, the intensity of this close-knit little company becomes almost frightening: "Where would it lead them? . . . They had been living so long on their surface feelings that they had almost forgotten the deeper wells of life."[11]

In insisting on the importance of organized, collective effort, the urban moral reformers of the 1890s revealed not only their sense of the awesomeness of the evils to be subdued but also a profound concern about the viability and spiritual well-being of the middle class. As Robert Wiebe, Richard Sennett, and others have noted, the urban middle class was in a disordered state as the nineteenth century closed. Old patterns of organization had broken down, and new ones were in the process of formation. The uneasiness generated by this situation pervades the literature of the period. Adna F. Weber, for example, in his 1899 study of urbanization, discussed the problem of "city degeneracy" not from the expected angle of the slums, but in terms of the "intellectual, mercantile, [and] employing class." In great detail he reported the theory of the German sociologist George Hansen that the dynamic of urban class mobility was itself "an instrument of social degeneration." In Weber's summary of Hansen's model, the urban elite is continually replenishing itself with fresh recruits who are initially full of "crude vigor and vitality" but who soon find the competitive pace so debilitating and disorienting that they fall by the wayside to join "the ever-increasing number of non-efficients"—to be replaced by a fresh crop of ambitious newcomers from the hinterlands.[12]

179
The Two
Faces of
Urban Moral
Reform in
the 1890s

By banding together in a massive moral-control effort, suggested Sheldon and Flower, members of the urban middle class would themselves be strengthened against the kind of disintegrative and devitalizing pressures Hansen had described. This theme was as old as the Jacksonian era, but in the nineties it was vastly broadened. By organizing for a great urban moral purification drive, promised the reform spokesmen, the middle class could not only become a powerful weapon for eradicating vice; it would also achieve a greater degree of internal order and cohesion, and overcome the social isolation and emotional aridity that seemed always to plague it.

The Positive Environmentalist Approach:
The City as Moral Habitat

While the coercive impulse loomed large in the 1890s, another strand interwoven with it would ultimately prove equally, if not more, influential: the attempt to elevate the moral character of city dwellers by transforming the physical conditions of their lives. If the brittle moralism of the coercive reformers harks back to the early nineteenth century, the subtler arguments of the environmentalists are recognizably modern. The idea of moral reform through environmental betterment dates to the mid-nineteenth century, but it had always been subordinated to other, more direct strategies. Now, as the century ended, the environmentalist approach began to come into its own. The author of an *Arena* article entitled "Morality and Environment" summed up the central argument: the child born and bred in a slum environment "has no chance but to become wicked. He is not free to choose good from evil . . . [A]ny practical philanthropist . . . will tell you how slight the chances are for children to be virtuous who grow up in that atmosphere."[13]

Slums meant tenements, and in the 1890s a vigorous tenement-reform movement in New York State and elsewhere reflected not only concern about the physical discomforts and public-health hazards of slum overcrowding but its moral consequences as well —an issue Dr. John H. Griscom had raised as early as 1845 in *The Sanitary Condition of the Laboring Population of New York*. But upgrading the tenements was only a preliminary step. The larger task was to replace the demoralizing detritus of years of urban growth with a consciously planned urban environment. The reformers of the 1890s pursued this overall goal on a variety of fronts, including the development of parks and playgrounds; public baths; children's clubs; gymns and swimming pools; and facilities for concerts, lectures, and art exhibits. Slum bathhouses, argued a New York State Tenement House Committee in 1895, would have a "favorable effect . . . upon character; tending to self-respect and decency of life"; more parks and playgrounds, agreed Mayor William Strong's Small Parks Advisory Committee (chaired by the ubiquitous Jacob Riis), would promote both the physical well-being and the "moral health" of the poor; free open-air concerts, suggested Washington Gladden, would counteract the "tendencies to vulgarity and dissipation and immorality" in the cities.[14]

As the foregoing suggests, urban leisure was a special concern of these environmental moralists. In *Civilization's Inferno*, Benjamin Flower's dismay over the few pleasures of slum life was nearly as great as his distress over the hardships. In a saloon in an immigrant section of Boston, he wrote disapprovingly, he had spotted "a company of young men and girls, laughing hilariously over their liquor." Such amusements, Flower pontificated, were actually "counterfeit coins; bearing small resemblance to true enjoyment, whose influence is ever refining and uplifting." Most of the commercialized pleasure available in the city, he added, bore "precisely the relation to its victim that the candle does to the moth." In place of such hellholes, Flower concluded, alternatives must be devised that would not only entertain but also help their patrons to be "pure, just, and noble."[15]

Again in common with the urban moral reformers of earlier decades, the environmentalists of the 1890s looked especially to the children. Benjamin Flower urged the formation of boys' and girls' clubs in which stories embodying "high ideals"; songs emphasizing the "noblest sentiments"; and, of course, the personal example of the club leaders would help impressionable city children avoid vice as a "loathsome contagion" and "give them what, in the nature of things, they have never before enjoyed—correct ideas and a new point of view." The ideas thus implanted in youthful minds would "silently work themselves into the hearts and homes of the unfortunates," Flower added, "becoming a wonderful factor in many lives."[16] (Old-timers who remembered the arguments advanced for urban Sunday schools in the 1830s must have experienced a strong sense of déjà vu upon reading Flower's proposals in 1893!)

One of the more articulate and influential champions of environmental reform in this decade was Josiah Quincy, mayor of Boston from 1895 to 1899. Believing that the duty of a city was to "promote the civilization, in the fullest sense of the word, of all its citizens," Quincy insisted that the playgrounds, bathhouses, swimming pools, gymns, and free concerts he had introduced in Boston's poorer districts represented powerful instruments for "the social and moral development of the masses of the people." Documenting his claim, Quincy asserted that youths who patronized the public swimming pools and gymns were proving "less likely to fall into vicious ways"; that areas around municipal bathhouses had seen a "decrease of juvenile disorder"; and that at city-sponsored concerts attracting as many as 10,000 people, "a very few policemen" had been "quite sufficient to prevent disorder."[17]

181
The Two
Faces of
Urban Moral
Reform in
the 1890s

Few areas of urban environmental betterment escaped the notice of these late–Gilded Age reformers, and always the moral-control aspect loomed large. Even improved refuse collection (insisted George E. Waring, Jr., street-cleaning commissioner during Mayor Strong's reform administration in New York) would create a more attractive city that would in turn inspire civic loyalty, encourage people to place the public interest above personal concerns, and ultimately raise the moral tone of city life. The slum child who joined a "Juvenile Street Cleaning League," Waring believed, was more likely "to grow up with an increased love for his city" and become "the sturdy, upright citizen which the times demand."[18] Perhaps Benjamin Flower best summed up the larger vision underlying all these efforts and pronouncements. A transformed urban environment, he declared, would give "new and joyous significance" to the lives of multitudes "long exiled from joy, gladness, and comfort."[19] Surely the moral dividends of such a change—in transformed lives and uplifted spirits— could not fail to be enormous!

For all their differences of rhetoric and strategy, most urban reformers of this decade saw the coercive and the environmentalist approaches as simply alternative paths to the same destination. Jacob Riis admired Theodore Roosevelt's repressive stance toward urban vice, and Roosevelt praised Riis's slum playgrounds for taking children from the streets and preventing them from "growing up toughs."[20] Throughout *In His Steps*, Charles Sheldon propagandizes for prohibition—the quintessential coercive reform—while simultaneously advocating more positive environmental reforms such as cooking schools and musical institutes in the slums.

This ambivalence as to strategy found its counterpart in the fluctuating moods of these reformers as they contemplated the urban situation. Sometimes they saw it in the bleakest possible terms, sometimes much more hopefully—and often they expressed both viewpoints simultaneously. "To the superficial observer the outlook may appear discouraging," wrote Walter Vrooman, but "if we probe more deeply we can rest assured of final triumph."[21]

Washington Gladden, despite his fears of an oncoming Armageddon between the forces of good and evil in the city, could also portray urbanization much more hopefully as a manifestation of a divine impulse drawing men together. The Apostle John displayed a "true insight," Gladden declared, when in the Apocalypse he portrayed a "glorified humanity dwelling in a city." In *Civilization's Inferno*, Benjamin Flower's nightmarish fantasy of a Boston decimated by plague is quickly supplanted by a gleaming vision in which vice-ridden slums have been replaced by beautiful, airy apartments and "temple-like" community centers complete with playgrounds, gardens, swimming pools, and lecture halls where "the wonders of other lands and ages" are unfolded with the aid of a "magnificent stereopticon."[22]

For those drawn to this vision of a redeemed city, yet dismayed and discouraged by the actual urban reality, the 1893 World's Columbian Exposition in Chicago—the great "White City"—seemed a portent of enormous significance. "If things looked dark in New York," wrote William Rainsford, "there was another city whose white, classic loveliness stood, for one summer . . . I first saw that city of the ideal as the sun sank behind it . . . , and the utter beauty of it entered my soul."[23]

The World's Fair site, an unpromising swamp on Chicago's lakefront transformed through the efforts of landscaper Frederick Law Olmsted and scores of architects under the general direction of Daniel H. Burnham, included an imposing array of exhibition halls around a majestic reflecting pool and promenade—the "Court of Honor." The overall effect struck millions of visitors with something like religious awe. Transmitted everywhere by photographs, newspaper and magazine stories, and word-of-mouth accounts, the impressive beauty of this ephemeral creation sank deep into the nation's consciousness. "A 'dream city' men called it then," wrote city planner Charles Mulford Robinson a decade later, "but the dream has outlived all else."[24]

For our urban reformers, of course, the fair's moral significance outweighed even its aesthetic satisfactions. A more orderly and uplifting urban environment *could* be achieved, with impressive effects upon human behavior. The moral destiny of a city *could* be influenced by its physical character! "Order reigned everywhere," William Rainsford went on; ". . . no boisterousness, no unseemly merriment. It seemed as though the beauty of the place brought gentleness, happiness, and self-respect to its visitors."[25]

This note was sounded over and over again in contemporary accounts of the fair. "No great multitude of people ever . . . showed more love of order," marveled John C. Adams in the *New England Magazine*. "The restraint and discipline were remarkable," agreed another observer. "Courtiers in . . . Versailles or Fontainebleau could not have been more deferential and observant of the decorum of the place and occasion than these obscure and anonymous myriads of unknown laborers . . . [I]n the presence of the ignorance, vice, poverty, misery, and folly of modern society, . . . pessimism seems the only creed; but doubt is banished here."[26]

183
The Two
Faces of
Urban Moral
Reform in
the 1890s

The World's Fair, in short, brought a heartening message to the prophets of urban awakening in the 1890s. "The White City . . . is not an apotheosis," insisted a writer in *Cosmopolitan*, "it is a hope." And what was that hope? John C. Adams well summed it up: "The great White City has disappeared," he wrote after the fair's close. "But . . . we shall yet see springing into being throughout the land cities which shall embody in permanent form [its] dignified municipal ideals."[27]

In reading such passages, one is reminded of Robert Wiebe's description of the emotional stance of many reformers in this Depression decade: "Accepting the current signs of disruption, even relishing them in a certain grim fashion, they described an enveloping moral unity to come as the very essence of their visions. In other words, they replaced threats with promise."[28] As Wiebe's observation suggests, the exalted hopes aroused by the White City did not resolve—indeed, they probably exacerbated —the ambivalence with which reformers contemplated the implications of urbanization. Lofty dreams continually gave way to deep apprehension. The tensions inherent in such uncertainty are painfully evident in the effort of the Reverend Lyman Abbott to sum up the moral import of the "bright, beautiful, but awful city": "On the one hand, the city stands for all that is evil—a city that is full of devils, foul and corrupting; and, on the other hand, the city stands for all that is noble, full of the glory of God, and shining with a clear and brilliant light."[29] In terms of moral-reform strategy, the contradictory impulses of the decade were distilled in an 1896 article in the *Congregationalist*: a city, it declared, was "something at once to be feared and loved, to be served and mastered."[30]

But when the afflatus was on them, these urban reformers saw themselves as standing on Mount Pisgah, viewing the Promised Land—a purified, ennobled urban America—that their successors would finally win. "What we have done so far has been practically nothing in actual achievement," wrote one of them in 1902, "but it has raised a little corner of the curtain, given us a glimpse, a foretaste, of what can be done."[31]

No book better captures the ferment and volatility of this decade's urban moral reformism than William T. Stead's *If Christ Came to Chicago* (1894). Having orchestrated the public gathering that led to the formation of the Chicago Civic Federation in November 1893, Stead remained in the city for six months more. He spent his time, that bleak Depression winter following the euphoria of the World's Fair, with politicians, prostitutes, businessmen, saloon keepers, reporters, ministers, gamblers, and settlement-house workers, discussing the city's political, commercial, and moral life. *If Christ Came to Chicago*, the book resulting from all this, is a long and somewhat disjointed work fused into a whole by Stead's white-hot moral passion.

This moralism is directed, in part, against the familiar manifestations of urban vice: the saloons, brothels, "gambling hells," and theaters whose "vulgarity and obscenity . . . would be more in place in Sodom and Gomorrah than in Chicago." While sympathetic toward the plight of individual prostitutes and even toward madams who tried to maintain orderly brothels, Stead left no doubt that he viewed prostitution as a "sin" and a direct affront to "the moral law." One chapter focuses on a single district—the Nineteenth Precinct of the First Ward—with its forty-six saloons, thirty-seven brothels, and eleven pawnshops, where "the policemen perambulating the beat . . . is the only human nexus which binds the precinct together." In describing these evils, Stead expressed in full measure the revulsion and apprehension that characterized so much of the urban reform literature of the decade. The precinct police station, with its drunks, tramps, and streetwalkers, he calls "the central cesspool whither drain the poisonous drippings of the city"; Chicago itself is "the *cloaca maxima* of the world."[32]

Concerned with political wrongdoing as well as with individual immorality, Stead devotes chapters to the dishonest aldermen —"the swine of our civilization"—who have turned city hall into an "Augean stable"; to the police who simultaneously tolerate and shake down the brothels; to the saloon keepers who double as ward bosses; and to the gambling interests that help finance political campaigns. He attacks the profiteers who control the city's utilities, and denounces the great capitalists whose neglect of civic affairs has left the field to more unsavory elements. Under such conditions, he warns, revolutionary upheaval is a real and immediate threat. Throughout these political and economic sections, Stead's moral animus remains clear. Chicago has been "possessed by a host of unclean spirits," he insists, and only a "revival of civic faith" will restore it to moral health.[33]

185
The Two
Faces of
Urban Moral
Reform in
the 1890s

How will this spiritual renewal be achieved? One after another, Stead explores and dismisses the various institutions that might offer hope. The press he finds timid and wholly subservient to the commercial interests. The local charity organization society is hopelessly limited in its outlook. And what of the churches? Here Stead unleashes some of his most stinging rhetoric. He offers ironic praise to the Catholic priesthood for its "weekly maneuvers on the ecclesiastical parade ground," but laments that it has "so little influence on the civic life of Chicago." As for the city's Protestant churches, they remind him of "huge fly-wheels driven at great expenditures of coal without any driving belt." Echoing Benjamin Flower, he denounces the churches' "lethargy and callous indifference" in the face of the "moral pestilence" menacing the city.[34]

Ultimately, says Stead, the political process offers the best hope; "it is by politics, through politics and in politics that the work of redemption must be wrought." But this will be no ordinary political movement, it will be a "quickening of spiritual life in the political sphere"—a great coalescence of the city's moral energies to achieve nothing less that the spiritual regeneration of the entire metropolis: "If Christ came to Chicago, the center from which he would work to establish his kingdom . . . would be the City Hall . . . He would do as he did in olden time and endeavor to band together those who loved Him and believed in Him in an organization which would work for the realization of His ideals, and for the removal of the evils which afflict the least of these His brethren."[35] In the emergence of the Chicago Civic Federation, Stead found hopeful evidence that this moral consolidation was beginning, and that a "Civic Revival" was underway.[36]

At times, Stead appears to see this development primarily in coercive moral-control terms. In the ideal Chicago, he writes, a morally awakened press would function as an "unsparing and unflinching . . . social pillory," and the churches would establish "a central executive empowered to wield the united force of all . . . against the common enemies of all." And if the "constituted authorities" shirked the task of moral oversight, "then the duty of action would devolve upon the committee of the [Civic] Federation charged with moral questions.[37]

Ultimately, however, Stead's optimism triumphs over his fears, and his commitment to environmental amelioration wins out over his coercive impulses. If Chicagoans could only acquire "a sense of the unity of their city and [the] greatness of its destinies," he declares, they could make it "the centre of the English-Speaking Race, so far as Moral Reform is concerned."[38] *If Christ Came to Chicago* closes with a remarkable utopian chapter, "In the Twentieth Century," set several decades in the future. In the Chicago of Stead's imagination—now the nation's capital—utilities have been socialized and other aspects of municipal life comparably transformed: garbage is recycled as a fuel source; a Saint Lawrence seaway has made Chicago an ocean port; Lake Michigan has been linked to the Mississippi (its waters thereby having become available for generating power); railroad grade crossings have been eliminated; and the broad, tree-lined thoroughfares are scrubbed daily by phenomenally efficient and dedicated sanitation crews. All the troublesome practical problems of modern city life have, in short, been brought under "perfect control."[39]

So, too, have the people. No vice, crime, disorder, or antisocial behavior disturbs the harmony of Stead's vision. This has been accomplished through a combination of environmental transformation, the effective utilization of the city's latent and diffuse moral force, and the emergence of a single civic ideal in place of self-seeking individualism. Now Chicago is dotted with playgrounds, parks, zoos, and lakefront promenades. Municipally sponsored circuses, parades, and civic celebrations occur almost daily; a widely circulated "official gazette" keeps every citizen informed about "the movement of the civic life"; and the theaters —controlled by a vaguely described official body that operates them for the public good rather than for private profit—function as powerful instruments for strengthening "the moral forces of the city."[40]

In a transformation no less breathtaking, Chicago's competing and ineffectual churches have federated, in Stead's utopian dream, and converted their edifices from centers of sectarian ritual into people's temples housing art galleries, reading rooms, and concert halls where at the lunch hour one may find "grimy, brawny workmen eating out of their dinner pails and listening to organ recitals and vocal and instrumental music." The churches also function in a powerful if ill-defined way as bastions of the collective moral code to which every Chicagoan is expected to adhere. "If any spiritual or moral evil occurs in one district, the whole of the massed forces of the associated churches can be depended upon to assist in its removal." Stead describes one church that is draped in black on a festival day in shame for "the birth of an illegitimate child in the block for which it had accepted responsibility."[41]

In common with Edward Bellamy and other utopian prophets of a redeemed city in the 1890s, Stead is hazy about the precise stages by which his transformed Chicago came into being. He does, however, in describing how a "great civic revival" unleashed the city's "hitherto unutilized moral force," ascribe an important catalytic role to the World's Fair. The White City of 1893, he says, "led the citizens to decide . . . that their black city should be transformed."[42]

Stead's sketchy yet compelling vision also leaves unresolved many nagging questions about the inner workings of the purified city he envisions. For example, he gives a key role to an organization of "helpers" who are "dedicated to the redemption of the municipal or social system." How are the "helpers" chosen? Who directs them? Who controls and edits the "official gazette"? Above all, by what process does everyone come to accept the all-pervasive moral code that the theaters, the press, and the churches so effectively enforce?

But all such questions are swept aside in the soaring conclusion of *If Christ Came to Chicago*: it is Mayor's Day, one of the great civic fetes that dot the calendar. The sun is shining, the flags are waving, city hall and the churches (all but one) are bedecked with bunting, and, as the book ends, Kaiser Wilhelm II of Germany marches up the steps of City Hall to pay a state visit to the mayor —Mrs. Potter Palmer!—and bestow his regal blessing upon Chicago—"the ideal city of the world."[43]

Such was the mood in which urban moral reformers confronted the twentieth century. The two broad approaches they had developed—the one confidently environmentalist, the other apprehensively coercive—would diverge more sharply after 1900 and, gaining momentum, powerfully shape the course of American social history in the years ahead.

187
The Two
Faces of
Urban Moral
Reform in
the 1890s

Four

The Progressives and the City

COMMON CONCERNS, DIVERGENT STRATEGIES

One century yielded to another, and the flow of humanity city-ward continued. In the census of 1920, with sixty-eight cities exceeding the 100,000 figure, America's urban population for the first time surpassed the symbolic 50 percent mark. In the first two decades of the new century, New York City grew by 2.2 million, Chicago by 1 million, Detroit by 425,000—and so on down the roster of established urban giants and fast-growing contenders. Even in the South (historically a laggard in urbanization), though the great surge still lay ahead, the early twentieth century saw a quickened pace of city growth.[1] Foreign immigration continued to account for a large share of this expansion. After a dip in the 1890s, immigration soared to unprecedented levels in these years —over 17 million from 1900 to 1917, with the single-year total exceeding 1 million for the first time in 1905—and most of these millions remained in the cities. By 1920, over 80 percent of all Russian, Irish, Italian, and Polish-born people in the United States were urban residents.[2] Only war and the Immigration Act of 1924 would finally stem the tide.

With such statistics as a backdrop, the familiar warnings persisted. Josiah Strong returned to the fray with *The Challenge of the City* (1907), giving his chapters such lugubrious titles as "The Modern City as Menace to State and Nation," and quoting Shelley's epigram: "Hell is a city much like London."[3] Even those who took a less alarmist view agreed that urban growth was a looming social reality whose full implications America had not yet begun to grasp. The problem of the city, declared the Boston sociologist Frank Parsons, in 1899, was "the problem of civilization." William B. Munro, professor of government at Harvard, agreed that cities were becoming the "controlling factor" in American life. "The modern city marks an epoch in our civilization," wrote Frederic Howe, adviser to Mayor Tom Johnson of Cleveland, in 1906; "Through it, a new society has been created."[4]

As this conviction deepened, the urban social-control impulse, its roots lying deep in the past, assumed fresh urgency. "How to reach the heart of the city and to change its life is, indeed, the question of questions," declared the American Methodist bishops as the new century dawned. William Munro quoted with approval Henry Drummond's challenging aphorism, "He who makes the city makes the world."[5]

Influenced by such battle cries, a large and diverse company of men and women sought a role in shaping the urban moral order. In part, their energies flowed into channels already explored in earlier chapters.[6] More typically, however, they turned to new approaches grounded in assumptions and strategies that had found inchoate expression in the intense urban reform climate of the 1890s.

Whereas the earlier voluntarist movements had concentrated on influencing individuals or families, those of the Progressive era were based on the conviction that the moral destiny of the city would be most decisively influenced through broad programs utilizing a full panoply of governmental power and aimed at a fundamental restructuring of the urban environment.

This central environmentalist assumption, however, led in two radically different directions. The divergent and even contradictory approaches that in the 1890s had coexisted under the capacious rhetorical umbrella of "urban awakening" now widened into two quite distinct branches of reform activity. On one hand, some reformers—"negative environmentalists," we might call them—pursued a coercive and moralistic approach, concentrating on eradicating two institutions that for them had come to epitomize urban moral and social breakdown: the brothel and the saloon. The other category of reformers—the "positive environmentalists"—took their cue from the more hopeful and visionary side of late-nineteenth-century urban reformism. Their goal was to create in the city the kind of physical environment that would gently but irresistibly mold a population of cultivated, moral, and socially responsible city dwellers.

Despite profound differences, however, these two approaches shared certain fundamental moral-control purposes: the elevation of character, the inculcation of a "higher" standard of individual behavior, the placing of social duty above private desire, the re-creation of the urban masses in the reformers' own image. At this basic level, both remained firmly linked to an urban social-control tradition extending back to the Jacksonian period.

13

Battling the Saloon and the Brothel

THE GREAT COERCIVE
CRUSADES

On June 25, 1910, President William Howard Taft signed into law
a bill introduced by Congressman James Mann of Illinois making
it a federal offense to transport a woman across a state line for
"immoral purposes." A death blow had been struck, so the fram-
ers of the Mann Act claimed, against prostitution, the brothel,
and the dread "white-slave traffic."

Seven and a half years later, on December 22, 1917, in the
midst of a world war, Congress submitted to the states a constitutional amendment barring the manufacture, sale, or importation
of intoxicating liquor within the United States. In January 1919,
the necessary thirty-six states having ratified, prohibition became
the law of the land. (By the terms of the Eighteenth Amendment,
actual enforcement began a year later: a final crumb tossed to
the liquor interests by the triumphant prohibitionists.)

These two measures were among the crowning achievements
of the great Progressive-era crusades against the "liquor evil"
and the "prostitution evil." Although these crusades hardly represent unexplored historical terrain, they are central to the present study, for the brothel and the saloon were widely perceived
as the great bastions of urban vice. So long as they stood, the
dream of an urban moral awakening would be no more than that;
if they could be subdued, the purified, morally homogeneous city
might at last become a reality.

Intemperance and prostitution were not, of course, discoveries of the Progressives. Both had been the object of reformist attention since the days of Lyman Beecher and John R. McDowall. In the Gilded Age, the Woman's Christian Temperance Union (1874) had revived the temperance cause, and the antiprostitution banner had been upheld by "social purity" leaders like Abby Hopper Gibbons of New York and the Philadelphia Quaker Aaron Macy Powell, as well as by local civic organizations campaigning against municipal regulation (and hence tacit acceptance) of prostitution.[1] The decade of the 1890s saw an intensification of both antialcohol and antiprostitution effort, including state campaigns to raise the legal age of consent, national temperance conventions and "purity" congresses, the formation of the Anti-Saloon League (1895) and the American Purity Alliance, and the organization of rescue work aimed at prostitutes and unwed mothers.[2]

For all this, the dawning century found both vices still deeply entrenched. In 1900 only three states had prohibition laws on the books; saloons, liquor stores, and the infamous "bucket shops" flourished in every major city; and per capita alcohol consumption—augmented by the new national favorite, German lager beer—stood at nearly twice the 1860 figure. As for prostitution, every city had its red-light district, including some now bathed in a nostalgic glow: Gayosa Street in Memphis; the Levee in Chicago; San Francisco's Barbary Coast; New Orleans' Storyville (named for the alderman who drafted the statute establishing its boundaries); "Hooker's Division" in Washington, an appelation immortalizing the Civil War general who had confined prostitutes to that section. In 1900, two Omaha madams, Ada and Minna Everleigh, felt confident enough of their prospects to invest thousands of dollars in a luxurious Chicago brothel, the Everleigh Club, which soon became the showplace of the Levee.[3]

In focusing attention on these evils—indeed, in making them stand symbolically for much that was unsettling about city life—urban moral reformers of the Progressive era succeeded in channeling the urban uplift enthusiasm of the 1890s into highly organized efforts involving specific goals and carefully planned strategies. In the prohibition drive, the Anti-Saloon League—supported by innumerable small contributors and a few very large ones like John D. Rockefeller, Jr., and dime-store baron S. S. Kresge—played the crucial organizational role. From the first, the ASL's single-minded goal was legal prohibition, and its major target, the cities. In counties and townships where prohibitionist sentiment was strong, the league organized local-option campaigns and worked for the election of sympathetic state legislators. The local groundwork laid, it moved to the state level, exhibiting the same skill in legislative lobbying that it displayed in marshaling public opinion. By concentrating on state legislatures (where the cities were underrepresented), the Anti-Saloon League gradually isolated urban America. In the campaign's final stages, thousands of ASL speakers promoted the cause in the nation's Protestant pulpits, and oceans of propaganda (including the League's principal organ, the *American Issue*) poured from ASL presses in Westerville, Ohio. The triumph of 1919 was thus the culmination of more than two decades of grass roots effort, reinforced by wartime moral fervor, grain-conservation enthusiasm, and anti-German-brewer sentiment.[4]

While the ASL was orchestrating the prohibition campaign, a more complex organizational effort was focusing diffuse sexual-purity impulses on a specific issue: urban prostitution. The issue first surfaced in New York City, where the number of saloons harboring prostitutes had increased sharply after 1896, when a revision of the state licensing code—dubbed the Raines Law after its sponsor—had inadvertently made it advantageous for them to add bedrooms and transform themselves into "hotels." The spread of these "Raines Law hotels" into well-to-do neighborhoods aroused a storm of indignation, and in November 1900 Episcopal Bishop Henry C. Potter penned a stinging protest to Tammany mayor Robert Van Wyck. (Unruffled, Van Wyck declared that New York had "the highest standard of morality in the world"; Tammany boss Richard Croker, taking a rather contradictory tack, argued that in any city there were "bound to be some unusually vile places.")[5]

A few days after Potter's letter, the New York Committee of Fifteen was formed. This organization of businessmen, publishers, academics, and other elite figures—the prototype of antiprostitution commissions that would soon emerge in scores of cities—set out quietly to investigate vice conditions and develop legislative remedies. It soon became involved in more stirring matters, however, through its support for a flamboyant young special-sessions judge, William T. Jerome—the "second Theodore Roosevelt," his admirers claimed—who had won celebrity for his dramatic raids on brothels and other vice dens. In the municipal elections of 1901, thanks in part to the support of the Committee of Fifteen and the Reverend Charles Parkhurst's City Vigilance League, Jerome was elected district attorney while Seth Low, a "fusion" candidate backed by the reformers, defeated Tammany's man in the mayoral race.[6]

Meanwhile, a team of prostitution investigators had been recruited by the Committee of Fifteen, and in 1902 its findings were published as *The Social Evil, with Special Reference to Conditions Existing in the City of New York*. A 1909 *McClure's* exposé, "The Daughters of the Poor: A Plain Story of the Development of New York City as a Leading Center of the White Slave Trade of the World, under Tammany Hall," helped sustain the cause, as did the 1910 investigations of a special grand jury under John D. Rockefeller, Jr.[7]

At the same time, Chicago was emerging as a second major center of the antiprostitution campaign. In a 1907 *McClure's* article, "The City of Chicago: A Study of the Great Immoralities," muckraker George Kibbe Turner accorded prostitution a prominent place in his catalog of evils. ("As in the stock-yards, not one shred of flesh is wasted.") Soon an ambitious assistant state's attorney named Clifford G. Roe was organizing a series of white-slave prosecutions. Thwarted by his superiors, Roe resigned, secretly arranged financial backing from a group of sympathetic Chicagoans, and proceeded with his investigations as a private citizen. In 1911 Roe organized the National Vigilance Society (with himself as director, secretary, and general counsel) and over the next few years published several lurid books on prostitution.[8]

Meanwhile, in January 1910, under pressure from the Chicago church federation, Mayor Fred Busse had appointed a thirty-member vice commission (twenty-eight men, two women), under the chairmanship of Walter T. Sumner, dean of the Cathedral of Saints Peter and Paul (Episcopal), to investigate prostitution in the city. Given a $5,000 appropriation, the Commission in 1911 produced *The Social Evil in Chicago*, a 394-page report ending with a set of recommendations aimed at implementing its motto: "Constant and Persistent Repression of Prostitution the Immediate Method; Absolute Annihilation the Ultimate Ideal." The report was based on data compiled by a research team under George J. Kneeland, a Yale Divinity School dropout who had worked as an editor with several New York magazines before becoming director of investigations for New York's Committee of Fifteen in 1908.[9]

Also involved in the antiprostitution crusade were the American Society of Sanitary and Moral Prophylaxis (founded 1905), a medical group headed by the prominent dermatologist Prince A. Morrow, whose influential *Social Diseases and Marriage* had appeared in 1904, and the Bureau of Social Hygiene (1910), a small, New York–based agency financed with Rockefeller money.[10] Among the latter's publications was *Commercialized Prostitution in New York* (1913), a somewhat popularized version of the various vice reports already in circulation.

Some order emerged in this organizational thicket in 1913 when the Rockefeller and Morrow groups, together with several other societies (including the old American Purity Alliance), merged to form the American Social Hygiene Association.[11] While no single group ever dominated the antiprostitution movement as the Anti-

Saloon League did the prohibition crusade, the ASHA and its magazine *Social Hygiene* played a central role.

Sparked by all this organizational activity, the antiprostitution drive had assumed the characteristics of a national crusade. "No movement devoted to the betterment and uplift of humanity has advanced more rapidly within recent years," reported the *New Encyclopedia of Social Reform* in 1909. From 1902 to 1916, 102 cities and three states conducted vice investigations modeled on those of New York and Chicago. By 1920 practically every state had outlawed soliciting, and more than 30 had passed Injunction and Abatement laws empowering the courts to close brothels upon the filing of citizens' complaints. At the federal level, the reform found expression not only in the Mann Act but also in President Roosevelt's 1908 announcement of America's adherence to an international white-slave convention recently adopted in Paris, as well as a series of reports on prostitution—"the most accursed business ever devised by man"—by the United States Immigration Commission.[12]

"White slavery" proved a gold mine to journalists, editors, moviemakers, and publishers. George Kibbe Turner's exposés are merely the best remembered of many in the periodicals of the day. *Traffic in Souls,* a film purporting to document the nationwide prostitution business, appeared in 1913.[13] As for books, the scores of vice commission reports simply added to a torrent of works including such diverse titles as Clifford Roe's *Horrors of the White Slave Trade* (1911), with its 448 pages and thirty-two illustrations; Jane Addams's thoughtful *A New Conscience and an Ancient Evil* (1912); and David Graham Phillips's novel *Susan Lenox; Her Fall and Rise* (1917).

Just as it provided the final impetus for prohibition, the wartime mood of 1917–18 also intensified the antiprostitution crusade. With the support of Secretary of War Newton D. Baker (who as mayor of Cleveland had taken a strong antiprostitution stand), the wartime Commission on Training Camp Activities closed a number of red-light districts hitherto resisting purification—an achievement perhaps praised more heartily in *Social Hygiene* than in the barracks.[14]

Moralism and Expertise: The Links between the Great Coercive Crusades and Progressivism

Historians have engaged in a lively debate over whether prohibition—and, by implication, the antiprostitution crusade—should be included within the canon of legitimate Progressive reforms. Writing in 1955, Richard Hofstadter said no. Prohibition, he contended, was "a ludicrous caricature of the reforming impulse"—

a "pinched, parochial substitute" for genuine reform, imposed by spiteful rural folk upon the more tolerant and urbane cities. In the same vein, Egal Feldman in 1967 described the coercive aspects of the antiprostitution crusade as "irrational, evangelical, uncompromising, and completely divorced from the humanitarianism of the early twentieth century." Other historians have challenged this thesis. Demonstrating the close connections—in terms of personnel, mutual affirmations of support, and overlapping organizational commitments—that can be established between the moral-control crusades and other strands of progressivism, they argue that the former must be considered an authentic expression of the broader Progressive impulse.[15]

Interestingly, the Progressives themselves had trouble reaching a consensus on this question. Although some reformers and ideologues welcomed the prohibition and antiprostitution campaigns, others denied any kinship between what they stood for and the coercive moral-control crusades. Walter Lippmann, for example, ridiculed the "raucous purity" of some antivice campaigners, and Charles A. Beard in 1912 criticized the "moral enthusiasts" who were "pushing through legislation which they are not willing to uphold by concentrated and persistent action." Herbert Croly in *The Promise of American Life* declared that reformers who functioned merely as "moral protestants and purifiers" were engaged in a fundamentally "misdirected effort." Only "personal self-stultification," he insisted, could result from such an "illiberal puritanism." True reform, Croly characteristically added, involved "an intellectual as well as a moral challenge."[16]

The answer depends in large part, of course, on where one looks on the Progressive spectrum and, indeed, on how one defines progressivism, and that, as Peter Filene has reminded us, can be a very difficult task.[17] But one trait common to most reformers of these years—and one which helped establish a bond between the coercive reformers and other Progressives—was an infinite capacity for moral indignation. For Progressives of all stripes, as for their predecessors in the 1890s, questions of social injustice, corporate wrongdoing, governmental corruption, and personal morality were inextricably linked. Almost every Progressive cause had its moral dimension; almost every condition Progressives set out to change was seen as contributing to a debilitating social environment that made it easier for people to go wrong and harder for them to go right. Child labor and the exploitation of women workers were evil not only because they were physically harmful, but also because they stunted the moral and spiritual development of their victims. (Society had the right to limit the hours of women in industry, Louis D. Brandeis argued before the United States Supreme Court in 1908, because the fatigue of long hours was undermining their moral fiber and driving them to "alcoholic stimulants and other excesses.") Urban graft and misgovernment were evil not only because they wasted taxpayers' money but also because they debased the moral climate of the city. ("The influence and example of bad municipal government . . . , of public servants dishonest with impunity and profit," cried an officer of the National Municipal League in 1904, echoing his reform predecessors of the Gilded Age, "constitutes a disease against which we have greater need of a quarantine than we ever had against yellow fever.") As Stanley K. Schultz has written of progressivism's journalistic advance guard the muckrakers, their writings often "assumed the nature of a moral crusade, . . . because ultimately their search was a moral endeavor."[18]

The moral substratum of progressivism is heavily underscored in the autobiography of Frederic C. Howe, in many respects a prototypical Progressive, in which he describes his intensely evangelical upbringing and its shaping influence on his later reform career: "Physical escape from the embraces of evangelical religion did not mean moral escape. From that religion my reason was never emancipated. By it I was conformed to my generation and made to share its moral standards and ideals . . . Early assumptions as to virtue and vice, goodness and evil remained in my mind long after I had tried to discard them. This is, I think, the most characteristic influence of my generation."[19]

Some historians have drawn sharp distinctions between progressivism's various facets, opposing the economic and political reforms to those that were explicitly moralistic. Such an approach, if too literally applied, does violence to the powerful moral thrust underlying *all* these reforms. For the Progressives, society had the right—indeed the duty!—to intervene at *any* point where the well-being of its members was threatened, since every such threat had its moral aspect. A 1914 article in a reform journal edited by Josiah Strong and W. D. P. Bliss put the matter plainly: "We are no longer frightened by that ancient bogy— 'paternalism in government.' We affirm boldly, it is the business of government to be just that—paternal . . . *Nothing human can be foreign to a true government.*"[20]

Within this intensely moralistic ambience, it was easy to see the coercive social-control crusades as simply one piece in the larger reform mosaic. In *The Shame of the Cities* (1904), for example, muckraker Lincoln Steffens frequently called attention to organized gambling and prostitution as byproducts of municipal political corruption. Similarly, a leading San Francisco Progressive, newspaper editor Fremont Older, in fighting boss Abraham Ruef in 1907–1909, revealed many seamy details of Ruef's involvement with organized vice.[21]

Those who were seeking to rid urban America of these vices,

for their part, never doubted that they were in the mainstream of the era's broader reform current. "We are tired of poverty, of squalor, of ignorance . . . , of the wretchedness of women and the degradation of men," wrote a prohibition leader in 1908. "Our hearts bleed when we look upon the misery of child life." Convinced that intolerable conditions of work and habitation were driving men into the saloons and women into the streets, they supported such Progressive reforms as wage-and-hour laws, tenement codes, and factory-safety legislation. "Is it any wonder," asked the Chicago Vice Commission rhetorically, "that a tempted girl who receives only six dollars per week working with her hands sells her body for twenty-five dollars per week when she learns there is a demand for it and men are willing to pay the price?"[22]

A second important respect in which the coercive moral reformers were closely attuned to the broader Progressive impulse was in their reliance on statistics, sociological investigation, and "objective" social analysis to buttress their cause—a strategy characteristic of many otherwise quite disparate Progressive reforms. For the antisaloon and antiprostitution forces, this represented a significant shift from earlier approaches. Through much of the Gilded Age, the temperance and social purity enthusiasts had concentrated on moral appeals to the individual, assuming that they and the objects of their benevolent attention shared, at some level, a common body of values and standards. (There were exceptions to this personalistic approach—the state drives to raise the legal age of consent, the quadrennial electoral campaigns of the Prohibition party—but in general the personal moral appeal was the preferred strategy.)

By the end of the century, as the old assumptions faded, overtly moralistic personal appeals were being supplanted by a more generalized emphasis on the reformers' technical expertise and superior factual grasp of urban issues. Moral reform must be rooted in careful investigation and social analysis, insisted Benjamin Flower in *Civilization's Inferno*. "Mere sentimentality will not answer. We must have incontrovertible data upon which to base our arguments." The first step of a prestigious Committee of Fifty for the Investigation of the Liquor Problem formed in New York City in 1893 was to "secure a body of facts which may serve as a basis for intelligent public and private actions." Even the WCTU established a Department of Scientific Temperance Instruction that lobbied for alcohol-education programs in the public schools.[23]

In the Progressive years this shift accelerated, and the personalistic approach was largely abandoned. Now, by contrast, intemperance and sexual deviation came to be viewed less as personal failings than as products of an urban environment that needed to be purified—by force of law if necessary. The Chicago Vice Commission expressed the prevailing view when it dismissed as "naive" those who looked for the sources of prostitution in the individual prostitute's flaws of character.[24] The emphasis was now on eliminating from the urban environment those *institutions* that undermined individual moral resistence—especially the saloon and the brothel.

With this development, the "scientific" aura of urban moral reform intensified. A *Scientific Temperance Journal* was established in Boston in 1906 by Cora Frances Stoddard. Muckraking journalists like George Kibbe Turner marshaled facts, statistics, dates, and names to buttress their indictment of the saloon, and the antiprostitution crusaders similarly strove for a tone of objective expertise as remote as possible from the thundering moral denunciations of earlier years. Indeed, in a number of cities the antiprostitution groups called themselves "Morals Efficiency Commissions." The 1902 report of New York's Committee of Fifteen exuded the scholarly aura appropriate to what its secretary called in the preface "a valuable scientific contribution," and *The Social Evil in Chicago*, a forbiddingly dry compendium of charts, statistics, appendixes, medical data, and analyses of interviews with 2,420 prostitutes, was similarly described by its sponsors as a "scientific study" based on the findings of "experts and trained investigators."[25]

The fetish of scientific objectivity took many forms. One national group concentrated on assigning exact numerical ratings to various cities' success in eradicating prostitution: Chicago, 37 percent; New York, 41 percent; Houston, 86 percent; and so on. In many vice commission reports, the antiseptic aura was heightened by the substitution of numbers and letters for actual names: "One woman, Mollie (X61), lives near Oak Park and solicits in (X62). Her husband is dying in (X62a)." The point of view underlying all this was summed up by the chairman of the Moral Survey Committee of Syracuse, New York. "It is a waste of time and energy to begin dealing with commercialized vice with talk, talk, talk," he wrote. "What we need is facts, facts, facts." The ASL's *National Issue* and its hefty annual *Yearbook* fairly bristled with charts, tables, and graphs purporting to establish positive or negative correlations between the saloon and death rates, arrest rates, tax rates, divorce rates, wages, insanity, pauperism, bank deposits, industrial efficiency, housing investment, and public-school enrollment. Drawing upon data compiled by Cora Frances Stoddard, the ASL in 1917 reported—with the usual flourish of graphs —that studies undertaken in Germany and Finland had proved conclusively a link between drinking, sloppy typing, and the inability to thread needles.[26]

This obsession with technical expertise and factual data completed the secularization of the urban moral-control movement. To be sure, these reforms ultimately depended on the moral energy of Protestant America, and denominational agencies like the Methodist Board of Temperance and Morals played an important role in rallying support. Yet appeals to the evangelical moral code do not figure strongly in either the prohibition or the antiprostitution movements, and the organizations promoting these reforms were not by any means overweighed with clergymen. The top ASL men were ministers, to be sure, but during the prohibition struggle they functioned almost entirely as secularized managers, lobbyists, and propagandists rather than as latter-day Jeremiahs pronouncing God's judgment on the saloon. The lower echelons of ASL administration were even more completely secular. The organization's general superintendent, Purley A. Baker, set the tone. "The narrow, acrimonious and emotional appeal is giving way," he declared in 1915, "to a rational, determined conviction that the [liquor] traffic . . . has no rightful place in our modern civilization."[27]

The antiprostitution movement, despite the prominence of an occasional cleric like Chicago's Dean Sumner, was even more completely divorced from the Protestant establishment. Indeed, by around 1910, antivice zealots among the clergy had become a distinct embarrassment. The Chicago Vice Commission roundly condemned an evangelist who was conducting prayer meetings in front of the city's leading brothels. An *Arena* writer in 1909 urged that the cause be pursued "sanely and scientifically" and not through " 'moral' rant from the pulpits." The local vice commissions usually had only token ministerial representation, and many delegated the actual investigative work to the team of New York–based researchers originally put together by George Kneeland for the Committee of Fifteen.[28] As an older generation of urban moral reformers passed from the scene, the movement came to exude more of the aura of the laboratory, law library, and university lecture hall than the pulpit.

Indeed, the very shift in terminology in the antiprostitution movement, from "social *purity*" to "social *hygiene*," is significant. The entire urban moral-control effort in these years was suffused with public-health terminology and rhetoric. A writer in *Social Hygiene* in 1917 predicted that New Orleans would soon conquer prostitution just as she had eradicated yellow fever, and in *The Challenge of the City*, Josiah Strong suggested that the polluters of the city's "moral atmosphere" should be considered as deadly as the "vermin of an Egyptian plague."[29] In Boston, the Watch and Ward Society won praise in these years from Harvard professor Francis G. Peabody for "unobtrusively working underground, guarding us from the pestiferous evil which at any time may come up into our faces, into our homes, into our children's lives." Picking up on these cues, the Watch and Ward, like similar moral-control agencies elsewhere, increasingly defined its mission in public-health terms. "The old idea of 'charity' . . . has gradually given way to a larger conception," it declared in 1915, "to prevent . . . the moral diseases which lead to misery and crime."[30]

The fullest elaboration of the public-health analogy in this period was probably that offered by the Massachusetts prohibitionist Newton M. Hall in *Civic Righteousness and Civic Pride* (1914). "The moral evil of the community does not remain in the foul pools in which it is bred," he wrote. "A moral miasma arises from those pools, and . . . enters not the poorest homes of the city alone, but the most carefully guarded, and leaves its trail of sorrow and despair . . . Why should the community have any more sympathy for the saloon . . . than . . . for a typhoid-breeding pool of filthy water, . . . a swarm of deadly mosquitoes, or . . . a nest of rats infected with the bubonic plague?"[31] For Hall, the logic of the analogy was irresistible: "Cut off the impure water and the typhoid epidemic is conquered"; destroy the saloon and the urban "moral epidemic" would vanish.[32]

The ubiquitous medical terminology in the utterances of these reformers had more than rhetorical significance, because recent advances in venereal disease research had made clear the ravages of the disease's advanced stages, the process of transmission, and the clear link with sexual promiscuity. For the antiprostitution reformers, the moral implications of these findings were no less important than the medical. "In all previous efforts to safeguard the morality of youth," wrote one reformer in *Social Hygiene*, "the ethical barrier was alone available," and "the situation seemed . . . hopeless"; now, happily, the "ethical ideal" could be "grounded upon the most convincing facts." Jane Addams welcomed these findings as a powerful force in the emergence of a "new conscience" on prostitution, and Dr. Prince A. Morrow expressed his pleasure that "punishment for sexual sin" no longer need be "reserved for the hereafter."[33]

Through lectures, tracts, posters, exhibits, and graphic films, the antiprostitution reformers warned of promiscuity's grim consequences—for the wrongdoer and his innocent progeny alike. The Chicago Vice Commission vividly spelled out VD's long-range effects—"the blinded eyes of little babes, the twisted limbs of deformed children, degradation, physical rot and mental decay"—and demanded that every brothel be quarantined forthwith as a "house of contagious disease." The control of sexual expression, in short, was simply another of the social constraints essential to modern urban life. Just as "the storage of gasoline and

other combustibles is controlled by the city," argued the Louisville Vice Commission, so dance halls and other "vice combustibles" had to be "carefully watched and controlled."[34]

One significant if inadvertent by-product of this preoccupation
with establishing the scientific legitimacy of the urban moral-
control effort—particularly through the accumulation of statistical data—was that the researchers often achieved a fragile but
authentic intimacy with the objects of their study, and their
reports provided glimpses of otherwise obscure facets of turn-
of-the-century urban social history. Budding young sociologists
danced and talked for hours with prostitutes and girls of the
street . . . though always (so far as we know) holding back from
the actual sexual encounter. One woman investigator, in particular, was praised by George Kneeland as "extraordinarily successful in winning the confidence of the girls with whom she
associated on easy and familiar terms."[35]

In the thousands of pages of vice commission reports lie buried
fascinating details illuminating the reality of urban prostitution
in this period: the business practices and domestic details of
brothel life; the prevalence of oral sex in the "better" houses
("$3.00 straight, $5.00 French"); the slang (in some cities, the
police assigned to the red-light district were called "fly cops");
the euphemistic advertising. (One madam who had moved sent
out postcards urging her former patrons to renew their "membership in the library." A selection of "new books," she promised,
could be found "on file in our new quarters.")[36]

Striving for objectivity, these investigators often evoked the
complexity of the urban sexual scene in ways that contradicted
the simplistic certitude of the antivice leadership. Even William
T. Stead, a first-rate journalist as well as an antivice crusader,
offered considerable evidence undermining the stereotyped image
of the brothel as a den of wild revels and unbridled sensuality.
"The rules and regulations . . . posted in every room," he wrote
of one Chicago brothel in *If Christ Came to Chicago*, "enforce
decorum and decency with pains and penalties which could
hardly be more strict if they were drawn up for the regulation
of a Sunday School."[37]

Such observations, with their implication that organized prostitution might sometimes function as a stabilizing and conservative urban social force, appear frequently in the early-twentieth-
century vice reports. In *Commercialized Vice in New York*, for
example, George Kneeland reported that many of the city's brothels were "cozy and homelike" institutions presided over by madams who possessed not only considerable business acumen but
also keen psychological insight and great capacity for human

warmth: "It is not uncommon for the girls as well as the customers to call her 'mother.' Strange as it may seem, some men marry these women and find them devoted wives."[38] Describing the various classes of men who patronized brothels, Kneeland wrote:

A numerous but pathetic group. is that made up of young clerks who, living alone in unattractive quarters, find in professional prostitutes companions in the company of whom a night's revel offsets the dullness of their lives at other times. There are thousands of these men in New York. No home ties restrain them; no home associations fill their time or thought. Their rooms are fit only to sleep in; close friends they have few or none. You can watch them on the streets any evening. Hour after hour they gaze at the passing throng; at length they fling themselves into the current,—no longer silent and alone.[39]

What YMCA leader of the 1850s could have described the plight of the young man in the city more eloquently?

Furthermore, one finds in these vice reports insights into the motivations of the prostitutes that go beyond such stock explanations as alcohol, slum life, early seduction and abandonment, or even the perils of the industrial order. This is particularly true of the often verbatim summaries of interviews with individual prostitutes that are included by the hundred—for no apparent reason except perhaps the investigators' wish that the rich complexities of their findings not be flattened out into a few pat conclusions and recommendations. What emerges most strongly from these interviews with women of the turn-of-the-century city is how many of them, old and young, appear reasonably well satisfied with their lot, insist that they are performing a useful social function for a satisfactory return, and reveal little sense of regret or inclination to reform. "No. 3 is refined looking; no one would take her for a public woman. She is fond of drink. She states, 'I have a lovely boss. He often takes me out in his car. Have made many friends in this town. If a girl is careful she can make good money here.' "[40]

What initially led these women to become prostitutes? The reasons that emerge in these interviews are varied, personal, and unpredictable. Sometimes, to be sure, it was economic, as with twenty-two-year-old Paulette, "interviewed on the corner of Curtis and West Madison" in Chicago, "who 'hustles' to support a two-year-old baby," or nineteen-year-old Tantine who snapped: "It is easier than waiting on table for $1.00 per day." More frequently, however, the impetus was a more complex combination of factors: the lure of the city, the fascination of activity and glitter ("I loved the excitement and a good time"), the drive to achieve a higher living standard, the unwillingness to pass one's life in subservient, deferential rôles: "The ladies when they got money to hire servants imagine they have some kind of a dog to kick around, and I didn't want to be kicked around."[41]

Time and again in these interviews one encounters real-life parallels to David Graham Phillips's Susan Lenox—spirited women who have chosen prostitution in preference to boring, demeaning, or otherwise intolerable situations: Bessie, the Indiana farm girl who "prefers city life"; another rural girl who "did not want to live among a lot of 'dead ones' "; the two small-town girls who "ran away from home so they would not have to go to school"; the Hartford young woman just beginning in the street life: "I want nice clothes and a good time . . . I am crazy to get to New York."[42] Many had walked out on husbands they found improvident, inadequate, or simply tiresome:

> "I was always fond of life. Married a dead one; he never goes out."

> "I married a fellow in Pennsylvania. He is all right but damn slow. He doesn't know he is alive; not the right kind of man for me."

> Her husband is employed in the AB164 store as salesman. "Too dumb to be alive. All he knows is work and he makes no money at that."

> Her husband is cold; she longs for affection, clothes and pleasure; he never leaves the house. She comes to Hartford two or three times a week from B155. She will go out with a man for a glass of soda.[43]

In the more lurid rhetorical flights of the antivice crusaders, to become a prostitute was to enter a life of "white slavery"; from the perspective of many of the women themselves (as revealed in the very reports generated by that crusade!), the decision represented a liberating *escape* from bondage.

Thus, buried in the interstices of the vice reports, one comes upon observations, insights, and personal revelations that suddenly illuminate the human reality of urban prostitution two generations ago—a complex reality that resists easy summation or judgment. Seeking to validate their moral-control impulse through sociological investigation, the urban moral reformers of the Progressive era unwittingly sponsored the collection of a wealth of social data that reveals far more about the actual contours of urban "vice" than they perhaps intended.

14

One Last, Decisive Struggle

THE SYMBOLIC COMPONENT
OF THE GREAT
COERCIVE CRUSADES

For all their scientific aura and trappings of objectivity, the prohibition and antiprostitution crusades touched countless Americans at a deep emotional level—a level where flourished profound apprehensions about the long-range implications of massive, unremitting urban growth. Though obviously shaped by the prevailing ethos of the Progressive era, these crusades were rooted in the long-standing impulse to subject the cities to a greater degree of conscious social control.

Repeatedly, almost obsessively, the prohibition and antiprostitution reformers emphasized that these were crusades against *urban* evil. True to its name, the Anti-Saloon League directed its propaganda less against alcohol per se than against that quintessentially urban institution: the saloon. ASL lecturers made shrewd use of large maps of the United States that showed in white the vast rural areas where prohibition had triumphed, and in sinister black the urban centers where the saloon still held sway. "The Gibraltar of the American liquor traffic," declared the ASL in 1914, "is the American city." The ASL *Yearbook* repeatedly called attention to dry strength in rural regions and the fact that half the nation's saloons were to be found in her six largest cities. It also noted the high correlation between urban liquor consumption and the large numbers of immigrants settling in the cities, especially New York, where the most "ignorant and vicious" of the newcomers were concentrating. "If there is a liquor problem in America—which every one seems to concede," wrote the ASL's strongest friend among the muckrakers, George Kibbe Turner, in 1909, "it is obviously of the city."[1]

Similarly, the Progressive sex reformers displayed less interest in the nation's general level of sexual morality than in a single limited phase of the subject: large-scale commercial prostitution —by its very nature a phenomenon of the city. Some vice commission investigators did call attention to the many urban prostitutes first "ruined" by farm boys back home and to the role of male visitors from the hinterlands in sustaining the big-city redlight districts, but in general these matters were played down. Prostitution was an evil of the city, and this connection was extremely important to those who fought it so vehemently. "The City—from scarlet Babylon to smoky Chicago—" declared George Kibbe Turner, "has always been the great marketplace of dissipation."[2]

Time and again in the literature of these reforms, the discussion "spills over" from the immediate issue to a broader consideration of urbanization's impact on personal behavior. The prototypical vice report, that of New York's Committee of Fifteen in 1902, set the tone. The problem of prostitution, it declared, was "intimately connected" with the rise of the city. In urban centers, young men who earned enough to maintain themselves but not enough to support a wife or family all too often turned to illicit sexual outlets—a practice made possible by that aspect of city life that had vexed urban moralists for a century: its anonymity. In the city, declared the committee:

> the main external check upon a man's conduct, the opinion of his neighbours, which has such a powerful influence in the country or small town, tends to disappear. In a great city one has no neighbours. No man knows the doings of even his close friends; few men care what the secret life of their friends may be. Thus, with his moral sensibilities blunted, the young man is left free to follow his own inclinations.[3]

For young women, too, the report added, the impersonality of city life made it possible "to experiment with immorality without losing such social standing as they may have, and thus many of them drift gradually into professional prostitution."[4]

This generalized concern over urban moral breakdown crops up repeatedly in the vice reports of various cities. Prostitution, declared the Louisville Vice Commission, was merely symptomatic of city dwellers' "craze for pleasure" and their "modern, careless way of upbringing the young."[5] The reports discuss all kinds of social behavior only peripherally related to commercialized prostitution, but which their authors clearly found dismaying: the New York dance hall where intoxicated young people were observed "hugging and kissing"; the girl on the Hudson River excursion boat who "became friendly" with an investigator and "offered to make a 'date' "; the Hartford hotel bar where a patient investigator one afternoon observed a "veritable 'carnival of fornication' . . . Eight men and five women were smoking, singing, and indulging in very suggestive dances. Couples frequently left the room and returned in about half an hour, and the remarks made . . . plainly indicated the nature of their occupation while they were away."[6]

This tendency to use the prostitution issue as a jumping-off point for a broader attack on moral decay in the city is especially evident in *The Social Evil in Chicago*. In listing prostitution's "contributing factors," the Chicago Vice Commissioners simply drew up a catalog of everything about the city that disturbed them: "immoral" movies; the high divorce rate; dance halls where short-skirted girls competed "in being 'tough' " as they whirled through the Turkey Trot and the Grizzly Bear; "coarse and . . . vulgar" vaudeville shows with their "suggestive and indecent songs"; ostensibly respectable theaters where scantily clad actresses displayed themselves "under the guise of art"; the "nauseous and repulsive" homosexual subculture (including "people of a good deal of talent"); the very streets, with their suggestive billboards, magazine stands, and countless other allurements to "vice and immorality."[7]

Still worse, the Chicago vice report went on, this same urban environment with its overcharged sexual atmosphere afforded endless opportunities for the gratification of artificially heightened desire. Pinpointing the particular danger spots, the commission listed not only the obvious places—brothels, dance halls, saloons with curtained booths and back rooms—but also lake excursion boats; amusement parks; darkened movie theaters in which "boys and men slyly embrace the girls near them"; and public parks, where girls "sit around on the grass with boys, or go with them into . . . the shrubbery."[8]

On and on goes the list: Turkish baths, state fairs, cheap hotels, massage and manicure establishments, even ice-cream parlors with their moveable screens. (Behind one such screen a keen-eyed investigator observed a youth fondling a girl's breast and taking "other liberties" with her as well.) The entire city, it seemed, was one vast place of concealment where men and women could pursue their pleasure safe from prying eyes. With so many opportunities for sexual gratification in the modern city, concluded another vice report presciently, the brothel would soon hardly be necessary.[9]

The Syracuse vice commission, describing a well-known "secluded spot" popular with the city's youth, summed up the frustration of the Progressive moral reformers as they tried to reduce their fears to a manageable shape: "It is so dark there that you can scarcely see your hand before your face. As you go slowly along you can *see* nothing, but you can *hear* whisperings all about."[10]

In answer to such diffuse fears, the prohibition and antiprostitution leaders offered a deceptively simple answer: the saloon and the brothel lay at the heart of urban immorality and social disorder. If they could only be rooted out, the entire character of the city could be transformed. Syracuse, reported the chairman of that city's vice committee, picking up a theme found everywhere in the antiprostitution crusade, was being "corrupted and rotted" by her brothels. The central refrain of the Anti-Saloon League's propaganda—that prohibition would remove at a single stroke most of the political, social, and moral problems associated with the city—emerges starkly in this 1914 pronouncement by the league's general superintendent:

> The vices of the cities have been the undoing of past empires and civilizations. It has been at the point where the urban population outnumbers the rural people that wrecked Republics have gone down . . . The peril of this Republic likewise is now clearly seen to be in her cities. There is no greater menace to democratic institutions than the great segregation of an element which gathers its ideas of patriotism and citizenship from the low grogshop . . . Already some of our cities are well-nigh submerged with this unpatriotic element, which is manipulated by the still baser element engaged in the unAmerican drink traffic and by the kind of politician the saloon creates . . . If our Republic is to be saved the liquor traffic must be destroyed.[11]

The task, of course, was a monumental one. Endlessly, the leaders of these purification crusades emphasized the enormous and sinister power of the men controlling these fountainheads of evil in the cities. While the individual prostitute or saloon keeper might be treated sympathetically as victims of the system, the higher-ups—the brewers, distillers, brothel owners, and shadowy "white slavers"—were portrayed as men of almost boundless malignant influence. An "invisible government," warned vice crusader Clifford Roe, was scheming to enlarge the sway of organized vice in urban America. Josiah Strong made the same point from the perspective of the prohibition cause. "What if the saloon·controls the city," he asked rhetorically in 1911, "when the city controls state and nation?"[12] Jane Addams painted a disturbing picture of the "multiplied ramifications" of the urban vice network. "Prostitution has become a business," declared George Kneeland, "the promoters of which continually scan the field for a location favorable to their operations . . . No legitimate enterprise is more shrewdly managed . . . , no variety of trade adjusts itself more promptly to conditions, transferring its activities from one place to another, as opportunities contract here and expand there."[13]

These magnates of vice were typically painted in loathsome colors. "A large diamond ring sparkled on his fat hand," begins Kneeland's description of a New York brothel owner; "a diamond horse shoe pin flashed in his tie, and a charm set with precious stones hung from a heavy gold watch chain." Clifford Roe pulled out all the stops in describing the "low and degenerate, grasping and avaricious" character of the leaders of the "great, hideous business" of commercialized prostitution. Ethnic stereotypes were employed to good effect. George Kibbe Turner informed *McClure's* readers that "the acute and often unscrupulous Jewish type of mind" was behind the liquor business, and that "the Jewish dealer in women" had done more than any other instrumentality to erode "the moral life of the great cities of America in the past ten years."[14]

By such means the conviction was subtly fostered that the social disruptions of urbanization were the work of alien and sinister men who collectively formed, in George Kneeland's words, a "whole network of relations . . . , elaborated below the surface of society." The most fundamental of these subterranean links was seen to be the one between the liquor interests and the prostitution interests. Readers of ASL literature or the vice commission reports might justifiably have concluded that most saloons were little more than fronts for illicit sex. The two were intimately related, contended settlement-house leader Robert Woods in 1919, predicting that the triumph of prohibition would deal a death blow to prostitution.[15]

The link between prostitution and the saloon was not wholly a product of reformers' overheated imaginations. New developments in brewing, transportation, and refrigeration squeezed out many local brewers in the late nineteenth century and concentrated beer production in the hands of a few major companies, all competing to open as many saloons as possible featuring their brand. Constantly pressured to increase sales, with the threat of franchise removal ever present, the local tavern keeper occupied somewhat the position of the modern gas-station owner vis à vis the oil companies. In the early twentieth century, the annual turnover of ownership in Chicago's more than 7,000 saloons was about

50 percent. Obviously, the more marginal saloon keepers had compelling economic reasons to stimulate sales by tolerating the presence of prostitutes. Some even provided bedrooms or curtained compartments with couches.[16] As we saw in chapter thirteen, such practices were inadvertently fostered in New York State by the Raines Law of 1896. This measure outlawed Sunday liquor sales except when the beverage was served with a meal in a hotel—defined as an establishment with at least ten bedrooms. The unanticipated consequences were the "free lunch" that magically transformed many a saloon into a restaurant (one magistrate held that seventeen beers and a pretzel constituted a meal, complained police commissioner Theodore Roosevelt) and the emergence of over 1,200 "Raines law hotels": saloons with the addition of ten tiny, shabby bedrooms. With no economic reason for existence, these "hotels" quickly became the haunts of prostitutes and their customers.[17]

But while there was some factual basis for this specter of a shadowy urban vice network masterminded by brewers, distillers, and "white slavers," the way the reformers wove these sinister themes together, and the melodramatic imagery in which they presented them, revealed more about their own frame of mind than it did about the urban reality. Earlier urban moral-reform rhetoric had to a degree been moderated by the self-corrective encounter with flesh-and-blood city dwellers. The Progressive-era struggles to purify the city were under no such constraints. Drained of much of their concrete meaning and specificity, terms like "the saloon" and "the brothel" became, at times, simply code words for the larger menace of urban social change.

Investigative reports, statistical analyses, and public-health analogies may have lent these crusades a scientific aura, but their central import was psychological and symbolic. They reduced the manifold threats of urbanization to manageable proportions. Robert Wiebe has noted how the complicated issues of the late nineteenth century were gathered into "rhetorical clusters" as "antagonists confronted each other behind sets of stereotypes [and] frozen images," and a similar process was at work in the great moral crusades of the Progressive era.[18] The disturbing aspects of the urban reality were the work of sinister but identifiable evil forces. If those forces could be exterminated, the larger threat would subside. Many members of this generation of Americans very much wished to believe the Anti-Saloon League promises that a constitutional amendment would purify the cities overnight, and the assurances of the antiprostitution reformers that urban sexual morality could be transformed with equal ease. They must have exulted when they read in Social Hygiene that organized prostitution in notorious Kansas City had been "abolished after a sharp campaign of one week in October 1913."[19] This was urban purification at lightening speed, achieving at a single stroke the elusive objectives to which earlier movements had devoted decades of frustrating effort!

As we grasp the symbolic component of these crusades, we begin to understand their strident and coercive quality. Mesmerized by their own rhetoric, these moral purifiers became increasingly vituperative in their charges and absolutist in their goals. In 1902, New York's Committee of Fifteen had taken a moderate line, concluding that since "the present state of . . . moral and social evolution" made the elimination of prostitution impossible, only its "public, obtrusive" manifestations were a proper object of reform effort and criminal prosecution.[20] As the white-slave crusade gained momentum, however, caution gave way to full-scale attack. Anything less than all-out war on vice, declared the Minneapolis Vice Commission in 1911, was "foreign to the sentiment and feeling of the American people, and repugnant to their high moral sense." Former President Theodore Roosevelt in 1913 described those who recruited women into prostitution as "far worse criminals than any ordinary murderers," and advocated public whipping as the proper punishment for such monsters; the only way to reach "brutes so low, so infamous, so degraded and bestial," he declared "is through their skins." The leader of the San Antonio, Texas, antiprostitution campaign (a "lean, gray-haired Yankee type of lawyer," according to *Social Hygiene*) announced at the organizational meeting, "I understand that we propose to fight vice and its allies with the cold steel of the law, and to drive in the steel from point to hilt until the law's supremacy is acknowledged." Clearly, the *Social Hygiene* account noted approvingly, the moral forces of San Antonio were "beginning to speak like 75 mm. guns."[21]

The leader of a 1914 prohibition campaign in Washington State, a Savonarola-like Seattle Presbyterian minister described as "six feet five inches tall, white-faced, red-lipped, angular and lean," blasted the saloon as "the most fiendish, corrupt and hell-soaked institution that ever crawled out of the slime of the eternal pit."[22] Perhaps the pinnacle of such bloodthirsty rhetoric was reached at the 1913 ASL convention, when a speaker declared: "Day and night we will pursue [the saloon]. And when it lies dying among its bags of bloody gold and looks up into our faces with its last gasp and whispers, 'Another million of revenue for just one breath of life,' we will put the heel of open-eyed national honor on its throat and say 'NO! Down to hell and say we sent thee thither!' "[23]

What groups were especially drawn to these purification crusades? One well-established interpretation going back to H. L. Mencken's day views them essentially as an uprising of the hinterlands against the cities. Prohibition enthusiasm was greatest among "rural and small-town Americans," wrote Richard Hofstadter in 1955; "the more sophisticated urban Progressive leadership" generally disdained it. With the Eighteenth Amendment, agreed Samuel P. Hays in 1957, "rural Protestant America at last subdued the urban menace to its traditional morals and culture."[24]

Unquestionably, rural support was central to the success of these crusades. Nor can it be denied that a simplistic rural/urban moral dichotomy often crops up in their propaganda. George Kibbe Turner in 1909 described the Anti-Saloon League as "a great semi-religious revival of rural feeling" against the city saloon. The ASL in 1903 portrayed prohibition as the natural moral expression of "the vast and virile countrysides where the bible is not yet effete, nor Christ a myth." The only way to save America, it added in 1915, was for "the pure stream of country sentiment and township morals to flush out the cesspools of cities." The best way for rural parents to protect their daughters' virtue, wrote one antivice leader, "is to keep them in the country." Taking such assertions at face value, the historian Charles A. Beard concluded as early as 1912 that these reforms were best understood as "attempts of rural communities to force upon the cities moral standards which the latter do not accept."[25]

What this rural/urban dichotomy obscures is the strength of prohibition and antiprostitution sentiment within the cities. The prostitution investigations were urban phenomena. The Committee of Fifteen, the Chicago Vice Commission, and the American Social Hygiene Association were hardly movements of farmers and small-town folk. Of 641 prohibition leaders investigated in a recent study, about 38 percent lived in cities of 100,000 or more in 1910—a year when the corresponding figure for the population at large was 22 percent.[26]

As for the rank-and-file support for these reforms, a number of recent studies have highlighted their strong urban component. In supposedly wide-open San Francisco, 36 percent of the voters supported a 1914 referendum aimed at suppressing prostitution.[27] The list of cities which went dry by local referenda prior to 1918 is long and impressive, including Portland, Spokane, Seattle, Tacoma, and Long Beach on the West Coast; Albuquerque, Duluth, and Denver in the central and mountain states; Birmingham, Jackson, and Raleigh in the South; and Worcester, Massachusetts, in the Northeast. Worcester went dry by a slim margin in 1907, and again in 1908, thereby becoming, according to the ASL, the largest dry city in the world. On the night of the 1908 vote, crowds jammed the downtown area as the results came in, and according to the local newspaper, "the no-license men seemed to be the most enthusiastic, for every time no-license made a gain there was a roar of approval." Of thirty-one successful state prohibition referenda from 1900 to 1918, ten were in states classified by the census bureau as predominantly urban. The Anti-Saloon League, for all its fulminations about urban hostility to prohibition, was able in 1911 to list fifty-two American cities that had abolished the saloon, including fourteen of 50,000 or more population. Even in cities that did not produce dry majorities, prohibition strength was often impressive. In Chicago, for example, 160 precincts had lined up in the dry column by 1907. In Boston, a strong minority of about 37 percent supported a prohibition referendum in 1916.[28]

Where was this urban support for coercive moral control concentrated, and where was the opposition strongest? Once again, the local prohibition referenda shed some light on this question. As the ASL never failed to point out, the poorer immigrant wards were the great bulwarks of opposition to the prohibition reform. In Worcester, for example, the successful antisaloon forces had to overcome pro-liquor majorites of well over 70 percent in the city's poorest wards. In at least some cities, however, a more complex pattern emerged in the prohibition referenda, as the business and professional elite joined the immigrants in opposition and the native-born middle-class and lower-middle-class voters, organized through the evangelical churches, provided enthusiastic support. In Richmond, Virginia, a 1914 state prohibition referendum was opposed by all the major newspapers and by the more influential business spokesmen, yet a strong contingent of evangelical middle-class voters nearly carried the city into the dry ranks. Emulating their contemporaries in Worcester six years earlier, many of them gathered on a downtown Richmond street corner on election night for prayers and hymns as the results, showing an overwhelming prohibition majority statewide, were flashed on a screen by the local ASL representatives. The Boston vote of 1916 saw the bankers, the commercial elite, and the Beacon Hill patricians line up with the Italian and Irish wards in opposition, while strong support came from the less affluent Yankee neighborhoods.[29]

If one uses the prohibition votes in the cities as an indicator, then clearly the coercive crusades of the Progressive years reveal a downward social shift in the locus of urban moral-control energy from where it had been in the 1870s and 1880s, when genteel, upper-class ladies had volunteered as friendly visitors for their local charity organization societies. We are now dealing with the kind of socially marginal people who in these same years were being drawn into the fundamentalist churches, with their literal

Biblical creeds and their rigid codes of personal morality.[30] They were perhaps closest to the anonymous city dwellers who had volunteered as tract distributors and Sunday school teachers a century before. Viewing the immigrant poor across barriers not only of physical distance but also of class and culture, they responded with alacrity to reform proposals that promised to purify and control "the city"—without requiring direct contact with the actual inhabitants of one's particular city.

But to explain the beleaguered tone of these crusades—a tone that belied their apparent successes—we must consider another fact which emerges clearly in the urban prohibition votes: at the more rarefied social and economic levels, the attitude toward these reforms ranged from tepid support to outright opposition. To be sure, determined efforts were made to win elite backing. The ASL in 1917 set up a special committee to rally business support. Prohibition spokesmen reminded industrialists that workers could not perform efficiently with "drink-befuddled brains," and their counterparts in the antiprostitution crusade contended that their reform was not only morally compelling but "a good thing from the businessman's standpoint," since streetwalkers and brothels damaged a city's reputation and commercial attractiveness.[31]

Despite such rhetoric, and the largesse of an occasional Rockefeller or Kresge, the picture of patricians and business leaders joining hands with an uneasy native-born middle class to clamp a rigid moral control upon the immigrant hordes is a misleading one. Certainly all these groups, for varying reasons, were interested in promoting morality and social order in the cities, but not all were equally drawn to the coercive approach. For the genteel elites, these crusades not only threatened aspects of their lifestyle (the wine with dinner, for example, that so befuddles Silas Lapham when he dines with the Brahmin Corey family in William Dean Howells's novel) but they often involved strategies and propagandistic excesses distasteful to patrician sensibilities. As for business support, it was vitiated by the awareness that these vices, however deplorable, were to an extent tied in with the larger commercial life of the city. The red-light district often involved substantial real-estate interests, some of it held in quite respectable portfolios. The bankers' national magazine might publish editorials favoring prohibition, but at the local level many banks were heavily involved in financing distillery and brewery expansion, not to mention their mortgages on countless thousands of saloons, liquor stores, and hotels and restaurants where liquor was served.[32] In cities like New Orleans, San Francisco, and Chicago, whose red-light districts were an established feature of the urban scene and even clandestine tourist attractions, business enthusiasm for vice reform remained well under control. The only way to "clean up San Francisco," advised a *Social Hygiene* writer in 1915, was to convince its *business leaders* that the denizens of the Barbary Coast were "parasites who not only contribute nothing of value to the city, but actually and literally pollute the life stream of society and drive away the better class of home-seekers and constructive workers." It was ambiguities such as this that led the Anti-Saloon League in 1911 to lash out bitterly at commercial interests hostile to the ASL cause, and to call for a boycott of businesses resisting the prohibition reform.[33]

Nor was business sympathy deepened by the anticapitalist rhetoric that periodically crept into these crusades. In Illinois, a state senate vice committee engaged in some sharp and hostile questioning of the major employers of women in Chicago, including Julius Rosenwald of Sears Roebuck, and asserted in its 1916 report that thousands of girls were being driven into prostitution out of a "sheer inability to keep body and soul together on the low wages received by them." The way to end the "curse" of prostitution, agreed the Wisconsin socialist congressman Victor Berger, was "by making women economically independent."[34] Such rhetoric (which was also occasionally used to explain why men sought comfort in the saloon) was hardly calculated to arouse enthusiastic business support.

And yet, the elite groups had no wish to appear as supporters of drunkenness or sexual vice. Nor were they in disagreement with the fundamental symbolic thrust of these crusades: the creation of greater moral cohesiveness in the sprawling and heterogeneous cities. Rather, they sought less obvious, less divisive, and less blatantly coercive avenues to that goal. Typically, then, while paying lip service to the moralistic objectives of the coercive crusades, they channeled their real energies into less explicit social-control efforts involving the beautification and enrichment of the city's physical environment.

While the upper class maintained its distance, the middle and lower-middle ranks—Protestant, native-born, typically rural or small-town in origin—supplied a solid core of support for the coercive moral reforms. It was men and women of this class level who responded positively when complex social phenomena were reduced to rhetorical formulas, who read with earnest attention descriptions of the "liquor power" and the "white-slave power" as parts of a hidden network controlling the life of the city, and who welcomed the simplistic clarity of the crusades to eradicate these foul sources of immorality and disorder.

As one might expect, given this pattern of support, the literature of these reforms frequently portrayed the moral threat as emanating from the higher as well as the lower social reaches of the city. The *Ladies' Home Journal* charged the "fashionable rich" with demanding the freedom to drink as a "class privilege." One prohibitionist characterized the reform as a struggle of the "little people" against the "vice-capitalists." The Hartford Vice Commission, in demanding the prosecution of all who consorted with prostitutes "regardless of their social standing," was only one of a number of antiprostitution bodies pointedly to note the involvement of the well-to-do in sustaining this vice. *The Social Evil in Chicago* charged that streetwalkers and brothels patronized by the "lowly" were more vulnerable to legal harrassment than the "silken clad prostitute[s]" to be found in "pretentious hotels and restaurants" and "gilded palaces of sin."[35] *Commercialized Prostitution in New York* called attention to the wide social spectrum spanned by the city's brothels, from the fifty-cent houses catering to "longshoremen, truck drivers, street cleaners, coal heavers, soldiers and sailors, [and] recently landed immigrants of low moral standards," to the most expensive establishments serving an affluent and even prestigious clientele. "One such individual is the New York agent for a famous automobile concern; another is the manager of a company which manufactures a well-known typewriter; another travels about from city to city selling hats; while still a fourth is connected with a celebrated watch company."[36]

From the wary perspective of many urban Americans of limited means and uncertain status in these years, it seemed that the social and moral order was being undermined at both extremities of city life. The response was a determined effort to reassert it through force of law. Throughout much of the nineteenth century, urban moral-control volunteers had felt sufficiently confident of their standing, or optimistic about their prospects, to adopt what Joseph R. Gusfield calls an "assimilative" approach: treating those who violated the prevailing norms as misguided wanderers who by persuasion could be brought back to the fold. In the prohibition and antiprostitution causes, by contrast, the focus shifted from reclaiming individual transgressors to proving that the reformers were still capable of asserting a jeopardized moral dominance. These were classic instances of what Gusfield calls "coercive reform"—the rigid social-control stance adopted by the individual who has begun to realize that "his norms may not be as respected as he has thought"; the person who is becoming "alien to his own society."[37]

In the YMCA and charity organization movements, the coercive approach had existed somewhat uneasily with the older, more confident assimilative outlook. Gaining ground in the turbulent 1890s, it emerged as a full-blown reform force in the early twentieth century. What Robert T. Handy (in discussing the rise of

Fundamentalism) has called the "hardening and . . . narrowing" of the Protestant moral tradition now found expression in efforts to subject specific aspects of urban social behavior to "the cold steel of the law."[38]

The intensity and inherent futility of this drive to reimpose earlier patterns of social conformity by force of law emerges with almost poignant clarity in the wide variety of recommendations advanced by the vice commissions for controlling prostitution: that the names of brothel owners be displayed on metal plates posted prominently by the front doors (the "brass plate" law, to embarrass absentee owners); that male patrons be arrested and publicly identified; that rooming houses be licensed and monitored; that motion pictures be censored; that sensational newspaper coverage of morals cases be strictly suppressed; that "sensuous plays" as well as "indecent vaudeville, picture-slot machines, nickleodeons, etc." be banished from the city. One vice commission even urged that the colonial "publishing of banns" be revived as a way of increasing community oversight of individual behavior![39]

The Chicago Vice Commission offered a particularly comprehensive array of recommendations to re-create earlier patterns of moral surveillance: the establishment of a Morals Commission and a Department of Inspection to oversee dance halls, ice-cream parlors, and excursion boats—all the hidden places of the city; an ordinance requiring that movies be shown only in "well-lighted halls"; the removal of park benches from the "deep shadows" and better park lighting, including searchlights to aid in "the proper policing of such spots as are not covered by arc lights." Grasping at straws, the Chicagoans even urged the city's newspapers to "publish an appeal . . . to parents that their children be not given too much liberty."[40]

People laughed at the mayor of this period who insisted that department store mannequins in his city be fully clothed at all times, and at the town fathers of another city who, taking a leaf from Gilbert and Sullivan, made it a misdemeanor for any man to "stare at, or make what is commonly called 'goo-goo eyes' at, or in any other manner look at or make remarks to or concerning, or cough or whistle at, or do any other act to attract the attention of any woman or female person." But these were simply logical extensions of the impulse toward the minute legal oversight of personal behavior that underlay the era's better-known moral-reform crusades.[41]

For all the energy and moral passion that flowed into them, the great coercive crusades ultimately failed. As Joseph Gusfield has observed, dying orders leave "their rear guards behind to fight delaying action"—and these reforms were just that.[42] One of the more familiar chapters of American social history recounts how the nation in the 1920s turned away from the moral-control obsessions that had loomed so large a few years before. Efforts to enforce the Eighteenth Amendment quickly showed the difficulties of changing social mores by law, and the Wickersham Commission report presented to President Hoover in 1931 pinpointed yet again the source of the prohibition enforcement problem: the city.[43] When repeal came at last in 1933, it simply underscored the obvious: prohibition had become a national headache. The white-slave hysteria faded even more quickly. New Orleans's famed Storyville, closed with great fanfare in 1917, was going full blast ten years later. In the early 1930s, a sociologist studying prostitution in New York City concluded that the reform crusade had reduced street solicitation and the number of wideopen brothels, but that it was "impossible to say with certainty" what effect, if any, it had had upon the actual incidence of prostitution in the city. Assessing the vice reform movement as a whole, he concluded that in most cities it had represented "no more than an emotional outburst with no permanent gain."[44]

In the 1920s the dregs of the coercive moral-control impulse were left to isolated fanatics; to pulpit showmen like the Birmingham minister who denounced his city as a place that contained "no Bible, but lots of bunnyhug; no Jesus, but plenty of jazz"; to anachronistic organizations like the New England Watch and Ward Society, surviving on the benefactions of earlier years; and to the Ku Klux Klan. With its whippings of "loose women," its raids on speakeasies, and its embittered anticity bias, the Klan became the pathetic residual legatee of generations of accumulated anxiety over the disappearance of a simpler America.[45]

But even in the Progressive-era heyday of these reforms, some of their more thoughtful adherents recognized that they were fundamentally misconceived. One vice commission warned against "hullabaloo crusades" that assumed the "immediate, peremptory annihilation" of urban vice. At some level, many of these reformers recognized from the outset that they faced a profoundly altered social reality rooted in the dynamics of urbanization and only marginally amenable to legislative coercion. Although sexual behavior could be controlled in a small community, noted the Chicago Vice Commission, "the situation is more difficult in a city the size of Chicago. Here an individual may, if he chooses, live any life he pleases, so far as his personal habits are concerned, and no one be the wiser." Certainly moral standards should be "definite and clearly understood," agreed the Louisville Vice Commission, "but much trouble in all cities arises because nobody seems clear as to just what should be allowed and what should be prohibited."[46]

In *A New Conscience and an Ancient Evil*, Jane Addams wrestled with the problem of how a common moral order could be sustained in large cities where "social relationships . . . are so hastily made and often so superficial," and where "the old human restraints of public opinion, long sustained in smaller communities, have . . . broken down." At one point her frustration with this dilemma even led her to express nostalgia for the "village gossip" whose "vituperative tongue after all performs a valuable function both of castigation and retribution." But where, in the modern industrial city, were to be found analogues to such ancient and time-tested modes of social control? Exhausting their arsenal of coercive proposals, the vice reformers often quietly acknowledged that, in the long run, repression was not the answer. As one antiprostitution leader conceded in 1915, "The law is an instrument much more difficult to use than is commonly supposed."[47]

15

Positive Environmentalism

THE IDEOLOGICAL
UNDERPINNINGS

It was 1914, and Newton D. Baker had a problem. He had been mayor of Cleveland for two years, and among such reform objectives as lower transit fares, municipal ownership of utilities, and the other familiar goals of municipal progressivism was the desire to achieve in this great industrial city, with its diverse immigrant population, at least an approximation of the moral order he remembered from his own West Virginia boyhood.

Focusing his attention on Cleveland's numerous dance halls, with their drunkenness, sexual laxity, and general ribaldry, he had first tried the familiar approach: denunciation and repression. But police surveillance, arrests, and padlocking all proved ineffective. The dance halls seemed only to grow more popular and more brazen.

In desperation, Baker tried a different tack. Instead of fighting the dance halls head-on, he opened several municipal dance pavilions in the city parks, seeing to it that they were attractive, well lit, alcohol-free, and "chaperoned by carefully selected men and women." Soon the disreputable private establishments were standing practically empty, outdistanced by the more wholesome publicly sponsored alternative. Early in 1918, Baker took time from his massive duties as secretary of war to recount this instructive experience for the American Social Hygiene Association.[1]

For Baker, as for many of his generation, the lesson was clear:

the most promising long-range strategy of urban moral control was not repression but a more subtle and complex process of influencing behavior and molding character through a transformed, consciously planned urban environment. Growing from the positive-environmentalist initiatives of the 1890s, this conviction found expression not only in muncipally sponsored amusements like Baker's dance pavilions but also in tenement reform, in park and playground development, in civic pageants and municipal art, and ultimately in the city-planning movement. While the crusades against the saloon and the brothel have traditionally shaped our image of urban moral reform in the Progressive era, these other efforts had an important moral-control dimension as well.

The positive environmentalists often shared the underlying moral assumptions of the coercive crusaders, but they differed fundamentally on basic strategy. Their aim (as they constantly stressed), was not to destroy urban vice through denunciatory rhetoric or legal repression, but by creating the kind of city where objectionable patterns of behavior, finding no nurture, would gradually wither away. In an influential 1904 work, *The American City*, Delos F. Wilcox yielded to no one in portraying urban immorality and vice as dire social threats "preying upon the vitals of municipal democracy," but with equal firmness he rejected coercive solutions to the problem. Instead of "repression" and "puritanic legislation," he called for "other and more effective weapons of warfare" to create in city dwellers "a wider social consciousness, a heartier spirit of cooperation, [and] a keener sense of responsibility to the future."[2]

Even the coercive moral reformers, implicitly conceding the drawbacks of their approach, occasionally endorsed positive environmentalist strategies. In *Substitutes for the Saloon*, for example, Raymond Calkins insisted that the answer to the saloon and other urban vices did not lie in forcing the masses into a rigid moral straitjacket. Instead, he argued, reformers must study the social needs met by the saloon, the dance hall, and so forth, and develop alternatives to meet those needs without the evil side effects. Among Calkins's "substitutes" were parks, playgrounds, municipal theaters, and "temperance saloons" offering camaraderie but not alcohol. (In one experimental temperance saloon, Calkins reported hopefully in 1919, the patrons were as convivial as ever, but instead of beer mugs at their tables, one now saw "milk chocolate, a peanut candy bar, or perhaps a soda or iced drink.") As such changes were effected in the city, Calkins concluded, "the coarser elements of the environment" would "exert a gradually diminishing influence."[3]

Among the antiprostitution crusaders, the Louisville Vice Commission contended that one way to produce "vice-proof or vice resisting young people" was to encourage "the wholesome use of their leisure hours." Similarly, Hartford's vice investigators, noting that one thoroughfare had been "cleansed of prostitutes in 1908 when it was broadened [and] paved," urged further environmental improvements as a means toward their city's moral purification. From its founding in 1914, the American Social Hygiene Association insisted that "remedial and constructive measures" were as important in the antiprostitution struggle as legal repression. "Legislation is essential . . . , but we must go deeper," argued on ASHA spokesman. "The ideal is to so mould the interests, activities, and organized volitions of youth, that it will put the brothel out of business through lack of patronage."[4]

The conviction that the most enduring moral advance would come through a gradual reshaping and enrichment of the urban environment found strong support among Social Gospel spokesmen in these years. In the ethical realm, argued Walter Rauschenbusch in *Christianity and the Social Crisis* (1907), "physical compulsion" was "impotent" unless it rested upon a "diffused, spontaneous moral impulse in the community." The law might represent the "stiff skeleton of public morality," but the "finer tissues . . . must be deposited by other forces." Even Josiah Strong, who continued to paint the urban menace in lurid colors, now concluded that the challenge was not to engage urban vice in frontal combat through "Draconian law," but to nurture the "awakening social conscience" of the urban masses and thereby "overcome evil with good."[5]

Among settlement leaders, Jane Addams emerged as a persuasive champion of the environmentalist outlook—an outlook which grew naturally from the settlements' emphasis on the role of environmental factors in shaping the lives of the immigrant masses. Although in *The Spirit of Youth and the City Streets* (1909) and other writings of the period Addams made no effort to conceal her distaste for the moral ambience of the modern city with its "vicious excitements and trivial amusements," she rejected preurban modes of social control as "totally unsuited to modern city conditions." If public authorities were to "intelligently foster social morality," they must offer municipally sponsored alternatives to the exploitative and debasing commercial amusements. Warming to her theme, Addams described a transformed city in which publicly supported recreational and leisure activities would become the social cement of a cohesive urban community. "We are only beginning to understand," she wrote, "what might be done through the festival, the street procession, the band of marching musicians, orchestral music in public squares or parks." In the urban future she envisioned, the stroller

in the city would encounter not the jangling distraction of raucous commercialized entertainment, but "spontaneous laughter,
snatches of lyric song, the recovered forms of old dances, and
the traditional rondels of merry games." The "delicious sensation
to be found in a swimming pool" would surely outweigh the
temptation "to play craps in a foul and stuffy alley, even with
the unnatural excitement which gambling offers."[6]

In her 1912 work on prostitution, *A New Conscience and an
Ancient Evil*, despite a fleeting nostalgia for the days when the
village gossip kept people in line, Addams conceded that the
new social reality demanded a rethinking of the entire question
of urban morality. The "new conscience" she envisioned was
rooted not in the coercive enforcement of a rigid moral code but
in a gradually maturing popular awareness that the imperatives
of urban life required the subordination of individual gratification
to the larger social good. "Fortunately . . . for our moral progress . . . , a new form of social control is slowly establishing itself . . . This new and more vigorous development . . . , while
reflecting something of that wholesome fear of public opinion
which the intimacies of a small community maintain, is much
more closely allied to the old communal restraints and mutual
protections to which the human will first yielded."[7] This new
urban moral consciousness could not be artificially imposed, Addams insisted; it would emerge only slowly, through careful nurture, from sources within individual city dwellers. In contrast to
"the forced submission that characterized the older forms of social restraint," the "new control" would be "based upon the voluntary cooperation of self-directed individuals."[8]

Other settlement leaders picked up the theme. The role of the
settlement house, wrote Chicago's Graham Taylor, was to help
create neighborhoods where it would be "easier to live right and
harder to go wrong." The way to deal with the "debasing" amusements and general ethical breakdown of the laboring masses,
agreed Mary Kingsbury Simkhovitch of New York's Greenwich
House in 1917, was not by plunging into repressive crusades but
by working to change the fundamental conditions of urban-industrial life.[9]

In charity-organization circles, too, the earlier tentative interest in environmentalist strategies intensified after 1900. As
in the 1890s, a crucial figure in articulating the new viewpoint
was Edward T. Devine, secretary of the New York COS from
1896 to 1912, editor of the influential social-work periodical *Survey*, and professor of "social economy" at Columbia University.
In a stream of books, articles, and speeches, Devine chipped away
at the COS's still deeply rooted preoccupation with personal
moral defects and its family-by-family approach. Devine's full-

est exposition of his ideas came in *Misery and Its Causes* (1909). Conceding that the belief in a direct causal connection between personal immorality and poverty was "thoroughly interwoven into a vast quantity of literature and into almost the whole of our charitable tradition," he nevertheless dismissed it as a "halfway explanation." The causes of destitution, he declared, were "economic, social, transitional, measurable, [and] manageable"; the urban vice and immorality that so distressed middle-class social workers were "more largely the results of social environment than of defective character." Charity organizations, he concluded firmly, should shift from "arbitrary and artificial" efforts at individual uplift to a broader program of environmental change.[10]

Clearly, this was an idea whose time had come. "Bad physical environment means bad moral environment," intoned an official of the General Federation of Women's Clubs that same year, as though reciting a self-evident truth. Chicago juvenile-court judge Julian W. Mack was another who added his voice to the chorus. Antivice laws were not enough, he declared. "Constructive help is the real thing." Give youth innocent pleasures to replace immoral ones, Mack urged, and "they will not go to their downfall."[11]

In a 1915 *Atlantic Monthly* article on his campaign to drive Cleveland's dance halls out of business by offering a wholesome municipal alternative, Newton D. Baker tried to sum up the new mode of thinking. In urban moral reform, he declared, both the "emotional excitability" of the "sensational pulpit" and the "rigid regimentation" of the coercive crusade were being supplanted by positive efforts to strengthen the city dwellers' innate preference for order and "social self-control." As this new outlook gradually spread through urban America, he concluded confidently, the chronic problem of moral breakdown in the cities would at last be solved.[12]

In turning to positive environmentalism as a technique of urban moral control, this generation of reformers was profoundly influenced by the larger thrust of early-twentieth-century social thought. Wherever one probes the intellectual life of this period, one finds a fundamental shift of interest away from the individual to the group. The study of human behavior would never become truly scientific, declared the young sociologist Luther Lee Bernard in 1911, until its practitioners "abandon[ed] the individual as the measure of all things social, and fix[ed] upon the group . . . as the unity which lives, acts, and progresses or deteriorates."[13] This shift reflected not merely an interest in *studying* social groups, but also in *controlling* them through the benevolent manipulation of their physical and social environment. To be sure, as home economist Ellen Richards put it in 1912, genuine moral advance ultimately depended on "evolution from within," but as she herself went on to note, "if the bale of hay is skillfully hung in front of the donkey's nose it will often serve to start the wheels on an easy road."[14]

A full exploration of this shift would be, in effect, an intellectual history of the United States from perhaps 1890 to 1920. It would require attention to scores of thinkers, including John B. Watson, Frederick W. Taylor, Herbert Croly, and, above all, John Dewey, with his insistence on the centrality of environment in shaping human behavior and his conviction (as he expressed it in 1908) that the most effective social control was "not merely physical or coercive, but moral"—not one based on the legal enforcement of rigid behavioral standards, but on "the intelligent selection and determination of the environments in which we act."[15] Although this shift of outlook influenced all Progressive social thought, four works of the period are particularly germane: Edward A. Ross's *Social Control* (1901), Charles H. Cooley's *Human Nature and the Social Order* (1902), Simon N. Patten's *The New Basis of Civilization* (1907) and Luther Lee Bernard's "The Transition to an Objective Standard of Social Control" (1911). Though their perspectives differ, each of these four studies confronts theoretically the social and moral implications of urban-industrial growth and tries to chart future strategies for maintaining social stability and ethical cohesiveness in a mass society. In so doing, they helped lay the ideological groundwork for the urban environmental reforms of these years.

Edward A. Ross, born in rural Illinois the year after Appomattox, received a doctorate in economics from Johns Hopkins in 1891 and then taught at Stanford and Nebraska before settling at Wisconsin, where he remained for many years. Sociology gradually supplanted economics as his major field of interest, and he played an important role in the development of that discipline. *Social Control*, his first book, remains his most important.[16]

Adopting the formulation introduced by the German sociologist Ferdinand Tönnies in 1887, Ross began by describing the evolution of the Western world from *Gemeinschaft* to *Gesellschaft*: that is, from a relatively static, close-knit, morally homogeneous order to a dynamic, impersonal, socially stratified, and morally fragmented urban-industrial order.[17] The historical groundwork laid to his satisfaction, Ross turned to his specific purpose: to trace the erosion of *Gemeinschaft* modes of social-control in the age of the city, and to propose alternative mechanisms by which modern urban society might protect itself against "vice and crime and that moral decay which is worse than either."[18]

As a substitute for the weakened moral bulwarks of the pre-urban era, Ross urged the development of a new "Social Religion" that would impress upon the masses "the conviction that there is a bond of ideal relationship between the members of a society."[19] This new social ideal would be promulgated by many means. The public schools, civic art, and municipal pageants and ceremonies would all play their part. Through the arts, the abstract ideal of social loyalty would be objectified and made seductively attractive. Art in the service of the state, a concept later brought to a high degree of refinement in various totalitarian societies, found

an early champion in E. A. Ross. "Art shows us Society, and bids us be content. The collective life is magnified till it fascinates with its spaciousness, glorified till it dazzles with its splendor. Thus the stream of dependence and awe that naturally sets out toward the universe is skilfully turned aside and caused to make fruitful the social garden."[20] The post-Darwinian crisis of faith might actually prove morally beneficial, Ross argued, in releasing a mass of religious feeling which, through skillful manipulation, could be redirected to the social ideal.[21]

While recognizing the (considerably weakened) role of religion and traditional moral maxims in the overall web of social control, Ross himself was an ethical relativist; morality, for him, simply reflected "the situation and needs of society" in any given period. The challenge was not to restore a fixed moral code but to develop "a rational theory of social relations which every 'good citizen' is expected to believe in," and to awaken "a sense of responsibility by dwelling on the social consequences of conduct." Such an approach, he pointed out, would be "simpler and more elastic than certain outworn means of control."[22]

Although denying any suggestion that his proposed "Social Religion" would be a "mere cement manufactured by shrewd men," Ross readily conceded that it would be at first little more than a useful fiction involving considerable verbal legerdemain and manipulation of symbols. "The passiveness of the average mind," he noted, "will make it safe to weave into . . . moral instruction certain convenient illusions and fallacies which it is nobody's interest to denounce."[23]

In a key section of *Social Control* aimed at differentiating his proposals from mere domination by the rich and powerful, Ross detailed with some specificity the groups he saw as the appropriate manipulators of the social-control machinery. After mentioning those for whom an interest in order was a kind of professional necessity—ministers, educators, jurists—and those with a strong economic interest in stability, he went on to hypothesize a crucial third component in the "party of order." This was the "ethical elite"—a moral cadre not drawn from any single vocation or economic group, but encompassing all citizens who "have at heart the general welfare and know what kinds of conduct will promote this welfare." The "surplus moral energy" of this guiding elite "recruited freely from the people and unspoiled by class spirit," he wrote, would both energize and inspire other elements in the "party of order" whose motives were less high-minded: "The others want *order*, any kind of order, while the elite stand for an order that is *right*."[24]

Under the benevolent oversight of the "ethical elite," Ross suggested, social control in the urban-industrial era would not involve "rude force," but "sweet seduction" through "inobvious . . . social suggestions."[25] If society were to master the "unpleasant slimy things lurking in the . . . undergrowth of the human soul," it must "quell one emotion with another, and supplement control by sanctions with control through the feelings." The goal, he insisted, was not to force a mere grudging conformity on mass man, but gently entice him to a spontaneous and even joyous inward affirmation of the larger social will.[26]

Ross's contemporary Charles H. Cooley was also a sociologist; he, too, taught at a big state university (Michigan); and his first book appeared within months of Ross's.[27] Indeed, the parallel extends still further, for the two books reflect a strikingly similar outlook. But while Ross's search for new modes of social control reflected his uneasy sense that society had entered a fundamentally new and uncharted era—the era of the industrial city—Cooley's approach was shaped by his understanding of certain immutable aspects of the human condition. Indeed, the entire structure of *Human Nature and the Social Order* is summed up in its title: human experience has meaning only as social experience; consciousness is social consciousness; "personality" is not a given, it is "built up" gradually through social encounters. For Cooley, as for the philosopher George Herbert Mead, the "self" was invariably a product of the interaction of the human organism with its social environment. Indeed, he argued, " 'society' and 'individuals' do not denote separable phenomena, but are simply . . . aspects of the same thing."[28]

For Cooley, the ramifications of this view of human nature were profound. It implied, for one thing, a radically altered understanding of ethics. For Cooley, as for Ross, morality was simply the "standard regarded as normal by the dominant sentiment of the group," and conscience merely the promptings of the "social self"—the constant modification of one's behavior according to the responses of others. Our behavior as adults, Cooley suggested, is primarily determined by "a circle of persons, more or less extended, whom we . . . imagine, and who thus work upon our impulses."[29]

The implications for social policy Cooley derived from all this were similar to Ross's. Although not as explicit in entrusting social control to a "party of order" led by an "ethical elite," he clearly implied that those in whom the "social self" was most fully developed were duty-bound to combat "degenerate tendencies" in others and promote the development of greater social responsiveness in the population at large. The "passion of self-aggrandizement" could never be eradicated entirely, but it could become "morally higher" if linked to "a larger conception of what constitutes the self." This enlargement of the social imagination was especially needed in the crowded cities where, ironically, people seemed most prone to withdraw into their private shells.[30]

Like Ross, Cooley insisted that what he envisioned was not simply new forms of "repressive discipline" or the "rule and habit" of a "mechanical" moral code. His proposal was both more subtle and more sweeping: the creation of the kind of urban environment in which the "social imagination" would be awakened and the "group conscience" experienced as something not rigid and remote, but "warm and fresh." Only when the social claim was made vividly real would the masses grasp "the highest vision of personality" and "make it the object of definite endeavor."[31] As urban moral reformers pondered the relative merits of coercive repression and positive environmentalism, Charles H. Cooley offered powerful support for the latter approach.

Simon N. Patten's work in some respects complemented that of Ross and Cooley, but it included some distinctive twists that were all his own. Born in 1852, Patten, like his friend and sometime rival E. A. Ross, spent his early years on an Illinois farm; again like Ross, he moved on. After a year and a half at Northwestern University he spent three years at the University of Halle in Germany, returning to America in 1879 with a doctorate in economics and a heady set of ideas inspired by the social-activist academics then gaining ascendency in Germany. A founder of the American Economic Association in 1885, Patten three years later took a position at the Wharton School of the University of Pennsylvania, where he would remain until his retirement in 1917. Although he published several books in the 1890s, *The New Basis of Civilization* was to prove his best known and most influential work, going through eight editions between 1907 and 1923.[32]

Patten's point of departure was the thesis with which his name is identified: that scarcity and want—the grim background of most nineteenth-century moral and social theorizing—were being rapidly supplanted by a new age of abundance. The ramifications of this development, he predicted, would touch almost every area of national life. In the scarcity era, for example, the prevailing moral climate was one of repression and restraint: the masses had to be persuaded or forced to curb their appetite for the pleasures and creature comforts of the rich, since the economy could supply such gratifications to only a few. Worked to exhaustion, with scant hope of bettering their lot, the urban poor turned to the "artificial stimuli of vice," accepting the saloon, the brothel, and the cheap dance hall as shabby counterfeits of the larger life they knew existed for a privileged few. This pursuit of false pleasures was a delusive, but understandable, effort to "enrich an impoverished, alien situation."[33]

In the dawning age of abundance, Patten prophesied, as the masses gained access to the cultural advantages once confined to the elite, the moral quality of life would be transformed along with the material. Recognizing the tawdriness of the pleasures they had perforce pursued in the past, the urban working class would begin to defer short-term gratifications in preference for the more rewarding and enduring opportunities now within reach. In the "age of surplus" with its "fuller life," he predicted, prostitution, the saloon, and other urban vices would vanish.[34]

As the newly affluent masses learned the rewards of delayed gratification, Patten went on, "restraint and morality"—once mere abstractions preached from above—would become experiential values rooted in economic reality and self-interest. Prosperity itself would teach the lesson that charity organization visitors had long been trying to inculcate. Once this process began, he wrote, the steps toward further ethical advance would prove "fairly well-paved." Prosperity would draw men into progressively larger cooperative groups that would "ultimately melt into a denationalized fraternal humanity."[35] Patten's utopian optimism knew no bounds: "Here is control that overcomes race, creed, and the natural differences of men; it is sustained by universal forces so attractive that it subdues vices and casts aside the crude traditions and punishments of our ancestors."[36]

Would the mere fact of abundance, then, of itself undergird the moral order in urban America? Were the efforts of moral reformers merely superfluous attempts to achieve what a maturing economic order would soon bring about willy-nilly? Patten went a long way toward suggesting just this, and (echoing Ross and Cooley) he repudiated coercive moral reformism as an anachronistic holdover from the era of scarcity with its ethic of "restraint, denial, and negation." Why bother with the prohibition of alcohol, for example, when the economic process itself would soon generate "new and better forms of social control"?[37]

Nevertheless, Patten did suggest that reform effort could hasten and, to an extent, guide a process whose central dynamic lay beyond direct control. As the age of abundance dawned for the industrial masses, for example, the enlightened reformer could help sensitize them to its enlarged possibilities. No longer con-

cerned with "restraining impulses and instincts," he could strive
to "free the[ir] imagination" and direct their aspirations toward
broader cultural interests and aesthetic pleasures.[38] Municipal
art, parks, lectures, concerts, cultural events—all would be important, Patten suggested, in awakening the urban throngs to the
broader vistas now open to them. The challenge confronting the
moralist of the future, in short, would not be to "suppress vices,"
but to "release virtues."[39]

Luther Lee Bernard, the final figure in this quartet of social
thinkers, differed from the others in important respects, but he
shared their conviction that the urban-industrial revolution had
profound implications for the future of the moral order. Born in
backwoods Kentucky in 1881, Bernard attended a Missouri Baptist college and the University of Missouri and in 1910 began
graduate study in sociology at the University of Chicago, where
Albion W. Small and others were pioneering the new fields of
urban sociology and social control.[40] The eager newcomer readily
assimilated the prevailing outlook, and his book-length monograph, "The Transition to an Objective Standard of Social Control," appeared in several successive issues of the *American Journal of Sociology* in 1911.

What was this "objective standard of social control"? For
Bernard, it was one based on a recognition that the harmonious
functioning of the social group must take precedence over the interests of its individual members. For too long, he insisted (with
copious documentation), individual happiness had been overrated
as a social and ethical good. The object of a properly run society,
he said, was not to make its members happy, but to turn them
into smoothly functional social components.

Bernard did not shrink from the practical implications of his
argument. "Means must be found," he insisted, "for the coercion
of individuals who stand in the way of efficient social functioning." In the face of this urgent goal, cherished dogmas about personal freedom had to give way. "The counterplea of 'interference
with individual liberty' should have no weight in court, for individuals have no liberties in opposition to a scientifically controlled
society but find all their legitimate freedom in conformity to and
futherance of such social functioning."[41]

How, precisely, would this objective social-control standard
be formulated? Edward A. Ross had dealt with this problem by
hypothesizing an "ethical elite" that would lead the way to a more
altruistic society. Charles Cooley had suggested that human nature itself, if allowed full expression, would bring individuals
into spontaneous harmony with the prevailing norms of the
group. Simon Patten had sidestepped the issue by contending that
the economic process, in generating an era of abundance, would

transform social behavior and morality, with a minimum of guidance and control.

Bernard, by contrast, bluntly insisted that the formulation and enforcement of standards of social behavior should be the responsibility of social-management professionals and that the "exploitation" of people by politicians must yield to "centralized administration by experts." Specifically, it would be *sociologists* who would curb "irresponsible" behavior by pointing out its "deleterious social effects." This did not imply "the rule of an elite in any objectionable sense," Bernard insisted, since these sociologist-masters, though operating independent of the political process, would always, in some unspecified way, remain "directly responsible to the people."[42]

Here was William T. Stead's vision of a perfectly managed urban world fleshed out in the imposing jargon of the fledgling sociologist. Once a "scientific social criterion of conduct" had been drawn up, and a "complete scientific social control" imposed, Bernard assured his readers, its sway would be absolute. "Where a social fact is established it should become as obligatory as the laws of astronomy or physics. The wilful disregard of the laws of health, of social hygiene, of public morality, should have as little tolerance as a wilful disregard of the law of falling bodies when the operation of this law has social consequences of equal importance."[43]

Though conceding that the specific details of his "objective standard of social control" awaited further sociological research, this Kentucky Baptist did give a few hints of what its general thrust might be—and it proved remarkably similar to the standard urban moral reformers had been trying to impose for a century. As the "reign of hedonism" gave way to an "ideal of social service," Bernard suggested, such glaring instances of "social waste" as prostitution, gambling, prize fighting and "the drink habit" would no longer be tolerated. The "butterfly life of pleasures" of the "modern woman of fashion," he sternly insisted, was precisely the kind of self-indulgence that would be unacceptable in the coming social order.[44]

Conventional moralist that he was, Bernard nevertheless shared the view of Ross, Cooley, and Patten that the era of overt repression had passed. In the future, he believed, social control would involve environmental strategies for rendering socially approved behavior emotionally gratifying to people, and proscribed behavior emotionally repugnant. Convinced that "feeling can easily be regulated socially through the control of habit formation, and . . . pleasant feeling . . . made to correspond to any useful social activity," he was confident that sociology and psychology, working hand in hand, would shortly develop effective means of directing individual behavior "in the service of a broader social control."[45]

Luther Lee Bernard, then, offered further support for what by 1911 had become a compelling set of assumptions in American social thought: that the city and the factory had radically transformed the social order; that this transformation required a fundamental rethinking of the processes by which a society achieved ethical consensus; and that in the future, social and moral control would depend not upon coercive repression, but upon a benign manipulation of the urban environment so as to evoke the desired behavior.[46] A few dissented from the prevailing consensus—most notably conservative New Humanists like Irving Babbitt and Paul Elmer More—but they were a tiny minority.[47] While Ross, Cooley, Patten, Bernard, and other theorists were laying the ideological foundation for a strategy of benevolent social control through environmental change, others of their generation were energetically exploring its practical ramifications.

16

Housing, Parks, and Playgrounds
POSITIVE ENVIRONMENTALISM
IN ACTION

Jacob Riis was, above all, a journalist; he knew the value of the dramatic and the concrete. Thus, when he sought to sum up the complex reality of New York's immigrant slums in his 1890 exposé *How the Other Half Lives,* he chose a single vivid example —Mulberry Bend near the infamous Five Points on the Lower East Side—and devoted an entire chapter to this "foul core of New York's slums."[1]

It was, therefore, of considerable symbolic significance when the municipal authorities in 1894 announced plans to raze the moldering tenements and criminal-infested alleys of Mulberry Bend and create a *park* in their place. Degeneracy and vice would yield to sunlight and fresh air; profanity and drunken brawling to the laughter of children at play! Where generations of tract distributors, Sunday school teachers, city missionaries, Children's Aid agents, and friendly visitors had trudged on their weary rounds of uplift, trees and green grass would flourish.

Bureaucratic delays held things up, but then tragedy struck: a collapsing wall in an abandoned building in the district Riis had made famous killed several children who had been playing inside. Here was epitomized the heartlessness of the urban environment, snuffing out not only the moral spark but now even the very lives of its innocent victims. The plans were pushed with fresh urgency, and by 1897 Mulberry Bend had, indeed, become a park.[2]

Such transformations were taking place in cities all over the country in the late nineteenth and early twentieth centuries, as Progressive reformers pursued the practical implications of the ideas explored in the last chapter. The most important of these positive-environmentalist efforts—tenement reform, the park and playground movements, and city planning—are familiar enough in broad outline. But viewed from the perspective of the larger urban moral-control movement, they take on interesting new dimensions and reveal some unexpected interconnections. Indeed, they might be viewed as a set of concentric circles, moving outward from the tenement all the way to the city itself, each circle in turn involving an enlarged conception of the scope of the environmentalist approach and its potential for reshaping the urban moral climate.

> One of the worst features of this
> overcrowding is the demoralizing
> lack of privacy.
> —Sophonisba P. Breckinridge and Edith Abbott,
> "Housing Conditions in Chicago,"
> American Journal of Sociology, January 1911

Interest in improved housing for America's urban poor—a matter of sporadic attention since Dr. John Griscom's 1845 exposé of slum conditions in New York, and a central part of the urban reformism of the 1890s—reached a peak in the Progressive years. A tenement exhibit by a committee of the New York Charity Organization Society in 1900 drew crowds in New York, Boston, and Chicago. In that same year, a highly publicized New York state tenement investigation (the follow-up to an earlier one in 1894–95) resulted in a tightening of the state's tenement code. In 1907, the steel executive Henry Phipps financed Phipps House, a model tenement in Harlem; two years later the vestrymen of New York's Trinity Church hired a well-known housing reformer as superintendent of its notorious slum properties, pledging to improve and upgrade them.[3] The movement spread to many other cities as well, thanks in large part to the efforts of the National Housing Association (founded in 1910) and its energetic director, Lawrence Veiller.[4]

As Roy Lubove has shown, this activity reflected not merely a disinterested urge to relieve the physical discomforts and health hazards of slum living but also a determination to influence the moral and social values of the urban poor by transforming their most immediate physical surroundings.[5] The evidence for such a conclusion abounds. The 1894 New York State Tenement House Committee (headed by Richard Watson Gilder, the editor of Century magazine) charged that "the promiscuous mixing of all ages and sexes" in cramped tenement apartments was "breaking down the barriers of modesty" and "conducing to the corruption of the young." Its successor, the New York Tenement House Commission of 1900, established a subcommittee on the "moral and social influences of tenement house life," and in its report pinpointed prostitution and gambling as tenement-linked vices.[6]

Almost every commentator on the urban moral challenge in these years agreed on the centrality of improved housing. "Familiarity with vice lessens the horror of it," reported tenement investigators in Cleveland: "the physical conditions under which these people live lessen their power of resisting evil."[7] In the tenement, declared Raymond Calkins in Substitutes for the Saloon, "moral standards are gradually lowered, and finally disappear"; slum housing congestion, agreed a writer in the American City magazine, "raises the death-rate and lowers the moral tone." Newton M. Hall saw the tenement as a "festering plague-spot of social corruption"; Frederic C. Howe echoed this judgment in The City: The Hope of Democracy; and Jacob Riis, writing in 1903, pulled out all the journalistic stops to make the same point: few tenements had "a chimney big enough to let in Santa Claus," he declared, "and you might as well give up at once as to have him excluded."[8]

The antiprostitution reformers devoted much worried attention to this question. Jane Addams charged that the tenement, in breaking down a girl's "natural safeguard of modesty and reserve," was a major factor in sexual immorality and prostitution. The very first recommendation of the New York Committee of Fifteen was for a campaign against the tenement overcrowding that was a "prolific source of sexual immorality."[9]

How to alleviate the tenement evil? Some reformers urged stricter housing codes, others favored model tenements underwritten by private philanthropy, and still others—noting the expansion of metropolitan transit systems in the 1890s—saw suburbanization as the long-range answer.[10]

Whatever the specific strategy, the underlying conviction remained constant: the behavior and morality of the urban masses could surely be influenced for the better by changing or upgrading their housing. Here was a fundamental beginning point for the positive environmentalism of the Progressive years.

Despite the high hopes which its partisans held out for its social and moral benefits, housing reform loomed in the Progressive era, no less than it does today, as a massive and complex task. It is hardly surprising, then, that many urban environmental reformers avoided a frontal assault on the tenement, concentrating instead on other approaches that seemed more promising and more attainable. One of the projects to which they turned was the municipal park.

Today, parks are so ubiquitous and familiar a feature of the urban scene that we give little thought, beyond a vaguely favorable feeling, to their social significance. Thus, it takes a considerable imaginative leap to realize that the park movement once had the force of a fresh social discovery that could arouse intense and passionate commitment, and that its moral implications were carefully explored and debated by moralists, urban reformers, social critics, landscape designers, and municipal authorities alike.

The movement arose in the 1840s, an outgrowth of the garden-cemetery vogue of the preceding decade. Throughout the forties, landscape gardener Andrew Jackson Downing urged cities to set aside land for parks while they could.[11] Belatedly heeding Downing's advice, New York City in 1856 acquired 840 acres in upper Manhattan for park purposes, and announced a design competition. The winners were two young men in their early thirties, Frederick Law Olmsted and Calvert Vaux; the result of their plan is Central Park. As its superintendent of construction from 1858 to 1878, Olmsted quickly emerged as the dominant figure in the Gilded Age park movement. Inspired by New York's example, and often with the assistance of Olmsted and Vaux, Brooklyn, Philadelphia, Chicago, Boston, and other cities developed large-scale parks in these years.[12]

The 1890s saw the emergence of a second and significantly different surge of interest. As cities continued to expand and slum wards became ever more congested with immigrant newcomers, it became obvious that a single municipal park, however vast or impressive, was inadequate. (In some instances, the existing park was so distant from the central city as to be practically inaccessible to the masses.) With this realization, the emphasis shifted to creating park systems, including small neighborhood parks in congested districts.

One of the first cities to move in this direction was Kansas City, which in 1890, prodded by editor William R. Nelson of the *Kansas City Star*, hired the young landscape designer George E. Kessler to develop such an overall park system. Kessler's 1893 report—plus a timely bequest of land and the influence of boss James Pendergast who was inspired by visions of patronage jobs—led to the creation of an enviable municipal park system.[13]

Meanwhile, back East, the Massachusetts legislature in 1892 created a Metropolitan Park Commission under landscape architect Charles Eliot (son of Harvard's president) to develop and implement a comprehensive, multimillion-dollar park plan for greater Boston. Two years later, New York's lawmakers appropriated several million dollars for the development of small parks in crowded urban districts. (The Mulberry Bend park was one of the results.) Chicago, too, went forward with an ambitious small-parks program. By 1920, practically every American city had its park commission and its network of parks in existence or under development.[14]

Like their counterparts in tenement reform, park advocates from the first saw an important moral dimension to their efforts. The mayor of New York, calling for a park appropriation in 1851, argued that such a retreat in the city would provide a morally preferable alternative for the thousands who were spending their Sundays "among the idle and dissolute, in porter-houses or in places more objectionable." Henry Ward Beecher welcomed Brooklyn's Prospect Park as a distinct moral asset to the city. "The divine element of beauty in nature," he felt, would inspire the poor to "gentle thoughts and grateful silence."[15]

The most persuasive and articulate nineteenth-century voice urging the moral significance of urban parks was that of Frederick Law Olmsted. Not only a gifted landscape designer but also an intellectual of wide-ranging interests, Olmsted had already achieved a substantial reputation as a social observer and commentator before winning the Central Park competition, and he continued throughout his career to bring a reflective intelligence to bear upon its larger social implications. If the Progressive-era park advocates diverged radically from Olmsted's vision, they nevertheless remained heavily in his debt.

Reared in the rural environs of Hartford (itself hardly more than an overgrown town during his boyhood in the 1820s), Olmsted early recognized that his childhood world was vanishing. Walk through the average New England village, he later wrote, and you will find "the meeting-house closed, the church dilapidated; the famous old taverns, stores, shops, mills, and offices dropping to pieces and vacant." Yet he was not one to pine for the irretrievable past. He sensed that the city was to be the shaping social force of the future and that the urbanization that had already occurred was "merely a premonition" of a "vastly greater enlargement."[16]

Although he rejected the view of those who saw the rise of the city as "a sort of moral epidemic,"[17] he did not adopt a blandly optimistic stance. Drawing upon his own experience and the ideas of friends (including Yale classmate Charles Loring Brace), he concluded that urbanization posed social and moral hazards all the more insidious for being intermingled with positive social gains. The moral problem of the city, he contended in 1870— rather atypically for the period—was not one of blatant vice, crime, and mob disorder, but rather the erosion of the social bond, the deadening of human sensitivity, and the loss of opportunities for reflection and repose. The city was an "enervating" place where selfish interests were pursued with "devouring eagerness" and where people eyed each other "in a hard if not always hardening way." The enforced intimacy with others on the crowded city street did not inspire a "friendly flowing toward them, but rather a drawing from them."[18]

Nor did Olmsted believe that "progress" in the form of a benign historical inevitability would ultimately resolve these problems. The only defense against the morally deadening effects of city life, he insisted, was "direct action" by urban leaders. Though influenced by liberal Protestantism's hopeful view of human nature, he never questioned that decisive intervention by a socially responsible elite was essential if urbanization were to prove beneficent in its social effects. As Albert Fein has suggested and Geoffrey Blodgett more recently documented, he assumed unquestioningly that men of his class were duty-bound to work to elevate the moral and social tone of city life—if not through politics, then through such means as presented themselves.[19]

That Olmsted chose the park as his fulcrum of social control was a consequence not only of his natural gifts but of the intellectual milieu in which he moved. Through such friends as the editor and socialist Parke Godwin he was in touch with the Fourierist/Brook Farm tradition and its interest in developing environmental analogues to social ideals.[20] For Charles Fourier, the material expression of his social vision had been the phalanstery; for Olmsted, it was the park.

A romantic in the Wordsworthian tradition, Olmsted believed implicitly in the elevating and restorative power of nature. Once those responsible for civic affairs had returned "nature" to the city in the form of parks, it would exert its beneficent influence with little further human intervention. He did not, however, believe that park planners should seek to arouse the sometimes turbulent "sublime" emotions associated with nature in its more awe-inspiring guises. Rather, they should provide grassy meadows, quiet vistas, and gentle streams that would bring "tranquility and rest to the mind." The ideal park, he wrote, would have at its heart a "broad, open space of clean greensward," with a surrounding screen of trees to "completely shut out the city."[21] Such a park, Olmsted believed, would exert upon the urban masses a "harmonizing and refining influence . . . favorable to courtesy, self-control, and temperance." More important, in this setting, the sense of community and fellow feeling would revive, competitive clamor would be muted, and class divisions would fade as each visitor "by his mere presence" contributed to "the pleasure of the others, all helping to the greater happiness of each." The park, in short, would function as an artfully contrived urban equivalent of the peaceful bucolic scene or the "familiar domestic gathering." In so doing, it would offer a powerful antidote to the forces of "degeneration and demoralization" in the city.[22]

Embodying this romantic naturalism in their design for Central Park (which they originally called "Greensward"), Olmsted and Vaux kept the artificial and the man-made to a minimum: rambling pathways followed the contours of the land, lookout points displayed the modest natural vistas to best advantage, and discreet landscaping subtly highlighted already existing features. As an early Central Park guidebook put it, their aim was to recapture the "delicate flavor of wildness, so hard to seize and imprison when civilization has once put it to flight."[23] With this carefully contrived "natural" setting as a stimulus, the organic harmony of a preurban era would be renewed, gradually spreading its influence through the larger life of the city.

While Olmsted enjoyed great professional success from the 1850s on, his vision of the social-control function of parks was at first neglected in favor of more direct strategies, such as those of the charity organization movement. As interest in environmentalist approaches quickened at the turn of the century, however, the park's larger social potential was rediscovered. Kansas City's George Kessler and Boston's Charles Eliot both echoed Olmsted in insisting that parks would promote the "moral growth" of the urban population. Walter Rauschenbusch portrayed the park movement as an expression of "enlightened moral sentiment" more promising than any repressive approach, and even the coercive moral crusaders sometimes praised it as a valuable adjunct to their efforts. A writer in *Social Hygiene* in 1917, for example, approvingly quoted one park superintendent's claim that with a larger budget he could reduce prostitution in his city by 98 percent![24]

Sometimes this Progressive rediscovery of the moral significance of parks followed quite literally Olmsted's belief in the elevating power of grass, foliage, and bubbling streams. The "green turf" and "waving trees" of Kansas City's parks, prophesied Kessler, would produce "innocent, joyous" children instead of "dirty, white-faced, and vicious gamins" early conversant with "immorality and vice." To Charles Eliot, it seemed axiomatic that the "more natural and agreeable" setting of the park would counteract the city's "confusion and excitement" and produce more "desirable types of humanity." When city dwellers "have Nature at hand," agreed another early-twentieth-century park enthusiast, "evil seems weakened . . . , the souls of children become freshened with joy, [and] the spirit of men [is] calmed and emboldened to virtue."[25]

Although the vision of the park as a "natural" counterweight to the morally destructive pressures of urban life never wholly faded, a quite different point of view found vigorous expression in the Progressive era. It was not enough, many park advocates now asserted, merely to create a sylvan retreat in the city and then sit back as it exerted its beneficent influence without further human intervention. To function as an instrument of urban social control, the park must be managed and administered. "There is no use trying to treat a place in the middle of a crowded city on the wilderness motif," wrote one Progressive park leader. "The thing to do is to frankly recognize that its beauty, if it is to have any, must be civic beauty."[26] The somewhat ominously named American Institute of Park Executives was founded in 1898, and throughout the Progressive years the manipulative, activist conception of urban park administration found frequent expression.

The shift in outlook is evident in a study of the municipal park movement which appeared in the 1920s. In part, the author simply reiterated familiar Olmstedian ideas: parks could help restore "lines of social contact" shattered by the city's "disintegrative forces"; their "quietness and beauty," in which city dwellers could rediscover "the first great instructor, Mother Nature," would surely produce a more "wholesome" urban life.[27] But Mother Nature, this author hastened to make clear, needed a good deal of human assistance: "the mere presence of open spaces is not enough, leisure itself is not enough." The up-to-date park administrator must also (as Simon Patten had advised) stimulate the cultural development of parkgoers by organizing musical and dramatic performances. He should publish manuals and guidebooks, organize classes in domestic landscaping (perhaps distributing shrubs and flowers to the masses "on condition that they be planted and cared for"), and recruit experts "whose sole function will be to lead people into the open spaces and *interpret* nature to them." Finally, he should utilize the park for community events that would promote the "spirit of neighborliness." A park's social effectiveness, he asserted briskly, was "largely a problem of organization," and "the predominating need is leadership." Indeed, leadership (rather than, say, nature) was his central motif: "Just as parents are the most important factor in the home, the teacher in the school, [and] the trained executive in the business organization," he insisted, so park administrators and other municipal recreation officials are "the most important and fundamental of all environmental factors"—the "chief agents" in restoring to the nation's cities "the spirit which made earlier life in America wholesome and desirable."[28]

The quintessential expression of the Progressive conception of the park as an urban social-control instrument was the influential *Parks: Their Design, Equipment, and Use* (1916) by George Burnap, landscape architect of public buildings and grounds in Washington, D.C. While sharing Olmsted's belief that parks had an important moral role in the city, Burnap's understanding of how that role should be played was a thoroughly contemporary one. For him, every detail of park design should reflect in a literal and explicit way the social values of its planners and administrators and, in a larger sense, symbolize the power of the municipality over its inhabitants. Entrance gates, for example, should express "the character and importance of the park." Paths should be of a "dignified width" to heighten "esteem" for the park, "exalting its features, increasing its authority." (By contrast, "narrow," "devious," or "irrelevant" trails would "fritter away the dignity of a park, belittling its features, decreasing its importance.") Fountains should be "dominating and forceful." Landscaping should emphasize "regularity of skyline, with avoidance of snaggle-toothed picturesqueness." Only "strong-growing plants" should be introduced, "the sort that do not need constant pampering but are able to withstand the buffets of the city, the varieties that represent the survival of the fittest."[29]

Burnap's interest was not in the park as a retreat from urban pressures or in nature as a moral counterpoise to the city—no Wordsworthian sermons in stone or lessons in babbling brooks for him!—but in deliberately shaping the park as a social artifact expressing the class realities of urban-industrial society and inculcating the social values and outlook of the dominant group. Accordingly, he insisted that park design be precisely calibrated to the particular social characteristics (and presumed needs) of the different economic levels of the city. In the slums, for example, parks should consist mainly of open space so that workers escaping from stifling, crowded tenements would "feel that a city is bestowing upon them a bountiful gift." Their landscaping and facilities "should be a grade higher than that to which they are accustomed, which will not form sufficient contrast to cause resentment, and yet encourage a desire in them for something better." In middle-class neighborhoods, Burnap went on, parks could be somewhat less austere, yet still "regular and formal" in design, expressing "restraint," "order," and "straightforwardness," and exerting a "steadying influence" to counteract "the present tendency of our middle classes to ape . . . those of larger means and to covet their extravagancies and indulgences." In upper-class neighborhoods, Burnap concluded, greater "liberty of design" might be indulged, but even here "a certain amount of government in naturalistic design" should be maintained.[30] Such were George Burnap's views of the meaning and function of the city park. Nowhere in the Progressive urban social-control literature were the assumptions underlying the positive-environmentalist position more starkly expressed or more literally applied.

Of all the Progressives preaching urban social control through environmental manipulation, none were more confident in their assertions than the champions of the playground movement. The lowly city playground, with its sandboxes, its slides and swings, its playing fields, and perhaps its swimming pool, they proclaimed, would be the womb from which a new urban citizenry —moral, industrious, and socially responsible—would emerge.

Like other urban reform strategies, the playground movement took shape in the turbulent closing years of the nineteenth century and gained momentum in the hopeful opening years of the next. The beginnings were modest enough. In the summer of 1886 (a few months after Haymarket), Boston's city fathers set aside a portion of the Charles River embankment as a play area for children and had wagon loads of sand dumped at various sites in the working-class sections of the city. In 1890 a small playground was opened on New York's Lower East Side by the Society for Parks and Playgrounds for Children (organized that year by Walter Vrooman and others), but it was soon vandalized and abandoned.[31]

A few years of comparative inactivity followed these small beginnings, but in the wake of the Depression of 1893–1897, with its sharpened fears of urban unrest, interest in the playground idea increased. Chicago's Associated Charities opened a playground in 1897, and in 1898 they were introduced (or reintroduced) in Philadelphia, New York, and Baltimore. That same year the Massachusetts legislature gave the Metropolitan Park Commission $500,000 to develop a comprehensive playground system.[32]

But it was in the Progressive years that the dramatic advance came. An important catalyst was Boston's Joseph Lee, "the father of American playgrounds," who worked tirelessly in these years to spread the playground message. "Play is the intensest part of the life of a child," Lee never tired of asserting, "and it is therefore in his play hours that his most abiding lessons are learned." In 1906 Lee joined with Dr. Luther H. Gulick, director of physical training in the New York City public schools, Henry Stoddard Curtis, and others to found the Playground Association of America. Through its conferences, its magazine *Playground*, and the travels of an energetic field secretary, the PAA publicized the idea widely.[33]

Chicago took the lead, expending some $15 million between 1899 and 1909 to develop thirty playground/recreation centers in the city's immigrant wards. In 1907, when 5,000 delegates descended on the Windy City for the first annual convention of the Playground Association of America, they were given tours of its extensive network of playgrounds and exposed to hours of speeches extolling the importance of the movement and Chicago's contribution to it. "The city which has made its reputation by killing hogs," declared settlement-house leader Graham Taylor, "has awakened to the fact that manufacturing good and sturdy citizenship is even more important." Chicago's commitment to playgrounds was duplicated on a more modest scale throughout urban America. In a 1908 referendum, to take one typical instance, all but two of Massachusetts's forty-two cities and towns voted by overwhelming majorities to support municipal playgrounds. By 1917 the reform had spread to more than five hundred cities nationwide.[34]

Like the housing and park reformers, the early playground champions were impelled by a social vision more sweeping than might appear at first glance. They were not concerned simply with brightening the existence of urban ragamuffins. Nor did even the obvious physical benefits of fresh air and exercise lie at the heart of their reform. The rhetoric may have differed, but these playground leaders were pursuing the same objective that their forerunners in urban moral reform had been seeking for a century: to shape a cohesive urban moral order.

This social-control purpose pervades the literature of the movement. In Pittsburgh, for example, the leaders of the reform assured their fellow citizens that money spent on playgrounds would pay high dividends in cultivating the "moral nature" of children, promoting "civic unity" and supplying the "social training and discipline" urgently needed among the immigrant masses. Another playground advocate put the matter more bluntly: the point of the reform, she declared in 1911, was to give city children "new social notions, and a better standard of what is acceptable to those 'higher up.'" To Luther H. Gulick, the playground was above all a social-control instrument for producing in urban youth the "corporate conscience" demanded by the "complex interdependence of modern life."[35]

Gulick's comments were spelled out more fully a decade later by Henry Stoddard Curtis, secretary of the PAA, in The Play Movement and Its Significance. Curtis began with the usual bleak assessment of the city's impact on the young. "Constantly overstimulated" by the pace of urban life and given few outlets for their pent-up energies, they idly congregated on street corners to "watch the drunken people, listen to the leader of the gang, hear the shady story, smoke cigarettes," and ultimately end in the poolrooms and dance halls "where drinking and the sex lure are the main enticements."[36]

The answer, wrote Curtis, lay not in repression but in creating "a different environment" as an alternative to the vice-ridden streets. As a central component in that "different environment," the playground would occupy children during those hours when they were beyond the scrutiny of either parents or teachers. ("No one who has observed children carefully in any city . . . between the close of school and supper," he observed in a profoundly insightful utterance, "has found that any considerable percentage of them were doing anything that was worth while.") It was the playground's potential as a "new force" for shaping urban character, Curtis insisted, that had given the movement its tremendous appeal. His point was graphically if unintentionally dramatized by the organizers of the 1910 conference of the PAA, held in Rochester, New York, when they took the delegates to a model playground where "at the stroke of the gong" the assembled children began to play, the younger ones turning out identical, symmetrical sand pies![37]

Convinced that here at last was a key to the problem of urban social control, the proponents of this latest panacea once again took the lead in discrediting their predecessors in reform. The playground, declared one of its champions, could instill "more ethics and good citizenship . . . in a single week than can be inculcated by Sunday school teachers . . . in a decade." Unlike the YMCA and other programs largely confined by their sectarian origins to work among "Protestant people of the evangelical type," observed another partisan somewhat smugly, playgrounds could accomplish their good offices just as easily in Catholic or Jewish neighborhoods. Furthermore, this writer went on, they were free of the typical charity organization society's preoccupation with procedural red tape and condescending aura of upper-class do-goodism.[38]

The playground proponents' self assurance even led to a rift with the reformers seemingly closest to them: the leaders of the park movement. Initially the playground movement was portrayed as wholly compatible with park reform, but as it attracted its own constituency and evolved its own organizational structure, its spokesmen increasingly criticized park administrators for their emphasis on preserving natural landscapes even when it meant severe limitations on park use—especially by children. Parks were aptly called urban "breathing spaces," commented one playground leader acidly, because *breathing* was about all one was permitted to do in them. ("The average playground enthusiast," retorted George Kessler, "understands the term only as applied to a group of swings, slides and all the other forms of violent exercise, disregarding almost entirely the value of natural beauty.")[39]

Such intramural sniping notwithstanding, most urban reformers found the confident, activist rhetoric of the playground movement irresistible. Few other reform strategies were discussed with more enthusiasm in Progressive-era explorations of the urban question. Jacob Riis ranked the playground high among the "wholesome counterinfluences to the saloon, street gang, and similar evils"; it would, agreed the urban planner Charles Mulford Robinson, help city children "keep their souls pure though they soil their hands." Housing reformer Lawrence Veiller gave the movement favorable notice; Raymond Calkins assigned it a "prominent place among the agencies favorably affecting the moral condition of society"; and Frederic C. Howe saw it as an admirable antidote to slum disorder and the "irregular life of the street and the saloon."[40]

Everyone, it seemed, had a good word to say for the playground, including, as one supporter boasted in 1908, "many eminent pedagogues, scientists, and sociologists." Jane Addams lent her prestige to the movement, praising it as the kind of positive social innovation that could drive out the debased commercial amusements of the modern city. The United States commissioner of education, the Social Gospel leader W. D. P. Bliss, ex-President Theodore Roosevelt, and the president of the American Civic Association were united in the belief (as the latter gentleman put it in 1916) that the playground was no "frill" but a powerful new weapon in the continuing struggle with "the forces of evil."[41]

This heavy investment of hope in playgrounds reflected not only the prevailing environmentalism of the period but also the belief that environmentalist strategies could be especially effective in influencing children. Since the early days of the Sunday school movement, many reformers had concluded that their best hope lay with those in whom the seeds of vice and degeneracy had not yet struck deep root, and this belief flowered exuberantly under the sunlight of progressivism. For the Progressives (as Roy Lubove has felicitously put it), the child was "putty ready for the hand of the social sculptor"—a perpetually beckoning, perpetually renewed symbol of the possibility of transforming the city's *moral* environment by transforming the *physical* environment of its youngest, most malleable inhabitants.[42]

This faith was reinforced by the then-fashionable recapitulation theory of human development. As formulated by psychologist G. Stanley Hall of Clark University and others, this theory held that each child reexperienced and displayed, in its own development, all the earlier stages of human social evolution. It followed, then, as one writer put it, that every child at a certain stage of its maturation was "essentially a savage, with the interests of a savage, the body of a savage, and to no small extent, the soul of one." The early playground advocates—notably Henry Stoddard Curtis, author of a doctoral thesis in psychology under Hall at Clark University—made effective use of recapitulationist ideas.[43] They (as well as spokesmen for the closely related boys' club movement) had little difficulty convincing their contemporaries that in the modern city, the "savagery" stage—especially as expressed in the adolescent gang impulse—was fraught with danger. The members of gangs, they pointed out, could easily be lured into vice simply by emulating an admired older leader. They found a ready ear when they pledged that playgrounds and boys' clubs would shepherd the child safely through the "savagery" stage to a fully socialized adulthood.

This would be accomplished, they explained, not by resisting the gang instinct, but by accepting it as natural and exploiting its positive components. Whenever a "competent leader" managed to "capture" a city gang, the head of Chicago's Juvenile Protective Association told a Chicago child-welfare conference in 1911, he could exert a "moral leverage" on it "almost beyond comprehension." The individual who could gain the trust of boys during the gang-forming stage, agreed a Protestant churchman addressing the same conference, was in an ideal position to "control them for a better and nobler citizenship . . . , having gained them at the time when they are liable to be lost to society and good government." Illustrating the same point, Raymond Calkins described the transformation in a once-dissolute Chicago gang that had been taken in hand by a youth worker and transformed into a "club." "Regular business meetings are held, and men of standing invited to discuss . . . various sociological problems and topics of current interest. As one of their members said: 'We used to do nothing but crack jokes, and plan how to have a good time. Now we have something serious to talk about.' "[44]

The most interesting effort to justify the playground movement's social-control objectives on the basis of recapitulationist psychology were those of Joseph Lee, playground pioneer and president of the Playground Association of America (and its successor the National Recreation Association) from 1910 until his death in 1937. In numerous articles in the *Playground* and in his books *Constructive and Preventive Philanthropy* (1902) and *Play in Education* (1915), Lee probed the "nervous disorders" of modern urban life and the role of the playground in healing them.[45]

For Lee, recapitulationist that he was, the "play instinct" was

CONDITIONS ON THE STREETS OF MANHATTAN IN MONTHLY PERIODS FROM JANUARY 24TH TO NOVEMBER 15TH, 1912, SHOWING STREET WALKERS COUNTED, AND NUMBER WHO SOLICITED MEN INVESTIGATORS

Period	All Streets in Manhattan			Broadway		
	Street Walkers Counted	Street Walkers who Solicited Investigators	Number of Reports	Street Walkers Counted	Street Walkers who Solicited Investigators	Number of Reports
Jan. 24th to Feb. 24th . .	482	104	157	38	8	9
Feb. 24th to Mar. 24th . .	492	133	149	105	25	22
Mar. 24th to Apr. 24th . .	490	104	179	195	25	28
Apr. 24th to May 24th . .	843	117	214	435	46	74
May 24th to June 24th . .	1203	118	299	962	60	69
June 24th to July 24th . .	696	72	245	479	25	114
July 24th to Sept. 1st . .	1048	52	201	593	20	87
Sept. 1st to Oct. 1st . .	451	45	69	209	18	22
Oct. 1st to Nov. 1st . .	738	34	134	352	16	55
Nov. 1st to Nov. 15th . .	876	14	39	207	12	12
TOTALS	6739	793	1596	3175	235	492

Of the total number of street walkers counted, over 47% were on Broadway.
Of the total number of street walkers who solicited investigators, nearly 30% were on Broadway.
Of the total number of reports on streets, about 31% related to Broadway.

Quantifying evil. This chart, from George J. Kneeland's *Commercialized Prostitution in New York City* (1913), reports the results of a street count of New York prostitutes from January to November 1912.

Statistics in the service of urban moral control. A 1913 Anti-Saloon League chart showing a close relationship—presumably a causal one—between the rate of alcoholic consumption and the rate of divorce.

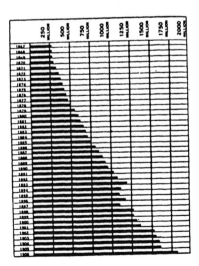
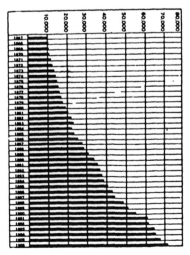

Dramatizing the antiprostitution crusade: An idealized portrayal of a white slave from Clifford G. Roe's *The Prodigal Daughter* (1911).

Fighting for purity on the homefront. In this scene from the 1917 War Department film "Fit to Fight," Kid McCarthy tries to entice a sorely tempted Hank into a bawdy house.

Fellow Citizens: What Will You Make of Me?

The efficiency of a community should not be gauged by the length of its "improved" water-front, the number of tall factory chimneys, and the size of its daily bank clearances, but by the answer to the question: "Does it afford a good setting for children and a good place for their up-bringing?"

THE SEED OF CIVIC RIGHTEOUSNESS FLOWERS IN ITS FUTURE CITIZENS

In the Progressive playground movement no less than in the Jacksonian Sunday school movement, children were seen as the key to the creation of a moral and cohesive urban order.

The playground ideal: physical, social, and moral development under skilled leadership. A Bronx, New York, playground scene in the 1890s.

A Chicago playground project of the early twentieth century: constructing an idealized city in miniature.

Inspiring civic idealism through drama: a scene from the Saint Louis Pageant and Masque of May 1914.

Charles Mulford Robinson: prophet
of the "City Beautiful."

Daniel Hudson Burnham: city planner, promoter, and social visionary.

Symbolizing the authority of the civic ideal. The proposed civic center from *Plan of Chicago.*

Social harmony through architectural harmony: Jules Guérin's painting of the proposed civic center plaza from *Plan of Chicago* (1909) by Daniel H. Burnham and Edward H. Bennett.

no light matter: it embodied some of the most primal human drives—the impulse to hunt, to fight, to pit oneself against a natural or human adversary, to join with the pack in battle and conquest. In these instincts, Lee was convinced, lay the "original and creative force in every man." Their reappearance in each generation he viewed as a vigorous instinctual revolt against the "soft and easy ways" of a "too civilized and peaceful life." Lee's hostility to modern urban-industrial society went deep. It was a social order somehow gone wrong—a civilization that thwarted man's deepest instincts and drained his "vital force and potentiality," leaving his life a "spiritual waste . . . , dessicated of all meaning." Cain, the tiller of the soil, slew Abel, the roaming herdsman, and now "Cain has in turn succumbed to Arkwright. Mankind has become a city dweller in a world no longer recognizable as that to which his inherited instincts still relate."[46]

As a crucible of character, the harsh wilderness or primordial jungle of, say, a Jack London or an Edgar Rice Burroughs story was for Lee far superior to Simon Patten's new age of affluence and ease. He felt a profound sympathy for the atavistic and antisocial impulses that rose to the surface during each child's unconscious recapitulation of the social evolution of the race. In trying to force the child "to settle softly into the mould," he wrote, society was battling "his moral nature as determined by his instincts."[47] Of all the urban moralists we have encountered, none, except perhaps Charles Loring Brace, felt more affinity with the objects of his reformist efforts.

For all his admiration of the primitive and the instinctual, Lee, like James Fenimore Cooper long before, finally opted for civilization and its restraints. "The remedy is not in a return to barbarism," he wrote; the primitive impulses underlying the "play instinct" must be domesticated and socialized. Here, he believed, the modern city had failed. In his own comfortable suburban boyhood in Brookline, Massachusetts, in the 1870s, the wild impulses of the "savagery" stage had been harmlessly expended in exuberant rivalries with other gangs and what he later recalled as innocent assaults on the dignity and propriety of the adult world. But the city, lacking such natural outlets, forced the youthful craving for challenge, conflict, and adventure into debased channels: petty crime; street brawling; and precocious experimentation with alcohol, illicit sex, and other vices.[48]

For Lee, the playground was a powerful mediating agent between man's instinctual nature and the restraints essential to urban-industrial society. Like the kindergarten pioneer Friedrich Froebel, he saw in guided play a primary instrument for socialization and the cultivation of the moral sense. As the child progressed from simple, unstructured play to more complex games and team sports, social and ethical values would gradually take root. These would not be imposed didactically; the play instinct itself would make their utility evident. "When a baseball game among boys over twelve breaks up in a riot, let them fight it out; they are too fond of the game not to arrive eventually at some *modus vivendi* . . . If at the end of several months they have worked out some system by which their disputes can generally be settled, they have traveled in that time as far as their ancestors progressed in some few hundred thousand years."[49] Through actual experience, in short, the children of the playground would realize "the disadvantages of anarchy, and . . . learn for themselves to overcome them."[50]

Not only the process of settling disputes but the total experience of participation in organized playground games would further the socialization process, as the young person learned the emotional satisfaction of "merging his own individuality in the common consciousness." Growing accustomed to holding a "regular responsible position" as part of a "permanent organism," the team member would gradually exhibit a "better state of discipline," achieve a higher "moral tone," and become "easier to manage."[51]

The early socializing influence of the playground was especially crucial, Lee argued (echoing generations of commentators on the urban moral problem), because once the child passed into the adult world, the external restraints on his behavior would be disturbingly few. Many a city dweller, he wrote in *Play in Education*, "is to all intents and purposes invisible so far as effective check upon his conduct is concerned. Nobody sees him whom he need ever see again or whose opinion he has any motive to conciliate. The people of his own street need know nothing of his life. There is nobody to whom he must give an account of himself or present a definite and comprehensible personality, no public opinion to which he is effectively amenable."[52] For Lee, the playground represented one of society's few opportunities to mold the urban child before he disappeared into the anonymous mass.

By a somewhat circuitous path, then, and with many nostalgic detours, Joseph Lee joined those Progressives who were seeking in environmental manipulation new modes of urban social control. For him, the playground was a place where the atavistic "play instinct" would not only find a safe and socially acceptable outlet, but where it would be permanently tamed.

In his discussions of the playground's social role, Lee placed great stress on the importance of adult supervision. A trained supervisor in the playground, he wrote, would "increase its effectiveness tenfold"; lacking such control, the bigger children would act as "petty tyrants," a "disorderly set" would take over, and the little playground community would degenerate into "anarchy and chaos."[53]

Lee's emphasis on leadership reflected a broader ideological shift in the playground movement analogous to that which occurred in the park movement. In the early years, playground enthusiasts paid little attention to the issue of supervision, portraying in rosy colors the joy and moral value of free and spontaneous childish play. The role of the city authorities, they implied, was simply to provide swings, slides, sandboxes, and a safe and pleasant setting, and then let the little ones enjoy themselves. Such supervision as did occur in the first playgrounds, writes one playground historian, tended to be by neighbor women who "brought their sewing to their windows and looked out occasionally to utter a reproof when a quarrel was on."[54]

In the later Progressive years, however, this laissez faire attitude was rejected as naive and dangerous. What went on in the playground could be "either moral or immoral," declared Henry Stoddard Curtis, and to channel those activities in a positive direction was "one of the most difficult feats of moral leadership." The playground's "moral value," agreed the head of Chicago's Juvenile Protective Association, depended completely on the presence of someone who could guide the children to a higher plane of "social consciousness." As in so many areas of Progressive social thought, expertise now became the rallying cry; only the "intelligently equipped social worker," insisted one leader, could "cultivate and harvest those finer fruits of the social nature" whose early tender buds the playground experience had called forth.[55]

This insistence on the need for leaders to control the little sandbox society was not mere rhetoric. Many cities hired trained playground managers in these years. Newton D. Baker, recounting his role in bringing playgrounds to Cleveland, recalled in 1918 that when he became mayor his aim had merely been to provide free play space, but that he had soon realized that one "could not reproduce in a city, by simply giving a piece of ground, those normal opportunities for play which occur in the sparsely settled countryside; . . . the artificiality of city life intruded." Wholesome play meant supervised play—"and so we began to train experts."[56]

In Chicago, a large cadre of playground leaders not only supervised day-to-day playground activities but also developed detailed weekly, monthly, and even annual schedules; planned pageants and other special events; classified their clientele in a variety of ways; and elaborated their own administrative hierarchy to a high degree of complexity. Their duty, as Chicago's director of playgrounds reminded them, was "to serve the public as experts," and they strove to live up to the title.[57] A 1908 Chicago playground handbook offers a revealing glimpse into the actual functioning of municipal playgrounds in the Progressive era. The playground leader, the handbook noted, "should praise every tendency of a boy or girl to sacrifice himself or herself for the good of the team. Show them that this is the only way to succeed—by unity of action. If you can develop this spirit you have laid the foundation of cooperation, politeness, and good morals."[58] Should a child fail to live up to the leader's expectations, it went on, "the disapprobation of the teacher and the other children" should be sufficient to bring him into line. If that failed, the offender should be "excluded from teams or games or, as a last resort, from the playground." By such techniques, children would gradually come to share the supervisor's values through "a copied politeness, gentleness, and justice."[59] A passage like this highlights the strong elements of continuity that underlay all the changes of strategy and personnel within the urban social control movement. With minor changes of terminology, it might have been lifted verbatim from almost any Sunday school handbook of the Jacksonian period!

In further unconscious imitation of their predecessors in the Sunday school movement, these playground enthusiasts convinced themselves that the children they reached would in turn influence their families and, ultimately, society as a whole. In Washington, D.C., Henry Stoddard Curtis reported, where playground athletic competitions were scored partly on the basis of conduct, children had been observed circulating among their parents warning: " 'Don't sass the umpire; don't say nothin'; we'll lose our points if you do.' " In describing the movement as "better calculated to raise the standard of good citizenship than any other single agency in the hands of public servants," Chicago's director of playgrounds summed up a widely held view.[60]

In their more expansive moods, playground ideologists saw this reform as simply one step toward a more comprehensive control of urban leisure. Henry Stoddard Curtis, for example, believed that municipal authorities should operate all dance halls and "sooner or later . . . also take over the moving picture." Raymond Calkins linked his praise of the playground movement to a recommendation for municipally controlled theaters that would drive out the "unspeakably disgusting" vaudeville theaters of the day. Delos Wilcox, writing in 1904, saw the "more detailed social regulation" made possible by the playground as the initial phase of an all-inclusive program of "direct or indirect control of leisure" in the cities. Soon, he predicted, authorities would "reach out beyond the training of the youth and include to a considerable extent the care of the morals and amusements of adults as well."[61]

A work which nicely captures the heady mood of the Progressive playground movement, and the leaders' vision of its larger meaning, is *The Play Movement in the United States* (1922), by Clarence A. Rainwater, a former Chicago playground director who had gone on to teach sociology at the University of Southern California. As an agency for teaching "collective behavior," Rainwater wrote, the playground represented a vitally important means for "the control of 'individuals' [sic]" in the city. While the movement still had far to go in overcoming the "disorganization" and "degeneration" of urban life, Rainwater confidently predicted that it would gradually extend its "field of approval and adoption." The long-range objective, he declared, should be to move from the supervision of children to the "control of the remaining 80 percent of the population during the sixty-four hours per week in which even the laboring element is at leisure."[62]

By 1922, when these ambitious words were penned, the social vision they embodied was in fact already on the wane. But for a brief interval in the early twentieth century, the playground represented one of the brightest beacons of hope for those who dreamed of an urban America whose moral level—indeed, whose whole tenor of life—could be elevated to an incomparably loftier plane through the benevolent guidance of the social engineer.

17

The Civic Ideal and the Urban Moral Order

During the final game of the 1977 World's Series, as the New York Yankee fans uproariously celebrated their heroes' victory with rocks and bottles, Howard Cosell burst out indignantly: "Behavior like this is disgraceful. It is terrible. It is unthinkable. It is not worthy of this great city." Though the fact may have occurred to few television viewers, Cosell was unwittingly drawing upon a social-control technique dating from the Progressive period.

Perennially tantalized by their vision of a cohesive and homogeneous urban moral order, some Progressive urban reformers were drawn to a strategy at once simpler and more sweeping in its assumptions than any examined so far. If a park or a playground could exert a unifying moral influence, they reasoned, what might not be possible through a far more comprehensive approach? Why could not "civic loyalty" itself—that elusive abstraction which rolled so easily from Progressive tongues—provide the foundation stone of an even more close-knit and harmonious urban moral order?

The tendency to bathe cities in a mystical aura had its roots in the tensions and visionary dreams of the 1890s. "The city, in many of its functions, is a greater Church than the Church," wrote Henry Drummond in 1893. "It is amid the whirr of its machinery and the discipline of its life that the souls of men are really made." George E. Waring, Jr., New York's street-cleaning commissioner during the administration of Mayor Strong, administered to thousands of school children an oath whose force depended upon a similarly spiritualized conception of the city. "We, who are soon to be citizens of New York, the largest city on the American continent, desire to have her possess a name that is above reproach. And we therefore agree to keep from littering her streets and as far as possible to prevent others from doing the same, in order that our city may be as clean as she is great, and as pure as she is free."[1]

In the Progressive years, efforts to exploit the social-control possibilities of civic idealism reached unprecedented levels of intensity. As Jean B. Quandt has noted, social thinkers were conscious in these years of the need to achieve "a greater psychic and moral integration to match the increasing physical integration of society," and the attempt to arouse civic loyalty among the urban masses was central to that undertaking. Urban reformers outdid each other in insisting that the city was no mere chance accumulation of free-floating human atoms, but a cohesive, interconnected social organism that deserved, indeed demanded, the dedicated loyalty of all its constituent parts. "We have passed the time when a city was simply a conglomerate of individuals . . . The city is becoming a unit in the minds of its people," wrote John Ihlder in *American City* magazine in 1911. "A city, like a man, is body, mind and spirit," agreed Henry Macfarland, a former president of the Washington, D.C., board of commissioners. "It is more than the individual citizens, for it lives on."[2]

Edward A. Ross had urged in *Social Control* that emotions once channeled toward the supernatural be redirected to the civic ideal, and urban writers followed his advice with a vengeance. Invoking the Apostle John's vision of the New Jerusalem, Richard T. Ely in 1902 exhorted Americans to adopt a comparably exalted view of the spiritual potential of their urban centers, and to learn to say with the psalmist: "If I forget thee, O Chicago, O New York, O St. Louis, let my right hand forget her cunning. If I do not remember thee, let my tongue cleave to the roof of my mouth, if I prefer thee not above my chief joy." As civic loyalty of this intensity was called into being, Ely concluded, "we may look forward with the brightest anticipations to the future of the twentieth-century city." Frederic C. Howe predicted in 1906 that as the urban masses came to perceive the city as "a common authority and [a] thing to be loved and cared for," degeneracy and vice would diminish, and the city—like ancient Athens or Rome—would become a "tremendous agency for human advancement."[3]

This belief found vivid expression, too, in Newton M. Hall's 1914 work *Civic Righteousness and Civic Pride*. While confessing his dismay over the moral depravity of actual cities, Hall also perceived a divine providence in the flow of humanity cityward. Indeed, since God Himself was the author of man's social nature, it followed that the city, as the supreme expression of that nature, was the means by which the race would fulfill its divine potential. Drawing inspiration, like Ely, from the book of Revelation, Hall conjured up a shimmering vision of the "invincible" city of the future, "refined in the fires of God's love and discipline until it shines like a jasper stone most precious, clear as crystal," a city with "every evil eliminated, every wrong righted, every life transformed."[4] But Hall was a Progressive as well as a Christian millenarian, and his dreaming had its operational side. Men of vision had to act if the city's spiritual potential were to be realized. The key to a "purer social atmosphere" in urban America lay in awakening the city dweller to an awareness of his role in the unfolding moral drama, and to the "communal spirit and civic pride" that role demanded.[5]

How was this to be accomplished? How could the urban masses, in all their diversity, be made to realize their abstract obligation to promote the "ethical well-being of the whole community" when their individual preoccupations were so much more tangible and compelling? The question was an urgent one, and urban moralists like Newton Hall strove determinedly through sermons, speeches, and the printed word to animate their vision of the civic ideal's awesome moral authority.

In doing so, they often resorted to anthropomorphic imagery, describing the nation's municipalities as conscious, sentient beings. "The city is . . . a spiritual entity; it has a soul," wrote Hall. "As in the man, so in the city," declared Henry Macfarland, "the spirit is the most important. As a city thinketh in its heart so is it." Delos Wilcox, in Great Cities in America (1910), was quite explicit about the aim of such rhetoric. "The need," he wrote, "is for . . . the magic wand of feeling and intelligence that will make all cities walk before us clothed in the habiliments of human personality."[6]

From a social-control perspective, the point is clear enough. If, by the "magic wand" of their prose, these reformers could convince their generation that America's cities were destined to become organic, cohesive social units, then every city dweller's existence would derive its meaning primarily in relation to the corporate whole. His values, his every action, would be informed by an awareness of his larger civic role. The mere fact of residence in a city would take on enormous ethical significance! As Woodrow Wilson put it in addressing a conference of civic leaders in 1911, when the members of a social group selfishly pursued their individual wants at the expense of the whole, it was "just as if you separated the organs of the human body and then expected them to produce life." Josiah Strong, always sensitive to the shifting current of social thought, had anticipated this theme as early as 1898. "Every organism is composed of numberless living cells which freely give their lives for the good of the organism," he wrote, and should those individual components begin to drift away in pursuit of their own private interests under the banner "every cell for itself," the organism would die. Pursuing the analogy, he clinched his point: the "diseases" afflicting America's cities were the fault of "cells" that had not yet learned the "great social laws of service and sacrifice" and were "introducing selfishness and disorder into the social organism."[7]

This nearly idolatrous insistence on the moral authority of the city represents an interesting development in the history of urban moral-control effort. For generations, moralists had sought mechanisms by which the traditional structure of social authority could be adapted to the city—mechanisms by which the "natural moral leaders" presumed to exist in every social group could make their influence felt, just as they had in the villages of pre-urban America. The Sunday school and tract societies, the revival and city mission movements, the AICP, the YMCA, the charity organizations, and, in the Progressive era itself, the coercive moral crusades—all were manifestations of this impulse. Now, or so hoped the civic-loyalty propagandists, it would no longer be individuals or organizations whose moral force would prevail, but a disembodied collective standard sustained by the psychologically energizing power of urbanization itself. In place of the actual village order, where moral authority had in fact reposed in tangible institutions and flesh-and-blood people, they offered a "community" of the imagination whose authority depended not on day-to-day experience, but upon the manipulation of ideas and images.

Progressives of all stripes were fond of invoking such abstractions in defense of their reformist prescriptions. Croly in *The Promise of American Life*, for example, wrote grandly of the perils and challenges facing the "American ship of state" and of the "stern discipline which may eventually be imposed upon the ship's crew."[8] Our reformers simply applied this formula to their particular area of concern, invoking "civic loyalty" as justification for the moral standard and patterns of behavior they wished to see prevail. They never defined "civic loyalty" very clearly or demonstrated why its moral authority was so compelling. Nor did they explain why it should be expected to work such wonders in transforming human behavior. They simply repeated and rephrased each other's rhetoric, wafted along on the billowing gusts of their own eloquence.

By the "magic wand" of their prose, they were trying to breathe new life into a very old tradition of organicist social thought and to use it against the moral disorder of the modern city. In place of the all-powerful monarch which a Thomas Hobbes or a Robert Filmer had proposed in the seventeenth century as a counterweight to society's centrifugal tendencies, these latter-day social theorists offered the "civic ideal" as the basis of cohesion and the font of authority.

And they did so not with nostalgia or regret, but with enthusiasm. Civic loyalty was not only a new basis for urban morality but a superior one. Thanks to "the religious enthusiasm of civic endeavor [and] civic patriotism," wrote Henry Macfarland in 1911, "the city more and more is repenting and beginning a new life." In the new urban-industrial age, Simon Patten insisted, there existed no greater agency of moral influence than the city itself, and "social workers should idealize and purify" it just as moralists once sanctified the home and tried to preserve it from the buffetings of social change.[9]

Patten's suggestion that the city would soon assume the moral role once held by the family (with its implication that the city therefore merited a comparable degree of loyalty and devotion) was echoed by many reformers. Newton Hall portrayed the city as benevolently overseeing "the lives of all its children, shielding them from evil, educating them in all good things, ministering to the sense of beauty, [and] stimulating the best and highest powers." Richard T. Ely put the matter in a nutshell: "All that is best in our nature," he wrote, "is called out by this ideal—the city a well-ordered household."[10]

How to awaken the masses to the imperative need for a higher level of civic loyalty? One way was to give the rather elusive concept of "civic idealism" tangible form through allegorical expression. By no coincidence, the Progressive years saw the production of many municipally sponsored pageants portraying symbolically various cities' history and aspirations—or at least the aspirations of the pageants' managers. As we have seen, playground leaders were often active in sponsoring such pageants. On Labor Day, 1913, for example, at a playground in Chicago's Palmer Park, an elaborate civic pageant was produced that included among its features a tableau in which Labor and Capital joined hands to symbolize their united commitment to harmony and progress. Such pageants, declared a committee of the Playground Association of America, were "the greatest and most characteristic form of democratic art" and an excellent way to "interpret the ideals of the people to themselves."[11]

The most enthusiastic exponent of the civic pageant idea was the poet Percy MacKaye, son of the well-known dramatist and theatrical innovator Steele MacKaye, who summed up his message in the titles of his two books on the subject: *The Civic Theatre in Relation to the Redemption of Leisure* (1912) and *Community Drama: Its Motive and Method of Neighborliness* (1917). Having written and produced an outdoor pageant at the summer home of the sculptor Augustus Saint-Gaudens in Cornish, New Hampshire, in 1905, MacKaye began to dream of extending this dramatic form to urban America. The "nobly sensuous symbolism" of the civic drama would not only provide an alternative to the "vicious and destructive" commercial theater, he contended, but, more important, it would transform "estrangement and conflict . . . into harmony" by awakening the urban masses to a "sense of their common citizenship and humanity." As a "science of cooperative expression," he was convinced, civic pageantry was the ideal medium for translating into the adult world the social harmony and cooperativeness of the playground. The "heaving ground-swell of idealism" that carried Woodrow Wilson to the White House in 1912, he believed, would also help establish the civic-theater idea in America's cities.[12]

The most ambitious effort to translate Percy MacKaye's ideas into practice and give dramatic expression to the moral potential of civic idealism was a great "Pageant and Masque" staged in Saint Louis in May 1914. Fourth in size among the nation's cities by 1914, Saint Louis's moral reputation still left something to be desired. In the 1870s had come the shocking "Whisky Ring" scandals and, for some, the even more shocking legalization of prostitution. In the nineties, the city's political corruption became so notorious that Lincoln Steffens placed his Saint Louis chapter first in *The Shame of the Cities* (1902). But the reformers had always fought back. Legalized prostitution was abolished and, thanks to District Attorney Joseph W. Folk, the boodlers were thrown out of city hall. The rehabilitation process was furthered by the Louisiana Purchase Exposition of 1904 ("Meet me in Saint Louie, Louie; Meet me at the Fair"), but the heavy immigration of the early twentieth century—including increasing numbers of southern blacks migrating northward—aroused profound uneasiness among the city's established elements.

It was against this backdrop that a group of "civic, business, improvement, and professional organizations" in 1913 launched plans for an outdoor pageant commemorating the 150th anniversary of the city's founding. The aim, according to Charlotte Rumbold, secretary of the St. Louis Public Recreation Commission, who originated the idea, was no less than to arouse Saint Louis to "a sense of its solidarity"—to weld its heterogeneous population of 800,000 into "a community under the spell of a unifying idealism." Roger N. Baldwin of the Saint Louis Civic League offered an even more revealing insight into the concerns that underlay the idea. "Behind the greatest civic drama ever projected in the United States," he wrote in the *Survey* as planning for the pageant went forward, "lies the idea of building on a spectacle of the past a new city unity for the future. . . . It was conceived and promoted . . . to rouse a great city to a sense of unity, of common understanding, of common effort. . . . Saint Louis needs to learn that lesson. Like many other cities, Saint Louis is divided within itself—geographically, racially, socially. Its very prosperity and even [its] growth have prevented that vitalizing of domestic relations on which democratic processes for the common welfare build. So the great drama is to visualize the city's life, and bring forth into expression all the latent power for a new citizenship."[13]

The event was a memorable success. For four successive spring nights, upwards of 100,000 Saint Louisans, drawn by a carefully orchestrated publicity campaign, thronged a vast natural amphitheater in Forest Park to marvel as a cast of 1,500 and a massed chorus of 750 voices performed the long historical drama. First to be performed was a long pageant by Thomas Wood Stevens, featuring realistic reenactments of scenes from the city's past. These were followed by an even more ambitious masque, from the pen of Percy MacKaye, treating that same history allegorically. In this part of the presentation the city was personified as Saint Louis himself, first as a baby, then as an awesome deity with commanding voice and gleaming sword. First come the pioneers, subduing in turn nature, the Indians, and the corrupting power of gold. "Our Trails are cleared; the Earth Spirits are tamed," Saint Louis exults. "What can withstand—Who shall defy us now?" "Lead us, Saint Louis!" shout the pioneers in response.[14]

But then come the immigrants—the World Adventurers—bearing their various national banners and followed by "haggard women and forlorn children, old men bowed over, and young men darkly brooding." Next Poverty stumbles on the scene with her frightening brood: Shame (draped in scarlet), Vice, Plague, and Rebellion. Alarmed as these menacing apparitions moan and groan at his feet, Saint Louis calls upon his fellow cities for aid, and as figures representing New York, Chicago, and New Orleans march across the stage in an impressive "Pageant of the Cities," Poverty, Vice, and the other stricken figures arise, "new clad in forms of light and graciousness."[15]

"O sisters—brothers—cities Leagued by Love!" Saint Louis cries,

> If we are dreaming, let us scorn to wake;
> Or waking, let us shape the sordid world
> To likeness of our dreams.[16]

The masque's stirring finale included fireworks, the release of a flock of pigeons, an airplane fly-by (the first use of the airplane to serve the "symbolism of dramatic poetry," MacKaye noted), and an anthem by the chorus beginning: "Out of the formless void, Beauty and Order are born."[17]

Even the sponsors were awed by what they had achieved, and in magazine articles and a printed report they reflected on its meaning. This "stupendous civic spectacle," wrote real-estate man John H. Gundlach, chairman of the pageant's executive committee, had sprung from "the breast of the people. The spirit of the playground, arch-enemy of caste, was the germ that animated the thought of this municipal art into life." The pageant spirit, he added, was "much akin to that awakened by a call to arms, in defense of country." Charlotte Rumbold, echoing Washington Gladden's vision of urban unity in *The Cosmopolis City Club*, emphasized that this was a cooperative achievement of people drawn from "every ward and precinct of the city," representing "every nationality, profession, trade, religion, and social status."[18]

Gundlach particularly emphasized the "efficiency of organization" by which the vast audience assembled each night "without perceptible noise, without disorder"—a "human mass, shoulder to shoulder, overflowing the crest of the hill, waiting in hushed silence and expectancy." And then had come "the great cast, like a well-trained corps of veterans, each one to his appointed place without confusion, without haste; a tribute to the men and women who were directing their respective departments to an end of harmony and beauty." (The chairman of the pageant's finance committee similarly marvelled at "the wonderful order shown, not only on the stage, but by the audience.")[19]

For many residents of Saint Louis, the Pageant and Masque was far more than simply a commemorative observance or a pleasant spring diversion. "The main reason for the Pageant," wrote Gundlach, "was to foster community spirit," and that goal had been achieved. "As the first strains of melody . . . floated upon the vast audience on that rare May evening, there came over all the sense of sanctified citizenship, of interest and confidence in neighbor, of pride in the city."[20]

But how deep was the impression? Would it all become only a

"pleasant but vague memory"? Would the "wonderfully aroused civic spirit" be sacrificed to the "immediate and petty personal interests that so often confuse and cloud issues of civic progress"? Was the "love of city" the drama had called forth simply the "froth and silver on the crest of the incoming wave, to be lost as it washes the sands of time," or would it prove to be "the tide of a mighty ocean of human cooperation which will carry us to a higher level of intimate human contact and consequent civic accomplishment"?[21]

The prospects were uncertain, but Gundlach inclined to optimism. The "civic consciousness" that had been aroused, he predicted, would permanently deepen the "understanding of neighbor toward neighbor" and enhance "the possibilities of common effort intelligently applied." Henceforth, Saint Louis, with its checkered past and its uneasy present, would-be animated by "a sustained public spirit" promoting civic advance and uplift.[22]

The Saint Louis Pageant and Masque and similar undertakings in other cities aroused keen interest in urban reform circles—an interest expressed in 1916 by an invitation from the American Civic Association to Percy MacKaye to address its national convention. At a moment when Progressive reform energies stood at their zenith, Saint Louis had offered an impressive symbolic portrayal of a conviction that underlay much of the urban uplift effort in these years: loyalty to the city itself—or to a rarefied, abstract civic ideal—could serve as a potent instrument for at last bringing harmony, order, and moral cohesion to urban America.

18

The Civic Ideal Made Real

THE MORAL VISION OF THE
PROGRESSIVE CITY PLANNERS

Woodrow Wilson, reform governor of New Jersey and rising star
in national politics, was in an impatient mood when he rose to
address a gathering of municipal reformers in October 1911. It
was all very well, Wilson declared, to proclaim that the key to
achieving a better social and moral climate in the city lay in creating a heightened sense of civic loyalty and community cohesiveness, but the central issue was *how*. "Don't you see that
you produce communities by creating common feeling?" he demanded. "What really counts in our action is *feeling*."[1]

Despite his characteristically hectoring tone, Wilson's point
was a shrewd one. If civic loyalty were to become an effective
instrument of urban social control, it had to be made compellingly
real, not just in ephemeral pageants, but through sustained appeals to people's feelings and emotions. "If you want a great
movement, a movement that shall penetrate to the depths," Felix
Adler told the National Municipal League in 1904, "you must appeal to the imagination." Herbert Croly, in a slightly different
context, made the same point in *The Promise of American Life*.
"There is only one way in which popular standards and prefer-
ences can be improved," he wrote; "The men whose standards
are higher must learn to express their better message in a popu-
larly interesting manner." Only when the higher standard had
been "made to look good to them" would the public rally behind
it.[2] In short, the problem Wilson posed was a real and urgent one:

How were the urban masses—their numbers swelling with every immigrant ship that docked—to be imbued with the conviction that civic loyalty ought decisively to shape their behavior and ethical outlook?

The challenge was heightened by the paucity of landmarks, traditions, and civic symbols in most American cities. Writers from Charles Brockden Brown to Henry James had lamented the "thinness" of America's urban scene for literary purposes, and in these years the social implications of that thinness attracted notice as well. Where were the American Arcs de Triomphe, Piazzas San Marco, or Trafalgar Squares? In the United States, lamented Josiah Strong in 1907, cities were "not old enough to be overgrown and beautified by legend and romance as ancient castles are with ivy. There is no twilight to stimulate the imagination." This rawness and bland anonymity, he concluded, had stunted the growth of civic interest and pride. James Bryce made the same point in *The American Commonwealth* (1888), and Edward Bellamy and William T. Stead liberally supplied their urban utopias with the fountains, squares, boulevards, and civic edifices the actual cities of their day so conspicuously lacked. The task of the moment, declared John Nolen, a Massachusetts landscape architect, in 1909, was "to develop the individuality of our cities" and to give every city a distinct "personality" as a way of promoting "love and pride in local traditions and local ideals." The focal point of a "Model Street" at the Saint Louis fair of 1904, a little monument called "Civic loyalty," was in fact a poignant reminder of how fragile that loyalty actually was, and what scant nourishment was available to it in the drab and faceless immigrant-industrial city.[3]

The conviction that an intimate link existed between a city's physical appearance and its moral state—and that America's cities were sadly deficient on this score—was central to the "city beautiful" movement, a surge of interest in civic betterment and beautification that began in the mid-1890s and crested in the first two or three years of the twentieth century. The city beautiful enthusiasm has proved difficult for historians to deal with, because its structure and objectives were so diffuse. By 1905, according to one partisan's happy report, no fewer than 2,426 "improvement societies" of various description were at work in cities throughout the land. Even mention of the leading organizations can quickly turn into a chronicle: the Municipal Art Society of New York (1893), the American Park and Outdoor Art Association (1897), the Architectural League of America and its National Committee on Municipal Improvements and Civic Embellishments (1899), the American League for Civic Improvement (1900), the American Civic Association (1904)—on and on the list could go. In periodicals like the *American City, Charities and the Commons,* the *Survey,* and *Municipal Affairs* (founded in 1897 by the Reform Club of New York), these groups kept in touch and traded improvement ideas. Superficially, their betterment projects seem impossibly diverse. Some campaigned to eliminate factory pollution, ugly billboards, unsightly fences, overhead electrical wires, and street refuse. (The latter goal seemed more attainable as horses were replaced ·by motorized vehicles.) Others planted trees, shrubs, and flower beds along city streets, cleaned up alleys and vacant lots, and sponsored home beautification contests. Still other groups, particularly those established by artists, called for the adornment of public buildings and squares with statuary, fountains, and murals, and the commissioning of more aesthetically pleasing boulevards, bridges, streetlights, and even trash cans. Around 1902, as city beautiful enthusiasm shifted toward the more comprehensive city-planning movement, many of these organizations began to propagandize for civic centers and other more ambitious undertakings.[4] But though the specific projects were piecemeal and particularistic in nature, the long-range goal of the city beautiful evangelists was no less than the physical transformation of the city.

The motivations underlying the city beautiful movement are nearly as difficult to sort out as its varied manifestations. The president of the American Civic Association saw it simply as a "bubbling and uprising of the desire for better things" and compared it to an irresistible natural phenomenon. "It takes a snowball to start an avalanche, and we have a thousand such snowballs gathering force in a thousand communities! With a little help we can have these associated avalanches roll in whitening purity over ten thousand dirt spots in America."[5] Accepting such contemporary assessments at face value, historians have typically portrayed this movement as the unselfish work of "public spirited citizens [who] gradually became aware of the gross deficiencies in their environment and determined to remedy matters."[6]

If a disinterested philanthropic impulse led some reformers into the city beautiful movement, the issue for others was primarily aesthetic: billboards, belching smokestacks, and filthy streets were ugly; sparkling fountains, wide boulevards, and gleaming marble public buildings were deeply gratifying to the senses. For still others, a nagging feeling of national inferiority and backwardness in the arts—a pained awareness of the squat plainness of the average American city in contrast to the great centers of Europe—played a role. Under the leadership of important figures in the arts such as the sculptor Augustus Saint-

Gaudens and the architects Charles McKim and Richard M. Hunt, turn-of-the-century American artists organized to remedy this situation and "convert city government to art patronage."[7]

Boosterism and status considerations played a part as well: the desire to enhance one's own self-image by enhancing the beauty of one's city. Thorstein Veblen, predictably, saw this as the motive. In *The Theory of the Leisure Class* (1899), Veblen dismissed Chicago's park programs and incipient city-planning projects as merely illustrative of the "great cultural principle of conspicuous waste."[8]

And for some capitalists, the appeal of the city beautiful lay no deeper than their pocketbooks: ugliness, dirt, and disorder were bad for business; a more attractive and orderly city would surely attract more customers and investors. In 1899, after a violence-plagued transit workers' strike in Cleveland, a local businessman called for accelerated work on a new civic center to counteract the city's image as a place of "rioting, bloodshed, and anarchy." Even Chicago architect Daniel H. Burnham, whose commitment to civic beautification had complex sources, was not above bald appeals to the profit motive. "Beauty has always paid better than any other commodity," he told the Chicago Commercial Club in 1907, "and always will."[9]

But none of these motives goes to the heart of the city beautiful movement. Fundamentally, it sprang from the conviction that a more livable and attractive urban environment would call forth an answering surge of civic loyalty from the urban populace, and that this in turn would retard or even reverse the decay of social and moral cohesiveness which seemed so inevitable a concomitant of the rise of cities. As an editorial in the Dayton, Ohio, *Daily Journal* put it in 1901, a more beautiful city would surely be a place of superior "moral development."[10]

If a tradition-laden urban past could not be summoned up, the city of today could be made more attractive, and thus a more compelling symbol of the moral authority of the civic ideal. A Boston University law professor developed the argument in very explicit terms in these years. "An important result of these city movements is the development of civic interest and pride on the part of the people. A city which does nothing except to police and clean the streets means little. But, when it adds schools, libraries, galleries, parks, baths, lights, heat, homes and transportation, it awakens interest in itself. The citizen cares for the city which shows some care for him. He looks upon it as his city, and not as a thing apart from him; and he becomes a good citizen because it is his city."[11] The motto of the New York Municipal Art Society conveyed the same point in twelve words: "To make us love our city, we must make our city lovely." Or, as Robert A. Pope, a

New York City landscape architect put it in 1909, "The beautiful city . . . makes possible a more beautiful life."[12]

The most influential Progressive-era exponent of this view was Charles Mulford Robinson, a Rochester journalist who became a major city beautiful publicist and consultant, and, from 1913 until his death in 1917, professor of civic design at the University of Illinois. In *The Improvement of Towns and Cities* (1901), the often-reprinted *Modern Civic Art; or, The City Made Beautiful* (1903), and numerous speeches and articles, Robinson expounded his belief that a "lovely and uplifting" urban environment was the key to "the forward . . . movement of the race." A beautiful city—and the dedicated effort required to achieve it—could awaken in city dwellers "high desires that had before been dormant," thereby spurring civic idealism and ethical growth. "He who loves his city," Robinson wrote, "is a better citizen and a better man."[13]

Civic beautification effort would be especially well received by the poor, Robinson believed, because it dealt with "conditions before their very eyes, to the avoidance of abstractions." While granting the aesthetic appeal of urban diversity and picturesque immigrant enclaves (so long as they observed "just standards of morality"), he insisted that the city's prime concern must be to promulgate a single civic ideal and impress "its own individuality on the poor districts." If vigorously pursued in the poorer wards, he predicted, beautification efforts would "awaken ambition," "encourage the love of the beautiful," and ultimately create "purer souls."[14]

Like Woodrow Wilson, Robinson assumed that for the masses "sentiment" was "the most powerful of forces for social and civic good or ill," and he offered specific suggestions for making the civic ideal more emotionally compelling. He proposed, for example, that every municipality adopt a distinctive official insignia and prominently display it on every structure and piece of apparatus, so that "by reiteration there will arise a consciousness and love of that abstract thing, the city." Just as the flag was loved as the national symbol, "so this insignia will be loved because it stands for a loved city."[15]

Robinson also urged the development of urban "focal points" as a way of heightening civic consciousness. Domes, fountains, and statuary, he wrote, would beautify the city "not merely in appearance, but in that higher sense . . . that demands the devotion, loyalty, and pride of its citizens."[16]

Recalling the memorable World's Fair "Court of Honor," Robinson contended that a comparably imposing civic center should be the capstone of any beautification scheme. The "dignity and importance" of stately municipal buildings, he believed, could exert a powerful moral force, in making the city "more pride-worthy . . . , more majestic, [and] better worth the devotion and service of its citizens." By the same token, such edifices should never be scattered in the "wilderness" of commercial structures, but grouped together and given "all the additional emphasis and conspicuousness that site can offer." Ideally, they should be situated on a promontory where they would "visibly dominate" the city: "To them the community would look up, seeing them lording over it at every turn, as, in fact, the government ought to do."[17]

For Charles Mulford Robinson, in short, the "civic battle between Ugliness and Beauty" was an ethical struggle no less than an aesthetic one, and its successful outcome would mean not mere surface prettification, but a "moral, intellectual, and administrative" gain of the highest significance. Whenever the "vision of a new London, a new Washington, Chicago, or New York breaks with the morning's sunshine upon the degradation, discomfort, and baseness of modern city life," he wrote in the soaring rhetoric of the day, "a new dream and a new hope" were born.[18]

Not all found the city beautiful ideal so seductive. At the 1912 convention of the American Civic Association a speaker still rooted in an earlier social-control tradition denounced the city beautifiers for concentrating on "frills and furbelows" while "the hideous slum, reeking with filth and disease, rotten with crime, is sapping the very life-blood of the city." Even Herbert Croly, despite his ideological affinity with the assumptions underlying Robinson's ideas, considered his "civic art millenium" a "bit of poetry," and warned that Robinson's dream city would be "less amusing, less suggestive, and in a real sense less habitable than the degraded but living cities of to-day."[19]

But Croly's skepticism was not the prevailing view. In its day, the city beautiful movement held a seductive appeal for many as an imaginative response to the ever-looming menace of the city. In statues, fountains, and tree-lined boulevards, its proponents believed, they had at last discovered an antidote to urban moral decay and social disorder.

From the City Beautiful to City Planning:
The Moral Dimension Remains Central

As the city beautiful movement evolved, many of its partisans became persuaded that piecemeal beautification and improvement must give way to more comprehensive, integrated approaches. A degree of planning had characterized American urban development since the eighteenth century, and in the 1840s Robert Fleming Gourlay had produced a plan for Boston involving a succession of circumferential streets radiating concentrically outward from the center. (Gourlay included eight such streets in his plan, beginning with Washington and ending with Van Buren, presumably believing that Boston's further growth and the accession of new presidents would proceed at an exactly equal pace.)[20]

It was in the early twentieth century, however, that the movement attracted public notice, gained professional stature, and took on a heavy freight of social meaning. The immediate impetus was the creation by Congress in 1901 of a prestigious commission of architects, artists, and landscape designers to draw up plans for the completion of Pierre L'Enfant's 1791 design for Washington, D.C. Olmsted's great nineteenth-century parks played a role, as did the Chicago World's Fair, contemporary city-planning advances in Germany, and the writings of the Britishers Ebenezer Howard and Patrick Geddes. In *Tomorrow: The Peaceful Path to Real Reform* (1898), Howard set forth his vision of a network of "garden cities" to house the English working class. As orderly and symmetrical as compass and ruler could make them, Howard's ideal cities featured greenbelts alternating with residential and business sections, and rapid transit to the factory. (Howard's ideals found partial expression in Letchworth, a planned community established near London in 1903.) A United States Garden City Association was founded in 1906 by W. D. P. Bliss, but the movement's American influence was less in inspiring the creation of new towns than in heightening interest in transforming existing ones.[21] Geddes, a Scottish biologist with a gifted amateur's interest in city planning, influenced American thought through a series of lectures in Boston in 1899 and still more through his 1904 work *City Development.*[22]

In actual city-planning effort, New York and San Francisco were the first to follow the lead of Washington. The New York City Improvement Commission was created by the aldermen in 1903 and charged with drawing up a plan, and in 1904 a group of civic and business leaders established an Association for the Improvement and Adornment of San Francisco and retained Daniel H. Burnham to develop a comprehensive plan for the Golden Gate city. (Burnham's sweeping proposals, submitted in 1905 but quickly superseded by the earthquake and fire of 1906, were never implemented.) The year 1907 saw the publication of *The New York City Improvement Plan* and the establishment in Hartford of a permanent city-planning agency—the first anywhere. Two years later came Benjamin Marsh's *Introduction to City Planning* and the landmark *Plan of Chicago* by Daniel Burnham and Edward H. Bennett, as well as the first national city-planning conference in Washington. The American City Planning Institute, a professional association, was founded in 1917, and by the end of the decade some 300 cities had established planning commissions. By this time even friends of the movement were complaining that "city planning has become a fad."[23]

Like the city beautiful vogue from which it sprang, the city-planning movement must be viewed against a background of profound apprehension about the moral fate of the city. It was, in fact, the culminating expression of the positive environmentalists' effort to achieve moral and social ends through environmental means. As Benjamin Marsh put it in 1909, "A city without a plan is like a ship without a rudder."[24]

The movement's moral significance, heavily emphasized in its literature and at the 1909 city-planning conference in Washington, was nowhere more pointedly underscored than in *What of the City* (1919), a hymn in praise of city planning by Walter D. Moody of the Chicago Plan Commission. For decades, he wrote, American cities had "stunted" the moral development of their inhabitants, and now—with newcomers pouring in and the maintenance of "good order" becoming increasingly problematic—they faced the threatening consequences. The answer was as obvious as it was urgent: "The remedy must be found in planning." (Displaying the usual cavalier attitude toward earlier urban moral-control efforts, Moody insisted that before the advent of city planning, "practically nothing" had been done for the "moral, sociological, and physical upbuilding" of city dwellers.) For Moody, as for Charles Mulford Robinson, the importance of planning lay not primarily in the physical transformation it promised, but in its effect upon the "conflict between the opposing elements of good and evil" raging in every great city.[25]

San Francisco offers a particularly graphic illustration of the way city planning could function as an alternative strategy for pursuing traditional moral-reform objectives. The Association for the Improvement and Adornment of San Francisco, sponsor of Daniel Burnham's city plan of 1905, was almost identical in composition to the group that had supported Mayor James D. Phelan's reform administration (1897–1901) in its crusades against prostitution, gambling, and other forms of urban vice. Defeated in 1901 by boss Abraham Ruef and his handpicked choice for mayor, the reformers turned to city planning as an alternative avenue to the kind of morally pure city they sought.[26]

At times, the moral-control objective was acknowledged quite openly. One of the advantages of the civic center proposed for Cleveland in 1903, its planners noted, was that it would require the razing of an area notorious for its brothels and saloons. In a speech at the Washington city-planning conference in 1909, New York banker and real-estate figure Henry Morgenthau (father of the future treasury secretary) declared that the planners' primary assignment should be to wipe out the slums that were the breeding places of "disease, moral depravity, discontent, and socialism."[27] In 1910, presenting a city plan for New Haven, Connecticut—a Yankee bastion reeling under the impact of immigration —Frederick Law Olmsted, Jr., spoke bluntly of the project's class basis and social objectives. "People of the old New England stock still to a large extent control the city, and if they want New Haven to be a fit and worthy place for their descendants it behooves them to establish conditions about the lives of *all* the people that will make the best fellow-citizens of them and of their children."[28]

Generally, however, the movement's social objectives were cast in terms that were both more hopeful and more artfully imprecise. The aim, wrote one enthusiast in 1909, was to create "a new sense of citizenship," and arouse "a new and vital interest in the city as our common heritage." The plan proposed for New York, declared that city's planning commission, would give it "monuments worthy of its importance," thereby enhancing "the civic pride of its citizens." Joseph Lee, welcoming city planning as a natural extension of the playground reform, defined its objectives in similarly lofty and generalized terms. "The child should be helped to carry his city and his country with him in imagination," Lee wrote in 1915; "to this end we must make much use of symbols . . . We must preserve and dignify our monuments, erect our public buildings in a spirit of reverence for the Commonwealth."[29] Even Olmsted retreated from his 1910 candor into the blander rhetoric of civic harmony. The modern city was "one great social organism," he wrote in 1916, and city planning was simply an effort to express that organic unity and the "interdependence" of all its elements.[30]

But whether expressed baldly or obliquely, such comments offer a revealing insight into the thinking of this first generation of city planners. Over the decades, a succession of reformers— Bible and tract distributors, Sunday school teachers, YMCA secretaries, charity organization workers, and the others who have passed through these pages—had seen themselves as indispensable instruments in controlling the moral and social development of the urban masses. Now, under the altered circumstances of the early twentieth century, the city planners translated familiar social-control objectives into the idiom of environmental improvement. "The making of the new city will mean the making of a new citizen," declared a confident Charles Zueblin of the University of Chicago in 1903, "and the process is in no sense visionary."[31] Ten years before, in a poem celebrating the Chicago World's Fair and the decorum its buildings seemed to inspire in the fairgoers, Richard Watson Gilder had anticipated some of the messianic spirit which soon would suffuse the city-planning movement:

> Ah, silent multitudes, ye are a part,
> Of the wise architect's supreme and glorious art.[32]

But it was the president of the New York City board of aldermen in the Progressive years, a staunch city-planning advocate, who perhaps best summed up the movement's social-control dimension as the planners preferred to view it. "City planning . . . is the guidance into proper channels of a community's impulses towards a larger and broader life. On the face it has to do with things physical . . . , [b]ut its real significance is far deeper; a proper city plan has a powerful influence for good upon the mental and moral development of the people."[33]

Few careers better illuminate the social outlook of the early city-planning movement than that of the man mainly responsible for the White City of 1893 that Gilder found so inspiring: Daniel Hudson Burnham. Sharing with his contemporary William James a deep mystical strain (perhaps, like James's, the product of a childhood saturated in Swedenborgianism), Burnham brought to all his projects an outlook summed up in his oft-quoted motto: "Make no little plans; they have no magic to stir men's blood."[34] This power to "stir men's blood" was, for him, what gave city planning its high moral significance.

Born in 1846 in upstate New York, Burnham's earliest social experiences beyond the family were, as for so many urban moral reformers, those of the country village. Soon, however, he came with his parents to Chicago where his father prospered in the wholesale drug business. Here, in 1873, after a period of drift and uncertainty, Daniel joined with John W. Root in the practice of architecture. For the next eighteen years, until Root's death in 1891, the two were heavily engaged in designing the mansions, churches, banks, and office buildings of the emergent commercial elites in the major cities. Burnham and Root played an important role in the development of the skyscraper in these years, in keeping with their underlying objective: to create an urban architecture that would "convey in some large elemental sense an idea of the great stable, conserving forces of modern civilization."[35]

Never veering from that objective, Burnham, after his partner's death, pursued it increasingly through public architecture and civic design. Clearly a decisive factor in this shift was his achievement as chief of construction for the Chicago World's Fair. The triumph of 1893 convinced Burnham of the social possibilities of municipal architecture, and from that year onward he turned his energies to a succession of large-scale civic design projects: in Washington, Cleveland, San Francisco, and, finally, his own Chicago. His periodic exhortations to Chicagoans—especially the commercial elite—to translate the ephemeral achievement of 1893 into a permanent reshaping of their city met with little response at first, but if the businessmen of Chicago were slower than their brethren elsewhere to catch the city-planning vision, their conversion, when it came, was complete. In 1906 the Merchants' Club retained Burnham to prepare a city plan, and with the merger of the Merchants' Club and the older Commercial Club a short time later, the organized business interests of Chicago were lined up solidly behind the idea.[36] This, then, was the background for the publication, on the Fourth of July, 1909, of the *Plan of Chicago*, in many respects the quintessential expression of the social vision underlying the Progressive city-planning movement.

No dry technical treatise, the *Plan of Chicago* was designed to persuade, and it still remains seductive after the passage of many chastening years. A beautifully crafted quarto volume, enhanced by delicate architectural drawings, sepia photographs, and dreamlike water-color renderings by the muralist Jules Guérin, this is a quietly passionate visual and verbal evocation of Burnham's vision of the city of the future.

Like Edward Bellamy and William T. Stead, Burnham effectively contrasted his dream city with the bleak reality of Chicago as it was: a city almost overwhelmed by rampant industrial expansion and a ceaseless influx of immigrants. Years of "formless growth" had spawned the familiar array of urban evils: poverty, congestion, immorality, ugliness, and "the frequent outbreaks against law and order which result from narrow and pleasureless lives." The "disorder, vice, and disease" among Chicago's poor, warned Burnham, menaced the "moral and physical health" of the population and indeed "the well-being of the city itself."[37]

But, happily, the period of drift was ending. The World's Fair had revealed that "the soul of Chicago" was "vital and dominant," and now at last the city's "practical men of affairs" had recognized that Chicago's larger problems could be mastered by a comparably determined effort. "Chicago, in common with other great cities, realizes that the time has come to bring order out of the chaos incident to rapid growth, and . . . the influx of people of many nationalities without common traditions or habits of life."[38]

How, precisely, did Burnham propose to deal with the social, moral, and physical challenges facing the city? In part, he hoped to combat them through direct and open social-control stratagems: "cutting . . . broad thoroughfares through the unwholesome district," for example, or, as a last resort, forcibly relocating those city dwellers "so degraded by long life in the slums that they have lost all power of caring for themselves." He also planned to enlarge Chicago's park system, in the spirit of Frederick Law Olmsted's belief in the moral power of grass and trees. The person who maintained "close contact with nature," Burnham contended, would develop "saner methods of thought" than one exposed only to "the artificiality of the city." Through the beneficent influence of parks, he believed, "mind and body are restored to a normal condition, and we are enabled to take up the burden of life in our crowded streets and endless stretches of buildings with renewed vigor and hopefulness."[39]

But Burnham's conception of the social mission of city planning was more subtle than the above might suggest. The idea was not just to build more parks or to uproot the slums. The fundamental object of Burnham's vast plan was to restore to the city a lost visual and aesthetic harmony, thereby creating the physical prerequisite for the emergence of a harmonious social order. The city planner's great opportunity—and solemn obligation—was to wage battle against the external physical disorder that was both a symptom and a cause of the city's deeper spiritual malaise.

The disarray and inharmoniousness of the city, observed Burnham in a striking passage, intruded even into the habitation of the dead. In the villages of bygone days, he wrote, "the old churchyards, with their serried ranks of slate headstones, their cypresses and weeping willows, and their rows of tombs, made a direct appeal to the deepest feelings of the human heart." In the city, by contrast, "the disorder of the modern . . . cemetery would seem to carry the idea of turbulence even to the grave itself."[40]

Burnham's ideal city was, above all, one that would foster the "love of good order." Indeed, the word *order*—along with *harmony* and *dignity*—runs like a leitmotif through the *Plan of Chicago*. Making the city more orderly meant beginning with its public areas: the parks, squares, boulevards, and especially the public buildings. Like Charles Mulford Robinson, Burnham viewed the design and arrangement of municipal edifices as the heart of city planning. It is hard to convey the enthusiasm and eloquence with which he described the great civic complexes that loomed over the Chicago of his dreams and discussed their role in the city's social and moral evolution.

Struck by the awe the human mind experiences in "contemplating orderly architectural arrangements of great magnitude," Burnham saw in this instinctive response an important instrument of social and moral leverage: "the city has a dignity to be maintained; ... good order is essential to material advancement," and "impressive groupings of public buildings" would promote those objectives.[41] In their magnitude, orderliness, and symmetry, these structures would express Chicago's "unity and dignity," and symbolize "in concrete form the feeling of loyalty to and pride in the city." When constructed, they would represent "a long step toward cementing together the [city's] heterogeneous elements."[42]

Furthermore—and most important—this "cementing together" of Chicago's diverse population would be achieved not by coercion or exhortation, but through a pervasive visual appeal to the "higher emotions of the human mind." Only in this way could a city "truly exercise dominion" over its inhabitants.[43]

This insistence on the importance of reinforcing architecturally the social values of order and dignity was no new theme for Burnham in 1909. Immediately before the Chicago project, he had designed an administrative capital for the Philippine Islands —newly acquired by the United States in the aftermath of the Spanish-American War—and in the Plan of Chicago he suggested that just as that design had symbolized the "power and dignity" of imperial America, so Chicago's municipal structures should express the superiority of the civic claim over personal interests or wants.[44]

In the Plan of Chicago, the reiteration of these themes becomes almost hypnotic: the complex of cultural institutions envisioned for Grant Park must be "impressive and dignified"; the design of the county courthouse must symbolize the "dignity, majesty and impartiality of justice"; a straightened and widened Michigan Avenue "would be to the city what the backbone is to the body"; the civic center must express the "dignity and importance of the city from the administrative point of view."[45]

The building on which Burnham lavished the greatest attention in the Plan of Chicago was the imposing and majestic city hall, the focal point of his proposed civic-center complex and the keystone of the whole plan. "The central building is planned not only to dominate the place in front of it, but also to mark the center of the city from afar and [to be] a monument to the spirit of civic unity . . . [I]n the center of all the varied activities of Chicago will rise the towering dome . . . , vivifying and unifying the entire composition."[46] Burnham gave his imagination full rein in evoking the awesomeness of his projected city hall: "Rising from the plain upon which Chicago rests, its effect may be compared to that of the dome of St. Peter's at Rome."[47]

Daniel Burnham's vast conception was well served by the brush of Jules Guérin. His delicate and tranquil paintings, with their softened light, muted colors, and subordination of technical exactitude to overall impression, exude the essential spirit of the *Plan of Chicago*. In Guérin's vision of Chicago, as in Burnham's, there is no hint of congestion, of discordant elements, or even of human diversity. The city he portrayed was large to be sure, but what catches the eye is not the undifferentiated blur of private structures stretching into the horizon, but the great primary civic elements: the sweeping boulevards, the imposing squares, the breathtaking lakefront development, and above all the overmastering civic center with its soaring city hall dominating a city that almost literally lies prostrate at its base.

Burnham and the plan in which he took such pride have not fared well at the hands of city-planning historians. John W. Reps faults his obsession with "monumental structures" and his neglect of the city's "more pressing social and economic ills." In the same vein, Mel Scott dismisses his "American Paris on the shores of Lake Michigan" as "an essentially aristocratic city, pleasing to the merchant princes who participated in its conception but not meeting some of the basic economic and human needs."[48] George F. Chadwick sees the *Plan of Chicago* as a mere exercise in aestheticism—"an architect's conception; an ordering of the city to visual ends." Burnham's projected city hall, scoffs Vincent Scully, was "a dome on a drum . . . attenuated to skyscraper proportions." The Cleveland civic-center plan of which he was principal author, write John Burchard and Albert Bush-Brown, was "an empty, lifeless memorial to the City Beautiful idea." And Burnham's most recent biographer notes the "paradoxical" contrast between his willingness to take on the architectural challenge of the modern industrial city and the "antique academic formulas" with which he answered that challenge.[49] Particularly puzzling has been Burnham's proposal to limit all private structures in Chicago to some twenty stories: a limitation which he of all men had reason to know was hopelessly unrealistic in the era of the skyscraper.

In accounting for the impracticality, archaic classicism, and seeming aesthetic megalomania of the *Plan of Chicago*, city-planning historians have placed the blame variously on the philistinism of Burnham's business sponsors, on his compulsion to re-create the success of the 1893 World's Fair, on the early removal of John W. Root's creative influence and Burnham's subsequent reliance on sterile classical models, and even on his supposed ambition to duplicate Baron Georges Haussmann's rebuilding of Paris along classical lines in the 1850s. As for the height limitation on private structures, Burnham's biographer can attribute it only to some deep and inexplicable revulsion against tall buildings.[50] (Why, then, a city hall that soared into the clouds?)

If The Plan of Chicago is viewed not from a narrow perspective, but as yet another product of the long-standing impulse to devise an effective mechanism of urban social control, its apparent contradictions and paradoxes begin to make sense. Burnham, after all, did not perceive his plan as anachronistic or irrelevant. He believed it to be a creative response to the moral challenge of the city, and, indeed, on one level it was. Like the Saint Louis Pageant and Masque of 1914, the Plan of Chicago was a daring effort to convey in compelling tangible form the city's moral claim upon its inhabitants. It was the supreme expression of some Progressives' dream of transforming the behavior and moral outlook of America's urban masses by transforming the cities in which they lived.[51]

This was the vision—not misguided classicism or a sycophant's desire to flatter Chicago's meat packers and grain merchants—that shaped Burnham's conception. His insistence that the city hall dwarf every other building in the city may have been outlandish in practical architectural terms, but it makes sense as an expression of his belief in the moral potential of civic idealism. "After all has been said," he wrote, "good citizenship is the prime object of good city planning." To contribute to the transformation of "the intellectual, social, moral, and aesthetic conditions" of the city—this was the long-range goal of the city planner's efforts.[52] In terms of architectural history, Burnham's ideological affinities were perhaps closest to those Enlightenment figures, especially Giambattista Piranesi, who saw in their urban designs a means of imposing a rational order on the city. Indeed, one could apply to the Plan of Chicago Manfredo Tafuri's characterization of Piranesi's 1761 plan for Rome as an epic expression of "the struggle between architecture and the city, between the demand for order and the will to formlessness."[53]

During the final stages of the preparation of the Plan of Chicago, after several bedside visits with the ailing Burnham, his young assistant Edward Bennett noted in his diary: "We talked of Swedenborg or rather I listened . . . and came away strengthened in purpose . . . We talked of the plan, but more of the philosophy of life—and his belief in the infinite possibilities of material expression of the spiritual." The man who perpetrated the leaden dictum "Beauty has always paid better than any other commodity, and always will" could also muse that "children must grow up dreaming of a beautiful city."[54] To understand the meaning of the Plan of Chicago, one must probe the implications of both comments.

Daniel Burnham was already mortally ill when the *Plan of Chicago* was published, and he lived for only three years more. But his dream found other champions whose zeal helps us gauge the depth of its appeal. A quasi-official Chicago Plan Commission, made up of 300 "representative citizens" was established under the direction of the merchant and brewery heir Charles H. Wacker. A booklet promoting the *Plan* was published in an edition of 165,000 copies, and a simplified version was adopted as a civics text in Chicago's schools.[55]

The publicists dwelt less on the plan's practical and aesthetic aspects than on the social vision underlying it. "Every generation has its burdens," declared one advocate; "to this is given the duty of curbing the individualism and establishing the collectivism of Democracy." The "noble character" of Burnham's proposed city hall, proclaimed Charles H. Wacker, would epitomize "the intellectual and moral quality of the city"; here Chicago's "best impulses" would "crystallize," and here her people would be "inspired . . . into devoted action for the public good." The physical transformation of Chicago envisioned by Burnham, added another supporter, would go far toward reversing the "physical and moral deterioration of the human race under bad conditions of city life" that was "one of the great problems of the age."[56]

But although Chicago spent $300 million on projects related to the Burnham plan in the fifteen years following its publication, the belief in the moral potential of city planning that found such passionate expression in the *Plan of Chicago* proved short-lived. In the 1920s bureaucratization set in, the focus narrowed to such matters as zoning, and city planners offered assurances that they had abandoned the sweeping pretensions of their predecessors and were now dealing with matters that were "ninety nine percent technical."[57] This development simply reflected a larger shift in post–World War I thinking about the city, but it must have been dismaying to the shade of Daniel Hudson Burnham. In his day, when city planning was in its infancy, its aspirations had been incomparably grander.

19

Positive Environmentalism and the Urban Moral-Control Tradition

CONTRASTS AND CONTINUITIES

The environmental reforms explored in the last four chapters were related in subtle and complex ways to the century-long cycle of urban moral-control effort examined earlier in this book. In certain important ways, of course, they represented a sharp break with the past. At a more fundamental level, however—or so I would contend—they were not only a continuation but indeed an apotheosis of the earlier movements.

Initially, perhaps, the discontinuities appear more evident than the continuities. The reformers we have just been examining do, after all, seem radically different from their predecessors in ostensibly focusing their primary attention not on the flaws and shortcomings of individuals and social groups, but on the deficiencies of the city's physical environment. The experience of turning to the positive environmentalists after a long immersion in the moralistic pronouncements of nineteenth-century city reformers can be refreshing indeed: here at last are urbane moderns with whose outlook and objectives one can at least begin to empathize.

Tactically, too, this shift of focus meant an end to the face-to-face encounters characteristic of nineteenth-century urban moral reform: the tract volunteer going from door to door, the YMCA secretary welcoming the young newcomer, the friendly visitor climbing tenement stairs. Explicitly or implicitly, all these earlier strategies shared the essentially preurban assumption that social control was best exercised through personal influence. As long as this personalistic approach held sway, the social-control motivation remained blatantly apparent.

Now (except perhaps for the playground proponents' flirtation with older strategies of direct oversight) the personal approach faded, and the social-control motive became correspondingly less obvious. Model tenements, parks, pageants, and inspiring civic centers would exert their beneficent influence, it was assumed in the heyday of positive environmentalism, with no direct contact between those responsible for them and those at whom they were aimed. They would operate, as it were, by remote control.

All this signified an important shift in attitudes toward the city. It reflected, at long last, a willingness to accept the city on its own terms—for tactical purposes, at any rate—as a new form of social organization whose structure and dynamic made it largely impervious to preurban modes of social control. In 1901, pointing out that the "living tissue" of *Gemeinschaft* had given way to "the rivets and screws of *Gesellschaft*, with its huge and complex aggregates," E. A. Ross had warned that the only viable modes of social control in the future would be "artificial rather than natural"—and the positive environmentalists assimilated Ross's message.[1]

A second feature distinguishing the positive environmentalists from the mainstream of nineteenth-century urban moral reform was their reliance on professional expertise and technical skill, rather than class dominance or an assumed moral superiority, as justification for their manipulation of the urban environment. These park administrators, playground supervisors, pageant directors, and city planners implicitly assumed that technical mastery of a specialized field was sufficient qualification for the exercise of social power and moral influence. If society was held together by "rivets and screws," who but disinterested technicians could be trusted to keep the machinery in good working order? Geoffrey Blodgett has recently shown how Frederick Law Olmsted professionalized urban landscape design as an instrument for exerting the influence being denied to men of his class in the municipal political arena, and we have seen how the prohibitionists and antiprostitution crusaders of the Progressive period invoked scientific arguments and sociological data to achieve their ends.[2] In the various facets of positive environmental reform, this tendency to subsume moral and social values into ostensibly technical issues found its fullest expression.

By this means, the secularlization of the urban social-control initiative, underway since the 1850s, was fully accomplished. Churchmen like Walter Rauschenbusch or the aging Josiah Strong might offer encouragement from the sidelines, but the center of gravity of positive-environmentalist reform lay with men and women whose claim to leadership was not their standing as moral or religious leaders, but their professional credentials. (The playground reform, Frederic C. Howe carefully noted, was not in the hands of moralists, but of "architects and social engineers.")[3] The movement's ideological underpinnings, as we have seen, were laid not by churchmen but by sociologists, economists, and political scientists.

279
*Positive
Environ-
mentalism
and the
Urban Moral-
Control
Tradition*

But if the strategies favored by the positive environmentalists, and the aura of professionalism with which they surrounded their activities, set them decisively apart from earlier urban reformers, in other respects they were the authentic heirs of an urban social-control tradition extending far back into the nineteenth century.

Sometimes the continuities can be established in the most direct and personal way. Joseph Lèe, for example, was first drawn to the playground movement when, as a volunteer with Boston's Charity Organization Society in the early 1890s, he undertook a survey of recreational facilities in the city's immigrant wards. Another playground ideologue, Luther H. Gulick, began his career as a YMCA worker in Springfield, Massachusetts, in the 1880s. (Earlier still, in the 1840s, his father had worked as a city missionary in New York City.) And the editor Richard Watson Gilder, who in the Progressive years saw tenement housing codes and inspiring civic architecture as keys to urban moral betterment, had first encountered city slums as a boy in the 1850s, when his minister father had taken him on a tour of Five Points, where the Ladies' Home Missionary Society had recently started a Methodist city mission.[4]

Intriguing as such direct links are, the continuity I am suggesting goes far deeper. No less than the earnest evangelicals who founded city Sunday schools and distributed tracts in Andrew Jackson's day, the Progressive reformers who preached social control through environmental means were convinced that planned, systematic, and organized effort by a concerned elite was essential if cities were not to collapse in degeneracy and disorder. The support which their proposals aroused sprang, in part, from a vast reservoir of anxiety built up by three generations of warnings about the wickedness and revolutionary potential of the city. Lyman Beecher, John R. McDowall, John Todd, S. Humphreys Gurteen, and the Josiah Strong of *Our Country* helped prepare the way for Joseph Lee, Percy MacKaye, and Daniel Burnham.

These latter-day urban moralists did not usually articulate an explicit code or spell out in detail the standards they sought to impose. Indeed, they frequently insisted that their aim was not to fasten a standardized norm of behavior upon the urban masses, but rather (as E. A. Ross put it in *Social Control*) to foster the emergence of a new "social type" attuned and responsive to the shifting demands of urban living.[5]

Nevertheless, most of the reformers and social thinkers who have populated the last four chapters remained consciously or unconsciously committed to a preurban model of social homogeneity as the ultimate goal of their efforts. At some deep level, they continued to believe that the key to stability in the cities lay in somehow re-creating a cohesive, organic community bound together by an enveloping web of shared moral and social values.

In 1904 a perceptive local historian characterized Indianapolis as "a town that became a city rather against its will," and the consequences of this reluctant, backward-looking response to urbanization were nowhere more apparent than in the tenacious survival of ingrained assumptions about the moral dimensions of urban life.[6] The civic ideal may have been less tangible than the orderly little communities the Jacksonian Sunday school teachers tried to create, but its grip upon the Progressive imagination was no less powerful. In a real sense, the urban vision animating the plans of Daniel Burnham and the pageants of Percy MacKaye was the culminating expression of a line of social thought dating from the Jacksonian era. It was the final, most soaring manifestation of an impulse that had sustained a century of urban social-control effort: the impulse to re-create in the city the cohesive moral order of the village.

In this respect, the coercive crusades and the positive environmentalist reforms simply represented two paths to the same end. While one group proposed to legislate morality, the other committed itself to creating the kind of urban environment that would gently but irresistibly engender an all-encompassing moral unity that would ultimately draw every city dweller within its orbit of influence.

Of course, the "community" pursued by the Progressive-era evangelists of civic idealism was very different from that sought by their predecessors in urban moral reform. Quixotic though they may have been, nineteenth-century efforts did require dealing with actual people and groups in the city and developing concrete strategies for bringing them up to what was seen as the prevailing moral standard. In the rhetorical flights of the Progressive urban environmentalists, by contrast, the communal ideal often becomes so abstract and rarefied as to be nearly drained of meaning.

One result was a blurring of the class realities of the movement. In retrospect, these realities are clear enough: Progressive urban environmental reform, especially as expressed in the city beautiful vogue, the civic-pageant enthusiasm, and the city-planning movement, was initiated, guided, and promoted by organized elements of the business elite—an elite still overwhelmingly native-born, "Anglo-Saxon," and Protestant. This was the same group that in these years, as Samuel P. Hays has shown, engineered various structural reforms in municipal government whose net result was to undermine the old ward politics and shift power to business-dominated organizations based on "specialized interests or functions."[7] The environmental reforms represented another avenue by which the elite extended its influence over the life of the city and expressed its interest in promoting urban social stability. There were exceptions to the pattern—bosses who supported civic projects for the jobs, patronage, or obvious tangible benefits they promised; working-class immigrant wards which welcomed playgrounds and parks without necessarily accepting or even realizing the nexus of upper-class assumptions that underlay such gestures; social workers who conscientiously tried to understand and articulate the interests of the poor; even the occasional socialist such as city-planning publicist Benjamin Marsh —but the general picture of business dominance in these reforms is clear. "Nobody now laughs [the city beautiful movement] to scorn," Charles Mulford Robinson observed; "Boards of Trade work for it; Chambers of Commerce appoint Commissioners to consider the local development." The Plan of Chicago was not the creation of "dreamers," Charles H. Wacker emphasized, but of "hard-headed businessmen." Burnham himself credited the project to the city's commercial leaders who were "accustomed to get together to plan for the general good."[8]

If the prohibition and antivice crusades energized the middle and lower-middle classes in the drive to achieve urban moral homogeneity, positive environmentalism was the characteristic mode adopted by the commercial elites to achieve the same goal. Although specific business interests may have opposed a particular reform (a factory affected by a smoke-abatement campaign, for example), the business class as a whole found the broad objectives of the positive environmentalists closely attuned to its own interests.

However, such realities were usually blurred by the misty rhetoric in which these reforms were shrouded. In an earlier day, urban moral reformers had often been quite candid in acknowledging that they sought to control or at least influence certain identifiable groups—usually groups below them on the economic scale. The publicists of Progressive environmental reform, by contrast, rarely acknowledged such a mundane class dimension to their cause. They represented the "civic ideal"—the collective

281
Positive
Environ-
mentalism
and the
Urban Moral-
Control
Tradition

stirring of the entire urban population toward a finer, purer collective life!

Again, the analogy to the municipal political reformers studied by Samuel P. Hays is close. Though the urban commercial elite clearly stood to benefit under the administrative reforms it promoted in these years—city commissioners elected on a citywide basis in place of the old ward aldermen were likely to be more responsive to business interests, for example—the elite backers of such reforms typically offered them as simply a more efficient and patently superior alternative to misgovernment and waste. They were presented as having been devised by disinterested, nonpartisan citizens in response to a great longing for better government that was sweeping the entire city.[9] A similar discrepancy between rhetoric and reality characterizes the environmental reforms as well. "Democracy is coming to demand and appreciate fitting monuments for the realization of its life," wrote Frederic C. Howe in a typical formulation, "and splendid parks and structures as the embodiment of its ideals."[10]

Not only did such inflation of rhetoric obscure the class basis of these reforms, but it also freed the reformers from almost all restraints in pursuing their objectives. In an earlier day, the moral values the reformers sought to transmit to the lower classes, parochial though they may have been, were at least fairly explicit, unambiguous, and historically rooted. But now that the moral-control initiative had passed to persons who saw themselves as simply conduits for the civic ideal or even democracy itself, what bounds were there, theoretically, to their high-minded efforts? The values they espoused were (to them) so obviously desirable that no reasonable person could possibly find them arbitrary, coercive, or colored by class assumptions. The issue was not social control at all, but simply one of awakening each city dweller to his true destiny as a part of the civic unity.

A few recognized the darker implications of this lofty vision. Frederick Law Olmsted, Jr., for example, while himself hardly immune to its lure, warned his fellow city planners in a thoughtful 1916 essay against assuming that their technical expertise and high motives gave them the right to determine "*what* the community should aim at as well as to direct the executive business of pursuing those aims." To assume that the interests of the masses were best served by "reliance on experts," Olmsted declared, was to repudiate the democratic ideal itself.[11] But Olmsted's was a lonely voice. To most of his contemporaries in urban environmental reform, it was an article of faith that public-spirited professionals and social technicians had not only the right but the urgent duty to use physical and environmental instrumentalities to mold a morally cohesive, homogeneous urban populace. They proposed in short, *Gesellschaft* means to *Gemein-schaft* ends.

But ends and means are in the long run inseparable, and in abandoning individual and family-based moral-control strategies in favor of the more amorphous environmental approach, these reformers severely undermined the fundamental assumption that homogeneity of values and behavior was a desirable or even an attainable urban objective. The supposed moral influence of playgrounds, gracious boulevards, and soaring civic centers, although vast in theory, was also so indirect and long-range that the shift of reform energies in this direction implied a tacit willingness to tolerate, in practice, much greater diversity in what a later generation would call urban "life-styles." So lofty was the great edifice of civic loyalty, one might say, that the masses scurrying about its base might be left free to pursue their own interests— even to cavort a bit—provided in some ultimate sense they acknowledged the moral claim of the civic ideal. In this sense, positive environmentalism pointed forward as well as back, not only concluding with a flourish the long cycle of urban moral-control effort but anticipating the post–World War I era when a very different set of controlling assumptions about urban life would emerge.

283
Positive
Environ-
mentalism
and the
Urban Moral-
Control
Tradition

20

Getting Right with Gesellschaft

THE DECAY OF THE URBAN
MORAL-CONTROL IMPULSE IN
THE 1920s AND AFTER

If Josiah Strong's *Our Country* distilled the antiurban feelings of the Gilded Age, then the comparable expression of the shifting mood of the post–World War I era was John G. Thompson's *Urbanization* (1927)—a 618-page salute to the city and repudiation of the "rural bias" in American thought. Exploring the city's impact in many areas of national life, Thompson concluded that in every instance earlier observers had exaggerated the evil aspects and underrated the positive. As to urban morality, Thompson cautiously observed that while "the city kettle may be as black as it has been painted . . . the rural pot is much too nearly the same hue to justify any invidious comparisons in its favor." All in all, he concluded, the "disparagement and depreciation of urban life" long prevalent in America was unjustified and injurious. Forget your village nostalgia and savor the urban reality was Thompson's message. "The 'golden age' lies before us and not behind us."[1]

Thompson's exercise in positive thinking reflected a fundamental shift in American social thought. Around the time of the First World War a set of attitudes toward the city that had dominated American thought for a century began to weaken dramatically, and by the end of the 1920s, as historian George Mowry has written, the United States was truly an urban nation—not only according to the census bureau but in "its cast of mind, in its ideals, and in its folk ways."[2]

To be sure, this profound shift was frequently obscured by the varied manifestations of antiurban, antimodern impulses that still tend to dominate our thinking about the decade: the Klan, the Scopes trial, prohibition and the book-censorship campaigns, the Fundamentalist movement in American Protestantism, the bucolic posturing of public figures like Henry Ford and Calvin Coolidge (dependent for its effect, ironically, on the publicity machinery of the big-city media), the village nostalgia of Norman Rockwell's *Saturday Evening Post* covers, the outpouring of ruralist sentimentality triggered by Lindbergh's flight. Nor was this activity all in the symbolic realm. This was, after all, the decade that effectively closed the door to foreign immigration and defeated Al Smith for the presidency at least in part because of his urban-immigrant roots and his brash big-city style.

When one looks more comprehensively at the social thought of the twenties, however, what strikes one is not merely the predictable tenacity of the antiurban animus but the spreading influence of the more affirmative outlook conveyed in John G. Thompson's 1927 work. At the popular culture level, even the most cursory survey reveals a massive exploitation of the city's potential to amuse and entertain. While the "lights-and-shadows" literary genre of an earlier day had been heavily moralistic in probing the shadows, the new literature of urban exploration displayed a frank delight in the totality of urban life. As early as 1904 grudging admiration had crept into Lincoln Steffens' description of Chicago in *The Shame of the Cities*. ("First in violence, deepest in dirt; loud, lawless, unlovely, . . . an overgrown gawk of a village; the 'tough' among cities, a spectacle for the nation. [etc.].") By the 1920s, journalists like Herbert Asbury and mystery writers like Dashiell Hammett could build careers exploiting and glamorizing the often gamey flavor of America's big cities.[3] With the rise of network radio in the mid-1920s, the major urban centers came to seem cornucopias of amusement, music, news, and entertainment to the listening millions. As for the movies, already in the pre-World-War-I era comedies like *Tillie's Punctured Romance* and *Easy Street* had offered a breezy picture of urban life—social turbulence and all!—and in the 1920s urban social disorder was most often reduced to the zany mayhem and misadventures of Laurel and Hardy, Harold Lloyd, and Buster Keaton.

At a quite different cultural level, this was the decade which made a culture hero of that quintessential urbanite H. L. Mencken, and a success of his determinedly sophisticated *American Mercury* magazine. Among intellectuals, the shift in attitudes toward the city was perhaps most clearly signaled in the writings of the urban sociologists who by the 1920s had largely replaced

ministers and social workers as the group most given to rumina-
tions about the larger meaning of urbanization. The tenor of this
era's sociological work on the urban theme was established as
early as 1915, when Robert Park of the University of Chicago
published a seminal essay, "The City," in the *American Journal
of Sociology*. Though coming only four years after Luther Lee
Bernard's labored effort to formulate an "objective standard of
social control" for an urban age, Park's work reflected a subtle

shift of tone. Where Bernard was apprehensive and hostile in
his view of urbanization, Park was comparatively more tolerant
and nonjudgmental in assessing the social meaning of the city,
which he characterized, significantly, as "the natural environment
of the free man."[4]

The positive tone established by Park was echoed in numerous
works of urban sociology in the years that followed. In *Principles
of Rural-Urban Sociology* (1929), for example, Pitirim Sorokin
and Carle C. Zimmerman portrayed urban and rural America
as existing in a state of dynamic tension, each with its unique
strengths, each making an essential contribution to the total social environment. If the country was the conservative social anchor, the city was the source of the cultural, intellectual, and
technological innovation that prevented society from stagnating.
Sorokin and Zimmerman gave short shrift to the long line of antiurban moralists whose gloomy pronouncements have dotted these
pages; "Urban and rural populations," they concluded, revealed
no "inherent differences of morality." Two years later, another
urban sociologist, Niles Carpenter, acknowledged that "the God-
less city" and "the wicked city" were "well-nigh universal clichés," but added: "They are seldom supported . . . by any concrete body of data. Indeed, it is difficult to see how they could
be." Louis Wirth, Robert Park's younger colleague at the University of Chicago and a leader with him of the influential Chicago
school of urban sociology, although offering a mixed assessment
of the social consequences of urbanization, fundamentally viewed
it from a positive perspective. Cities, he wrote, were not only the
"dwelling-place and the workshop of modern man"; they were
centers where "the fulfilling and socially meaningful life" could
best be achieved.[5]

Why this shift in attitudes? The sources are complex. They
include, certainly, the increased cultural influence of an urban-
based mass media and the altered pace and character of urban
growth. (The latter development was in turn linked, of course, to
the post-1914 drop in foreign immigration.) Nor should one overlook the decline in the kinds of mass disorder and violence that
had so alarmed earlier generations. Certainly there continued to

be disorders in the 1920s and after, particularly race riots, and the urban historian who has recently written that despite the social and economic stresses of the 1920–1940 period "the cities remained surprisingly peaceful" is perhaps overstating the case, but in contrast to the pervasive and often bloody violence of the 1830–1900 years, the generalization is not wholly unfounded.[6]

Then, too, as more Americans observed the often prosaic reality of urban life at first hand, either as residents or—in this age of the automobile—as tourists, the old stereotype of the city as a cesspool of wickedness and a seedbed of revolution lost much of its force. That stereotype—the cumulative product of countless tracts, sermons, dime novels, admonitory works, and journalistic exposés—did not disappear after 1920, but never again would it exert so direct a shaping influence on the national consciousness. After a century of urbanization, despite all its attendant strains, people at last began to recognize that the rise of the city was not necessarily a signal for the inevitable collapse of morality and the social order.

This larger process of coming to terms with the city had important implications for the urban moral-control effort. As the disturbing anomaly became the familiar norm, and resistance gave way to acceptance, concerns that had preoccupied generations of uplifters seemed less compelling. Imperceptibly but decisively, the impulse to impose moral uniformity on the city—an impulse that had found so many diverse institutional outlets since the 1820s—was drained of much of its vitality. Initially, of course, this development was related to the general decline of reformism in the 1920s which Arthur S. Link and others have noted.[7] Yet when reform energies revived in the 1930s, the urban social-control component was almost totally lacking.

In earlier years, urban moralists and uplifters had viewed the city's heterogeneity and seeming lack of moral cohesiveness as a threatening social deviation requiring urgent remedial attention. In the post-1920 years, by contrast, that same heterogeneity was often treated as a positive social gain, adding to the richness and creative diversity of American life. Horace Kallen, a Harvard-trained philosopher of urban immigrant stock, coined the term *cultural pluralism* in 1924, and it aptly summed up the more appreciative view of urban heterogeneity that was taking shape.[8] Once again, Robert Park anticipated the trend in his 1915 essay, not deploring but *welcoming* the city's capacity for "breaking down . . . local attachments" and weakening "the restraints and inhibitions of the primary group." Urbanization, he contended, had produced a stimulating variety of "new and divergent individual types" and given rise to "an element of chance and adventure, which adds to the stimulus of city life and gives it for young and fresh nerves a peculiar attractiveness." The "booming confusion" of the city, Park went on, was at once its greatest asset and the source of its moral and cultural vitality. "Among the varied manifestations of city life," he wrote, every person could find "the moral climate in which his peculiar nature obtains the stimulations that bring his innate qualities to full and free expression . . . The small community often tolerates eccentricity. The city, on the contrary, rewards it."[9]

For Park, the breakdown of preurban social restraints was a small price to pay for such benefits. The morally defective person might be freer to express himself in the city, but so, too, was the genius. That cities contained many different "moral regions," including some in which "vagrant and suppressed impulses" could for a time "emancipate themselves from the dominant moral order," was for him no cause for concern; indeed, he saw it as a safety valve assuring the long-term viability of that dominant order.[10]

Though not totally dominant, this celebratory tone toward the diversity and openness of urban life pervades much of American social thought of the post-1920 era. The city, wrote Louis Wirth in 1938, summing up two decades of work by urban sociologists, was the essential seedbed for "the ideas and practices that we call civilization." A similar feeling for urban heterogeneity is present in Lewis Mumford's *The Culture of Cities* (1938), a work whose outlook is summed up in Mumford's quotation from Aristotle: "Men come together in cities in order to live; they remain together in order to live the good life." Like Park and other urban sociologists, Mumford welcomed the city's corrosive effects on preurban forms of social organization. Before a people can become "fully humanized," he wrote, "the social man must break up into a thousand parts: so that each grain of aptitude, each streak of intelligence, each fiber of special interest, may take a deeper color by mingling with other grains, streaks and fibres of the same nature." Indeed, for Mumford, this "transfer of emphasis from the uniformities and common acceptances of the primary group to the critical choices, the purposive associations, and the rational ends of the secondary group" represented the crowning achievement of the urbanization process.[11]

With this heightened regard for urban diversity came a more critical attitude toward all schemes for reimposing in the city the moral and social homogeneity of the village. Robert Park, writing when the antiprostitution and antisaloon crusades were at their peak, found them "interesting and important as subjects of investigation," but expressed a cool skepticism toward the long-range efficacy of such "arbitrary" moral efforts. Prostitution, wrote Niles Carpenter in 1931, was rooted in "the fundamental character of city life and of human bio-psychology" and would inevitably remain a facet of urban society. By 1939, even Luther Lee Bernard had concluded that the social-control stratagems for which he had once tried to build an ideological foundation were, after all, mainly used for "the subordination of the weak or the underprivileged to the service of the powerful and the over-privileged."[12]

This skepticism extended not only to coercive urban social-control efforts, but to positive environmentalism as well. Robert Park was unpersuaded by the claim that playgrounds, model tenements, and civic centers would "elevate the moral tone" of the urban masses. "The inevitable processes of human nature," he observed drily, would in time give even the best-planned city "a character which it is less easy to control."[13] In *The Culture of Cities*, written in the shadow of Albert Speer's grandiose architectural monuments to Nazi power in Germany, Lewis Mumford delivered an even harsher verdict. Sweeping civic-design proposals of the *Plan of Chicago* variety, he wrote

> seek a harmony too absolute, an order whose translation into actual life would stultify the very purpose it seeks to achieve . . . [T]he weakness that lies in perfectionism . . . has now been made manifest in the new totalitarian states . . . What is lacking in such dreams is not a sense of the practical: what is lacking is a realization of the essential human need for disharmony and conflict, elements whose acceptance and resolution are indispensable to psychological growth.[14]

The aim of anyone truly concerned about the moral life of the city, Mumford went on, ought not be to promote a factitious "harmony" or subservience to a monolithic "civic ideal," but to work for an urban climate even more favorable to individual diversity: a "poly-nucleated city" where "more significant kinds of conflict, more complex and intellectually stimulating kinds of disharmony, may take place . . . ; an environment broad enough and rich enough never to degenerate into a 'model community.' "[15]

Even many who did not necessarily share Mumford's enthusiasm for a "poly-nucleated" city came in these years to view organized urban social-control effort as unnecessary and redundant. They now recognized that the urban-industrial order itself, even while freeing people of certain traditional social restraints, was generating its own powerful social-control instrumentalities: the pervasive influence of radio, the movies, and mass-circulation periodicals; the potency of advertising and the emerging field of public relations; the commercialization of mass spectator sports; the standardization of consumption.[16]

Some welcomed this development. Confronting an urban mass with "no common ancestry, no common tradition, . . . and no cohesive intelligence," declared public-relations expert E. L. Bernays in 1923, it was the responsibility of public-relations men to mold a common outlook. Though still unfortunately linked in the public mind with hucksterism and show-business flummery, he wrote, their future mission was a lofty one: "It is in the creation of a *public conscience* that the counsel on public relations is destined, I believe, to fulfill his highest usefulness to the society in which he lives."[17] Writing from a quite different perspective, Norman F. Harriman, author of *Standards and Standardization* (1928), reached a parallel conclusion. In all areas of life, including many hitherto "unsuspected fields," he declared, the unsystematic and the idiosyncratic were succumbing to the overriding need for uniformity in an increasingly systematized technological age. Standardization was becoming "a primary aspect of all well-ordered activity," he noted approvingly, imposing uniformity in countless areas of human endeavor with "a rigor superior to legal enactment."[18]

For other social observers of the 1920s, however, this same development was a source of profound apprehension. Just as the city's fostering of diversity was coming to be viewed as a positive good, powerful pressures rooted in the dynamic of urbanization itself threatened to snuff it out! That these pressures were simply the by-products of technological innovation in the service of a profit-oriented capitalism, rather than the consequence of deliberate schemes of social control, did not diminish their power.

Among urban sociologists, such apprehension was widespread. Modern city dwellers, wrote Sorokin and Zimmerman, were being reduced to the condition of " 'robots' or automatons" controlled by "standardized, half-mechanical, ready-made [behavior] patterns." In his behavior, they declared, the typical urbanite "may be compared to a victrola; he simply and half mechanically changes one standard for another (like one record for another)." The social conditioning forces of urban life, agreed sociologist Niles Carpenter, "attend the city dweller's life from his arrival into the urban community and dog his every footstep while he remains within it." The great danger of urbanization, he suggested, was not moral deviance or social disintegration—the classic concerns of earlier generations—but the loss of individuality and autonomy through the routinization of social function in the city.[19]

In his 1925 work *Means of Social Control*, sociologist Frederick E. Lumley took an equally bleak view of the forces promoting a sterile conformity in contemporary urban America. Though "rarely articulated" and not "organized into one mighty engine of control," he wrote, these forces were almost irresistible in their cumulative effect. Indicative of Lumley's point of view is his discussion of modern techniques of advertising. "Somewhere and somehow, somebody has appropriated the right to stand before us, stare us out of countenance, point accusing fingers at us, and otherwise gain ascendancy over us . . . In a thousand ways the advertisers invade our private lives and issue never-ending ultimatums. With some people this everlasting peppering with commands inspires opposition. With the majority, however, it is effectual. . . . There are many of us who like to be ordered about."[20] "From the cradle to the grave," concluded Lumley, a vast array of social-control pressures—from the derisive chuckle to the glaring neon sign—were subtly shaping the behavior of everyone; "there is no possible escape."[21]

The American city, viewed by generations of moralists as a seething human mass that might explode at any moment, came to be perceived by many in the 1920s as the dwelling place of millions of docile conformists daily subjected to a barrage of influences that shaped their behavior and values in ways they themselves hardly realized. The most famous urbanite of the 1920s —Sinclair Lewis's George F. Babbitt—invited only derision or pity, certainly not fear, as he feebly struggled against the social pressures that determined his every action. In their 1929 study Middletown, sociologists Robert and Helen Lynd provided a disturbing picture of the conformist lives and standardized thinking of Babbitt's real-life counterparts in the city of Muncie, Indiana. The progression of Charlie Chaplin from the cop who subdues the brawling toughs of Easy Street (1917) to the urban worker who is the hapless victim of his boss's insane infatuation with efficiency and standardization in Modern Times (1933) sums up a crucially important transition in American social thought.

Inevitably, all of this had a fatally corrosive effect on the assumptions that had underlain a century of urban social-control effort. Strategies for controlling urban behavior that had once seemed so promising now appeared as only a tiny and largely ineffectual part of the total process by which behavior and values were shaped in a modern social order. By 1941, examining "The Concept of Social Control" in the American Sociological Review, A. B. Hollingshead of Indiana University concluded that, in the past, far too much attention had been paid to "the instruments men use to manipulate selected aspects of behavior," to the neglect of the great variety of subtle but pervasive influences tending to produce "common attitudes and behavior modes" within any society.[22]

The nexus of concerns and assumptions that had guided the

reform efforts of so diverse a group of Americans as Arthur Tappan, Eleazer Lord, Robert Hartley, Verranus Morse, Josephine Shaw Lowell, Clifford Roe, Joseph Lee, Charles Mulford Robinson, and Daniel Burnham had broken up at last. After decades of worry about how to achieve greater order and moral cohesiveness in the city, the dominant thrust of urban thought shifted 180 degrees after 1920. The pressing urban danger was now seen not in disorder and degeneracy, but in a sterile conformity. The city's fostering of diversity now seemed not a harbinger of imminent social collapse, but a valuable social asset, to be safeguarded from the conformist pressures that seemed to be intensifying with every passing year. With this shift, the effort to re-create in the city the moral homogeneity of the village—an effort that for a century had been so powerful and protean a social force in America—was effectively abandoned.

Of course politicians, educators, churchmen, social workers, and urbanologists of all description would continue to wrestle with the social problems of the city, but they would do so within an intellectual framework that was itself an artifact of urbanization. The city might be the spawning ground of many of the central problems and challenges of modern life, but its mere existence was no longer seen as a massive challenge to the social order —it *was* the social order! The experience of a century had borne home at least one lesson: if the city in all its moral and social diversity was a powerful solvent of older modes of social organization, it also contained within itself strong elements of cohesion and tenacious powers of survival and renewal.

Notes
Index

Notes

A note on citation form: To avoid cluttering the text with numbers, all quotes and factual references in a given paragraph are usually covered by a single note. The quote or factual reference *closest* to the number in the text is cited *first* in the note, with the others following in the order in which they occur in the text.

1 THE URBAN THREAT EMERGES

1. George Rogers Taylor, "American Urban Growth Preceding the Railway Age," *Journal of Economic History*, 27 (Sept. 1967), 317; Alexis de Tocqueville, *Democracy in America* (New York, Random House, Vintage Books, n.d.), I, 300; *The American Puritans: Their Prose and Poetry*, ed. Perry Miller (Garden City, N.Y., Doubleday, 1956), p. 83 (Winthrop quote); Thomas Jefferson, *Notes on the State of Virginia*, ed. William Peden (Chapel Hill, University of North Carolina Press, 1955), p. 165.

2. Taylor, "American Urban Growth," p. 309.

3. Ibid., table 1, p. 311.

4. Raymond A. Mohl, "Poverty in Early America, A Reappraisal: The Case of Eighteenth-Century New York City," *New York History*, 50 (Jan. 1969), 5–27; Sam Bass Warner, Jr., *The Private City: Philadelphia in Three Periods of Its Growth* (Philadelphia, University of Pennsylvania Press, 1968), pp. 15–17 (Franklin reference on p. 15); Carl Abbott, "The Neighborhoods of New York, 1760–1775," *New York History*, 55 (Jan. 1974), 35–54, esp. 51.

5. Walter Hugins, *Jacksonian Democracy and the Working Class: A Study of the New York Workingmen's Movement, 1829–1837* (Palo Alto, Calif., Stanford University Press, 1960), pp. 203–206; Edward Pessen, *Riches, Class and Power before the Civil War* (Lexington, Mass., D.C. Heath, 1973), pp. 172–201, esp. 178–179, 188; Robert A. McCaughey, "From Town to City: Boston in the 1820s," *Political Science Quarterly*, 88 (June 1973), 191–213; Robert Ernst, *Immigrant Life in New York City, 1825–1863* (New York, King's Crown Press, Columbia University, 1949), pp. 20–21.

6. Peter R. Knights, *The Plain People of Boston, 1830–1860: A Study in City Growth* (New York, Oxford University Press, 1971), chaps. IV and VI; Stuart M. Blumin, "Residential Mobility Within the Nineteenth-Century City," in *The Peoples of Philadelphia: A History of Ethnic Groups and Lower-Class Life, 1790–1940*, ed. Allen F. Davis and Mark H. Haller (Philadelphia, Temple University Press, 1973), pp. 37–51; Raymond A. Mohl, "Humanitarianism in the Preindustrial City: The New York Society for the Prevention of Pauperism, 1817–1823," *Journal of American History* 57 (Dec. 1970), 576–578 (on early nineteenth-century economic distress and its social consequences).

7. The best account here, for one city, is Ernst, *Immigrant Life in New York City.* See also Robert T. Handy, *A Christian America: Protestant Hopes and Historical Realities* (New York, Oxford University Press, 1971), p. 58; Hugins, *Jacksonian Democracy and the Working Class*, p. 203. On the "young men in the city," see Joseph F. Kett, "Growing Up in Rural New England, 1800–1840," in *Anonymous Americans: Explorations in Nineteenth Century Social History*, ed. Tamara K. Hareven (Englewood Cliffs, N.J., Prentice-Hall, 1971), p. 15 (note 14), and Knights, *Plain People of Boston*, p. 27, which notes that in the 1830s from 110 to 120 males lived in Boston's central area for every 100 females.

8. Richard C. Wade, *The Urban Frontier: The Rise of Western Cities, 1790–1830* (Cambridge, Mass., Harvard University Press, 1959), p. 310 (Pittsburgh quote); Henry Bradshaw Fearon, *Sketches of America: A Narrative of a Journey of Five Thousand Miles through the Eastern and Western States* (New York, Benjamin Blom, 1969 [reissue of 1818 edition]), p. 11.

9. See, e.g., Mrs. Frances Trollope, *Domestic Manners of the Americans*, ed. Donald Smalley (New York, Vintage Books, n.d. [orig. pub. 1832]), p. 43.

10. "Town and Country," *The Knickerbocker*, 8 (Nov. 1836), 537–539, reprinted in *Urban America: A History With Documents*, ed. Bayrd Still (Boston, Little, Brown, 1974), p. 196.

11. John R. Bodo, *The Protestant Clergy and Public Issues, 1812–1848* (Princeton, Princeton University Press, 1954), p. 162. See also M. J. Heale, "Patterns of Benevolence: Charity and Morality in Rural and Urban New York, 1783–1830," *Societas*, 3 (Autumn 1973), 339, and T. Scott Miyakawa, *Protestants and Pioneers: Individualism and Conformity on the American Frontier* (Chicago, University of Chicago Press, 1964), pp. 16–17.

12. Wade's *Urban Frontier* is the standard history of Midwestern urbanization.

13. McCaughey, "Town to City," p. 196.

14. Roderick N. Ryon, "Moral Reform and Democratic Politics: The Dilemma of Roberts Vaux," *Quaker History*, 59 (Spring 1970), 3–14; Warner, *Private City*, pp. 86–91.

15. Hugins, *Jacksonian Democracy and the Working Class*, pp. 30–48, 235; Mohl, "Humanitarianism in the Preindustrial City," p. 593 ("total aversion" quote); Lewis Tappan, *The Life of Arthur Tappan*

(New York, 1870; reissued, Westport, Conn., Negro Universities Press, 1970), p. 123 ("profligate jurors" quote).

16. Quoted in McCaughey, "Town to City," p. 199. For a contrasting interpretation see M. J. Heale, "From City Fathers to Social Critics: Humanitarianism and Government in New York, 1790–1860," *Journal of American History*, 63 (June 1976), 21–41. Heale argues that down to around the 1840s there was a close correspondence in membership and ideology between New York's political and moral-uplift leadership, and that only by the 1850s did a distinct divergence take place. While the divergence certainly grew more pronounced in the later antebellum period, the shift in political power away from the elite, and a clear distinction between the political leadership and the moral-reform leadership, was already in evidence by the 1820s.

17. Bodo, *Protestant Clergy and Public Issues*, pp. 44–47 (quoted passage, p. 47); Joseph L. Blau, "The Christian Party in Politics," *Review of Religion*, 11 (Nov. 1946), 18–35; Elizabeth M. Geffen, "Philadelphia Protestantism Reacts to Social Reform Movements before the Civil War," *Pennsylvania History*, 30 (April 1963), 192–212, esp. p. 208.

18. Bertram Wyatt-Brown, "Prelude to Abolitionism: Sabbatarian Politics and the Rise of the Second Party System," *Journal of American History*, 58 (Sept. 1971), 316–341, esp. pp. 328–338; Charles C. Cole, *The Social Ideas of the Northern Evangelists, 1826–1860* (New York, Columbia University Press, 1954), pp. 107–108.

19. John Todd, *The Sabbath School Teacher: Designed to Aid in Elevating and Perfecting the Sabbath School System* (Northampton, Mass., 1837), pp. 346, 348, 349; Charles G. Finney, *Lectures on Revivals of Religion* (New York, 1835; reprinted, Cambridge, Mass., Harvard University Press, 1960, William G. McLoughlin, ed.), p. 304.

20. Wyatt-Brown, "Prelude to Abolitionism," pp. 327, 340. President Jackson's refusal to call a national day of prayer during the 1832 cholera epidemic, despite numerous appeals, was another pointed slap at evangelicals. Charles E. Rosenberg, *The Cholera Years: The United States in 1832, 1849, and 1866* (Chicago, University of Chicago Press, 1962), pp. 47–50.

21. Robert H. Bremner, *From the Depths: The Discovery of Poverty in the United States* (New York, New York University Press, 1956), pp. 33–34; William Ellery Channing, "Discourse on the Life and Character of the Rev. Joseph Tuckerman, D.D." (1841), in *The Works of William E. Channing* (Boston, American Unitarian Association, 1903), VI, 113–114; Ward Stafford, A.M., *New Missionary Field: A Report to the Female Missionary Society for the Poor of the City of New York* (New York, 1817), pp. 3, 5, 16 (quoted passage); Bertram Wyatt-Brown, *Lewis Tappan and the Evangelical War against Slavery* (Cleveland, Case Western Reserve Press, 1969; reissued, New York, Atheneum, 1971), p. 65; Charles C. Cole, Jr., "The Free Church Movement in New York City," *New York History*, 51 (July 1953), 290–293; Lewis Tappan, *Life of Arthur Tappan*, pp. 89–90.

22. Wyatt-Brown, *Lewis Tappan*, p. 71; Richard Carwardine, "The Second Great Awakening in the Urban Centers: An Examination of

Methodism and the 'New Measures,' " *Journal of American History*, 59 (Sept. 1972), 327–340; Trollope, *Domestic Manners of the Americans*, pp. 75–81; comment on the Rochester revival quoted in Cole, *Social Ideas of the Northern Evangelists*, p. 91; *Memoirs of Rev. Charles G. Finney, Written by Himself* (New York, A. S. Barnes, 1876), pp. 238–245, 275–277, 318–320; the *Methodist Review*, established in 1818, contains numerous reports of urban revivals. See, e.g., May 1821, p. 197 (Pittsburgh); June 1821, pp. 229 (New Haven) and 231 (Providence).

23. John Todd, *The Story of His Life Told Mainly by Himself* (New York, 1876), pp. 264, 283; Wade C. Barclay, *A History of Methodist Missions* (6 vols., New York, Board of Missions and Church Extension of the Methodist Church, 1949), I, 230–231.

24. Wade, *Urban Frontier*, p. 134; Cole, *Social Ideas of the Northern Evangelists*, pp. 23, 80 (George W. Gale to Finney quoted); Catharine M. Sedgwick, *Clarence; or, A Tale of Our Own Times* (Philadelphia, 1830), p. 177. See also Timothy L. Smith, *Revivalism and Social Reform: American Protestantism on the Eve of the Civil War* (Nashville, Abingdon Press, 1957; reprinted, New York, Harper Torchbooks, 1965), pp. 47–49, and Bernard A. Weisberger, *They Gathered at the River; the Story of the Great Revivalists and Their Impact upon Religion in America* (Boston, Little, Brown, 1958; reprinted, New York, Quadrangle Books, 1966), p. 132.

25. Gardiner Spring, *Personal Reminiscences of the Life and Times of Gardiner Spring* (2 vols., New York, 1866), I, 226; Wyatt-Brown, *Lewis Tappan*, p. 65.

26. Finney, *Lectures on Revivals of Religion*, pp. 67, 143, 154.

27. Finney, *Memoirs*, p. 321; Cowardine, "The Second Great Awakening in the Urban Centers," p. 329; H. Pomeroy Brewster, "The Magic of a Voice: Rochester Revivals of Rev. Charles G. Finney" [1892], Rochester Historical Society, *Publication Fund Series*, 4 (1925), 283.

28. *The Sixth Annual Report of the Board of Managers of the American Bible Society* (New York, 1822), p. 112.

29. The Reverend William Nevins, "Are You a Sabbath School Teacher?" *Tracts of the American Tract Society, General Series* (New York, n.d. [but ca. 1825]), X, no. 396, p. 4. While urban church members were enjoying "ice-creams and silks," agreed the Reverend John Todd, "a great population" was being "shut out from places of worship, or denied the common privileges of the Sabbath." Todd, *Story of His Life*, p. 265. See also Stafford, *New Missionary Field*, pp. 7, 25, and *The Teacher Taught: An Humble Attempt to Make the Path of the Sunday School Teacher Straight and Plain* (Philadelphia, American Sunday School Union, 1839), p. 67.

30. For general discussions of the evangelical moral-reform efforts of these years, see Charles I. Foster, *An Errand of Mercy; The Evangelical United Front, 1790–1837* (Chapel Hill, University of North Carolina Press, 1960), and Clifford S. Griffin, *Their Brothers' Keeper: Moral Stewardship in the United States, 1800–1850* (New Brunswick, N.J., Rutgers University Press, 1960). See also Gregory H. Singleton's interesting essay, "Protestant Voluntary Organizations and the Shap-

ing of Victorian America," in *Victorian America,* ed. Daniel Walker Howe (Philadelphia, University of Pennsylvania Press, 1976), pp. 47–58, which explores the links—both ideological and familial—between the great antebellum Protestant voluntary associations and the emergence of a national corporate economic order later in the nineteenth century.

31. Lyman Beecher, *The Autobiography of Lyman Beecher,* ed. Barbara M. Cross (2 vols., Cambridge, Mass., Harvard University Press, 1961), I, 185–191, quoted phrase, p. 187; Richard J. Purcell, *Connecticut in Transition, 1775–1818* (Middletown, Conn., Wesleyan University Press, 1963), p. 182.

32. Beecher, *Autobiography,* pp. 192, 194.

33. John A. Krout, *The Origins of Prohibition* (New York, Alfred A. Knopf, 1925), p. 87.

34. Beecher, *Autobiography,* I, 255.

35. Quoted in Handy, *Christian America,* p. 45, and Cole, *Social Ideas of the Northern Evangelists,* p. 100.

36. Lyman Beecher, *A Reformation of Morals Practical and Indispensable* (1814), quoted in Ibid.

37. Beecher, *Autobiography,* I, 252, 253.

38. Geffen, "Philadelphia Protestantism Reacts to Social Reform Movements before the Civil War," p. 202; Edwin W. Rice, *The Sunday-School Movement, 1780–1917, and the American Sunday-School Union, 1817–1917* (Philadelphia, American Sunday School Union, 1917), p. 53; Heale, "Patterns of Benevolence," p. 345; Purcell, *Connecticut in Transition,* p. 21 (on Dwight).

39. Krout, *Origins of Prohibition,* pp. 90–93.

40. Beecher, *Autobiography,* II, 107, 108.

41. Foster, *Errand of Mercy,* pp. 275–279; Wade, *Urban Frontier,* p. 220 (Louisville). See also Handy, *Christian America,* pp. 57–58, and Heale, "Patterns of Benevolence," pp. 344–346.

42. Pessen, *Riches, Class, and Power before the Civil War,* pp. 252–278. Pessen heavily emphasizes the role of the established patrician elite in these moral-reform efforts, giving correspondingly less attention to rising newcomers of evangelical persuasion, but his evidence is ambiguous because in his statistical presentations he combines involvement in moral-reform organizations with membership in such undertakings as library trust boards, historical societies, and cultural groups.

43. Beecher, *Autobiography,* II, 107n.

44. Keith Melder, "Ladies Bountiful: Organized Women's Benevolence in Early Nineteenth-Century America," *New York History,* 48 (July 1967), 231–254; Carroll Smith-Rosenberg, *Religion and the Rise of the American City: The New York City Mission Movement, 1812–1870* (Ithaca, Cornell University Press, 1971) is valuable on women's role in these movements.

45. Lewis Tappan, *Life of Arthur Tappan,* pp. 13, 19–32; Wyatt-Brown, *Lewis Tappan,* pp. 1–14.

46. Lewis Tappan, *Life of Arthur Tappan,* pp. 339–344.

47. Ibid., pp. 33–69; quoted passages on pp. 10, 59, 69.

48. Wyatt-Brown, *Lewis Tappan*, pp. 17, 35.

49. Ibid., pp. 26–42.

50. Lewis Tappan, *Life of Arthur Tappan*, p. 88.

51. John R. McDowall, *Magdalen Facts*, New York, 1 (Jan. 1832), pp. 59, 80; *Memoir and Select Remains of the Late Rev. John R. McDowall, the Martyr of the Seventh Commandment in the Nineteenth Century* (New York, 1838), pp. 101–127, 181–184; John W. Kuykendall, "Martyr to the Seventh Commandment: John R. McDowall," *Journal of Presbyterian History*, 50 (Winter 1972), 288–305.

52. Lewis Tappan, *Life of Arthur Tappan*, p. 118; Kuykendall, "Martyr to the Seventh Commandment," pp. 294–295.

53. Melder, "Ladies Bountiful," p. 245; Carroll Smith-Rosenberg, "Beauty, the Beast, and the Militant Woman: A Case Study in Sex Roles and Social Stress in Jacksonian America," *American Quarterly*, 23 (October 1971), 562–584; Cole, *Social Ideas of the Northern Evangelists*, pp. 125–129; Kuykendall, "Martyr to the Seventh Commandment," pp. 298–299.

54. Stafford, *New Missionary Field*, pp. 29, 30, 31 (italics added).

55. Quoted in Smith-Rosenberg, *Religion and the Rise of the American City*, pp. 106, 110.

56. The New York legislature in 1848 did outlaw seduction—one of the goals of the Female Moral Reform Society. See Smith-Rosenberg, "Beauty, the Beast, and the Militant Woman," pp. 570–574. What effect this legislation had on sexual behavior in New York State has not been ascertained.

57. *Memoir and Select Remains of the Late Rev. John R. McDowall*, pp. 199, 213, 222–225, 271, 291 (quoted passage), 294, 299.

58. *The Diary of Philip Hone, 1828–1851*, ed. Allan Nevins (New York, Dodd, Mead, 1936), p. 45; Wyatt-Brown, *Lewis Tappan*, pp. 61–68, includes a useful discussion of the tensions between the old Knickerbocker elite and the newer commercial class. See also, on this subject, Robert Greenhalgh Albion, *The Rise of New York Port, 1815–1860* (New York, Charles Scribner's Sons, 1939; reissued, London, David and Charles, 1970), pp. 250–251; Dixon Ryan Fox, *Yankees and Yorkers* (New York, New York University Press, 1940), pp. 199–215.

59. The *Advocate of Moral Reform* did print numerous communications from rural and small-town subscribers describing illicit sexual activity and occasionally naming or offering detailed descriptions of the men involved. Smith-Rosenberg, "Beauty, the Beast, and the Militant Woman," p. 573. See also idem, *Religion and the Rise of the American City*, p. 111 ("serious and industrious" quote).

60. *Report of the [New York] Mercantile Library Association, 1834*, quoted in Allan Stanley Horlick, *Country Boys and Merchant Princes: The Social Control of Young Men in New York* (Lewisburg, Pa., Bucknell University Press, 1975), p. 257; *New York Post* quoted in Mohl, "Humanitarianism in the Preindustrial City," p. 592.

2 THE TRACT SOCIETIES

1. John Tebbel, *A History of Book Publishing in the United States* (New York, R. R. Bowker, 1972), I, 207, 257–262.

2. W. P. Strickland, *History of the American Bible Society from Its Organization to the Present Time* (New York, 1849), pp. 26–29, 53; *First Annual Report of the Board of Managers of the American Bible Society, Presented May 8, 1817* (New York, 1817), p. 9 (hereafter, ABS, AR).

3. "Constitution of the American Bible Society" (New York, 1816, bound with vol. I of the annual reports), pp. 2, 16, 17; Edward Pessen, *Riches, Class and Power before the Civil War* (Lexington, Mass., D. C. Heath, 1973), p. 262. The names of the first board of directors are printed in the first annual report.

4. Strickland, *History of the ABS*, pp. 62, 63, 79; ABS, AR (1820), p. 11, and (1841), p. 89.

5. Strickland, *History of the ABS*, p. 80. For the reports from the various big-city Bible societies, see almost any annual report of the American Bible Society, e.g., 1822, p. 114 (Boston); 1824, p. 102 (Philadelphia); and 1825, p. 21 (New York).

6. Ibid. (1835), p. 86; (1820), p. 38; (1823), p. 83; (1822), p. 132.

7. Ibid. (1822), p. 167; (1823), pp. 22, 86; (1832), p. 18; Strickland, *History of the ABS*, p. 58.

8. ABS, AR (1839), p. 64; *American Sunday School Magazine* (Oct. 1827), p. 311.

9. ABS, AR (1833), p. 77.

10. Malcolm Vivian Mussina, "The Background and Origin of the American Religious Tract Movement" (Ph.D. diss., Drew University, 1936), chap. I and pp. 102, 176–186; Lawrence Thompson, "The Printing and Publishing Activities of the American Tract Society from 1825 to 1850," *The Papers of the Bibliographical Society of America*, 35 (Second Quarter, 1941), 84–85.

11. Justin Edwards, "Usefulness of Tracts," *Tracts of the American Tract Society*, general series (n.d., New York), III, no. 104, pp. 5, 19 (hereafter, ATS, *Tracts*); William A. Hallock, *"Light and Love": A Sketch of the Life and Labor of the Rev. Justin Edwards, D.D.* (New York, 1855[?]), pp. 103, 204; Thompson, "Printing and Publishing Activities of the ATS," p. 86; "Address of the [American Tract Society] Executive Committee, New York, June 1825" (bound with ATS, *Tracts*, vol. I), p. 16 (membership of first Executive Committee); biographical data from *National Cyclopedia of American Biography*; Bertram Wyatt-Brown, *Lewis Tappan and the Evangelical War against Slavery* (Cleveland, Case Western Reserve University Press, 1969; reissued, New York, Atheneum, 1971), p. 50. The four New York City ministers on the first ATS Executive Committee were James Milnor (Episcopal), Gardiner Spring (Presbyterian), John Knox (Reformed), and Charles Sommers (Baptist).

12. "Address of the [ATS] Executive Committee," pp. 4, 5, 6, 12.

13. Ibid., p. 5.

14. Ibid., pp. 12, 13.

15. Thompson, "Printing and Publishing Activities of the ATS," pp. 83, 90–97; 102–106.

16. Edwin W. Bonner, "Distributing the Printed Word: The Tract Association of Friends, 1816–1966," *Pennsylvania Magazine of His-

tory and Biography, 91 (July 1967), 348; Thompson, "Printing and Publishing Activities of the ATS," pp. 83, 90–97, 102–106; Keith Melder, "Ladies Bountiful: Organized Women's Benevolence in Early Nineteenth Century America," *New York History*, 48 (July 1967), 236; Carroll Smith-Rosenberg, *Religion and the Rise of the American City: The New York City Mission Movement, 1812–1870* (Ithaca, Cornell University Press, 1971), pp. 79–83; Wyatt-Brown, *Lewis Tappan*, p. 53; Lewis Tappan, *The Life of Arthur Tappan* (New York, 1870; reissued, Westport, Conn., Negro Universities Press, 1970), p. 88. Both Tappan brothers were active in the tract movement as financial supporters and volunteer distributors. Somewhat later, the Chicago Tract Society (founded 1838) adopted a plan of saturation distribution closely modeled on the one developed in New York City. See Bessie L. Pierce, *A History of Chicago*, 3 vols. (New York, Alfred A. Knopf, 1937–1957), vol. II, p. 374.

17. Rev. J. Scudder, "Knocking at the Door: an Appeal to Youth," ATS, *Tracts*, I, no. 31, p. 19; "Friendly Conversation," ibid., IV, no. 118, p. 1.

18. "Conversation with a Young Traveler," ibid., VI, no. 203, p. 1. See also "Conversation with an Infidel," ibid., II, no. 64, and "The One Thing Needful," ibid., I, no. 6.

19. "To a Person Engaged in a Lawsuit," ibid., V, no. 168, p. 3; "To the Afflicted," ibid., II, no. 47, p. 4; "To a Lady in Fashionable Life," ibid., VIII, no. 289. During the cholera outbreak of 1832 in New York City, the ATS printed and distributed 160,000 tracts entitled "An Appeal on the Subject of the Cholera to the Prepared and Unprepared." Charles E. Rosenberg, *The Cholera Years: The United States in 1832, 1849, and 1866* (Chicago, University of Chicago Press, 1962), p. 50.

20. "Friendly Suggestions to an Emigrant. By an Emigrant," ATS, *Tracts*, XI, no. 468, pp. 2, 7.

21. "Importance of Consideration," ibid., VI, no. 202, p. 1; Scudder, "Knocking at the Door," p. 19.

22. "Family Worship," ibid., I, no. 18, p. 3; "The Downward Course of Sin," ibid., no. 15, p. 5; "Return Poor Wanderer," a tract for prostitutes reprinted in John R. McDowall, *Magdalen Facts*, New York, I (Jan. 1832), 101, 103; "The Warning Voice," ATS, *Tracts*, I, no. 5, p. 5; "A Friendly Visit to the House of Mourning," ibid., no. 3, p. 5.

23. "Sabbath Occupations," ibid., IV, no. 116, p. 8; ibid., I, no. 25 (Benjamin Rush's temperance tract).

24. "Counsels to a Young Man," ibid., X, no. 402, pp. 5, 9, 10, 11; Rev. Robert Hall, "The Work of the Holy Spirit," ibid., I, no. 2, p. 13; "To a Lady in Fashionable Life," ibid., VIII, no. 289, p. 5; "The Advantages of Sabbath Schools," ibid., VIII, no. 272, p. 4; "God is a Refuge," ibid., I, no. 23, p. 5.

25. "Parental Faithfulness," ibid., V, no. 171, p. 1; "Family Worship," ibid., I, no. 18, p. 15. For the graphic story of a boy who goes bad through the lack of just such parental oversight, see W. G. Brownlee, "The Spoiled Child," ibid., I, no. 28.

26. Rev. James Bean, "The Christian Minister's Affectionate Advice to a Married Couple," ibid., II, no. 67, p. 1.

27. "Conviction at the Judgment Day," ibid., II, no. 54, p. 1; "The Misery of the Lost," ibid., no. 51, p. 9. See also Edward Payson, "How Sin Appears in Heaven," ibid., no. 40, pp. 2, 4.

28. "To the Inhabitants of New Settlements," ibid., V, no. 182, p. 10.

29. Hannah More, "The Shepherd of Salisbury Plain," ibid., I, no. 10, p. 15.

30. "David Baldwin, or The Miller's Son," ibid., VIII, no. 282. See also "The Moral Man Tried, in Three Dialogues," ibid., I, no. 19, and "The Village Prayer Meeting," ibid., VI, no. 199, p. 2.

31. "My Father's Prayer. An Authentic Narrative," ibid., IX, no. 312, p. 6; "A dying Mother's Counsel to her only Son," ibid., II, no. 52. See also, in the same vein, "The Mother's Last Prayer," ibid., X, no. 354, and "Give Me Thy Heart," ibid., II, no. 44, p. 13. In their use of tangible, emotion-charged images to convey the moral message, the American tract writers were much influenced by British precedent. Only through "strong, pithy expressions" and "lively representations of truth," a British tract leader had advised in 1813, could one "allure the listless to read." Quoted in Mussina, "Background and Origin of the American Religious Tract Movement," p. 296.

32. Leigh Edwards, "The Dairyman's Daughter," ibid., I, no. 9, p. 15.

33. "The Widow's Son," ibid., I, no. 35, p. 9.

34. Edwards, "The Dairyman's Daughter," p. 22.

35. "The Widow's Son," pp. 15, 16, 18, 21, 24.

36. "The Young Cottager," ibid., III, no. 79, p. 41; "The Village Funeral," ibid., I, no. 36, p. 1; Philippe Ariès, *Western Attitudes toward Death: From the Middle Ages to the Present* (Baltimore, Johns Hopkins University Press, 1974), chap. III; Ann Douglas, "Heaven Our Home: Consolation Literature in the Northern United States, 1830–1880," in *Death in America*, ed. with an introduction by David E. Stannard (Philadelphia, University of Pennsylvania Press, 1975), pp. 49–68. For another pathetic village funeral, see "The Cottager's Wife," ATS, *Tracts*, II, no. 63, esp. p. 27.

3 THE SUNDAY SCHOOL IN THE CITY

1. *American Sunday School Magazine* (Feb. 1826), p. 53. This American Sunday School Union publication, issued in Philadelphia, is cited hereafter as *ASSM*. In January 1830, the name was expanded to *American Sunday School Teachers Magazine*.

2. Edwin W. Rice, *The Sunday-School Movement, 1780–1917, and the American Sunday-School Union, 1817–1917* (Philadelphia, American Sunday-School Union, 1917), p. 66.

3. American Bible Society, *Annual Report* (1821), p. 11; (1829), p. 11; (1833), p. 23; *The History of American Methodism*, ed. Emory S. Bucke, 3 vols. (New York, Abingdon Press, 1964), I, 585.

4. *Christian Observer* quoted in *ASSM* (Jan. 1827), p. 11. New York Sunday School Union, *Plain and Easy Directions for Forming Sunday Schools, Presenting Complete and Approved Plans for Their Management and Instruction* (New York, 1826), p. iii (hereafter, *Plain*

and *Easy Directions*); American Sunday School Union, *The Teacher Taught. An Humble Attempt to Make the Path of the Sunday School Teacher Straight and Plain* (Philadelphia, 1839), p. 28 (hereafter, *Teacher Taught*). See also Rice, *Sunday-School Movement*, pp. 53, 195, 202.

5. *Teacher Taught*, pp. 379, 382; *ASSM* (Feb. 1828), p. 56; (May 1830), p. 159 (quoting the Reverend Samuel S. Schmucker, a Lutheran leader); (Nov. 1830), p. 324. See also, for similar sentiments, American Sunday School Union, *Annual Report* (Philadelphia, 1832), p. 41 (hereafter, ASSU, AR).

6. *ASSM* (Dec. 1826), pp. 374–375; (Mar. 1826), p. 84.

7. *Memorials of William E. Dodge*, ed. D. Stuart Dodge (New York [1887]), pp. 224, 231; Rice, *Sunday-School Movement*, pp. 55–57; *Dictionary of American Biography*, XI, 405–406 (Eleazer Lord); *ASSM* (Nov. 1824), p. 147 (obituary of Divie Bethune); Mary S. Benson, "Bethune, Joanna Graham," *Notable American Women*, ed. Edward T. James, Janet W. James, and Paul S. Boyer (Cambridge, Mass., Harvard University Press, 1971), I, 138–140. In 1871, listening to a Philadelphia Sunday school recite the catechism, the aged William E. Dodge exclaimed: "You have taken me back to-night to my old New England home, . . . when at my father's knee I mastered these very answers, these very words, just as you have done." (Dodge, ed., *Memorials of William E. Dodge*, p. 231).

8. ASSU, AR (1848), pp. 12–16 (obituary of Alexander Henry); Massachusetts Sabbath School Society, *Annual Reports*, lists of officers (hereafter, Mass. S.S. So., AR); *Dictionary of American Biography*, I, 360–361 (Samuel T. Armstrong); *National Cyclopedia of American Biography*, XXV, 91 (Alfred D. Foster). Foster and Armstrong served as presidents of the Massachusetts Sabbath-School Society, a Congregationalist body founded in 1829. Another prominent Philadelphia Sunday school leader whose career follows the pattern described was Joseph H. Dulles. See Rice, *Sunday-School Movement*, pp. 98–99.

9. *ASSM* (Nov. 1824), p. 148.

10. Ibid. (Mar. 1826), p. 77; (May 1829), p. 133. Cf. the Reverend Ward Stafford's comment on immorality in New York in 1817: "Multitudes are as yet uncontaminated, especially of the rising generation. but vice is spreading like a contagion." Stafford, *New Missionary Field: A Report to the Female Missionary Society for the Poor of the City of New York and Its Vicinity* (New York, 1817), p. 16.

11. Silas Farmer, *History of Detroit and Wayne County and Early Michigan* (New York, 1890; reissued, Gale Research, 1969), p. 631; Rice, *Sunday-School Movement*, p. 437 (Raikes quote); Mass. S.S. Soc., AR (1837), pp. 27, 28; *Sunday School Repository* (New York, Sept. 1817), p. 181 (Troy, N.Y., report).

12. *ASSM* (Mar. 1830), p. 74; (Feb. 1830), p. 58. For similar sentiments, see also Mass. S.S. Soc., AR (1843), p. 84.

13. *Teacher Taught*, pp. 121–123, 380; "Apprentices in Cities," *ASSM* (Jan. 1828). See also ibid. (Feb. 1828), p. 56.

14. Ibid. (Jan. 1828), p. 25; (Feb. 1828), p. 56; *S.S. Repository* (Apr. 1818), p. 31; *Teacher Taught*, p. 380.

15. Ibid., p. 18; *ASSM* (Apr. 1831), p. 38.

16. *ASSM* (Jan. 1830), p. 14; Anne Mary Boylan, " 'The Nursery of the Church': Evangelical Protestant Sunday Schools, 1820–1880" (Ph.D. diss., University of Wisconsin, 1973), pp. 282–286 (on Taylor); John Todd, *The Sabbath School Teacher: Designed to Aid in Elevating and Perfecting the Sabbath School System* (Northampton, Mass., 1837), pp. 66, 67. See also, for a similar argument, "The Advantages of Sabbath Schools," American Tract Society, *Tracts* (New York, n.d.), VIII, no. 272, p. 7.

17. "To the Parents of Sabbath School Children," ibid., V, no. 157, pp. 2, 3; *ASSM* (Aug. 1824), p. 39, (Sept. 1830), p. 267; ASSU, *AR* (1838), p. 19; *S.S. Repository* (June/July, 1817) p. 157. For similar denials of any intention of preempting the parental role, see *ASSM* (Feb. 1830), p. 42, and ASSU, *AR* (1847), p. 35.

18. *ASSM* (Oct. 1826), p. 303; (Dec. 1828), p. 556; ASSU, *AR* (1835), p. 21.

19. *ASSM* (Apr. 1831), p. 44; Barbara Welter, "The Cult of True Womanhood, 1820–1860," *American Quarterly*, 18 (Summer 1966), 151–174.

20. *ASSM* (Sept. 1824), p. 82 ("moral deformities"); (Oct. 1831), p. 189; ASSU, *AR* (1830), p. 21; ibid. (1836), p. 30; ibid. (1849), p. 21; Todd, *Sabbath School Teacher*, p. 262.

21. *ASSM* (June 1825), p. 196.

22. ASSU, *AR* (1848), pp. 16, 17; ibid. (1830), p. 21. For an earlier expression of the same view, see *S.S. Repository* (June/July 1817), p. 156. The same rhetorical strategy was employed by supporters of the "infant school" movement which enjoyed a brief vogue in Boston in the late 1820s and early 1830s. See Dean May and Maris A. Vinovskis, "A Ray of Millennial Light: Early Education and Social Reform in the Infant School Movement in Massachusetts, 1826–1840," in *Family and Kin in Urban Communities, 1700–1930*, ed. Tamara K. Hareven (New York, Franklin Watts, 1977), pp. 81–82.

23. Stafford, *New Missionary Field*, p. 4; "Sunday Schools in Philadelphia," *ASSM* (May 1825), p. 135; ibid. (Feb. 1829), p. 43. See also *Teacher Taught*, p. 350 (New York City attendance statistics for 1837); Mass. S.S. Soc., *AR* (1837), p. 60; Rice, *Sunday-School Movement*, p. 60; Bessie L. Pierce, *History of Chicago*, 3 vols. (New York, Alfred A. Knopf, 1937–1957), I, 253–254.

24. *ASSM* (June 1825), p. 185; ibid. (June 1829), p. 184 (quoted passage); Pierce, *History of Chicago*, I, 254.

25. *ASSM* (Jan. 1827), p. 11 (quoting the New York *Christian Advocate*).

26. *ASSM* (May 1825), p. 135 (on Philadelphia); Mass. S.S. Soc., *AR* (1837), p. 27; ibid. (1833), p. 10; *Teacher Taught*, p. 31.

27. Boylan, " 'Nursery of the Church,' " p. 89; ASSU, *AR* (1832), p. 32 (denominational breakdown of officers).

28. *Teacher Taught*, p. 169; ASSU, *AR* (1833), p. 21; (1830), p. 21. References to the reservations and even hostility of some church people toward the Sunday school idea are frequent in the early literature of the movement. See, *e.g.*, Stafford, *New Missionary Field*, p. 18;

Rice, *Sunday-School Movement*, pp. 48, 62; Boylan, " 'Nursery of the Church,' " pp. 71–74, and Stephen H. Tyng, *Forty Years' Experience in Sunday-Schools* (New York, 1860), pp. 137–141. The religion taught in the Sunday schools, declared the *American Sunday School Magazine* (Apr. 1831, p. 47) should be of the variety that "soothes, restrains, and establishes by its own peculiar sanctions the relations of government with people, and of man with man."

29. Ibid. (Mar. 1828), p. 76; ibid. (July 1831), p. 125; "The Advantages of Sabbath Schools," p. 4; Tyng, *Forty Years' Experience in Sunday-Schools*, p. 61.

30. *S.S. Repository* (June 1818), pp. 61, 62.

31. ASSU, *AR* (1849), p. 36.

32. Ibid., p. 26; Raymond A. Mohl, "Education as Social Control in New York City, 1784–1825," *New York History*, 51 (Apr. 1970), p. 234; *Teacher Taught*, p. 33. In the same vein, the Reverend John Todd argued (*Sabbath School Teacher*, p. 249), that the Sunday school's main object was to "*form right HABITS in the scholar.*"

33 *S.S. Repository* (Apr. 1818), p. 11.

34. *Plain and Easy Directions*, p. 154.

35. *ASSM* (Feb. 1825), p. 71.

36. Ibid. (Oct. 1827), p. 302; ibid. (Oct. 1831), p. 188; ibid. (June 1826), p. 181. See also *S.S. Repository* (June 1818), p. 67, and Tyng, *Forty Years' Experience in Sunday-Schools*, p. 65.

37. Ibid., p. 80; *ASSM* (Sept. 1824), p. 82; ibid. (Feb. 1826), p. 54; *John Todd: The Story of His Life Told Mainly by Himself* (New York, 1876), p. 310; ASSU, *AR* (1849), p. 22. In *Philosophy of Manufactures*, an 1835 work written for English mill owners, Andrew Ure urged the mill owner to "organize his moral machinery on equally sound principles with his mechanical."—specifically, by establishing Sunday schools for his workers. Quoted in E. P. Thompson, *The Making of the English Working Class* (London, Gollancz, 1963; reissued, New York, Vintage Books, 1963), p. 361. I have benefited from Thompson's discussion of the role of Methodism—including Methodist Sunday schools—in shaping working class values in early nineteenth century England. See chap. IX, "The Transforming Power of the Cross."

38. *Teacher Taught*, p. 46.

39. Ibid., pp. 117–118.

40. *Plain and Easy Directions*, pp. 9–11.

41. Todd, *Sabbath School Teacher*, p. 129 (arabic numbers written out in the original).

42. Ibid., p. 83; *ASSM* (Mar. 1826), p. 82; "Directions for the Management of a Sunday School," ibid. (Sept. 1827), p. 259; *Teacher Taught*, pp. 36, 105.

43. *Plain and Easy Directions*, p. 24.

44. Ibid., p. 36.

45. ABS, *AR* (1822), p. 166; *The Diary of Michael Floy, Jr., Bowery Village, 1833–37*, ed. Richard A. E. Brooks (New Haven, Yale University Press, 1941), pp. 74–75, 110, 247; *Teacher Taught*, p. 119 ("I Am Late" placard); *ASSM* (July 1831), p. 175.

46. *Plain and Easy Directions*, pp. 3–4.

47. Ibid., pp. 119–120. On the monitorial vogue: Carl F. Kaestle, *Joseph Lancaster and the Monitorial School Movement* (New York, Teachers College Press, 1973).

48. *Plain and Easy Directions*, pp. 66, 73; Todd, *Sabbath School Teacher*, p. 135; ASSM (Oct. 1831), p. 347 (age of teachers).

49. Tyng, *Forty Years Experience in Sunday-Schools*, pp. 115–116; ASSM (Sept. 1827), p. 260; Todd, *Sabbath School Teacher*, p. 78.

50. *Teacher Taught*, pp. 106, 127. See also H. Clay Trumball, *A Model Superintendent: A Sketch of the Life, Character, and Methods of Work of Henry P. Haven* (New York, 1880), pp. 25–30.

51. ASSU, AR (1848), p. 17, 51, 52. In this respect the Jacksonian Sunday schools resembled—certainly by no coincidence—the colonial primary schools where, as James Axtell has recently pointed out (*The School upon a Hill: Education and Society in Colonial New England* [New Haven, Yale University Press, 1974; reissued New York, W. W. Norton, 1976], p. xv), "lessons in social conformity and obedience to authority" were implicit not only in the textbooks but also in "the very physical, pedagogical, and social conditions" under which the schools were conducted.

52. ASSM (Oct. 1827), p. 300; ibid. (Mar. 1828), p. 65. See also *S.S. Repository* (Apr. 1818), p. 13.

53. Sometimes the suggestion of a direct monetary advantage to Sunday school attendance was quite blatant. One tract urged parents to keep their children in Sunday school so their teachers would "take notice of them, and . . . employ them as they grow up, or recommend them to persons who can provide better for them." "To the Parents of Sabbath-School Children," American Tract Society, p. 3.

54. *Teacher Taught*, p. 108.

55. Ibid. (quoted passage); *Plain and Easy Directions*, p. 78; illustration following p. 72 of screen to hide face of misbehaving pupil.

56. Todd, *Sabbath School Teacher*, pp. 84–85.

57. William Ellery Channing, "The Sunday School," *Works* (Boston, American Unitarian Association, 1903), IV, 361–362.

58. Arthur E. Bestor, Jr., "Patent-Office Models of the Good Society: Some Relationships between Social Reform and Westward Expansion," *American Historical Review*, 58 (Apr. 1953), 505–526; Todd, *Sabbath School Teacher*, p. 290 (quoting Wesley).

59. John Dewey, *The School and Society* (Chicago, University of Chicago Press, 1900).

60. *S.S. Repository* (Apr. 1818), p. 28; ASSM (Jan. 1829), p. 3; ibid. (Sept. 1829), p. 260.

61. Ibid. (Feb. 1826), p. 34; ibid. (Oct. 1831), p. 188; ibid. (Apr. 1831), p. 67.

4 URBAN MORAL REFORM IN THE EARLY REPUBLIC

1. American Sunday School Union, *Annual Report* (1849), p. 26 (hereafter, ASSU, AR).

2. Quoted in Brian Harrison, "Religion and Recreation in Nineteenth Century England," *Past and Present*, 38 (Dec. 1967), 119–120.

3. David Montgomery, "The Working Classes of the Pre-industrial

American City, 1780–1830," in *The American City, Historical Studies,* ed. James F. Richardson (Waltham, Mass., Xerox College Publishing, 1972), p. 81; Joseph M. Hawes, *Children in Urban Society: Juvenile Delinquency in Nineteenth Century America* (New York, Oxford University Press, 1971), p. 27.

4. William Ellery Channing, "Ministry for the Poor: Discourse before the Benevolent Fraternity of Churches" (April 9, 1835), *The Works of William E. Channing* (Boston, American Unitarian Association, 1903), IV, 275; "Discourse on the Life and Character of the Rev. Joseph Tuckerman, D.D." [1841], ibid., VI, 95–96.

5. Carroll Smith-Rosenberg, *Religion and the Rise of the American City: The New York City Mission Movement, 1812–1870* (Ithaca, Cornell University Press, 1971), pp. 58, 83.

6. "Are You a Sabbath School Teacher?" American Tract Society, *Tracts* (New York, 1836), X, no. 396, p. 4; Smith-Rosenberg, *Religion and the Rise of the American City,* pp. 92–93.

7. Clifford S. Griffin, *The Ferment of Reform, 1830–1860* (New York, Thomas Y. Crowell, 1967), p. 19; Lois W. Banner, "Religious Benevolence as Social Control: A Critique of an Interpretation," *Journal of American History,* 60 (June 1973), 23; Raymond A. Mohl, "Education as Social Control in New York City, 1784–1825," *New York History,* 51 (April 1970), 234; Charles I. Foster, "The Urban Missionary Movement, 1814–1837," *Pennsylvania Magazine of History and Biography,* 75/76 (Jan. 1951), p. 58.

8. Quoted in John R. Bodo, *The Protestant Clergy and Public Issues, 1812–1848* (Princeton, Princeton University Press, 1954), p. 29. Walter Hugins, *Jacksonian Democracy and the Working Class: A Study of The New York Workingmen's Movement, 1829–1837* (Palo Alto, Stanford University Press, 1960), p. 135. On Calvin Colton, see *Dictionary of American Biography,* IV, 320–321.

9. ASSU, *AR* (1847), p. 35; Mohl, "Education as Social Control in New York City," p. 234; *American Sunday School Magazine* (Feb. 1826), pp. 43–44 (hereafter, *ASSM*).

10. Robert W. Lynn and Elliott Wright, *The Big Little School: Sunday Child of American Protestantism* (New York, Harper and Bros., 1971), p. 21; Banner, "Religious Benevolence as Social Control: A Critique of an Interpretation," pp. 25–27. Of the twenty-four New York City men on the first board of directors of the American Bible Society, eleven were from the wealthiest 1 percent of the population. A similar pattern can be found among the early leaders of the American Tract Society and the American Sunday School Union. Edward Pessen, *Riches, Class and Power before the Civil War* (Lexington, Mass., D. C. Heath, 1973), pp. 262–263.

11. "On Preaching the Gospel to the Poor," Channing, *Works,* V, 270. This point is interestingly touched on in William A. Muraskin, "The Social-Control Theory in American History: A Critique," *Journal of Social History* 9 (Summer 1976), 566.

12. John Paul Scott, "Science and Social Control," in *Social Control and Social Change,* ed. John Paul Scott and Sarah F. Scott (Chicago, University of Chicago Press, 1971), p. 5; Gerald N. Grob, "Wel-

fare and Poverty in American History," *Reviews in American History*, 1 (Mar. 1973), 49–50.

13. Paul Faler, "Cultural Aspects of the Industrial Revolution: Lynn, Massachusetts, Shoemakers and Industrial Morality, 1826–1860," *Labor History*, 15 (Summer 1974), 381, 391; J. B. Horton, tract volunteer, quoted in John H. Griscom, M.D., *The Sanitary Condition of the Laboring Population of New York* (New York, Harper and Bros., 1845), p. 29.

14. *Sunday School Repository* (Oct. 1818), p. 121.

15. For a useful discussion of the upper ranks of the urban class structure in the Jacksonian period see Pessen, *Riches, Class and Power before the Civil War*.

16. Catharine M. Sedgwick, *Clarence; or, A Tale of Our Times* (Philadelphia, 1830), I, 52.

17. Charles C. Cole, *The Social Ideas of the Northern Evangelists, 1826–1860* (New York, Columbia University Press, 1954), p. 112.

18. A real-life parallel to the hero of the tract was young William Merrill, who arrived in the burgeoning Ohio River town of Cincinnati in 1823. Of pious background and originally intent upon a career in the ministry, William soon found himself attracted by the theater and other urban temptations. With distress he confessed in his diary that he was coming to prefer reading novels in the isolation of his room to attendance at prayer meeting. Recognizing his danger, he volunteered to teach a Sunday school for black children and in 1825 organized his own slum Sunday school. Having given his life focus and disciplined seriousness at a crucial stage, Merrill went on to a successful career as head of a large pharmaceutical house. Richard C. Wade, *The Urban Frontier: The Rise of Western Cities, 1790–1830* (Cambridge, Mass., Harvard University Press, 1959), pp. 266–268.

19. New York Sunday School Union, *Plain and Easy Directions for Forming Sunday Schools, Presenting Complete and Approved Plans for Their Management and Instruction* (New York, 1826), pp. 16, 17, 57, 66; John Todd, *The Sabbath School Teacher* (Northampton, Mass., 1837), pp. 123, 127; American Sunday School Union, *The Teacher Taught; An Humble Attempt to Make the Path of the Sunday-school Teacher Straight and Plain* (Philadelphia, 1839), p. 271; "The Advantages of Sabbath Schools," ATS, *Tracts*, VIII, no. 272, p. 8 (1833 estimate of nearly 100,000 Sunday school teachers in the United States).

20. *Plain and Easy Directions*, pp. 67–68, 69; "The Advantages of Sabbath Schools," p. 12; Todd, *The Sabbath School Teacher*, p. 90; Edwin W. Rice, *The Sunday-School Movement, 1780–1917, and the American Sunday-School Union, 1817–1917* (Philadelphia, American Sunday-School Union, 1917), p. 76.

21. *ASSM* (Feb. 1830), p. 54; ibid. (Apr. 1831), p. 60.

22. Stephen H. Tyng, D.D., *Forty-Years' Experience in Sunday-Schools* (New York, 1860), p. 101; *ASSM* (Feb. 1828), p. 41; Todd, *Sabbath School Teacher*, p. 142.

23. Ibid., pp. 83, 91, 113.

24. *Plain and Easy Directions*, p. 13; Todd, *Sabbath School Teacher*, p. 142.

25. *Teacher Taught*, p. 300; *ASSM* (Oct. 1827), p. 301; Todd, *Sabbath School Teacher*, p. 410.

26. ASSU, *AR* (1844), p. 43; *ASSM* (Jan. 1827), p. 11.

27. Ibid. (Feb. 1828), p. 55.

5 HEIGHTENED CONCERN

1. Oscar Handlin, *Boston's Immigrants, A Study in Acculturation. Revised and Enlarged Edition* (Cambridge, Mass., Harvard University Press, 1959), chap. II, and app., tables II and VII; United States Bureau of the Census, *Historical Statistics of the United States, Colonial Times to 1970, Bicentenial Edition*, 2 vols. (Washington, D.C., Government Printing Office, 1975), I, 12, 106; Robert Ernst, *Immigrant Life in New York City, 1825–1863* (New York, King's Crown Press, Columbia University, 1949), pp. 187, 191, 193; Sam Bass Warner, Jr., *The Private City: Philadelphia in Three Periods of Its Growth* (Philadelphia, University of Pennsylvania Press, 1968), pp. 49–50, 51. Ira Rosenwaike, *Population History of New York City* (Syracuse, N.Y., Syracuse University Press, 1972), pp. 33–48, 52–54. In this paragraph I have defined the urban population as those living in cities of 25,000 or more population.

2. Allan Stanley Horlick, *Country Boys and Merchant Princes: The Social Control of Young Men in New York* (Lewisburg, Pa., Bucknell University Press, 1975), p. 40; *The Diary of Philip Hone, 1828–1851*, ed. Allan Nevins (New York, Dodd Mead, 1936), pp. 394–395; Peter R. Knights, *The Plain People of Boston, 1830–1860: A Study in City Growth* (New York, Oxford University Press, 1971), p. 18; Warner, *Private City*, p. 50.

3. Bayrd Still, "Patterns of Mid-Nineteenth Century Urbanization in the Middle West," *Mississippi Valley Historical Review*, 28 (Sept. 1941), 187–206; Richard C. Wade, *The Urban Frontier: The Rise of Western Cities, 1790–1830* (Cambridge, Mass., Harvard University Press, 1959), quoted phrase, p. 341; Bessie L. Pierce, *A History of Chicago*, 3 vols. (New York, Alfred A. Knopf, 1937–1957), I, 171.

4. Handlin, *Boston's Immigrants*, pp. 106 (quoted phrase), 256. Of the 21,300 prison commitments in New York City in 1850, some 15,500 were foreign-born; by 1860, 86 percent of the paupers on the relief rolls in New York were foreign-born (Ernst, *Immigrant Life in New York*, pp. 56–59, 202). In Boston, expenditures for poor relief soared from $37,122 in 1830 to $168,389 in 1860 (Handlin, *Boston's Immigrants*, app., table III). For a graphic account of slum conditions in this period see John H. Griscom, M.D., *The Sanitary Condition of the Laboring Population of New York, with Suggestions for Its Improvement* (New York, 1845), esp. pp. 6–10. See also Samuel C. Busey, M.D., *Immigration: Its Evils and Consequences* (New York, 1856; reissued, New York, Arno Press, 1969), esp. p. 126, where immigration is linked to "disease, disorder, and immorality."

5. Knights, *Plain People of Boston*, p. 58; Theodore N. Ferdinand, "The Criminal Patterns of Boston since 1849," *American Journal of Sociology*, 73 (July 1967), 84–99; Stephen Thernstrom and Peter R.

Knights, "Men in Motion: Some Data and Speculations about Urban Population Mobility in Nineteenth-Century America," in *Anonymous Americans: Explorations in Nineteenth-Century Social History*, ed. Tamara K. Hareven (Englewood Cliffs, N.J., Prentice-Hall, 1971), quoted phrase, p. 20. See also Roger Lane, "Crime and Criminal Statistics in Nineteenth-Century Massachusetts," *Journal of Social History*, 2 (Winter 1968), 156–163, and Stuart M. Blumin, "Residential Mobility within the Nineteenth-Century City," in *The Peoples of Philadelphia: A History of Ethnic Groups and Lower Class Life, 1790–1940*, ed. Allen F. Davis and Mark H. Haller (Philadelphia, Temple University Press, 1973), pp. 37–51, esp. p. 49.

6. Wade, *Urban Frontier*, pp. 106–107, 121–122, 206–220; Joseph M. Hawes, *Children in Urban Society* (New York, Oxford University Press, 1971), p. 91 (Dickens); Blumin, "Residential Mobility," p. 44 (Dandy Hill); Ernst, *Immigrant Life in New York*, p. 39.

7. Adrian Cook, *The Armies of the Streets: The New York City Draft Riots of 1863* (Lexington, The University Press of Kentucky, 1974); [Louisa Goddard Whitney], *The Burning of the Convent. A Narrative of the Destruction by a Mob, of the Ursuline School on Mount Benedict, Charlestown, as Remembered by One of the Pupils* (Cambridge, Mass., 1877); [Asa Greene], *A Glance at New York* (New York, 1837), p. 96 (Baltimore as "Mob City"); Joel Tyler Headley, *The Great Riots of New York, 1712 to 1873* (New York, 1873; reissued, New York, Dover, 1971), pp. 97–135; Herbert Asbury, *The Gangs of New York* (New York, Alfred A. Knopf, 1928; reissued, New York, Capricorn Books, 1970), pp. 21–173, esp. p. 113 (quoted passage on 1857 gang war); Elizabeth M. Geffen, "Violence in Philadelphia in the 1840s and 1850s," *Pennsylvania History*, 36 (Oct. 1969), 381–410; Paul O. Weinbaum, "Temperance, Politics, and the New York City Riots of 1857," *New York Historical Society Quarterly*, 59 (July 1975), 246–270.

8. Arlen R. Dykstra, "Rowdyism and Rivalism in the St. Louis Fire Department, 1850–1857," *Missouri Historical Review*, 69 (Oct. 1974), 48–64; John C. Schneider, "Riot and Reaction in St. Louis, 1854–1856," *ibid.*, 68 (Jan. 1974), 171–185; James F. Richardson, *Urban Police in the United States* (Port Washington, N.Y., Kennikat Press, 1974), p. 35. See also, in addition to the sources already cited: Vincent P. Lannie and Bernard C. Diethorn, "For the Honor and Glory of God: The Philadelphia Bible Riots of 1840," *History of Education Quarterly*, 8 (Spring 1968), 44–95; Russell F. Weigley, " 'A Peaceful City': Public Order in Philadelphia from Consolidation [1854] through the Civil War," in *Peoples of Philadelphia*, ed. Davis and Haller, pp. 155–174; *Clemens of the "Call": Mark Twain in San Francisco*, ed. Edgar M. Branch (Berkeley, University of California Press, 1969), pt. II: "Crime and Court Reporter"; John Thomas Scharf, *The Chronicles of Baltimore* (Baltimore, 1874), pp. 550–552, on an 1856 election riot. Even this brief listing barely scratches the surface of the vast literature on antebellum urban violence. For a brief overview and summary of this literature, see Richard M. Brown, "Historical Patterns of Violence in America," in *Violence in America: Historical and Comparative Perspectives. A*

Report Submitted to the National Commission on the Causes and Prevention of Violence, ed. Hugh Davis Graham and Ted Robert Gurr (New York, Bantam Books, 1969), pp. 53–54, 78–79.

9. George Rudé, The Crowd in History: A Study of Popular Disturbances in France and England, 1730–1848 (New York, John Wiley and Sons, 1964); Eric J. Hobsbawm, Primitive Rebels: Studies in Archaic Forms of Social Movement in the Nineteenth and Twentieth Centuries (Manchester, Manchester University Press, 1969); Leonard L. Richards, "Gentlemen of Property and Standing": Anti-Abolition Mobs in Jacksonian America (New York, Oxford University Press, 1970); David Grimsted, "Rioting in Its Jacksonian Setting," American Historical Review, 77 (Apr. 1972), 361–397; John Runcie, " 'Hunting the Nigs' in Philadelphia: The Race Riot of August 1834," Pennsylvania History, 39 (April, 1972), 187–218; Michael Feldberg, "The Crowd in Philadelphia History: A Comparative Perspective," Labor History, 15 (Summer 1974), 323–336. For a sociological study focused on more recent urban violence but analytically relevant to the earlier period, see Irving Louis Horowitz and Martin Liebowitz, "Social Deviance and Political Marginality: Toward a Redefinition of the Relation between Sociology and Politics," Social Problems, 15 (Winter 1968), 280–296.

10. Philip Schaff, America: A Sketch of the Political, Social and Religious Character (New York, 1855; reissued, Cambridge, Mass., Harvard University Press, 1961, ed. Perry Miller), p. 9; [Greene], Glance at New York, p. 95.

11. Cook, Armies of the Streets, p. 197; Hone, Diary, p. 451; Geffen, "Violence in Philadelphia," p. 391; Dykstra, "Rowdyism and Rivalism in the St. Louis Fire Department," pp. 55, 57 (quoted passage). Christopher Lasch, commenting on David J. Rothman's The Discovery of the Asylum: Social Order and Disorder in the New Republic (Boston, Little, Brown, 1971) has dismissed as "trite" Rothman's argument that fear of social disorder figured in such antebellum social-control innovations as the asylum. No doubt this explanation is often used glibly, but it is impossible to read extensively in the writings about the city in the 1830–1860 period without being struck again and again by the pervasiveness of the fears aroused by street violence, riots, rowdiness, crime, and moral degeneracy in the slums. I fail to see how calling attention to these fears contradicts Lasch's assertion that "the asylum arose out of conditions that were general in modern society rather than specific to the United States." General conditions manifest themselves in specific ways. Christopher Lasch, The World of Nations; Reflections on American History, Politics, and Culture (New York, Alfred A. Knopf, 1973), p. 316.

12. Michael H. Cowan, City of the West: Emerson, America, and the Urban Metaphor (New Haven, Yale University Press, 1967), pp. 61, 138, 191 (Thoreau). See also John Henry Raleigh, "The Novel and the City: England and America in the Nineteenth Century," Victorian Studies, 11 (Mar. 1968), 291–328.

13. Eugene Arden, "The Evil City in American Fiction," New York History, 52 (July 1954), 259–279; Catharine M. Sedgwick, Clarence; or, A Tale of Our Own Times, 2 vols. (Philadelphia, 1830), I, 109; Herman

Melville, *Pierre; or, The Ambiguities* (New York, 1852; reprinted New York, Grove Press, n.d.), p. 336. See also George A. Dunlap, *The City in the American Novel, 1789–1900* (Philadelphia, University of Pennsylvania Press, 1934), esp. pp. 14, 68–69.

14. David Brion Davis, *Homicide in American Fiction, 1798–1860* (Ithaca, Cornell University Press, 1957), pp. 161–163, 262–263; James L. Crouthamel, "James Gordon Bennett, The *New York Herald*, and the Development of Newspaper Sensationalism," *New York History*, 54 (July 1973), 294–316, esp. p. 303.

15. Arden, "The Evil City in American Fiction," p. 262; Davis, *Homicide in American Fiction*, p. 165.

16. Though refracted through a lurid and perhaps deranged imagination, Lippard's urban vision was rooted in experience. Born on a farm in 1822, orphaned, and brought to Philadelphia, his life was a continual struggle against poverty and obscurity. At his death of tuberculosis in 1854, he was immersed in a fantastic scheme to build up a mystical secret brotherhood with himself as "Supreme Washington" —a doomed effort, perhaps, to re-create the kind of close-knit community whose breakdown he had so obsessively explored in his fiction. Roger Butterfield, "George Lippard and His Secret Brotherhood," *Pennsylvania Magazine of History and Biography*, 79 (July 1955), 285–301 (quoted passage, p. 288); Carsten E. Seecamp, "The Chapter of Perfection: A Neglected Influence on George Lippard," ibid., 94 (April 1970), 192–212.

17. Among the contributions to this genre were Peter Stryker's *The Lower Depths of the Great American Metropolis* (1866), George Ellington's *The Women of New York; or, The Underworld of the Great American City* (New York, 1869), and James D. McCabe Jr.'s *Lights and Shadows of New York Life* (Philadelphia, 1872).

18. N. N. Luxon, *Niles Weekly Register, News Magazine of the Nineteenth Century* (Baton Rouge, Louisiana State University Press, 1947); Glyndon G. Van Deusen, *Horace Greeley: Nineteenth-Century Crusader* (New York, Hill and Wang, 1964), p. 165.

19. Quoted in Davis, *Homicide in American Fiction*, p. 165.

20. John Todd, *The Moral Influence, Dangers, and Duties, Connected with Great Cities* (Northampton, Mass., 1841), pp. 18, 41, 130, 247.

21. John Todd, *The Story of His Life, Told Mainly by Himself* (New York, 1876), quoted passages, pp. 262, 285.

22. Todd, *Great Cities*, pp. 119, 79–80, 118.

23. A. D. Mayo, *The Symbols of the Capital; or, Civilization in New York* (New York, 1859), p. 51, quoted in R. Richard Wohl, "The 'Country Boy' Myth and Its Place in American Urban Culture: The Nineteenth-Century Contribution," *Perspectives in American History*, 3 (1969) 106; Lydia Maria Child, *Letters from New-York* (Boston, 1843), pp. 82, 182.

24. Rev. E[dwin] H. Chapin, *Moral Aspects of City Life* (New York, 1853), pp. 19, 33, 61, 181.

25. Ibid., pp. 14, 17, 19.

26. Stephan Thernstrom, *Poverty and Progress: Social Mobility in*

a *Nineteenth Century City* (Cambridge, Mass., Harvard University Press, 1964; reissued, New York, Atheneum, 1969), p. 45; Kenneth T. Jackson, "Urban Decentralization in the Nineteenth Century: A Statistical Study," in *The New Urban History: Quantitative Explorations by American Historians*, ed. Leo F. Schnore (Princeton, Princeton University Press, 1975), pp. 113, 128–132; David Ward, *Cities and Immigrants: A Geography of Change in Nineteenth-Century America* (New York, Oxford University Press, 1971), chap. 4, "Immigrant Residential Quarters," pp. 105–121, esp. p. 105; John Modell, "The Peopling of a Working-Class Ward: Reading, Pennsylvania, 1850," *Journal of Social History*, 5 (Fall 1971), 77; Rosenwaike, *Population History of New York City*, pp. 48–52 (geographic expansion).

27. Quoted in Asbury, *Gangs of New York*, pp. 12–13.

28. *The Life of Charles Loring Brace, Chiefly Told in His Own Letters*, Edited by His Daughter (New York, 1894), p. 192; Hone, *Diary*, p. 331; Horlick, *Country Boys and Merchant Princes*, p. 249 (New York Association for the Suppression of Gambling). On the frustrations moralists and reformers felt with the political process in these years see Griscom, *The Sanitary Condition of the Laboring Population of New York*, preface and p. 2; Timothy L. Smith, *Revivalism and Social Reform: American Protestantism on the Eve of the Civil War* (Nashville, Abingdon Press, 1957; reissued, New York, Harper Torchbooks, 1957), p. 151; and M. J. Heale, "From City Fathers to Social Critics: Humanitarianism and Government in New York, 1790–1860," *Journal of American History*, 63 (June 1976), pp. 33–36.

29. Richardson, *Urban Police in the United States*, pp. 19–37; Dykstra, "Rowdyism and Rivalism in the St. Louis Fire Department," pp. 60–62.

30. Quoted in Lee Benson, *The Concept of Jacksonian Democracy: New York as a Test Case* (Princeton, N.J., Princeton University Press, 1961; reissued, New York, Atheneum, 1965), p. 207.

31. J. B. Horton, New York City tract volunteer, quoted in Griscom, *Sanitary Condition of the Laboring Population of New York*, p. 30; Hone, *Diary*, p. 335 (entry for June 19, 1838).

32. Clifford S. Griffin, *Their Brothers' Keepers: Moral Stewardship in the United States, 1800–1850* (New Brunswick, N.J., Rutgers University Press, 1960), p. 238; Warner, *Private City*, p. 94, n. 25.

33. Child, *Letters From New-York*, p. 7; Isaac Orchard quoted in Griscom, *Sanitary Condition of the Laboring Population of New York*, p. 37; Chapin, *Moral Aspects of City Life*, pp. 113–114.

34. John Marsh, *Temperance Recollections* (New York, 1866), p. 87 (Marsh was corresponding secretary of the American Temperance Union for its first thirty years); Alice Felt Tyler, *Freedom's Ferment* (New York, Harper Torchbooks, 1962), pp. 316–338; John A. Krout, *The Origins of Prohibition* (New York, Alfred A. Knopf, 1925), p. 141; Child, *Letters From New-York*, II, 285 (description of a "Cold Water Army" parade).

35. Norman H. Clark, *Deliver Us from Evil: An Interpretation of American Prohibition* (New York, W. W. Norton, 1976), pp. 32–34;

Krout, *Origins of Prohibition*, pp. 185, 190, 192, 208–09; Marsh, *Temperance Recollections*, pp. 78, 80 (quoted passage), 217.

36. Weinbaum, "Temperance, Politics, and the New York City Riots of 1857," pp. 246–250; W. R. Halloway, *Indianapolis: A Historical and Statistical Sketch of the Railroad City* (Indianapolis, 1870), p. 101; Pierce, *History of Chicago*, II, 437; Richardson, *Urban Police in the United States*, p. 38 (on Wood); Ernest H. Cherrington, *The Evolution of Prohibition in the United States of America* (Westerville, Ohio, The American Issue Press, 1920), pp. 136–138.

37. Ibid., p. 143; Clark, *Deliver Us from Evil*, p. 48.

38. Henry A. Miles, *Lowell as It Was and as It is* (Lowell, 1846; reprinted, New York, Arno Press, 1972), pp. 144–145, 132, 128. An 1847 novel by a Lowell physician aimed at the mill operatives made the point even more bluntly: "A single deviation from the path of rectitude may cause the fairest of the fair to sink, like a meteor, into oblivion, and be forgotten." Ariel I. Cummings, *The Factory Girl; or, Gardez la Coeur* (Lowell, 1847), p. 50. For a similar effort at the moral control of female factory workers—one which also ultimately failed—see Vera Shlakman, *The Economic History of a Factory Town: A Study of Chicopee, Massachusetts* (Smith College Studies in History, vol. xx, nos. 1–4, Northampton, Mass., 1935; reprinted, New York, Octagon Books, 1969), pp. 50–53, 138.

39. Michel Chevalier, *Lettres sur l' Amérique du Nord*, 2 vols. (Paris, 1836), I, 235 ("Lowell n'est pas amusant, mais Lowell est propre et décent, paisable et sage"); Constance M. Green, *Holyoke, Mass.; A Case History of the Industrial Revolution in America* (New Haven, Yale University Press, 1939), p. 31.

40. Bertram Wyatt-Brown, *Lewis Tappan and the Evangelical War Against Slavery* (Cleveland, Ohio, The Press of Case Western Reserve University, 1969; reissued, New York, Atheneum, 1971), pp. 43–44.

41. Pierce, *History of Chicago*, II, 375; Smith, *Revivalism and Social Reform*, pp. 49, 72–73; Bernard A. Weisberger, *They Gathered at the River: The Story of the Great Revivalists and their Impact upon Religion in America* (Boston, Little, Brown, 1958; reissued, New York, Quadrangle, 1966), pp. 135–138.

42. *The New York Pulpit in the Revival of 1858. A Memorial Volume of Sermons* (New York, 1858), p. 26; Neal, *True Womanhood*, pp. 9, 99; Smith, *Revivalism and Social Reform*, pp. 63–72, quote re hymns, p. 70.

43. Noyes L. Thompson, *The History of Plymouth Church (Henry Ward Beecher) 1847 to 1872* (New York, 1873), p. 154; Smith, *Revivalism and Social Reform*, pp. 170–72.

44. American Bible Society, *Annual Report* (New York, 1857), quoted in Griffin, *Their Brothers' Keepers*, p. 50.

45. Quoted in Robert W. Lynn and Elliott Wright, *The Big Little School: Sunday Child of American Protestantism* (New York, Harper and Row, 1971), p. 33. See also, in the same vein, American Sunday School Union, *Annual Report* (1847), p. 34.

46. Silas Farmer, *History of Detroit and Wayne County and Early*

Michigan, 3rd ed. (New York, 1890; reissued, Detroit, Gale Research, 1969), pp. 634, 642; Smith, *Revivalism and Social Reform*, pp. 65–66; ASSU, *AR* (1849), pp. 31–32, 39.

47. *Life of Charles Loring Brace*, p. 181; Robert Baird, *Religion in America: A Critical Abridgment*, introduction by Henry Warner Bowden (New York, Harper and Bros., 1970), p. 169; Robert T. Handy, *A Christian America: Protestant Hopes and Historical Realities* (New York, Oxford University Press, 1971), chapter 2.

48. Rev. Samuel B. Cruft, Boston city missionary, quoted in Knights, *Plain People of Boston*, p. 48; Wade C. Barclay, *A History of Methodist Missions*, 6 vols. (New York, The Board of Missions and Church Extension of the Methodist Church, 1949); Thompson, *History of Plymouth Church*, pp. 154–155.

49. Quoted in L. L. Doggett, *History of the Boston Young Men's Christian Association* (Boston, The Young Men's Christian Association, 1901), p. 54; Dorothy G. Becker, "The Visitor to the New York City Poor, 1843–1920," *Social Service Review*, 35 (Dec. 1961), 391 (comment on tracts).

50. ASSU, *AR* (1847), pp. 18, 31 (quoted passage); Shlakman, *Economic History of a Factory Town*, p. 97; Todd, *Great Cities*, p. 128; Charles Loring Brace, *Short Sermons to News Boys: With a History of the Formation of the News Boys' Lodging-House* (New York, 1866), p. 13. A similar note of discouragement, with the desire to revive the enthusiasm of an earlier day, pervades the Reverend Stephen Tyng's *Forty Years' Experience in Sunday-Schools* (New York, 1860), esp. pp. 27, 163, 164.

51. ASSU, *AR* (1849), pp. 34, 35.

52. *Advance* (Nov. 7, 1867), p. 4, quoted in James F. Findlay, Jr., *Dwight L. Moody, American Evangelist, 1837–1899* (Chicago, University of Chicago Press, 1969), p. 80. William R. Moody, *The Life of Dwight L. Moody* (Chicago, Fleming H. Revell, 1900), pp. 57–59; *Some Recollections of John V. Farwell* (Chicago, R. R. Donnelley and Sons, 1911), pp. 101–06.

53. Quoted in Anne Mary Boylan, " 'The Nursery of the Church': Evangelical Protestant Sunday Schools, 1820–1880" (Ph.D. diss., University of Wisconsin, 1973), p. 68. The same point is made in Tyng, *Forty Years' Experience in Sunday-Schools*, p. 160.

54. Wade, *Urban Frontier*, p. 145.

55. Paul R. Lucas, "The Church and the City: Congregationalism in Minneapolis, 1850–1890," *Minnesota History*, 44 (Summer 1974), 62; Farmer, *History of Detroit*, pp. 201–202; Grimsted, "Rioting in Its Jacksonian Setting," p. 220; John C. Schneider, "Riot and Reaction in St. Louis," p. 176.

56. Quoted in Horlick, *Country Boys and Merchant Princes*, pp. 246, 249.

57. Richard N. Havens in *First Annual Report of the New York Association for the Suppression of Gambling* (New York, 1851), p. 8.

6 NARROWING THE PROBLEM

1. Blanche D. Coll, "The Baltimore Society for the Prevention of

Pauperism, 1820–1822," *American Historical Review*, 61 (Oct. 1955), 77–87, quoted phrase, p. 83; Raymond A. Mohl, "Humanitarianism in the Preindustrial City: The New York Society for the Prevention of Pauperism, 1817–1823," *Journal of American History*, 57 (Dec. 1970), 576–599; M. J. Heale, "The New York Society for the Prevention of Pauperism, 1817–1823," *New-York Historical Society Quarterly*, 55 (April 1971), 153–176. The leaders of these antipauperism societies were often Quakers: men like insurance broker Thomas Eddy and merchant John Murray, Jr., in New York, and banker Philip Thomas in Baltimore.

2. *Memoir and Writings of James Handasyd Perkins*, ed. William H. Channing, 2 vols. (Cincinnati, 1851), I, 114, 115, 117, 118, 119; Dorothy G. Becker, "The Visitor to the New York City Poor, 1843–1920," *Social Service Review*, 35 (Dec. 1961), 383–384 (on Tuckerman); R[obert] C. Waterston, *An Address on Pauperism, Its Extent, Causes, and the Best Means of Prevention* (Boston, 1844), p. 11 (on Tuckerman).

3. ·Mohl, "Humanitarianism in the Preindustrial City," pp. 592–594; Coll, "Baltimore Society for the Prevention of Pauperism," pp. 85–86; Becker, "Visitor to the New York City Poor," p. 384; Channing, ed., *Perkins*, p. 122.

4. Isaac S. Hartley, *Memorial of Robert Milham Hartley* (Utica, N.Y., 1882), pp. 18, 27, 37, 38, 41; New York Association for Improving the Condition of the Poor, *First Annual Report* (1845), p. 15 ("a number of gentlemen" quote; hereafter, NYAICP, *AR*); Roy Lubove, "The New York Association for Improving the Condition of the Poor: The Formative Years," *New-York Historical Society Quarterly*, 43 (July 1959), 308 (hereafter: "NYAICP").

5. Hartley, *Memorial*, pp. 71, 83, 85, 92, 203.

6. Ibid., pp. 191–209; Lubove, "NYAICP," p. 313; *Dictionary of American Biography* (sketches of Brown, Lenox, Minturn, and Wetmore).

7. Lilian Brandt, "Growth and Development of the AICP and COS (A Preliminary and Exploratory Review)," Report of the Committee on the Institute of Welfare Research, Community Service Society of New York, mimeographed (New York, 1942), pp. 12–13; Hartley, *Memorial*, quoted passage, p. 192.

8. If the AICP should fail, warned a Baltimorean in 1849, "no man would be safe walking our streets at night, nor . . . in his bed." A Boston philanthropic society agreed in 1854 that if poverty were not dealt with, American cities would soon witness "such scenes as have been once and again enacted in the streets of Paris." Margaretta Culver, "A History of the Baltimore Association for the Improvement of the Condition of the Poor from Its Foundation in 1849 to Its Federation with the Charity Organization Society in 1902," (M.A. thesis, Johns Hopkins University, 1923), p. 14; Lubove, "NYAICP," p. 314.

9. Rev. E[dwin] H. Chapin, *Moral Aspects of City Life* (New York, 1843), pp. 18, 146, 147; William Ellery Channing, "Discourse on the Life and Character of the Rev. Joseph Tuckerman, D.D.," in *The Works of William E. Channing* (Boston, American Unitarian Association, 1903), VI, 103.

10. NYAICP, *AR* (1851), p. 18, quoted in Robert H. Bremner, *From the Depths: The Discovery of Poverty in the United States* (New York, New York University Press, 1956), p. 5; John H. Griscom, M.D., *The Sanitary Condition of the Laboring Population of New York, with Suggestions for Its Improvement* (New York, 1845), p. 23.

11. Channing, *Works*, IV, 267–268, 278; Mohl, "Humanitarianism in the Preindustrial City," p. 583.

12. Quoted in Frank D. Watson, *The Charity Organization Movement in the United States* (New York, Macmillan, 1922), p. 84. Culver, "History of the Baltimore AICP," p. 17, quotes a typical listing of these vices: "imprudence, extravagance, idleness, and intemperance."

13. Ibid.; Brandt, "Growth and Development of AICP and COS," p. 11 (Hartley quote); Hartley, *Memorial*, pp. 189, 193 (quoting the New York AICP *Visitor's Manual*).

14. "Rules for Visiting," *American Sunday School Magazine* (July 1829), pp. 217, 218, 219; ibid. (Feb. 1826), p. 44; (May 1829), p. 134. As early as 1825 the New York City Sunday school association inaugurated a slum visitation program that even included a rudimentary system of classifying families as "reputable," "indifferent," or "careless"; ibid. (Apr. 1825), pp. 106–107. The American Sunday school movement was influenced in this respect by the work of the Reverend Thomas Chalmers of Scotland, who in the early 1820s devised a program of systematic visitation, relief, and moral uplift for the Glasgow slums. See ibid. (Dec. 1824), pp. 163–167, for a review of Chalmers's work.

15. Samuel Russell, Jr., quoted in Griscom, *Sanitary Conditions of the Laboring Population of New York*, p. 31; Hartley quoted in Becker, "Visitor to the New York City Poor," p. 385.

16. Channing, *Works*, VI, 93, 94, 97; IV, 293, 295.

17. Waterston, *Address on Pauperism*, pp. 16, 23, 43.

18. Ibid., pp. 7, 13, 41, 43.

19. Lubove, "NYAICP," p. 323.

20. Chapin, *Moral Aspects of City Life*, p. 157; Channing, *Works*, IV, 274; Griscom, *Sanitary Conditions of the Laboring Population of New York*, pp. 22–38. As a public-health officer, Griscom was especially forceful in linking the physical circumstances of slum life with the moral state of the poor. When people are jammed into unsanitary, disease-ridden tenements, he asked with asperity, can one be surprised that they lose "the nice moral distinctions so necessary to a life of virtue" and become "hardened against the teachings of the moralist?" (p. 23). Griscom sent questionnaires to a number of tract volunteers soliciting their opinions on this point, and he printed their extremely interesting replies verbatim (pp. 25–38).

21. Brandt, "Growth and Development of AICP and COS," pp. 64–65.

22. Lubove, "NYAICP," pp. 309, 311.

23. Brandt, "Growth and Development of AICP and COS," p. 26; Timothy L. Smith, *Revivalism and Social Reform: American Protestantism on the Eve of the Civil War* (Nashville, Abingdon Press, 1957; reissued, New York, Harper Torchbooks, 1957), p. 167.

24. Becker, "Visitor to the New York City Poor," pp. 391–393.

25. Culver, "History of the Baltimore AICP," p. 136.

26. See David J. Rothman, *The Discovery of the Asylum: Social Order and Disorder in the New Republic* (Boston, Little, Brown, 1971).

27. Ibid., chap. 9, "The Well-Ordered Asylum," pp. 206–236. See also Joseph M. Hawes, *Children in Urban Society; Juvenile Delinquency in Nineteenth Century America* (New York, Oxford University Press, 1971), esp. pp. 27–41, 54, 80; and Robert M. Mennel, *Thorns and Thistles: Juvenile Delinquents in the United States, 1825–1940* (Hanover, N.H., University Press of New England, 1973), p. 5. The Roman Catholic hierarchy, disturbed by the Protestant cast of these institutions, organized a number of its own, notably Boston's Home of the Guardian Angel (1851). Ibid., p. 64.

28. Rothman, *Discovery of the Asylum*, p. 207. In Massachusetts it was not until 1847, fifteen years after the opening of a privately sponsored boys' asylum, that a state institution with similar purposes was established. Hawes, *Children in Urban Society*, pp. 33–34, 82, 86.

29. For typical formulations of these objectives see ibid., p. 36, and Rothman, *Discovery of the Asylum*, p. 229.

30. Ibid., pp. 225–230 (quoted passage, p. 229).

31. Ibid., pp. 227, 230, 235; Hawes, *Children in Urban Society*, pp. 45–46 (quoted passage).

32. Rothman, *Discovery of the Asylum*, pp. 234–235. See also Hawes, *Children in Urban Society*, p. 28, and Mennel, *Thorns and Thistles*, p. 23.

33. Rothman, *Discovery of the Asylum*, p. 210; Samuel Perkins, *The World As It Is* (n.p., Thomas Belknap, 1839), p. 81.

34. *The Life of Charles Loring Brace. Chiefly Told in His Own Letters*, Edited by His Daughter (New York, 1894), p. 170; Charles Loring Brace, *The Dangerous Classes of New York and Twenty Years Work among Them*, 3rd ed., with addenda (New York, 1880; orig. published 1872), pp. 105, 236, 381; New York Children's Aid Society, *Annual Report* (1857), p. 8; (1858), p. 7; (1860), pp. 31–33, 86. Hereafter: NYCAS, AR.

35. Miriam Z. Langsam, *Children West; A History of the Placing-Out System of the New York Children's Aid Society, 1853–1890* (Madison, State Historical Society of Wisconsin and the University of Wisconsin Department of History, 1964), pp. 1, 2; NYCAS, AR (1854), pp. 3, 4; ibid. (1855), pp. 3, 11.

36. Brace, *Dangerous Classes*, pp. 29, 317; NYCAS, AR (1854), p. 14.

37. Brace, *Dangerous Classes*, p. 176.

38. Ibid., pp. 97, 344; *Life of Brace*, p. 493; NYCAS, AR (1856), p. 6.

39. Jacob A. Riis, *How the Other Half Lives* (New York, 1890; reprinted, New York, Hill and Wang, 1957), p. 148; Bremner, *From the Depths*, p. 92. See also George C. Needham, *Street Arabs and Gutter Snipes* (New York, 1884).

40. NYCAS, AR (1855), p. 15; (1857), p. 9; Brace, *Dangerous Classes*, pp. 107, 342.

41. Langsam, *Children West*, p. viii; *Life of Brace*, p. 501; Hawes, *Children in Urban Society*, p. 107; R. Richard Wohl, "The 'Country

Boy' Myth, and Its Place in American Urban Culture: The Nineteenth-Century Contribution," ed. Moses Rischin, *Perspectives in American History*, 3 (1969), 108, n. 51.

42. *Life of Brace*, pp. 224–225; Riis, *How the Other Half Lives*, p. 153; Brace, *Dangerous Classes*, pp. 104–105, 106. To give slum boys "the first taste of the pleasure of saving," rudimentary savings banks were established at all CAS lodging houses. NYCAS, *AR* (1855), p. 14.

43. Brace, *Dangerous Classes*, pp. 79–81.

44. A. D. Mayo, *Symbols of the Capital* (New York, 1859), quoted in Anselm L. Strauss, *The American City: A Sourcebook of Urban Imagery* (Chicago, Aldine, 1968), p. 174; NYAICP, *AR* (1850), p. 27, quoted in Bremner, *From the Depths*, p. 38. George Henry Evans's National Reform Association, leader of the free-land movement of the later 1840s and 1850s, stressed that such legislation would help "carry off our superabundant labor to the salubrious and fertile West"—Douglas T. Miller, *Jacksonian Aristocracy: Class and Democracy in New York, 1830–1860* (New York, Oxford University Press, 1967), p. 143. See also Carl N. Degler, "The West as a Solution to Urban Unemployment," *New York History*, 36 (Jan. 1955), 63–84.

45. NYCAS, *AR* (1856), p. 55.

46. Ibid. (1860), p. 86 (Brace was here quoting a *New York Sun* editorial which he may have written and with whose sentiments he was, in any event, thoroughly in accord); Charles Loring Brace, *Short Sermons to News Boys; With a History of the Formation of the News Boys' Lodging House* (New York, 1866), p. 46 (comment on the bootblack brigades).

47. Brace, *Dangerous Classes*, pp. 114, 265.

48. NYCAS, *AR* (1858), pp. 7, 52 ("Little Butch" story); (1857), p. 9; Brace, *Dangerous Classes*, p. 242. Horatio Alger, a great admirer of Brace and his work, wove favorable references to the CAS and its philosophy into a number of his stories, including *Ragged Dick* (1867) and *Julius the Street Boy* (1874). In the latter, the bright and resourceful young hero gladly abandons the city which "had been a harsh stepmother to him" (p. 28) to go West under CAS auspices. After capture by the Indians and other adventures, he goes into real estate.

49. NYCAS, *AR* (1856), p. 10; Brace, *Dangerous Classes*, p. 243. The western states often did not share Brace's vision, and by the 1890s many of them had passed legislation regulating out-of-state child-placement agencies like the CAS. Hawes, *Children in Urban Society*, p. 107; Langsam, *Children West*, pp. 26, 30.

50. NYCAS, *AR* (1855), p. 35; (1856), p. 9; Charles Loring Brace to Mrs. Asa Gray, April 23, 1853, in *Life of Brace*, pp. 160–161. See also, in the same vein, NYCAS, *AR* (1857), p. 5; (1860), p. 4; and (1861), p. 8. For a brief but suggestive article noting the similarities between Brace's ideas and those expressed in 1970 by Daniel Patrick Moynihan toward black ghetto families, see Francesco Cordasco, "Charles Loring Brace and the Dangerous Classes: Historical Analogues of the Urban Black Poor," *Journal of Human Relations*, 20 (Nov. 1972), 379–386.

51. NYCAS, *AR* (1861), p. 8; Brace, *Dangerous Classes*, pp. 47, 49.

52. Account of the Reverend E. P. Smith, leader of the 1854 emigrant party, reprinted in *Life of Brace*, app. B, pp. 489–501, quoted passages pp. 493, 495, 508; Brace, *Dangerous Classes*, p. 235; Langsam, *Children West*, p. 26. In later years, stung by charges of "kidnapping," the CAS transported children to the West only after court authorization. This aspect of the CAS program sharply diminished from the 1890s on, and was eliminated entirely in 1929 (ibid., p. 22).

53. Brace, *Dangerous Classes*, pp. 177, 233, 235, 244, 266.

54. Brace, *Short Sermons to News Boys*, pp. v, 9–10, 15; Brace, *Dangerous Classes*, p. 137.

55. Richard Hofstadter, *Social Darwinism in American Thought* (Philadelphia, University of Pennsylvania Press, 1944; reissued, Boston, Beacon Press, 1955), pp. 16, 22. In neglecting the social Darwinist element in Brace's thought, Thomas Bender in his *Toward an Urban Vision: Ideas and Institutions in Nineteenth-Century America* (Lexington, University Press of Kentucky, 1975) misses what was, in fact, a central component of his ideological position. Brace's program was rooted less in his vision of community than in his desire to promote a larger human progress through a radical laissez-faire individualism of the Herbert Spencer variety. In other respects, however, Bender's thoughtful and intelligent appraisal of Brace (which came to my notice too late for me to incorporate its insights into this and other chapters) parallels my own. This is particularly true of his emphasis on Brace's antiasylum views, his discussion of Brace's positive view of the city's power to break up and disperse pauperized families, and his rejection of the conventional view of Brace as an agrarian sentimentalist.

56. Brace, *Short Sermons to News Boys*, p. 33; Brace, *Dangerous Classes*, p. 345; NYCAS, *AR* (1863), p. 12.

57. *Life of Brace*, pp. 58–59 (quoted passage), 1–59 passim.

58. Ibid., pp. 64, 88.

59. Ibid., p. 114.

60. Ibid., p. 155; NYCAS, *AR* (1858), p. 5.

61. Ibid., p. 77.

62. Ibid., pp. 183–184; Brace, *Dangerous Classes*, pp. 76, 84.

63. NYCAS, *AR* (1854), list of trustees. Biographical information from *Dictionary of American Biography, National Cyclopedia of American Biography*, and *Trow's Guide to New York*.

64. *Life of Brace*, pp. 317–319 (quoted passage, p. 318).

65. Ibid., pp. 160–161.

66. Ibid., p. 464.

7 YOUNG MEN AND THE CITY

1. Emmett Dedmon, *Great Enterprises; 100 Years of the YMCA of Metropolitan Chicago* (Chicago, Rand McNally, 1957), p. 16; *The Seventh Census of the United States: 1850* (Washington, 1853), pp. 694 (Cook County, Ill. [Chicago]), 88–89 (New York City), 154 (Philadelphia). Although the superabundance of young males in the cities was matched by a similar bulge in the population as a whole (see ibid., p. xliii), their urban concentration made the males of this age group more

highly visible, and thus a greater source of social concern. See also Carlos Martyn, *William E. Dodge: The Christian Merchant* (New York, 1890), p. 147.

2. Quoted in Bernard Wishy, *The Child and the Republic: The Dawn of Modern American Child Nurture* (Philadelphia, University of Pennsylvania Press, 1968), p. 57; John Todd, *The Moral Influence, Dangers, and Duties, Connected with Great Cities* (Northampton, Mass., 1841), p. 219.

3. *First Annual Report of the New York Association for the Suppression of Gambling* (New York, 1851), p. 28, quoted in Allan Stanley Horlick, *Country Boys and Merchant Princes: The Social Control of Young Men in New York* (Lewisburg, Pa., Bucknell University Press, 1975), p. 249.

4. *Quarterly Reporter of the Young Men's Christian Association in North America* (Jan. 1857), p. 38.

5. Verranus Morse, M.D., *An Analytical Sketch of the Young Men's Christian Association in North America from 1851 to 1876* (New York, International Committee of Young Men's Christian Associations, 1901), pp. 45–46. This work includes a number of addresses made by Morse in the 1850s and 1860s before the New York YMCA.

6. Ibid., p. 46.

7. Ibid., p. 54 (from an 1866 address). See also "City Boarding Houses," *Young Men's Magazine* (Sept. 1857), p. 199.

8. See also Jared Waterbury, *Considerations for Young Men* (New York, 1832), William Alcott, *The Young Man's Guide* (Boston, 1833), John James, *The Young Man from Home* (New York, 1840), and "Counsels to a Young Man," American Tract Society, *Tracts* (New York, n.d.), X, no. 402. Allan Stanley Horlick has noted the interesting fact that in the later antebellum period these works were increasingly addressed to young men in the cities. In 1828, for example, Joel Hawes directed his *Lectures to Young Men on the Formation of Character* mainly to rural and small-town youths; in an 1856 revision, however, he devoted much more attention to urban young men such as clerks and salesmen. Horlick, *Country Boys and Merchant Princes*, pp. 148–150.

9. T. S. Arthur, *Advice to Young Men on Their Duties and Conduct in Life* (Boston, 1848), p. 81, quoted in Horlick, *Country Boys and Merchant Princes*, p. 198.

10. Morse, *Analytical Sketch*, pp. 59, 60; Todd, *Great Cities*, pp. 46, 205.

11. Morse, *Analytical Sketch*, pp. 59, 60.

12. Ibid., p. 54; *American Sunday School Magazine* (Jan. 1828), p. 25.

13. C. Howard Hopkins, *History of the YMCA in North America* (New York, Association Press, 1951), pp. 19–21; Horlick, *Country Boys and Merchant Princes*, pp. 252–259; Bayrd Still, "Patterns of Mid-Nineteenth Century Urbanization in the Middle West," *Mississippi Valley Historical Review*, 28 (Sept. 1941), pp. 202–203; idem., *Milwaukee; The History of a City*, 3 vols. (Madison, State Historical Society

of Wisconsin, 1965), vol. III, p. 214; Richard Wade, *The Urban Frontier; The Rise of Western Cities, 1790–1830* (Cambridge, Mass., Harvard University Press, 1959), pp. 106, 255.

14. *Memorials of William E. Dodge*, ed. D. Stuart Dodge (New York, [1887]), p. 51; Horlick, *Country Boys and Merchants Princes*, pp. 252–260 (on origins of New York Mercantile Library Association); Arlen R. Dykstra, "Rowdyism and Rivalism in the St. Louis Fire Department, 1850–1857," *Missouri Historical Review*, 69 (Oct. 1974), 61.

15. William E. Dodge, quoted in Martyn, *William E. Dodge*, p. 148; New York Mercantile Library Association, 1825 annual report, quoted in Horlick, *Country Boys and Merchant Princes*, pp. 253–254; George S. Hillard, "Success and the Man of Culture," address before the Boston Mercantile Library Association, Nov. 13, 1850, reprinted in Anselm L. Strauss, *The American City: A Sourcebook of Urban Imagery* (Chicago, Aldine, 1968), p. 185.

16. Philip Hone, *Address Delivered before the Mercantile Library Association at the Odeon in Boston, Oct. 3, 1843* (Boston, 1843), p. 20.

17. Hopkins, *History of the YMCA*, pp. 4–5.

18. Ibid., pp. 22–24; Mayer N. Zald, *Organizational Change: The Political Economy of the YMCA* (Chicago, University of Chicago Press, 1970), p. 31; Theodore Grivas, "A History of the Los Angeles Young Men's Christian Association: The First Twenty Years," *California Historical Society Quarterly*, 44 (Sept. 1965), 205–206; Terry Donoghue, *An Event on Mercer Street: A Brief History of the YMCA of the City of New York* (New York, privately printed, 1952), pp. 12, 15–16, 21; L. L. Doggett, *History of the Boston Young Men's Christian Association* (Boston, The Young Men's Christian Association, 1901), pp. 1–2, 113–114 (reprint of Van Derlip letter to the *Christian Watchman and Reflector*, Oct. 30, 1851).

19. Hopkins, *History of the YMCA*, pp. 18, 106; Dedmon, *Great Enterprises*, p. 39; Donoghue, *Event on Mercer Street*, p. 41.

20. *Dictionary of American Biography*, X, 61–62 (Morris K. Jesup); Alfred S. Roe, *The Worcester YMCA* (Worcester, 1901), pp. 9, 11 (Moen); *New York Times* (Mar. 6, 1905), p. 7 (Ward obituary). In Los Angeles, the YMCA founder was twenty-six-year-old Samuel Morrill, a native of upstate New York who had moved West with the railroads and was in 1882 beginning a successful career in hardware. Grivas, "History of the Los Angeles YMCA," p. 206.

21. *Some Recollections of John V. Farwell* (Chicago, R. R. Donnelley and Sons, 1911), pp. 1–36 (quoted passage, p. 36).

22. *Reminiscences of John V. Farwell by His Elder Daughter*, 2 vols. (Chicago, R. F. Seymour, [1928]), I, 100, 115, 123, 171.

23. Dedmon, *Great Enterprises*, p. 39.

24. Doggett, *History of the Boston YMCA*, p. 15.

25. Hopkins, *History of the YMCA*, pp. 43–45, 187; Dedmon, *Great Enterprises*, p. 42.

26. Ibid.; Roe, *Worcester YMCA*, p. 55; William R. Moody, *The Life of Dwight L. Moody* (Chicago, Fleming H. Revell, 1900), p. 81.

27. Hopkins, *History of the YMCA*, p. 37 (quoted passage re Balti-

more); Donoghue, *Event on Mercer Street*, pp. 51, 55; Roe, *Worcester YMCA*, p. 33 (quoted passage re Worcester); Dedmon, *Great Enterprises*, pp. 130–132.

28. Hopkins, *History of the YMCA*, pp. 6 (quoted passage), 239.

29. Dedmon, *Great Enterprises*, p. 126.

30. Hopkins, *History of the YMCA*, p. 44 (Rowland quote); Morse, *Analytical Sketch*, p. 47. The apparent lack of direction in the 1850s was heightened by divisions over abolitionism, which in some cities nearly destroyed the new movement before it was well launched. Donoghue, *Event on Mercer Street*, p. 30.

31. Doggett, *History of the Boston YMCA*, p. 12. Similarly, the New York YMCA invited newcomers to join the "vast harmonious band" of YMCA members. *Constitution of the New York YMCA, Organized June 1852* (New York, 1852), p. 7.

32. Roe, *Worcester YMCA*, pp. 61–63.

33. Dedmon, *Great Enterprises*, p. 30; Roe, *Worcester YMCA*, p. 35 (quoted passage).

34. Dedmon, *Great Enterprises*, pp. 68–69; Isaac Ferris, *Address Delivered at a Meeting of Young Men Convened for the Formation of the Young Men's Christian Association* (New York, 1852), "home feeling" quote, cited in Horlick, *Country Boys and Merchant Princes*, p. 231 (italics added); Doggett, *History of Boston YMCA*, p. 19 (quote re newspapers), 44; Hopkins, *History of the YMCA*, pp. 40–41 (Wanamaker).

35. Morse, *Analytical Sketch*, p. 51 (from an 1866 address).

36. Ibid., pp. 49, 54, 55; Ferris, *Address*, in Horlick, *Country Boys and Merchant Princes*, p. 230 ("social want").

37. John A. Krout, *The Origins of Prohibition* (New York, Alfred A. Knopf, 1925), p. 213; Walter Hugins, *Jacksonian Democracy and the Working Class; A Study of the New York Workingmen's Movement, 1829–1837* (Palo Alto, Calif., Stanford University Press, 1960), p. 58.

38. T. D. Seymour Bassett, "The Secular Utopian Socialists," in *Socialism and American Life*, ed. Donald Drew Egbert and Stow Persons, 2 vols. (Princeton, Princeton University Press, 1952), I, 153–211, esp. 157, 175–183.

39. "Have We Life within Us?" YMCA of North America, *Quarterly Reporter* (Apr. 1856).

40. Morse, *Analytical Sketch*, p. 61 (from an 1866 address); Horlick, *Country Boys and Merchant Princes*, p. 238 (Bethune quote).

41. Morse, *Analytical Sketch*, pp. 57, 61; M. Hamlin Cannon, "The United States Christian Commission," *Mississippi Valley Historical Review*, 37 (June 1951), 61–80.

42. Hopkins, *History of the YMCA*, pp. 383–384.

43. Paul S. Boyer, *Purity in Print: The Vice Society Movement and Book Censorship in America* (New York, Charles Scribner's Sons, 1968), p. 5.

44. Hopkins, *History of the YMCA*, p. 190; Aaron I. Abell, *The Urban Impact on American Protestantism* (Cambridge, Mass., Harvard University Press, 1943), pp. 43–45.

INTRODUCTION TO PART THREE

8 "THE RAGGED EDGE OF ANARCHY"

1. Dixon Ryan Fox, editor's foreword, in Arthur Meier Schlesinger, *The Rise of the City, 1878–1898* (New York, Macmillan, 1933), p. xiv.

1. United States Bureau of the Census, *Historical Statistics of the United States, Colonial Times to 1970, Bicentennial Edition*, 2 vols. (Washington, D.C., Government Printing Office, 1975), II, 12; Donald B. Cole, *Handbook of American History* (New York, Harcourt, Brace and World, 1968), p. 166; J. Cutler Andrews, "A Century of Urbanization in Pennsylvania, 1840–1940," *Pennsylvania History*, 10 (Jan. 1943), 11–25.

2. John A. Garraty, *The New Commonwealth, 1877–1890* (New York, Harper and Row, 1968), p. 179; Herbert G. Gutman, "Work, Culture, and Society in Industrializing America, 1815–1919," *American Historical Review*, 78 (June 1973), 555; *Historical Statistics of the U.S.*, vol. I, p. 106; Fred A. Shannon, *The Farmer's Last Frontier: Agriculture, 1860–1897* (New York, Holt, Rinehart and Winston, 1945; reissued, New York, Harper Torchbooks, 1968), p. 357; Ira Rosenwaike, *Population History of New York City* (Syracuse, N.Y., Syracuse University Press, 1972), pp. 62–76.

3. Sam B. Warner, Jr., *Streetcar Suburbs: The Process of Growth in Boston, 1870–1900* (Cambridge, Mass., Harvard University Press, 1962; reissued, New York, Atheneum, 1968), p. 2; *Chicago Sunday Times*, May 4, 1873, quoted in *The American City: A Documentary History*, ed. Charles N. Glaab (Homewood, Ill., Dorsey Press, 1963), pp. 229, 230; Rosenwaike, *Population History of New York City*, pp. 82–85.

4. Robert H. Wiebe, *The Search for Order, 1877–1920* (New York, Hill and Wang, 1967), p. 3; Sam Bass Warner, Jr., "If All the World Were Philadelphia: A Scaffolding for Urban History," *American Historical Review*, 74 (Oct. 1968), 33. This process is poignantly documented in Edmund H. Chapman, *Cleveland: Village to Metropolis. A Case Study of Problems of Urban Development in Nineteenth-Century America* (Cleveland, Western Reserve Historical Society, 1964).

5. Wiebe, *Search for Order*, p. 50; *The City Boss in America: An Interpretive Reader*, ed. Alexander B. Callow, Jr. (New York, Oxford University Press, 1976), esp. editor's "Commentary," pp. 3–13, 51–57, 91–97, 141–148.

6. Theodore N. Ferdinand, "The Criminal Patterns of Boston since 1849," *American Journal of Sociology*, 73 (July 1967), 84–99, esp. p. 87. In his recent statistical study of late-nineteenth-century crime rates in Franklin County (Columbus), Ohio, Eric H. Monkkonen challenges the widespread view that the urban crime rate rose sharply in that period. Except for theft and "theft by trick," he finds that the crime rate in Columbus remained fairly stable from 1860 to 1885, and that the rural and urban rates were not very different. He begins his book, however, with extensive documentation showing that the assumption of a high correlation between urbanization and a rising crime rate was widely held in the Gilded Age. Eric H. Monkkonen, *The Dangerous*

Class: Crime and Poverty in Columbus, Ohio, 1860–1885 (Cambridge, Mass., Harvard University Press, 1975), pp. 6–10, 70, 162.

7. Joy J. Jackson, New Orleans in the Gilded Age: Politics and Urban Progress, 1880–1896 (Baton Rouge, Louisiana State University Press, 1969), pp. 83–96, 232–257, quoted passage p. 232; Joel Tyler Headley, The Great Riots of New York, 1712–1873 (New York, 1873; reissued, New York, Dover Publications, 1971), pp. 289–306, esp. pp. 302–304; Zane L. Miller, "Boss Cox's Cincinnati: A Study in Urbanization and Politics, 1880–1914," Journal of American History, 54 (Mar. 1968), 827; Emilius O. Randall and Daniel J. Ryan, History of Ohio, IV (New York, 1912), 357–364. Less dramatic but perhaps more typical were the difficulties of Springfield, Massachusetts, where rapid growth spurred by the city's Civil War role as an arms-production center brought a sharp upsurge of petty disorders. Michael H. Frisch, From Town to City: Springfield, Massachusetts, and the Meaning of Community, 1840–1880 (Cambridge, Mass., Harvard University Press, 1972), p. 92.

8. Henry David, History of the Haymarket Affair (New York, Farrar and Rinehart, 1936); James M. Morris, "No Haymarket for Cincinnati," Ohio History, 83 (Winter 1974), 17–32; Jerry M. Cooper, "The Wisconsin National Guard in the Milwaukee Riots of 1886," Wisconsin Magazine of History, 55 (Autumn 1971), 31–48. On the Railroad Strike of 1877 see Wiebe, Search for Order, p. 10; Zane L. Miller, The Urbanization of Modern America: A Brief History (New York, Harcourt Brace Jovanovich, 1973), pp. 47–48; and, for a vivid narrative of its impact on one major rail center, Philip English Mackey, "Law and Order, 1877: Philadelphia's Response to the Railroad Riots," Pennsylvania Magazine of History and Biography, 96 (Apr. 1972), 183–202.

9. Quoted in Henry F. May, Protestant Churches and Industrial America (New York, Harper and Bros., 1949; reissued, New York, Octagon Books, 1963), pp. 92–93; New York Labor Standard, July 28, 1877, quoted in Mackey, "Law and Order, 1877," p. 196. Philadelphia and Saint Louis newspapers similarly called for forcible repression of rioters. Ibid., p. 198; David T. Burbank, Reign of the Rabble: The St. Louis General Strike of 1877 (New York, Augustus M. Kelley, 1966).

10. John Hay, The Bread-Winners (New York, 1883; reprinted, Ridgewood, N.J., Gregg Press, 1967), pp. 192, 215. See also Frederic Cople Jaher, "Industrialism and the American Aristocrat: A Social Study of John Hay and His Novel The Bread-Winners," Journal of the Illinois State Historical Society, 66 (Spring 1972), 69–93.

11. Wiebe, Search for Order, pp. 78–79; Morris, "No Haymarket for Cincinnati," p. 27; May, Protestant Churches and Industrial America, pp. 93, 101 (quoting the Congregationalist); John Higham, Strangers in the Land: Patterns of American Nativism, 1860–1925 (New Brunswick, N.J., Rutgers University Press, 1955; reissued, New York, Atheneum, 1963), pp. 54–55; Frederic Cople Jaher, Doubters and Dissenters: Cataclysmic Thought in America, 1885–1918 (New York, Free Press, 1964), p. 44 (quoting the New York Tribune). For similar expressions in the Baptist press see Lawrence B. Davis, Immigrants, Baptists,

and the *Protestant Mind in America* (Urbana, University of Illinois Press, 1973), pp. 58–61.

12. David Brody, *Steelworkers in America; The Nonunion Era* (Cambridge, Mass., Harvard University Press, 1960); Almont Lindsey, *The Pullman Strike* (Chicago, University of Chicago Press, 1942), pp. 122–235, esp. pp. 207–209, 214, 234.

13. Charles Hoffman, "The Depression of the Nineties," *Journal of Economic History*, 16 (June 1956), 137–164, esp. 138, 145–146.

14. Lindsey, *Pullman Strike*, pp. 245 (Olney quote), 308–334; Ray Ginger, *The Bending Cross: A Biography of Eugene Victor Debs* (New Brunswick, N.J., Rutgers University Press, 1949), pp. 130, 141–142; Douglas W. Steeples, "The Panic of 1893: Contemporary Reflections and Reactions," *Mid-America*, 47 (July 1965), 155–175.

15. George W. Walling, *Recollections of a New York Chief of Police* (New York, 1887, reissued, Montclair, N.J., Patterson Smith, 1972), p. 480; "The Wickedest Man in New York," *Packard's Monthly* (July 1868); R. M. Offord, *Jerry McAuley, An Apostle to the Lost*, 7th ed. (New York, American Tract Society, 1907; reissued, Freeport, N.Y., Books for Libraries Press, 1970), p. 157 (impact of the *Packard's* article); Anthony Comstock, *Traps for the Young* (New York, 1883), p. 241. See also, in this genre, George Ellington, *The Women of New York* (New York, 1869) and James D. McCabe, Jr., *Lights and Shadows of New York Life* (Philadelphia, 1872).

16. Walter Rauschenbusch, *Christianity and the Social Crisis* (New York, Macmillan, 1907; reissued, New York, Harper and Bros., 1964), pp. 251–252.

17. Edmund Pearson, *Dime Novels: or, Following an Old Trail in Popular Literature* (Boston, Little, Brown, 1929; reissued, Port Washington, N.Y., Kennikat Press, 1968), p. 138.

18. Richard Sennett, "Middle-Class Families and Urban Violence: The Experience of a Chicago Community in the Nineteenth Century," in *Nineteenth-Century Cities: Essays in the New Urban History*, ed. Stephan Thernstrom and Richard Sennett (New Haven, Yale University Press, 1969), pp. 391–397; Richard Sennett, *Families Against the City: Middle-Class Homes of Industrial Chicago, 1872–1890* (Cambridge, Mass., Harvard University Press, 1970; reissued, New York, Vintage Books, 1974), p. 53 (Dreiser quote); Warner, *Streetcar Suburbs*, p. 162. See also Samuel Lane Loomis, *Modern Cities and Their Religious Problems* (New York, 1887), pp. 63, 65; Bessie L. Pierce, *A History of Chicago*, 3 vols. (New York, Alfred A. Knopf, 1937–1957), III, 63.

19. Sennett, "Middle Class Families and Urban Violence," p. 397; Warner, *Streetcar Suburbs*, p. 159.

20. John L. Hart, *In the School-Room* (Philadelphia, 1879), quoted in Gutman, "Work, Culture, and Society in Industrializing America," p. 585 (Gramsci quoted in ibid., pp. 584–585).

21. George Nelson, "National Plague-Spots," *North American Review*, 145 (Dec. 1887), 687; Henry George, *Social Problems* (New York, 1883), p. 317.

22. Adna F. Weber, *The Growth of Cities in the Nineteenth Century: A Study in Statistics* (New York, 1899), p. 407; Frank W. Blackmar, "The Smoky Pilgrims," *American Journal of Sociology*, 2 (Jan. 1897), 485.

23. Edward Bellamy, *Looking Backward* (New York, 1888; reissued, New York, New American Library, 1960), p. 213.

24. From an 1896 address before the National Education Association, quoted in William A. Bullough, " 'It Is Better to Be a Country Boy': The Lure of the Country in Urban Education in the Gilded Age," *Historian*, 35 (Feb. 1973), 185; Eugene Arden, "The Evil City in American Fiction," *New York History*, 52 (July 1954), 265 (quote from J. F. Hume's *Five Hundred Majority; or, The Days of Tammany* [New York, 1872]); Robert H. Walker, "The Poet and the Rise of the City," *Mississippi Valley Historical Review*, 49 (June 1962), 87.

25. Jacob A. Riis, *How the Other Half Lives* (New York, 1890; reissued, New York, Hill and Wang, 1957), p. 226.

26. Josiah Strong, *Our Country, Its Possible Future and Its Present Crisis* (New York, 1885; reissued, Cambridge, Mass., Harvard University Press, 1963), pp. 177, 182, 186, and introduction by Jurgen Herbst. See also May, *Protestant Churches and Industrial America*, pp. 113–116.

27. Jaher, *Doubters and Dissenters*, pp. 100–121 (quoted passage, p. 110); Arden, "Evil City in American Fiction," p. 266 (quote from *The Destruction of Gotham*). For further warnings about the urban menace see the Reverend Lyman Abbott's introduction to Helen Campbell, *Darkness and Daylight; or, Lights and Shadows of New York Life* (Hartford, 1892), pp. 37, 40; Samuel Lane Loomis, *Modern Cities and Their Religious Problems* (New York, 1887), pp. 6, 63, 65, 104; *The Child in the City: A Series of Papers Presented at the Conference Held during the Chicago Child Welfare Exhibit* (Chicago, Department of Social Investigation, Chicago School of Civics and Philanthropy, 1912), p. 462 (quote from the Reverend Henry Drummond's 1893 Lowell Lectures in Boston).

9 AMERICAN PROTESTANTISM AND THE MORAL CHALLENGE OF THE INDUSTRIAL CITY

1. George F. Magoun, "Church Architecture and the Masses," *Congregational Quarterly*, 4 (Jan. 1862], 30; Robert T. Handy, *A Christian America: Protestant Hopes and Historical Realities* (New York, Oxford University Press, 1971), p. 79. Church membership data were not collected by the Census Bureau prior to 1890. Estimates of membership before that year must be based on extrapolations from figures available for a limited number of denominations. See United States Bureau of the Census, *Historical Statistics of the United States, Colonial Times to 1970*, Bicentennial Edition, part 1 (Washington, D.C., Government Printing Office, 1975), p. 389.

2. Harriet Beecher Stowe, *We and Our Neighbors* (New York, 1873), pp. 386, 439–440.

3. W. S. Rainsford, "What Can We Do for the Poor?" *Forum*, 11 (Apr. 1891), 123; Josiah Strong, *Our Country: Its Possible Future and*

Its Present Crisis (New York, 1885; reissued, Cambridge, Mass., Harvard University Press, 1963), pp. 177, 179; Samuel Lane Loomis, Modern Cities and Their Religious Problems (New York, 1887), esp. pp. 82, 83, and 201. See also Handy, Christian America, p. 78; Aaron I. Abell, The Urban Impact on American Protestantism, 1865–1900 (Cambridge, Mass., Harvard University Press, 1943), p. 91; and, on the Evangelical Alliance, Philip D. Jordan, "The Evangelical Alliance for the United States of America: An Evangelical Search for Identity in Ecumenicity during the Nineteenth Century" (Ph.D. diss., University of Iowa, 1971). The Evangelical Alliance was formed in 1867 to promote evangelical unity, support urban religious effort, and resist the Catholic religious dominance in the cities. Josiah Strong became general secretary in 1886.

4. Loomis, Modern Cities and Their Religious Problems, pp. 86–87. For some representative expressions of Catholic concern about the moral consequences of urbanization, see Charles F. Wingate, "The Moral Side of the Tenement House Problem," Catholic World, 41 (May 1885), 160–164; American Catholic Thought on Social Questions, ed. Aaron I. Abell (Indianapolis, Bobbs-Merrill, 1968), pp. 100–140; Ira Rosenwaike, Population History of New York City (Syracuse, N.Y., Syracuse University Press), pp. 85–89.

5. Rev. H. Francis Perry, "The Mission Sunday-School as a Social and Ethical Lever," Biblioteca Sacra, 56 (1899), 481–504 (quoted passage, p. 492). See also Wade C. Barclay, The Methodist Episcopal Church, 1845–1939: Widening Horizons, 1845–1895, I (New York, 1957), 109 (tract activity); Anne Mary Boylan, " 'The Nursery of the Church': Evangelical Protestant Sunday Schools, 1820–1880" (Ph.D. diss., University of Wisconsin, 1973), pp. 140–152.

6. William R. Moody, The Life of Dwight L. Moody (Chicago, Fleming H. Revell, 1900), pp. 274–281 (quoted passage, p. 281).

7. Stowe, We and Our Neighbors, pp. 375, 378.

8. Lawrence B. Davis, Immigrants, Baptists, and the Protestant Mind in America (Urbana, University of Illinois Press, 1973), pp. 97–112 (Antoshevski, p. 112); Joseph B. Clark, Leavening the Nation: The Story of American Home Missions (New York, Baker and Taylor, 1903), pp. 267 (quoted passage), 268; Abell, Urban Impact on American Protestantism, pp. 35–43, 176; Barclay, Methodist Episcopal Church, pp. 222–226; Charles Edwin Jones, Perfectionist Persuasion: The Holiness Movement and American Methodism, 1867–1936 (Metuchen, N.J., Scarecrow Press, 1974), p. 70. One of the more successful of the new urban-based sects was the Zion's Watchtower Society—"Jehovah's Witnesses"—founded in 1884. See Charles S. Braden, These Also Believe: A Study of Modern American Cults and Minority Religious Movements (New York, Macmillan, 1949), pp. 358–384.

9. J. Orin Oliphant and Ambrose Saricks, Jr., "Baptists and Other Home Missionary Labors in the Pacific Northwest, 1865–1890," Pacific Northwest Quarterly, 41 (Apr. 1950), 132.

10. Bessie L. Pierce, A History of Chicago, 3 vols. (New York, Alfred A. Knopf, 1937–1957), II, 370–371; III, 442; Benjamin O. Flower, Civilization's Inferno; or, Studies in the Social Cellar (Boston, 1893),

p. 50 (Bethel Mission); Abell, *Urban Impact on American Protestantism*, p. 95 (John C. Collins).

11. Jerry McAuley, *An Apostle to the Lost*, ed. R. M. Offord, 7th ed. (New York, American Tract Society, 1907; reissued, Freeport, N.Y., Books for Libraries Press, 1970).

12. Pierce, *History of Chicago*, III, 442; Abell, *Urban Impact on American Protestantism*, p. 176; Offord, *Jerry McAuley*, pp. 56, 152, 227; *New York Times*, May 14, 1904, p. 9 (A. S. Hatch obituary).

13. Abell, *Urban Impact on American Protestantism*, pp. 95–98.

14. Moody, *Life of D. L. Moody*, pp. 264, 276.

15. Ibid., pp. 285, 530. See also James F. Findlay, Jr., *Dwight L. Moody, American Evangelist, 1837–1899* (Chicago, University of Chicago Press, 1969), pp. 266–274.

16. Bernard A. Weisberger, *They Gathered at the River; The Story of the Great Revivalists and Their Impact upon Religion in America* (Boston, Little, Brown, 1958; reissued, New York, Quadrangle Books, 1966), pp. 213–217; Findlay, *Dwight L. Moody*, pp. 289–300.

17. George P. Mains, "The Church and the City," *Methodist Review*, 76 (Mar., 1894), 227–228; Davis, *Immigrants, Baptists, and the Protestant Mind in America*, pp. 113, 127; Barclay, *Methodist Episcopal Church*, p. 225. One Methodist missionary of the period reported "discouragements such as seldom have attended a humane and evangelical enterprise." Ibid., p. 223.

18. Clark, *Leavening the Nation*, pp. 279, 280.

19. William S. Rainsford, *The Story of a Varied Life: An Autobiography* (Garden City, N.Y., Doubleday, Page, 1922; reissued, Freeport, N.Y., Books for Libraries Press, 1970), pp. 199, 248.

20. Davis, *Immigrants, Baptists, and the Protestant Mind in America*, p. 110. See also Clark, *Leavening the Nation*, p. 280.

21. Abell, *Urban Impact on American Protestantism*, pp. 151–161 (quoted passage, p. 161); Rainsford, *Story of a Varied Life*, pp. 12, 124, 151, 197–204, 243, 249, 282, 309 (quoted passages pp. 198, 199); Genevieve C. Weeks, "Oscar C. McCulloch Transforms Plymouth Church, Indianapolis, into an 'Institutional' Church," *Indiana Magazine of History*, 64 (June 1968), 87–108. The first institutional church, dating from 1845, is said to have been the Reverend William A. Muhlenberg's Church of the Holy Communion (Episcopal) in New York. See Alvin W. Skardon, *Church Leader in the Cities: William Augustus Muhlenberg* (Philadelphia, University of Pennsylvania Press, 1971).

22. Paul R. Lucas, "The Church and the City: Congregationalism in Minneapolis, 1850–1890," *Minnesota History*, 44 (Summer 1974), 55–69; Raymond Calkins, *Substitutes for the Saloon* (Boston, Houghton-Mifflin, 1901), p. 128.

23. *The Churchman* [Episcopal], (Oct. 15, 1898), quoted in Abell, *Urban Impact on American Protestantism*, p. 253.

24. C. Allyn Russell, "William Bell Riley: Architect of Fundamentalism," *Minnesota History*, 43 (Spring 1972), 14–30, quoted passage, p. 20.

25. Herbert A. Wisbey, Jr., *Soldiers without Swords: A History of the Salvation Army in the United States* (New York, Macmillan,

1955), pp. 1–131; Abell, *Urban Impact on American Protestantism*, pp. 118–135.

26. William Booth, *In Darkest England and the Way Out* (London, 1890); Herman Ausubel, "General Booth's Scheme of Social Salvation," *American Historical Review*, 56 (April 1951), 519–525; William R. Stewart, *The Philanthropic Work of Josephine Shaw Lowell* (New York, Macmillan, 1911), quoted passage, p. 179.

27. Wisbey, *Soldiers without Swords*, pp. 130–131.

28. Ibid., p. 88; Maud Ballington Booth, "Salvation Army Work in the Slums," *Scribner's Magazine*, 17 (Jan. 1895), 102–114.

29. Abell, *Urban Impact on American Protestantism*, p. 255.

30. Benjamin O. Flower, *Civilization's Inferno*, p. 27. See also idem, "The Power and Responsibility of the Christian Ministry," *Arena*, 4 (June/Nov., 1891), 767–768.

31. Rowland Berthoff, "The Social Order of the Anthracite Region, 1825–1902," *Pennsylvania Magazine of History and Biography*, 89 (July 1965), 261; Loomis, *Modern Cities and Their Religious Problems*, pp. 63, 65; Mains, "The Church and the City," pp. 229–232.

10 BUILDING CHARACTER AMONG THE URBAN POOR

1. William R. Stewart, *The Philanthropic Work of Josephine Shaw Lowell* (New York, Macmillan, 1911), pp. 3–133.

2. David J. Pivar, *Purity Crusade; Sexual Morality and Social Control, 1868–1900* (Westport, Conn., Greenwood Press, 1973); Paul S. Boyer, *Purity in Print; Book Censorship in America* (New York, Charles Scribner's Sons, 1968), pp. 1–22; Joseph M. Hawes, *Children in Urban Society: Juvenile Delinquency in Nineteenth-Century America* (New York, Oxford University Press, 1971), pp. 138–142. Through the efforts of the Gerry society, juveniles in Manhattan were barred from saloons, theaters, and brothels, and action was taken to clear the streets of the "flower girls" who were often simply under-age prostitutes.

3. Stanley Buder, *Pullman: An Experiment in Industrial Order and Community Planning, 1880–1930* (New York, Oxford University Press, 1967), pp. 64, 69. For a discussion of another, less well known experiment along these lines—Vandergrift, Pa., "The Pullman of Western Pennsylvania" founded in the 1890s by the Apollo Iron and Steel Company—see Roy Lubove, *Twentieth Century Pittsburgh: Government, Business, and Environmental Change* (New York, John Wiley and Sons, 1969), pp. 17–18.

4. S. Humphreys Gurteen, *A Handbook of Charity Organization* (Buffalo, N.Y., 1882), pp. 41, 42, 72; Verl S. Lewis, "The Development of the Charity Organization Movement in the United States, 1875–1900. Its Principles and Methods" (D.S.W. diss., Western Reserve University, School of Applied Social Sciences, 1954), pp. 24–28.

5. Kathleen Woodroofe, *From Charity to Social Work in England and the United States* (London, Routledge and Paul, 1962), p. 28.

6. Gurteen, *Handbook*, p. 45.

7. Ibid., p. 48; Lewis, "Development of the Charity Organization Movement," p. 61.

8. More recently, in 1866, the Detroit City Mission Board had pro-

posed a scheme for systematic visitation and moral uplift among the poor that, in the view of one admiring contemporary, was "almost utopian in its completeness." Silas Farmer, *History of Detroit and Wayne County and Early Michigan*, 3rd ed. (New York, 1890; reissued, Detroit, Gale Research, 1969), p. 650.

9. Gurteen, *Handbook*, p. 18; Lewis, "Development of the Charity Organization Movement," p. 2; Nathan Irvin Huggins, *Protestants against Poverty: Boston's Charities, 1870–1900* (Westport, Conn., Greenwood Pub., 1971), p. 9.

10. Gurteen, *Handbook*, pp. 21, 38; Constance M. Green, *Washington: Capital City, 1879–1950* (Princeton, N.J., Princeton University Press, 1963), p. 70; Mrs. Glendower Evans, "Scientific Charity," *Proceedings of the National Conference of Charities and Correction, Sixteenth Annual Session, San Francisco, 1889* (Boston, 1889), p. 27 (hereafter, NCCC, *Proc.*). See also Huggins, *Protestants against Poverty*, p. 73, quoting Anna L. Meeker in *Lend-a-Hand* (1886) and S. Humphreys Gurteen, *Provident Schemes* (Buffalo, 1879), p. 76.

11. Lewis, "Development of the Charity Organization Movement," p. 120, quoting Lenora Hamlin, a Saint Paul, Minnesota, COS leader; Gurteen, *Handbook*, p. 49; Stewart, *Philanthropic Work of Josephine Shaw Lowell*, p. 179. See also Mary Willcox Brown, *The Development of Thrift* (New York, 1899), p. 6; NCCC, *Proc.* (1889), p. 27 (Mrs. Glendower Evans); Charles S. Fairchild, "Objects of Charity Organization," ibid. (1884), p. 68.

12. Stewart, *Philanthropic Work of Josephine Shaw Lowell*, pp. 16 (quote from diary), 35 (the theater incident).

13. Josephine Shaw Lowell, *Public Relief and Private Charity* (New York, 1884), pp. 68, 94; Stewart, *Philanthropic Work of Josephine Shaw Lowell*, pp. 146, 212–213.

14. Gurteen, *Handbook*, p. 32 (see also pp. 12, 109); Stewart, *Philanthropic Work of Josephine Shaw Lowell*, pp. 172, 212.

15. Gurteen, *Handbook*, p. 67; Lewis, "Development of the Charity Organization Movement," p. 131; Mary E. Richmond, *Friendly Visiting among the Poor; A Handbook for Charity Workers* (New York, [1899]; reissued, Montclair, N.J., Patterson Smith, 1969), p. 173. See also Gurteen, *Provident Schemes*, p. 17. This hostility to church-sponsored philanthropy also reflected the COS's desire to rationalize urban charity by eliminating the competition and overlapping efforts of numerous special-interest benevolent organizations.

16. Fairchild, "Objects of Charity Organization," p. 66.

17. NCCC, *Proc.* (1887), p. 134.

18. Gurteen, *Handbook*, pp. 109, 39; Fairchild, "Objects of Charity Organization," p. 66.

19. Ibid., p. 65.

20. Frank D. Watson, *The Charity Organization Movement in the United States* (New York, Macmillan, 1922), p. 218; Gurteen, *Handbook*, p. 30. In 1894 one COS spokesman urged the development of a standardized COS telegraph code to facilitate intercity COS communications. Amos G. Warner, *American Charities: A Study in Philanthropy and Economics* (New York, 1894), p. 382.

21. Gurteen, *Handbook*, pp. 160–161.

22. George D. Holt, "The Relation of Charity Problems to Social Problems," NCCC, *Proc.* (1891), pp. 120–121; Mrs. Glendower Evans, "Scientific Charity," p. 26. See also comments by Charles D. Kellogg quoted in NCCC, *Proc.* (1887), p. 125.

23. Lewis, "Development of the Charity Organization Movement," p. 190; Robert H. Bremner, *From the Depths; The Discovery of Poverty in the United States* (New York, New York University Press, 1956), p. 52.

24. NCCC, *Proc.* (1887), pp. 132–133 (Kellogg); Fairchild, "Objects of Charity Organization," p. 68.

25. Gurteen, *Handbook*, pp. 116, 113; Gurteen, *Provident Schemes*, pp. 72, 74.

26. "Rules and Suggestions for Visitors of the Associated Charities" (Boston, 1879), p. 8. (This pamphlet is reprinted as app. C in Lewis, "Development of the Charity Organization Movement.")

27. Marian C. Putnam, "Friendly Visiting," NCCC, *Proc.* (1887), p. 151; ibid. (1889), p. 27 (Mrs. Glendower Evans); Gurteen, *Handbook*, p. 176. See also Lenora Hamlin, "Friendly Visiting," *Charities Review*, 6 (June 1897), 322.

28. Robert Treat Paine, 1879 address quoted in Lewis, "Development of the Charity Organization Movement," p. 120.

29. Frances A. Smith, "Continued Care of Families," NCCC, *Proc.* (1895), p. 87.

30. See, e.g., Gurteen, *Handbook*, pp. 39, 182 (quoted phrase); Lewis, "Development of the Charity Organization Movement," pp. 114 (quoting the constitution of the Boston Associated Charities) and app. C ("Rules and Suggestions for Visitors of the Associated Charities.")

31. Ibid.; Gurteen, *Handbook*, pp. 224, 225.

32. Alexander Mackay-Smith, "The Power of Personality in Redemptive Work," NCCC, *Proc.* (1890), p. 20.

33. Holt, "Relation of Charity Problems to Social Problems," p. 121.

34. Green, *Washington: Capital City*, p. 70; "Rules and Suggestions for Visitors of the Associated Charities," p. 4.

35. Smith, "Continued Care of Families," p. 89.

36. Holt, "Relation of Charity Problems to Social Problems," p. 121; Smith, "Continued Care of Families," p. 90.

37. Gurteen, *Handbook*, p. 117; Gurteen, *Provident Schemes*, p. 32.

38. Jane Addams, *Democracy and Social Ethics* (New York, Macmillan, 1902; reissued, Cambridge, Mass., Harvard University Press, 1964, edited with introduction by Anne Firor Scott), pp. 27–28.

39. "Report of the Committee on the Organization of Charity," NCCC, *Proc.* (1891), p. 113. See also, for similar pessimism, Charles D. Kellogg, "Charity Organization in the United States," ibid. (1893), p. 84.

40. Quoted in Roy Lubove, *The Professional Altruist: The Emergence of Social Work as a Career* (Cambridge, Mass., Harvard University Press, 1965; reissued, New York, Atheneum, 1971), p. 17.

41. "Destitution in Boston: A Symposium," *Arena*, 2 (Nov. 1890), 734. The author of this comment was Edward Hamilton.

42. John Graham Brooks, "The Future Problem of Charity and the Unemployed," *Annals of the American Academy of Political and Social Science*, 5 (July 1894), 14–15.

43. Jeffrey R. Brackett, "The Charity Organization Movement: Its Tendency and Its Duties," NCCC, *Proc.* (1895), p. 83; Warner, *American Charities*, p. 390.

44. For a good recent study see Allen F. Davis, *Spearheads for Reform: The Social Settlements and the Progressive Movement, 1890–1914* (New York, Oxford University Press, 1967).

45. Bremner, *From the Depths*, pp. 60–61; Davis, *Spearheads for Reform*, pp. 8–12.

46. Mary E. McDowell, "Friendly Visiting," NCCC, *Proc.* (1896), p. 254.

47. Quoted in Lewis, "Development of the Charity Organization Movement," p. 122.

48. Stewart, *Philanthropic Work of Josephine Shaw Lowell*, pp. 185–186.

49. Eleanor H. Woods, *Robert A. Woods: Champion of Democracy* (Boston, Houghton Mifflin, 1929), pp. 198–202, 238–248, 250–256; Davis, *Spearheads for Reform*, pp. 75–76, 92.

50. Jane Addams, *The Spirit of Youth and the City Streets* (New York, Macmillan, 1909; reprinted, Urbana, University of Illinois Press, 1972, introduction by Allen F. Davis), pp. 14, xxvi–xxvii (Davis quote). When the sexual behavior of urban youth did not follow "the traditional line of domesticity," she wrote, it was "a cancer in the very tissues of society and . . . a disrupter of the securest social bonds" (ibid., p. 15).

51. Davis, *Spearheads for Reform*, chap. 6: "The Settlements and the Labor Movement."

52. Quoted in ibid., p. 75.

53. Addams, *Democracy and Social Ethics*, pp. 16, 25, 26, 44, 64.

54. This did not represent a total about-face, for the question of the physical circumstances of slum life had had a distinct if subordinate place in COS writings from the beginning. As early as 1879, for example, S. Humphreys Gurteen had written of "people who live huddled together in vile tenements and overcrowded dwellings and who have been allowed through the guilty negligence of their fellow-townsmen to float down the stream and through the floodgates of sanitary neglect and to land at last in physical, moral, aye, and spiritual degradation." Gurteen, *Provident Schemes,* p. 35. See also Gurteen, *Handbook*, p. 181.

55. P. W. Ayres, "Report of the Committee on Charity Organization," NCCC, *Proc.* (1896), p. 238.

56. Edward T. Devine, "The Value and the Dangers of Investigation," ibid. (1897), p. 194.

57. Charles F. Weller, "Friendly Visiting as a Social Force," ibid. (1897), pp. 201–202.

58. Warner, *American Charities*, pp. 26, 28; Brown, *The Development of Thrift*, p. 6.

59. Richmond, *Friendly Visiting among the Poor*, pp. 45, 180, 57; and introduction by Max Siporin, esp. pp. xix–xx ("good laugh" quote from Mary Richmond's *The Good Neighbor in the Modern City* [1907]).

60. It was on these grounds that Warner opposed supplying birth-control information to the poor: it would simply "promote sensuality." Warner, *American Charities*, pp. 28, 67–68.

61. Richmond, *Friendly Visiting among the Poor*, pp. 9, 45, 47, 73, 86, 109. Richard Sennett has suggested that concern by middle-class reformers about family stability in the slums was in part a projection of their interest in preserving and strengthening the *middle-class* family as a "bulwark against confusion" in new suburbs where traditional community structures were much weakened or absent altogether. Richard Sennett, *Families against the City: Middle-Class Homes of Industrial Chicago, 1872–1890* (Cambridge, Mass., Harvard University Press, 1970; reissued, New York, Vintage Books, 1974), pp. 42–43, 237 (quoted passage).

62. Ibid., p. 92.

63. Ibid., pp. 12, 45.

11 THE URBAN MORAL AWAKENING OF THE 1890s

1. Charles H. Parkhurst, *Our Fight with Tammany* (New York, 1895), pp. 267–285, esp. p. 272.

2. John Higham, "The Reorientation of American Culture in the 1890's," in *The Origins of Modern Consciousness*, ed. John Weiss (Detroit, Wayne State University Press, 1965), pp. 25–48, esp. pp. 26–28, 34–39.

3. Ross E. Paulson, *Radicalism and Reform; The Vrooman Family and American Social Thought, 1837–1937* (Lexington, University of Kentucky Press, 1968), pp. 80–90.

4. B[enjamin] O. Flower, *Progressive Men, Women, and Movements of the Past Twenty-Five Years* (Boston, The New Arena, 1914), pp. 128–129. An Illinois native, Flower arrived in Boston in the mid-1880s, and founded the *Arena* in 1889, when he was thirty-one.

5. Paulson, *Radicalism and Reform*, pp. 92–94.

6. Ibid., p. 83; Walter Vrooman, "First Steps in the Union of Reform Forces," *Arena*, 9 (Mar. 1894), 540–547, quoted passage pp. 544–545.

7. George E. Mowry, *The California Progressives* (Berkeley, University of California Press, 1951; reissued, New York, Quadrangle, 1963), p. 38; Joy J. Jackson, *New Orleans in the Gilded Age: Politics and Urban Progress, 1880–1896* (Baton Rouge, Louisiana State University Press, 1969), pp. 115–134, esp. p. 129; David J. Pivar, *Purity Crusade: Sexual Morality and Social Control, 1868–1900* (Westport, Conn., Greenwood Press, 1973), p. 148.

8. Walter Vrooman, "First Steps in the Union of Reform Forces," p. 540; William H. Tolman, *Municipal Reform Movements in the United States* (New York, Fleming H. Revell, 1895), p. 159 and sec. II, "Municipal Reform Movements"; Benjamin O. Flower, "Union for Practical Progress," *Arena*, 8 (June 1893), 79, 83.

9. Joseph O. Baylen, "A Victorian's 'Crusade' in Chicago, 1893–1894," *Journal of American History*, 51 (Dec. 1964), 418–434, quoted passages pp. 421, 430.

10. Parkhurst, *Our Fight with Tammany*, pp. 10, 126, 161.

11. Ibid., pp. 111, 240–243; Tolman, *Municipal Reform Movements*, pp. 185, 408.

12. Parkhurst, *Our Fight with Tammany*, pp. 256–260; Gerald W. McFarland, *Mugwumps, Morals, and Politics, 1884–1920* (Amherst, University of Massachusetts Press, 1975), p. 95.

13. James F. Richardson, *Urban Police in the United States* (Port Washington, N.Y., Kennikat Press, 1974), p. 69; McFarland, *Mugwumps, Morals, and Politics*, pp. 95–101; Parkhurst, *Our Fight with Tammany*, p. 272.

14. Washington Gladden, "The Cosmopolis City Club," *Century Magazine*, n.s. 23 (Jan., Feb., and Mar., 1893), 397, (after serialization in the *Century*, from which my citations are taken, this novel was published in book form); Flower, "Union for Practical Progress," p. 83.

15. The Reverend Madison C. Peters, 1891 address quoted in "Public Parks and Playgrounds: A Symposium," *Arena*, 10 (July 1894), 282.

16. Hiram Vrooman, "The Organization of Moral Forces," *Arena*, 9 (Feb. 1894), 353, 354; Walter Vrooman, "First Steps in the Union of Reform Forces," pp. 540, 545, 546 (italics added).

17. Paul S. Boyer, "*In His Steps*: A Reappraisal," *American Quarterly*, 23 (Spring 1971), 60–78; Gladden, "Cosmopolis City Club," pp. 397, 398.

18. "Public Parks and Playgrounds: A Symposium," p. 283; Diana Hirschler, "Union in Philadelphia," *Arena*, 9 (Mar. 1894), 548–552, esp. pp. 551–552.

19. Gladden, "Cosmopolis City Club," p. 399 (see also p. 574); Boyer, "*In His Steps*: A Reappraisal," p. 66. One Chicago minister in Sheldon's novel resigns when his congregation resists his vision of a morally regenerated city.

20. Hiram Vrooman, "The Organization of Moral Forces," p. 352; Benjamin O. Flower, *Civilization's Inferno; or, Studies in the Social Cellar* (Boston, 1893), p. 27.

21. Walter Vrooman, "First Steps in the Union of Reform Forces," p. 541.

22. Thomas E. Will, "The City Union for Practical Progress," *Arena*, 10 (July 1894), 263–273, quoted passages p. 268.

23. James Bryce, *The American Commonwealth*, 2 vols. (New York, Macmillan, 1888; reissued, 1919), I, 642.

24. E. L. Godkin, *Problems of Modern Democracy* (New York, 1896), p. 142.

25. Washington Gladden, *Social Facts and Forces* (New York, G. P. Putnam's Sons, 1897; reissued, Port Washington, N.Y., Kennikat Press, 1971), pp. 186–187.

26. See entries on "Municipal Reform" and "National Municipal League" in W. D. P. Bliss, ed., *New Encyclopedia of Social Reform* (New York, Funk and Wagnalls, 1909).

27. Melvin G. Holli, *Reform in Detroit: Hazen S. Pingree and Ur-*

ban *Politics* (New York, Oxford University Press, 1969), p. 169; Gladden, *Social Facts and Forces*, pp. iii, 161.

28. Adna F. Weber, *The Growth of Cities in the Nineteenth Century: A Study in Statistics* (New York, 1899), pp. 433, 434, 435.

29. Adeline Knapp, "San Francisco and the Civic Awakening," *Arena*, 12 (Apr. 1895), 242–243, 247.

30. Flower, *Civilization's Inferno*, pp. 48, 92, 226, 227, 228.

31. Ibid., pp. 5, 24, 104.

32. Zane L. Miller, "Boss Cox's Cincinnati: A Study in Urbanization and Politics, 1880–1914," *Journal of American History*, 54 (Mar. 1968), 823–838, esp. p. 829; Lyle W. Dorsett, "The City Boss and the Reformer," *Pacific Northwest Quarterly*, 63 (Oct. 1972), 153. For a discussion of the way Gilded Age reformers exaggerated "corruption" in government for their own purposes, see Ari Hoogenboom, "Spoilsmen and Reformers: Civil Service Reform and Public Morality," in *The Gilded Age: A Reappraisal*, ed. H. Wayne Morgan (Syracuse, N.Y., Syracuse University Press, 1963), pp. 69–90.

33. Theodore Roosevelt, *An Autobiography* (New York, Macmillan, 1913), p. 175; Tolman, *Municipal Reform Movements*, pp. 9, 30; Parkhurst, *Our Fight with Tammany*, p. 261.

34. Ibid., pp. 126, 270, 271, 275, 276.

35. Quoted in Tolman, *Municipal Reform in the United States*, p. 37.

36. Gladden, "Cosmopolis City Club," pp. 574, 575, 576.

37. Philip S. Benjamin, "Gentlemen Reformers in the Quaker City, 1870–1912," *Political Science Quarterly*, 85 (Mar. 1970), 61–79, quoted passages pp. 77, 79; Holli, *Reform in Detroit*, pp. 163, 169.

38. Gladden, "Cosmopolis City Club," p. 395.

39. Walter Vrooman, "First Steps in the Union of Reform Forces," pp. 543, 545, 547; Parkhurst, *Our Fight with Tammany*, p. 261.

40. Gladden, "Cosmopolis City Club," pp. 397, 399, 405; Charles M. Sheldon, *In His Steps* (Chicago, 1896; reissued, Chicago, Moody Press, 1956), p. 48.

41. Gladden, "Cosmopolis City Club," p. 789.

12 THE TWO FACES OF URBAN MORAL REFORM IN THE 1890s

1. William S. Rainsford, "What Can We Do for the Poor?" *Forum*, 11 (Apr. 1891), 117; Theodore Roosevelt, *An Autobiography* (New York, Macmillan, 1913), pp. 178, 202; Jacob Riis, *How the Other Half Lives* (New York, 1890; reissued, New York, Hill and Wang, 1957), p. 207 (italics added).

2. Charles M. Sheldon, *In His Steps* (Chicago, 1896; reissued, Chicago, Moody Press, 1956), pp. 73, 93, 111, 156; Walter Vrooman, "Playgrounds for Children" *Arena*, 10 (July 1894), 284.

3. Benjamin O. Flower, *Civilization's Inferno; or, Studies in the Social Cellar* (Boston, 1893), pp. 79, 218.

4. Washington Gladden, *Social Facts and Forces* (New York, 1897; reissued, Port Washington, N.Y., Kennikat Press, 1971), pp. 189–190.

5. Sheldon, *In His Steps*, pp. 72, 123.

6. Charles H. Parkhurst, *Our Fight with Tammany* (New York, 1895), pp. 20, 22, 23, 38.

7. Hubert Howe Bancroft, *Works* (San Francisco, 1887; reprinted, New York, McGraw Hill, n.d.), XXXVI and XXXVII (*Popular Tribunals*), quoted passages, XXXVII, 649, 655, 662.

8. Edward Everett Hale, in "Destitution in Boston: A Symposium," *Arena*, 2 (Nov. 1890), 741, 742. Such a scheme, Hale suggested, would simply be the urban equivalent of a village order in which the minister has "the moral oversight of every person in the town" (p. 741).

9. Flower, *Civilization's Inferno*, pp. 150, 152.

10. Ibid., p. 149; William H. Tolman, *Municipal Reform Movements in the United States* (New York, 1895), p. 198.

11. Sheldon, *In His Steps*, pp. 120, 122, 130. See also Paul S. Boyer, "*In His Steps*: A Reappraisal," *American Quarterly*, 23 (Spring 1971), pp. 73–74.

12. Adna F. Weber, *The Growth of Cities in the Nineteenth Century: A Study in Statistics* (New York, 1899), pp. 369, 386, 389, 397. (Weber did not endorse Hansen's depressing analysis, but his only counterargument was the rather lame one that in the recent Spanish-American War, "American city lads marched to victory on Cuban soil side by side with the rough cowboys of the western plains," p. 397); Robert H. Wiebe, *The Search for Order, 1877–1920* (New York, Hill and Wang, 1967), chaps. II–IV; Richard Sennett, *Families against the City: Middle-Class Homes of Industrial Chicago, 1872–1890* (Cambridge, Mass., Harvard University Press, 1970).

13. Arthur Dudley Vinton, "Morality and Environment," *Arena*, 3 (Apr. 1891), 574.

14. Gladden, *Social Facts and Forces*, p. 177; Roy Lubove, *The Progressives and the Slums: Tenement House Reform in New York City, 1890–1917* (Pittsburgh, University of Pittsburgh Press, 1962, pp. 88–89, 91 (quoted passage re bathhouses); James B. Lane, *Jacob A. Riis and the American City* (Port Washington, N.Y., Kennikat Press, 1974), p. 125. For similar comments on the moral importance of playgrounds see Thomas E. Will in "Public Parks and Playgrounds: A Symposium," *Arena*, 10 (July 1894), 276–277. The New York State Tenement Committee was a seven-member investigative body authorized by the legislature and appointed by the governor in 1894 under journalistic pressure. Its report appeared a year later.

15. Flower, *Civilization's Inferno*, pp. 110, 111, 177, 232.

16. Benjamin O. Flower, "Union for Practical Progress," *Arena*, 8 (June 1893), pp. 86, 87.

17. Josiah Quincy, "Municipal Progress in Boston," *Independent*, 52 (Feb. 15, 1900), p. 426; idem, "The Development of American Cities," *Arena*, 17 (Mar. 1897), 536; Geoffrey Blodgett, *The Gentle Reformers: Massachusetts Democrats in the Cleveland Era* (Cambridge, Mass., Harvard University Press, 1966), chap. 9, "Mayor Quincy's Boston," esp. pp. 249–253. In the same period the Philadelphia Union for Practical Progress sponsored penny concerts and entertainments to give Philadelphia's poor (according to one sympathizer) "a taste of those

gentler and more refined pleasures which alone can displace vice and coarse sports." Diana Hirschler, "Union in Philadelphia," *Arena*, 9 (Mar. 1894), 551.

18. George E. Waring, Jr., *Street Cleaning and the Disposal of a City's Waste: Methods and Results and the Effect upon Public Health, Public Morals, and Municipal Prosperity* (New York, 1897), p. 186. See also Martin V. Melosi, " 'Out of Sight, Out of Mind,' The Environment and Disposal of Municipal Refuse, 1860–1920," *Historian*, 35 (Aug. 1973), 621–640, esp. pp. 626, 632, 639.

19. Flower, *Civilization's Inferno*, p. 47.

20. Roosevelt, *Autobiography*, p. 174.

21. Walter Vrooman, "First Steps in the Union of Reform Forces," *Arena*, 9 (Mar. 1894), 546. See also Tolman, *Municipal Reform Movements*, p. 38.

22. Flower, *Civilization's Inferno*, pp. 219, 220; Gladden, *Social Facts and Forces*, p. 157. See also, for similar rhetoric, Sheldon, *In His Steps*, pp. 253–255.

23. William S. Rainsford, *The Story of a Varied Life* (Garden City, N.Y., Doubleday, Page, 1922; reissued, Freeport, N.Y., Books for Libraries Press, 1970), p. 329.

24. Charles Mulford Robinson, *Modern Civic Art; or, The City Made Beautiful* (New York, G. P. Putnam's Sons, 1903), p. 371. See also Charles Zueblin, " 'The White City' and After," *Chautauquan*, 38 (Dec. 1903), 372–384.

25. Rainsford, *Story of a Varied Life*, pp. 329, 330.

26. John J. Ingalls, "Lessons of the Fair," *Cosmopolitan*, 16 (Dec. 1893), 141–149, quoted passages pp. 143, 144; John Coleman Adams, "What a Great City Might Be—A Lesson from the White City," *New England Magazine*, new series 14 (Mar. 1896), 3–13, quoted passage p. 6. For similar sentiments see Paul Bourget, "A Farewell to the White City," *Cosmopolitan*, 16 (Dec. 1893), 134–140; and Alice Freeman Palmer, "Some Lasting Results of the World's Fair," *Forum*, 16 (Dec. 1893), 517–523.

27. Adams, "What a Great City Might Be," p. 13; Bourget, "Farewell to the White City," p. 135. See also John W. Reps, *The Making of Urban America: A History of City Planning in the United States* (Princeton, Princeton University Press, 1965), p. 498; David F. Burg, *Chicago's White City of 1893* (Lexington, Ky., The University Press of Kentucky, 1975), chap. 7, "Visions of the Celestial City" (pp. 286–348). For the influence of the White City on another reformer of the day, Henry Demarest Lloyd, see John L. Thomas, "Utopia for an Urban Age: Henry George, Henry Demarest Lloyd, Edward Bellamy," *Perspectives in American History*, 6 (1972), 154–155.

28. Wiebe, *Search for Order*, p. 155.

29. Lyman Abbott, introduction in Helen Campbell, *Darkness and Daylight; or, Lights and Shadows of New York Life* (Hartford, 1892), p. 41; Josiah Strong, *The Challenge of the City* (New York, Eaton and Mains, 1907), p. v (quoting Abbott).

30. William J. Tucker, "The Spiritual Life of the Modern City," *Congregationalist*, Dec. 31, 1896, p. 1038.

31. Joseph Lee, *Constructive and Preventive Philanthropy* (New York, Macmillan, 1902), p. 237.

32. William T. Stead, *If Christ Came to Chicago* (Chicago, 1894; reissued, New York, Living Books, 1964), pp. 377, 259, 248, 123–133 (chap. VI, "The Nineteenth Precinct of the First Ward"), 128, 129, 21, 19; Joseph O. Baylen, "A Victorian's 'Crusade' in Chicago, 1893–94," *Journal of American History*, 51 (Dec. 1964), 418–434.

33. Stead, *If Christ Came to Chicago*, 51–121, 228, 231–241, 370; quoted passages pp. 357, 182, 342.

34. Ibid., pp. 141, 264, 266, 269, 277, 327–328.

35. Ibid., pp. 281, 282, 337, 342.

36. Ibid., p. 322.

37. Ibid., pp. 272, 329, 372.

38. Ibid., p. 335; Baylen, "A Victorian's 'Crusade,'" p. 421 ("centre of the English-Speaking race").

39. Stead, *If Christ Came to Chicago*, pp. 409–428 (chap. 25, quoted passage, p. 413).

40. Ibid., pp. 414, 420, 427.

41. Ibid., pp. 417, 425.

42. Ibid., p. 410.

43. Ibid., pp. 426, 428.

INTRODUCTION TO PART FOUR

1. T. Lynn Smith, "The Emergence of Cities," in *The Urban South*, ed. Rupert B. Vance and Nicholas J. Demerath (Chapel Hill, University of North Carolina Press, 1955), pp. 24–37; Donald B. Cole, *Handbook of American History* (New York, Harcourt, Brace and World, 1968), p. 241; United States Bureau of the Census, *Historical Statistics of the United States, Colonial Times to 1970, Bicentennial Edition*, 2 vols. (Washington, D.C., Government Printing Office, 1975), I, 11.

2. Ibid., I, 105; David Ward, *Cities and Immigrants: A Geography of Change in Nineteenth-Century America* (New York, Oxford University Press, 1971), p. 56. The level of domestic migration cityward also remained high in these years, reinforced now by southern rural blacks migrating to northern (as well as southern) cities. By 1920 Saint Louis's black population stood at about 100,000, Chicago's at 130,000, that of New York and Philadelphia at about 250,000 each. See David Kinley, "The Movement of Population from Country to City," in *Cyclopedia of American Agriculture*, ed. Liberty Hyde Bailey (New York, Macmillan, 1909), IV, 113–119; George E. Haynes, "Negro Migration: Its Effect on Family and Community Life in the North," *Opportunity*, 2 (Sept. 1924), 274; August Meier and Elliott Rudwick, *From Plantation to Ghetto*, revised ed. (New York, Hill and Wang, 1970), pp. 214–216; Reynolds Farley, "The Urbanization of Negroes in the United States," *Journal of Social History*, 1 (Spring 1968), 241–258.

3. Josiah Strong, *The Challenge of the City* (New York, Eaton and Mains, 1907), p. 199. See also, for similar sentiments, Amory H. Bradford, "The Cry of the City," *Baptist Standard*, 53 (Nov. 18, 1905), 9,

quoted in Lawrence B. Davis, *Immigrants, Baptists, and the Protestant Mind in America* (Urbana, University of Illinois Press, 1973), p. 136.

4. Frederic C. Howe, *The City: The Hope of Democracy* (New York, Scribner's, 1906), p. 9; Frank Parsons' comment, from his 1899 book *The City for the People*, quoted in Arthur Mann, *Yankee Reformers in the Urban Age* (Cambridge, Mass., Harvard University Press, 1954), p. 139; William B. Munro, *The Government of American Cities* (New York, Macmillan, 1912), p. 51. See, in the same vein, Richard T. Ely, *The Coming City* (New York, T. Y. Crowell, 1902), p. 19.

5. Munro, *Government of American Cities*, p. 51; Robert T. Handy, *A Christian America: Protestant Hopes and Historical Realities* (New York, Oxford University Press, 1971), p. 144 (quoting the Northern Methodist bishops' Episcopal Address of 1900).

6. On urban revivalism and city mission effort in these years, for example, see Bernard A. Weisberger, *They Gathered at the River: The Story of the Great Revivalists and Their Impact upon Religion in America* (Boston, Little, Brown, 1958; reissued, New York, Quadrangle Books, 1966), pp. 220–265, and Norris Magnuson, *Salvation in the Slums: Evangelical Social Work, 1865–1920* (Metuchen, N.J., Scarecrow Press, 1977).

13 BATTLING THE SALOON AND THE BROTHEL

1. The regulatory approach, prevalent in Europe and advocated in Dr. William W. Sanger's *History of Prostitution: Its Extent, Causes, and Effects Throughout the World* (New York, 1858), was adopted for a time in Saint Louis in the early 1870s—hence the crusade against it. David J. Pivar, *Purity Crusade; Sexual Morality and Social Control, 1868–1900* (Westport, Conn., Greenwood Press, 1973), pp. 18, 32, 34, 83–85; John C. Burnham, "The Social Evil Ordinance—A Social Experiment in Nineteenth Century St. Louis," *Bulletin of the Missouri Historical Society*, 27 (Apr. 1971), 203–217; Robert E. Riegel, "Changing American Attitudes toward Prostitution (1800–1920)," *Journal of the History of Ideas*, 29 (July/Sept., 1968), 446 (Sanger). Dr. Sanger was resident physician at the women's prison on Blackwell's Island in New York.

2. In 1890 Mrs. Sidney Whittemore, a New Yorker drawn into mission work by Jerry McAuley, founded the Door of Hope Mission for prostitutes—the first of some sixty such centers eventually established throughout urban America. In 1895 a New York businessman founded the National Florence Crittenton Mission Association in memory of his deceased daughter, and under the leadership of Kate Waller Barrett, Florence Crittenton homes for unwed mothers were soon in operation in more than fifty cities. Carol L. Urness, "Barrett, Kate Harwood Waller," in *Notable American Women*, ed. Edward T. James, Janet W. James, Paul S. Boyer, 3 vols. (Cambridge, Mass., Harvard University Press, 1971), I, 97–99; R. M. Offord, ed., *Jerry McAuley, An Apostle to the Lost*, 7th ed. (New York, American Tract Society, 1907; reissued, Freeport, N.Y., Books for Libraries Press, 1970), p. 244; Pivar, *Purity Crusade*, pp. 139, 187.

3. Herman Kogan, "Everleigh, Minna," *Notable American Women*, I, 589–591; George Kibbe Turner, "Beer and the City Liquor Problem," *McClure's*, 33 (Sept. 1909), 528; Stanley Baron, *Brewed in America: A History of Beer and Ale in the United States* (Boston, Little, Brown, 1962), pp. 212–220. Joseph Mayer, "The Passing of the Red Light District—Vice Investigations and Results," *Social Hygiene*, 4 (Apr. 1918), 197; William D. Miller, *Memphis during the Progressive Era, 1900–1917* (Memphis, Memphis State University Press, 1957), pp. 89–90; Joy J. Jackson, *New Orleans in the Gilded Age; Politics and Urban Progress, 1880–1896* (Baton Rouge, Louisiana State University Press for the Louisiana Historical Association, 1969), p. 254; Constance M. Green, *Washington: Capital City: 1879–1950* (Princeton, Princeton University Press, 1963); p. 167.

4. Peter H. Odegard, *Pressure Politics; The Story of the Anti-Saloon League* (New York, Oxford University Press, 1928), pp. 30–32, 73, 75, 116–126, 176, 181–218; Norman H. Clark, *Deliver Us from Evil: An Interpretation of American Prohibition* (New York, W. W. Norton, 1976), pp. 98, 113 (on ASL financial support); Jack S. Blocker, Jr., *Retreat from Reform: The Prohibition Movement in the United States, 1890–1913* (Westport, Conn., Greenwood Press, 1976), pp. 154–213, esp. pp. 158, 199–201, 214, 236–239 (on state successes); Ross Evans Paulson, *Women's Suffrage and Prohibition: A Comparative Study of Equality and Social Control* (Glenview, Ill., Scott, Foresman, 1973), p. 157. For a picture of ASL operations at the state and local levels see Robert E. Wenger, "The Anti-Saloon League in Nebraska Politics, 1898–1910," *Nebraska History*, 52 (Fall 1971), 267–292; James A. Burran, "Prohibition in New Mexico, 1917," *New Mexico Historical Review*, 48 (Apr. 1973), 133–149; James E. Hansen II, "Moonshine and Murder: Prohibition in Denver," *The Colorado Magazine*, 50 (Winter 1973), 1–23; Gilman M. Ostrander, *The Prohibition Movement in California, 1848–1933*, 57 (Berkeley, University of California Publications in History, 1957); Norman H. Clark, *The Dry Years: Prohibition and Social Change in Washington* (Seattle, University of Washington Press, 1965); and Robert A. Hohner, "The Prohibitionists: Who Were They?" *South Atlantic Quarterly*, 68 (Autumn 1969), 491–505 (on Virginia).

5. Jeremy P. Felt, "Vice Reform as a Political Technique; The Committee of Fifteen in New York, 1900–1901," *New York History*, 54 (Jan. 1973), 24–51. For more on the Raines Law hotels, see chapter 14.

6. Felt, "Vice Reform as a Political Technique," pp. 29–48; John P. Peters, D.D., "The Story of the Committee of Fourteen of New York," *Social Hygiene*, 4 (July 1918), 347–388. In 1905, a reconstituted Committee of Fourteen was set up under ASL auspices to focus attention on saloons catering to prostitutes. Its report, emphasizing legal aspects of the question, appeared in 1910. See ibid., p. 371.

7. George Kibbe Turner, "The Daughters of the Poor," *McClure's*, 34 (Nov. 1909), 45–61; *The Social Evil With Special Reference to Conditions Existing in the City of New York. A Report Prepared [in 1902] under the Direction of the Committee of Fifteen*, ed. Edwin R. A. Selig-

man, 2nd ed., revised with new material (New York, G. P. Putnam's Sons, 1912), p. 210.

8. Clifford W. Barnes, "The Story of the Committee of Fifteen of Chicago," *Social Hygiene*, 4 (Apr. 1918), 145–146; George Kibbe Turner, "The City of Chicago: A Study of the Great Immoralities," *McClure's*, 28 (Apr. 1907), 575–592, quoted passage, p. 582; Roy Lubove, "The Progressives and the Prostitute," *Historian*, 24 (May 1962), 308, 313.

9. Barnes, "Story of the Committee of Fifteen of Chicago," pp. 146–156; Vice Commission of Chicago, *The Social Evil in Chicago* (Chicago, Gunthorp-Warren Printing, 1911), pp. 1–8, 25 (motto); *Who Was Who in America*, V (Chicago, A. N. Marquis, 1973), 402 (George J. Kneeland).

10. John D. Rockefeller, Jr., introduction in George J. Kneeland, *Commercialized Prostitution in New York City* (New York, Century, 1913), pp. vii–x; John C. Burnham, "The Progressive Era Revolution in American Attitudes toward Sex," *Journal of American History*, 59 (Mar. 1973), 885–908, esp. pp. 892–895 (on Morrow).

11. Ibid., pp. 897–898.

12. Lubove, "The Progressive and the Prostitute," p. 313; Jane Addams, *A New Conscience and an Ancient Evil* (New York, Macmillan, 1912), p. 23; "Social Purity," *The New Encyclopedia of Social Reform*, ed. W. D. P. Bliss (New York, Funk and Wagnalls, 1908), pp. 1126–28; Mayer, "The Passing of the Red Light District," pp. 199, 204.

13. Russel Nye, *The Unembarrassed Muse: The Popular Arts in America* (New York, Dial Press, 1970), p. 367.

14. Walter Clarke, "Social Hygiene and the War," *Social Hygiene*, 4 (April 1918), 259–306; Raymond B. Fosdick, "The Program of the Commission on Training Camp Activities with Relation to the Problem of Venereal Disease," ibid. (Jan. 1918), 71–76. For a specific instance: James R. McGovern, " 'Sporting Life on the Line': Prostitution in Progressive Era Pensacola," *Florida Historical Quarterly*, 54 (Oct. 1975), 131–144.

15. Richard Hofstadter, *The Age of Reform: From Bryan to FDR* (New York, Alfred A. Knopf, 1955; reissued, New York, Vintage Books, 1960), p. 289; Egal Feldman, "Prostitution, the Alien Woman and the Progressive Imagination, 1910–1915," *American Quarterly*, 19 (Summer 1967), p. 197. For the revisionist view see, inter alia, James H. Timberlake, *Prohibition and the Progressive Movement, 1900–1920* (Cambridge, Mass., Harvard University Press, 1963) passim, esp. pp. 1–3, 33–36, 61–66, 100–106, 164–168; Clark, *The Dry Years*, pp. 122–127; Ostrander, *The Prohibition Movement in California*, pp. 114–116; Lubove, "The Progressive and the Prostitute" esp. pp. 310–311; and Hohner, "The Prohibitionists: Who Were They?" On the basis of his study of Virginia prohibitionism, Hohner confirms the link between it and the broader Progressive reform movement but notes (p. 503) that the Progressives' support for prohibition was more consistent than was the prohibitionists' support for other Progressive reforms.

16. Herbert Croly, *The Promise of American Life* (New York, Mac-

millan, 1910; reprinted Indianapolis, Bobbs Merrill, 1965), p. 150. Walter Lippmann, *Drift and Mastery* (New York, Mitchell Kennerley, 1914; reprinted Englewood Cliffs, N.J., Prentice-Hall, 1961), p. 118; Charles A. Beard, *American City Government: A Survey of Newer Tendencies* (New York, Century, 1912), p. 159.

17. Peter G. Filene, "An Obituary for 'The Progressive Movement,'" *American Quarterly,* 22 (Spring 1970), 20–34.

18. Stanley K. Schultz, "The Morality of Politics: The Muckrakers' Vision of Democracy," *Journal of American History,* 52 (Dec. 1965), p. 529; *Women in Industry: Decision of the United States Supreme Court in Curt Muller vs. State of Oregon . . . and Brief for the State of Oregon by Louis D. Brandeis assisted by Josephine Goldmark* (New York, National Consumers' League, n.d.; reissued, New York, Arno Press, 1969), p. 44; Charles J. Bonaparte in *Proceedings of the Chicago Conference for Good City Government and the Tenth Annual Meeting of the National Municipal League* (Philadelphia, National Municipal League, 1904), p. 384. For similar sentiments see ibid. (1905), p. 378 (Amos Parker Wilder); and (1907); pp. 95 (Clinton R. Woodruff) and 387 (Albert Bushnell Hart).

19. Frederic C. Howe, *The Confessions of a Reformer* (New York, Charles Scribner's Sons, 1925; reissued, Chicago, Quadrangle, 1967), pp. 16–17.

20. *The Gospel of the Kingdom,* 6 (July 1914), 97–98, quoted in Timberlake, *Prohibition and the Progressive Movement,* p. 27.

21. Walton Bean, *Boss Reuf's San Francisco* (Berkeley, University of California Press, 1967), pp. 40–54; Lincoln Steffens, *The Shame of the Cities* (New York, McClure, Phillips, 1904; reissued, New York, Sagamore Press, 1957), e.g. pp. 115–116, 154. Progressives campaigning for a new city charter in Los Angeles in 1908–09 similarly charged the mayor and police chief with links to the city's prostitution trade. Robert M. Fogelson, *The Fragmented Metropolis: Los Angeles, 1850–1930* (Cambridge, Mass., Harvard University Press, 1967), p. 213.

22. *The Social Evil in Chicago,* p. 43; Charles F. Aked, "Man and His Neighbor," *Appleton's Magazine,* 12 (July 1908), 9. See also, in the same vein, Walter Rauschenbusch, *Christianity and the Social Crisis* (New York, Macmillan, 1907; reissued, New York, Harper and Bros., 1964, ed. Robert D. Cross), pp. 240–247. George Kneeland's *Commercialized Prostitution in New York,* financed by Rockefeller money, stands almost alone in failing to discuss low wages and bad working conditions among the factors leading girls into prostitution.

23. Benjamin O. Flower, *Civilization's Inferno; or, Studies in the Social Cellar* (Boston, 1893), p. 152; Mary H. H. Hunt, *A History of the First Decade of the Department of Scientific Temperance Instruction in Schools and Colleges* (Boston, 1891); Raymond Calkins, *Substitutes for the Saloon* (Boston, Houghton Mifflin, 1901; reissued with a new pref. and app., 1919), p. 310; Robert H. Bremner, *From the Depths; The Discovery of Poverty in the United States* (New York, New York University Press, 1956), pp. 80–81 (quoted passage); Timberlake, *Prohibition and the Progressive Movement,* pp. 17, 40–51. The Committee of Fifty was headed by the future mayor of New York, Seth Low, then

president of Columbia University; it also included the presidents of Johns Hopkins and Harvard universities, as well as other academic notables. Examples of the individualistic approach in the Gilded Age social purity movement, supplanted by other strategies in the Progressive years, are the White Cross Army, an idea imported from England in 1886, which pledged young people to sexual abstinence before marriage; and Grace Hoadley Dodge's Working Girls' Society of New York, which sought to safeguard the virtue of working-class women. Pivar, *Purity Crusade*, pp. 108–109, 111–115, 177–178; and Abbie Graham, *Grace H. Dodge: Merchant of Dreams* (New York, The Woman's Press, 1926), pp. 66, 89, 103.

24. *The Social Evil in Chicago*, p. 263.

25. Ibid., pp. 30, 69, 163; Timberlake, *Prohibition and the Progressive Movement*, pp. 51–55; Frederick L. Schepman, "Stoddard, Cora Frances," *Notable American Women*, III, 380–381. The secretary of the Committee of Fifteen was Edwin R. A. Seligman, McVickar Professor of Political Economy at Columbia University.

26. "Recent Scientific Facts," *Anti-Saloon League Yearbook, 1917* (Westerville, Ohio, The American Issue Press, 1917), pp. 291–292; Frederick W. Betts, "History of the Morals Survey Committee of Syracuse," *Social Hygiene*, 1 (Mar. 1915), 192; David G. McComb, *Houston, The Bayou City* (Austin, University of Texas Press, 1969), p. 155; *The Social Evil in Chicago*, p. 79.

27. *ASL Yearbook* (1915), p. 31; Odegard, *Pressure Politics*, pp. 5–24, 274–275; Blocker, *Retreat from Reform*, pp. 220–221.

28. Peters, "Story of the Committee of Fourteen," p. 371; Theodore Schroeder, "Prostitution as a Social Problem," *Arena*, 41 (Feb. 1909), 198; *Who Was Who*, V, 402 (Kneeland entry).

29. Josiah Strong, *The Challenge of the City* (New York, Eaton and Mains, 1907), pp. 106, 107; *Social Hygiene*, 3 (July 1917), 404. .

30. Quoted in Paul S. Boyer, *Purity in Print: The Vice Society Movement and Book Censorship in America* (New York, Charles Scribner's Sons, 1968), pp. 13, 25.

31. Newton D. Hall, *Civic Righteousness and Civic Pride* (Boston, Sherman, French, 1914), pp. 84, 99.

32. Ibid., p. 97.

33. Addams, *A New Conscience and an Ancient Evil*, p. 182; Donald R. Hooker, "Social Hygiene—Another Great Social Movement," *Social Hygiene*, 2 (Jan. 1916), 9; Burnham, "The Progressive Era Revolution in American Attitudes toward Sex," p. 899 (Morrow quote).

34. *Report of the Vice Commission* (Louisville, Ky., Smith and Dugan, 1915), p. 74; *The Social Evil in Chicago*, pp. 25, 57.

35. Kneeland, *Commercialized Prostitution in New York*, p. 101.

36. Ibid., p. 28; Morals Survey Committee, *The Social Evil in Syracuse* (Syracuse, N.Y., 1913), p. 23; *The Social Evil in Chicago*, p. 129.

37. William T. Stead, *If Christ Came to Chicago* (Chicago, 1894; reissued, New York, Living Books, 1964), p. 248.

38. Kneeland, *Commercialized Prostitution in New York*, p. 92.

39. Ibid., p. 110.

40. *Report of the Hartford Vice Commission*, p. 56.

41. *The Social Evil in Chicago*, pp. 133, 93, 134; Kneeland, *Commercialized Prostitution in New York*, p. 104.

42. *Report of the Hartford Vice Commission*, p. 57; *The Social Evil in Chicago*, pp. 95, 133; *The Social Evil in Syracuse*, p. 69.

43. *Report of the Hartford Vice Commission*, pp. 62, 56, 63, 61.

14 ONE LAST, DECISIVE STRUGGLE

1. George Kibbe Turner, "Beer and the City Liquor Problem," *McClure's*, 33 (Sept. 1909), 529; "The City Liquor Problem in the United States," *Anti-Saloon League Yearbook, 1914* (Westerville, Ohio, The American Issue Press, 1914), p. 6; "Immigration and the Liquor Traffic," ibid. (1913), p. 9; Peter H. Odegard, *Pressure Politics; The Story of the Anti-Saloon League* (New York, Oxford University Press, 1928), pp. 30–31.

2. George Kibbe Turner, "The City of Chicago; A Study of the Great Immoralities," *McClure's*, 28 (Apr. 1907), 576.

3. *The Social Evil with Special Reference to Conditions Existing in the City of New York. A Report Prepared* [in 1902] *under the Direction of the Committee of Fifteen*, ed. Edwin R. A. Seligman, 2d ed., revised with new material (New York, G. P. Putnam's Sons, 1912), p. 8.

4. Ibid., p. 10.

5. *Report of the Vice Commission* (Louisville, Ky., Smith and Dugan, 1915), pp. 21, 57.

6. *Report of the Hartford Vice Commission* (Hartford, 1914), p. 33; George J. Kneeland, *Commercialized Prostitution in New York* (New York, The Century Co., 1913), pp. 70, 73.

7. The Vice Commission of Chicago, *The Social Evil in Chicago* (Chicago, Gunthorp-Warren Printing Co., 1911), pp. 31, 35, 41, 159, 199, 224, 230, 247, 249, 297.

8. Ibid., pp. 213, 215, 247, 252.

9. *Report of the* [Louisville] *Vice Commission*, p. 58; *The Social Evil in Chicago*, p. 250.

10. Morals Survey Committee, *The Social Evil in Syracuse* (Syracuse, N.Y., 1913), pp. 44–45.

11. Purley A. Baker, "The Next and Final Step," *ASL Yearbook* (1914), p. 16; Frederick W. Betts, "History of the Morals Survey Committee of Syracuse," *Social Hygiene*, 1 (Mar. 1915), 184.

12. Josiah Strong, *The Challenge of the City* (New York, Eaton and Mains, 1911), p. 64; Clifford G. Roe, *The Girl Who Disappeared* (Chicago, American Bureau of Moral Education, 1914), p. 200.

13. Kneeland, *Commercialized Prostitution in New York*, p. 84; Jane Addams, *A New Conscience and an Ancient Evil* (New York, Macmillan, 1912), p. 25. See also *The Social Evil in Chicago*, p. 88, and Robert E. Riegel, "Changing American Attitudes toward Prostitution (1800–1920)," *Journal of the History of Ideas*, 29 (July/Sept., 1968), 450.

14. Turner, "Beer and the City Liquor Problem," p. 537; idem, "The Daughters of the Poor," *McClure's*, 34 (Nov. 1909), 45–52; Egal Feldman, "Prostitution, the Alien Woman and the Progressive Imagination, 1910–1915," *American Quarterly*, 19 (Summer 1967), 193–196; Kneeland, *Commercialized Prostitution in New York*, p. 81; Clifford

G. Roe, *The Prodigal Daughter; The White Slave Evil and the Remedy* (Chicago, L. W. Walter, 1911), pp. 185, 189.

15. Robert A. Woods, "Prohibition and its Social Consequences," *National Conference of Social Work, Proceedings, 1919* (Chicago, 1920), p. 763; "Liquor and Vice," *ASL Yearbook* (1912), pp. 121–123. Kneeland, *Commercialized Prostitution in New York*, p. x. See also Feldman, "Prostitution, the Alien Woman and the Progressive Imagination," p. 194, quoting a 1907 antiprostitution reformer: "What forces are there, hidden in American cities, which are dragging them . . . into a state of semibarbarism?"; and Jack S. Blocker, Jr., *Retreat from Reform: The Prohibition Movement in the United States, 1890–1913* (Westport, Conn., Greenwood Press, 1976), p. 219.

16. Stanley Baron, *Brewed in America: A History of Beer and Ale in the United States* (Boston, Little, Brown, 1962), pp. 257–273; Norman Clark, "The 'Hell-Soaked Institution' and the Washington Prohibition Initiative of 1917," *Pacific Northwest Quarterly*, 56 (Jan. 1965), 2 (impact of railroads and refrigeration in liquor and beer marketing); Turner, "Beer and the City Liquor Problem," pp. 528–538, 541; idem, "Chicago, A Study of the Great Immoralities," pp. 577–579; Arthur H. Gleason, "The New York Saloon," *Collier's*, 40 (Apr. 25, 1908), 16–17; *The Social Evil in Chicago*, p. 108; George Kneeland, "Commercialized Prostitution and the Liquor Traffic," *Social Hygiene*, 2 (Jan. 1916), 69–80.

17. John P. Peters, D.D., "The Story of the Committee of Fourteen of New York," ibid., 4 (July 1918), 348–353, 376n; Theodore Roosevelt, *An Autobiography* (New York, Macmillan, 1913), p. 197; Kneeland, *Commercialized Prostitution in New York*, p. 35.

18. Robert H. Wiebe, *The Search for Order, 1877–1920* (New York, Hill and Wang, 1967), pp. 96, 97.

19. *Social Hygiene*, 2 (July 1916), 467.

20. Committee of Fifteen, *The Social Evil in the City of New York*, p. 153.

21. Harrol B. Ayers, "Democracy at Work—San Antonio Being Reborn," *Social Hygiene*, 4 (Apr. 1918), 211–217, quoted passages pp. 213, 215, 216, 217; Committee of Fifteen, *The Social Evil in the City of New York*, p. 239 (quoting Minneapolis Vice Commission, in material added in the 1912 revision of this work); Roosevelt, *Autobiography*, p. 202.

22. Clark, "The 'Hell-Soaked Institution,' " p. 8. This minister, the Reverend Mark Matthews, was a Protestant leader of national standing, having served as moderator of the Presbyterian General Assembly in 1912. Norman H. Clark, *Deliver Us from Evil: An Interpretation of American Prohibition* (New York, W. W. Norton, 1976), p. 4.

23. Quoted in Odegard, *Pressure Politics*, p. 150.

24. Richard Hofstadter, *The Age of Reform: From Bryan to FDR* (New York, Alfred A. Knopf, 1960; reissued, New York, Vintage Books, 1960), p. 288; Samuel P. Hays, *The Response to Industrialism, 1885–1914* (Chicago, University of Chicago Press, 1957), p. 115. Another work treating prohibition as a product of rural hostility to the city is Andrew Sinclair, *Era of Excess: A Social History of the Prohibition*

Movement (Boston, Little, Brown, 1962; reissued, New York, Harper and Row, 1964). In fairness to Mencken, one should note that, although he delighted in lambasting rural America for its alleged fanatical puritanism, he frequently directed his criticisms to a *state of mind* which could crop up in cities as well as in the country. In 1913, for example, he published in his magazine *Smart Set* an article on Los Angeles which describes that city's political leaders as people who brought with them to the city "a complete stock of rural beliefs, pieties, superstitions and habits" and who therefore governed it "as they would a village"; Willard Huntington Wright, "Los Angeles: The Chemically Pure," quoted in Robert M. Fogelson, *The Fragmented Metropolis, Los Angeles 1850–1930* (Cambridge, Mass., Harvard University Press, 1967), p. 190.

25. Charles A. Beard, *American City Government; A Survey of Newer Tendencies* (New York, Century, 1912), p. 159; Turner, "Beer and the City Liquor Problem," p. 540; Anti-Saloon League *Proceedings* (1915), p. 231; *American Issue*, June 26, 1903; Feldman, "Prostitution, the Alien Woman, and the Progressive Imagination," p. 194.

26. Blocker, *Retreat from Reform*, pp. 11, 156.

27. Franklin Hichborn, "The Organization That Backed the California Red Light Abatement Bill," *Social Hygiene*, 1 (March 1915), 199–200.

28. Robert A. Hohner, "The Prohibitionists: Who Were They?" *South Atlantic Quarterly*, 68 (Autumn 1969), 495–497; Clark, *Deliver Us from Evil*, pp. 101, 102, 109; James A. Burran, "Prohibition in New Mexico, 1917," *New Mexico Historical Review*, 48 (Apr. 1973), 145; James E. Hansen II, "Moonshine and Murder: Prohibition in Denver," *Colorado Magazine*, 50 (Winter 1973), 2; Blocker, *Retreat from Reform*, p. 240 (analysis of state referenda); ASL *Yearbook* (1911), p. 52; James H. Timberlake, *Prohibition and the Progressive Movement, 1900–1920* (Cambridge, Mass., Harvard University Press, 1966), p. 169 (on Boston); *Worcester Union Gazette*, Dec. 9, 1908), p. 3.

29. Ibid. (ward-by-ward break-down of prohibition vote); *The Worcester of Eighteen Hundred and Ninety-Eight*, ed. Franklin P. Rice (Worcester, 1899), p. 359 (ward-by-ward population and property-valuation data); William D. Miller, *Memphis during the Progressive Era, 1900–1917* (Memphis, Memphis State University Press, 1957), p. 123; Hohner, "The Prohibitionists: Who Were They?" p. 497; Norman H. Clark, *The Dry Years; Prohibition and Social Change in Washington* (Seattle, University of Washington Press, 1965), pp. 118–122; Virginius Dabney, *Richmond: The Story of a City* (Garden City, N.Y., Doubleday, 1976), pp. 281–282; Timberlake, *Prohibition and the Progressive Movement*, p. 169. Another of Hohner's findings further confirming the interpretation offered here is that, of 314 urban WCTU leaders in Virginia in the 1887–1917 period, 55 percent were the wives of men of the lower middle class: bookkeepers, clerks, grocers, etc., "The Prohibitionists: Who Were They?" pp. 499–500.

30. See Gregory H. Singleton, "Fundamentalism and Urbanization: A Quantitative Critique of Impressionistic Interpretations," in *The New Urban History: Quantitative Explorations by American Histo-*

rians, ed. Leo F. Schnore (Princeton, Princeton University Press, 1975), pp. 205–227. See also the perceptive comments on the urban strength of the Nebraska prohibition reform in Robert E. Wenger, "The Anti-Saloon League in Nebraska Politics, 1898–1910," *Nebraska History*, 52 (Fall 1971), 273. While the precise locus of urban support for the anti-prostitution cause is more difficult to pin down, in the absence of local referenda or similar data, one may speculate from the themes that are emphasized in the vice reports and the white-slave exposés that they found their natural audience among the same people who were providing the urban votes for prohibition.

31. Roe, *The Prodigal Daughter*, p. 203; Timberlake, *Prohibition and the Progressive Movement*, pp. 77, 79; Odegard, *Pressure Politics*, p. 187; Harry Emerson Fosdick, *The Prohibition Question* (New York, Park Avenue Baptist Church, 1928), p. 9.

32. For some high-level business pronouncements in favor of prohibition see Timberlake, *Prohibition and the Progressive Movement*, pp. 73–75, 79–80, and Robert H. Wiebe, *Businessmen and Reform: A Study of the Progressive Movement* (Cambridge, Mass., Harvard University Press, 1962; reissued, Chicago, Quadrangle, 1968), p. 200. But, for a useful corrective to such rhetoric, note that in a 1914 prohibition referendum campaign in Seattle, the local chamber of commerce voted 625–45 against endorsing the reform, Clark, " 'The Hell-Soaked Institution,' " pp. 8–9.

33. "Real War," *ASL Yearbook* (1912), [p. 4]; Bascom Johnson, "Moral Conditions in San Francisco and at the Panama-Pacific Exposition," *Social Hygiene*, 1 (Sept. 1915), 609.

34. *Report of the [Illinois] Senate Vice Committee* (Chicago, 1916), pp. 28 (quoted passage), 177–260 (testimony of merchants); Paul H. Hass, "Sin in Wisconsin: The Teasdale Vice Committee of 1913," *Wisconsin Magazine of History*, 49 (Winter, 1965–66), 149 (Berger quote). See also Margaret Dreier Robins, "The Menace of Low Wages," *Social Hygiene*, 1 (June 1915), 358–363.

35. *The Social Evil in Chicago*, p. 31; Paul A. Carter, "Prohibition and Democracy: The Noble Experiment Reassessed," *Wisconsin Magazine of History*, 56 (Spring 1973), p. 190 (quoting *Ladies' Home Journal*); *Report of the Hartford Vice Commission*, p. 85. See also Blocker, *Retreat from Reform*, pp. 14, 241.

36. Kneeland, *Commercialized Prostitution in New York*, pp. 110, 108.

37. Joseph R. Gusfield, *Symbolic Crusade: Status Politics and the American Temperance Movement* (Urbana, University of Illinois Press, 1966), pp. 69–87 (quoted phrases, p. 87). For discussions of Gusfield's status interpretation of the temperance movement, see Blocker, *Retreat from Reform*, p. 168, and Ross Evans Paulson, *Women's Suffrage and Prohibition: A Comparative Study of Equality and Social Control* (Glenview, Ill., Scott, Foresman, 1973), p. 55.

38. Robert T. Handy, "The Protestant Quest for a Christian America, 1830–1930," *Church History*, 22 (Mar. 1953), 13.

39. *Report of the Hartford Vice Commission*, p. 85; Mayer, "The Passing of the Red Light District," p. 201 (general summary of the rec-

ommendations of the various vice commissions); *Report of the* [Ill.] *Senate Vice Committee*, p. 55 (newspaper censorship); Maude E. Miner, "Report of Committee on Social Hygiene" (of the National Conference on Charities and Correction), *Social Hygiene*, 1 (Dec. 1914), 85 ("sensuous plays"). The Bridgeport, Connecticut, vice commission urged the closing of all "private booths and side rooms" in restaurants—"Notes and Comments," ibid., 3 (Jan. 1917), 132.

40. *The Social Evil in Chicago*, pp. 51, 60, 61, 65, 252.

41. David G. McComb, *Houston, The Bayou City* (Austin, University of Texas Press, 1969), pp. 155–156 (quoted passage); Dabney, *Richmond*, p. 275.

42. Gusfield, *Symbolic Crusade*, p. 9.

43. Commission on Law Enforcement and Observance, *Enforcement of the Prohibition Laws of the United States* (United States Congress, House Doc. 722, Seventy-first Cong., 3d sess., 1931), summary, pp. 79–80, quoted in Sinclair, *Era of Excess*, pp. 367–368. This Commission, chaired by former Attorney General George W. Wickersham, was appointed by President Hoover in 1929.

44. Willoughby C. Waterman, *Prostitution and Its Repression in New York City, 1900–1931* (New York, Columbia University Press, 1932), pp. 99, 150; Blaine A. Brownell, "The Urban South Comes of Age, 1900–1940," in *The City in Southern History: The Growth of Urban Civilization in the South*, ed. Blaine A. Brownell and David R. Goldfield (Port Washington, N.Y., Kennikat Press, 1977), p. 149. For a more optimistic assessment, see Joseph Mayer, "The Passing of the Red Light District—Vice Investigations and Results," *Social Hygiene*, 4 (Apr. 1918), 197–209.

45. Kenneth T. Jackson, *The Ku Klux Klan in the City: 1915–1930* (New York, Oxford University Press, 1967), pp. 18–19, 32; Brownell, "The Urban South Comes of Age," p. 148 (quoted passage); Paul S. Boyer, *Purity in Print: The Vice Society Movement and Book Censorship in America* (New York, Charles Scribner's Sons, 1968), chaps. VI and VII, esp. pp. 126–127, 129–130, 137–138, 143, 197–198, and 206.

46. *Report of the* [Louisville] *Vice Commission*, pp. 28, 31, 75; *The Social Evil in Chicago*, p. 143.

47. Martha P. Falconer, "Report of the Committee on Social Hygiene" (of the National Conference of Charities and Correction), *Social Hygiene*, 1 (Sept. 1915), 524; Addams, *A New Conscience and an Ancient Evil*, pp. 104, 199.

15 POSITIVE ENVIRONMENTALISM

1. Newton D. Baker, "Expression versus Suppression," *Social Hygiene*, 4 (July 1918), 309–316.

2. Delos F. Wilcox, *The American City: A Problem of Democracy* (New York, Macmillan, 1904), pp. 91, 156, 157, 158.

3. Raymond Calkins, *Substitutes for the Saloon* (Boston, Houghton Mifflin, 1901; reissued 1919, with new apps.), pp. 149, xiii. See also E. C. Moore, "The Social Value of the Saloon," *American Journal of Sociology*, 3 (July 1897), 1–12, which anticipates many of Calkins' themes.

4. Clark W. Hetherington, "Play Leadership in Sex Education," *Social Hygiene*, 1 (Dec. 1914), 42; *Report of the Vice Commission, Louisville, Ky.* (Louisville, Smith and Dugan, 1915), p. 74; *Report of the Hartford Vice Commission* (Hartford, n.p., 1914), pp. 72, 73, 82 (quoted passage); Joseph Mayer, "The Passing of the Red Light District—Vice Investigations and Results," *Social Hygiene*, 4 (Apr. 1918), p. 206. See also C. Walker Hayes, "Public Morals and Recreation," ibid., 3 (July 1917), 331–339, esp. pp. 332, 338–339.

5. Josiah Strong, *The Challenge of the City* (New York, Eaton and Mains, 1907), pp. 49, 55, 141, 208 (quoted passage); idem, *The Twentieth Century City* (New York, Baker and Taylor, 1898), pp. 76, 118, 122 (quoted passage), 123–125, 173 (quoted passage); Walter Rauschenbusch, *Christianity and the Social Crisis* (New York, Macmillan, 1907; reissued, New York, Harper and Bros., 1964, ed. Robert D. Cross), pp. 373, 374, 376–377.

6. Jane Addams, "Public Recreation and Social Morality," *Charities and the Commons*, 18 (Aug. 3, 1907), pp. 492, 494; idem, *The Spirit of Youth and the City Streets* (New York, Macmillan, 1909; reissued, Urbana, University of Illinois Press, 1972, introduction by Allen F. Davis), pp. 15, 20, 98; see also, for expressions of dismay over the urban moral climate, pp. 4, 7, 12, 15, 20, 27, 79.

7. Jane Addams, *A New Conscience and an Ancient Evil* (New York, Macmillan, 1912), pp. 206–207.

8. Ibid.

9. Mary K. Simkhovitch, *The City Worker's World in America* (New York, Macmillan, 1917), pp. 109, 114; Graham Taylor, *Pioneering on Social Frontiers* (Chicago, University of Chicago Press, 1930), p. 366.

10. Edward T. Devine, *Misery and Its Causes* (New York, Macmillan, 1909), pp. 7, 11, 163, 267; *Who Was Who in America* (Chicago, A. N. Marquis, 1950), II, 154 (E. T. Devine). See also Max Siporin, introduction to Mary E. Richmond, *Friendly Visiting among the Poor* (New York, 1899; reissued, Montclair, N.J., Patterson Smith, 1969), pp. x–xii.

11. *The Child in the City. A Series of Papers Presented at the Conferences Held during the Chicago Child Welfare Exhibit* (Chicago, Department of Social Investigation, Chicago School of Civics and Philanthropy, 1912), p. 9 (Julian W. Mack comment); Mrs. Imogen B. Oakley, "The More Civic Work, the Less Need of Philanthropy," *American City*, 6 (June 1912), 805.

12. Newton D. Baker, "Law, Police, and Social Problems," *Atlantic Monthly*, 116 (July 1915), 13, 14, 16, 20.

13. Luther Lee Bernard, "The Transition to an Objective Standard of Social Control," *American Journal of Sociology*, 16 (Jan. 1911), 171.

14. Ellen H. Richards, *Euthenics: The Science of Controllable Environment* (Boston, Whitcomb and Barrows, 1910), pp. 20–21.

15. John Dewey, "Intelligence and Morals" (1908), in John Dewey, *The Influence of Darwin on Philosophy* (New York, Henry Holt, 1910; reissued, Bloomington, Indiana University Press, 1965), quoted passage p. 74. See also John B. Watson, "Psychology as the Behaviorist

Views It," *Psychological Review*, 20 (March 1913), 158–177; idem, *Psychology from the Standpoint of a Behaviorist* (Philadelphia, Lippincott, 1924), pp. xi–xii; David Bakan, "Behaviorism and American Urbanization," *Journal of the History of the Behaviorial Sciences*, 2 (Jan. 1966), 5–28; John Chynoweth Burnham, "The New Psychology: From Narcissism to Social Control," in *Change and Continuity in Twentieth Century America: The 1920s*, ed. John Braeman, Robert H. Bremner, and David Brody (Columbus, Ohio State University Press, 1968), pp. 351–398; Samuel Haber, *Efficiency and Uplift: Scientific Management in the Progressive Era, 1890–1920* (Chicago, University of Chicago Press, 1964), on F. W. Taylor and his influence; and Herbert Croly, *The Promise of American Life* (New York, Macmillan, 1909; reissued, Indianapolis, Bobbs-Merrill, 1965), pp. 139, 409, 443, 454.

16. Edward Alsworth Ross, *Social Control: A Survey of the Foundations of Order* (New York, Macmillan, 1901; reissued, Cleveland, Case Western Reserve Press, 1969), pp. vii–lv (introduction by Julius Weinberg, Gisela J. Hinkle, and Roscoe C. Hinkle).

17. Ibid., pp. 1–6, 432–435. For a critique of Tönnies and Ross, see Richard T. LaPiere, *A Theory of Social Control* (New York, McGraw-Hill, 1954), pp. 9–16.

18. Ross, *Social Control*, p. 177.

19. Ibid., p. 199.

20. Ibid., pp. 263–264.

21. Ibid., pp. 414–416.

22. Ibid., pp. 245, 302.

23. Ibid., pp. 207, 415 (quoted passage).

24. Ibid., pp. 212, 363, 371.

25. Ibid., p. 337.

26. Ibid., pp. 197, 337.

27. "Cooley, Charles Horton," *International Encyclopedia of the Social Sciences*, ed. David L. Sills (New York, Macmillan and the Free Press, 1968), vol. III, pp. 378–383.

28. Charles H. Cooley, *Human Nature and the Social Order* (New York, Scribner's, 1902), pp. 1–2; *George Herbert Mead: Essays on His Social Philosophy*, ed. with an introduction by John W. Petras (New York, Teachers College Press, 1968).

29. Cooley, *Human Nature and the Social Order*, pp. 136, 360, 376.

30. Ibid., pp. 113, 227, 390.

31. Ibid., pp. 107, 336, 349, 363, 371, 390.

32. Daniel M. Fox, *The Discovery of Abundance: Simon N. Patten and the Transformation of Social Theory* (Ithaca, Cornell University Press, 1967), pp. 13–25, 41, 126.

33. Simon N. Patten, *The New Basis of Civilization* (New York, Macmillan, 1907), p. 123.

34. Ibid., pp. 136–37; idem, "The Social Basis of Prohibition," *Charities and the Commons*, 20 (Sept. 19, 1908), 708.

35. Patten, *New Basis of Civilization*, pp. 141, 143, 180–181.

36. Ibid., p. 181.

37. Ibid., pp. 129, 190; Patten, "Social Basis of Prohibition," p. 708.

38. Patten, *New Basis of Civilization*, pp. 125, 126.

39. Ibid., pp. 125, 126, 213 (quoted phrases).

40. "Bernard, Luther Lee," *Who Was Who in America*, vol. 3 (Chicago, A. N. Marquis, 1960), p. 71. For a brief but perceptive discussion of Bernard's 1911 work see Henry F. May, *The End of American Innocence: A Study of the First Years of Our Own Time, 1912–1917* (New York, Alfred A. Knopf, 1959; reissued, New York, Quadrangle, 1964), pp. 157–158.

41. Luther Lee Bernard, "The Transition to an Objective Standard of Social Control," *American Journal of Sociology*, 16 (1911), 171–212, 309–341, 518–537, quoted passages, pp. 536–537.

42. Ibid., pp. 523, 533, 534.

43. Ibid., pp. 210, 532–533.

44. Ibid., pp. 209, 330, 334, 533, 535.

45. Ibid., p. 527, 531.

46. For an interesting discussion of this dimension of Progressive reform thought, which came to my notice after the completion of this chapter, see Don S. Kirschner, "The Ambiguous Legacy: Social Justice and Social Control in the Progressive Era," *Historical Reflections*, 2 (Summer 1975), 69–88. Kirschner suggests, correctly in my view, that urban moral decay and incipient disorder were central concerns of the Progressives, but that their most creative responses to these menaces were the indirect strategies that I have called "positive environmentalism." He discusses at length one particular manifestation of this approach: the neighborhood center.

47. J. David Hoeveler, Jr., *The New Humanism: A Critique of Modern America, 1900–1940* (Charlottesville, University Press of Virginia, 1977), pp. 129–130.

16 HOUSING, PARKS, AND PLAYGROUNDS

1. Jacob A. Riis, *How the Other Half Lives* (New York, 1890; reissued, New York, Hill and Wang, 1957), p. 41.

2. James B. Lane, *Jacob A. Riis and the American City* (Port Washington, N.Y., Kennikat Press, 1974), pp. 114–115.

3. Robert H. Bremner, *From the Depths: The Discovery of Poverty in the United States* (New York, New York University Press, 1956), p. 208; Allen F. Davis, *Spearheads for Reform: The Social Settlements and the Progressive Movement, 1890–1914* (New York, Oxford University Press, 1967), p. 68; Joseph Lee, *Constructive and Preventive Philanthropy* (New York, Macmillan, 1902), p. 63; Gilbert Osofsky, *Harlem: The Making of a Ghetto* (New York, Harper Torchbooks, 1968), p. 61; John Griscom, M.D., *The Sanitary Condition of the Laboring Population of New York* (New York, 1845).

4. Roy Lubove, *The Progressives and the Slums: Tenement House Reform in New York City, 1890–1917* (Pittsburgh, University of Pittsburgh Press, 1962), p. 144.

5. Ibid., pp. 131, 174, 252. Although I generally agree with Lubove's interpretation of tenement reform, I question his contention (pp. 66–67, 174–175, inter alia) that the environmental determinism underlying it was a "crude" formulation which the housing reformers "accepted with no reflection." As we have seen, the rationale for an environmen-

tal approach to urban social control was being elaborated with considerable subtlety and sophistication in the early twentieth century, and its acceptance by urban reformers was not casual but rooted in the dynamic of decades of moral-control effort.

6. *The Tenement House Problem, including the Report of the New York State Tenement House Commission of 1900*, ed. Robert W. DeForest and Lawrence Veiller, 2 vols. (New York, Macmillan, 1903), vol. I, p. 3; vol. II, pp. 17, 27; Lubove, *The Progressives and the Slums*, p. 95.

7. Quoted in Frederic C. Howe, *The City; The Hope of Democracy* (New York, Charles Scribner's Sons, 1906; reissued, Seattle, University of Washington Press, 1967), p. 199.

8. Jacob A. Riis, *The Peril and the Preservation of the Home* (Philadelphia, G. W. Jacobs, 1903), p. 34; Raymond Calkins, *Substitutes for the Saloon* (Boston, Houghton Mifflin, 1901; reissued with a new pref. and app., 1919), p. 276; *American City*, 1 (Sept. 1909), unnumbered page setting forth the magazine's purposes; Newton M. Hall, *Civic Righteousness and Civic Pride* (Boston, Sherman, French and Co., 1914), p. 8; Howe, *The City*, pp. 196–201. See also, for similar sentiments, Walter Rauschenbusch, *Christianity and the Social Crisis* (New York, Macmillan, 1907; reissued, New York, Harper and Bros., 1964, ed. Robert D. Cross), p. 227, and Josiah Strong, *The Challenge of the City* (New York, Eaton and Mains, 1907), p. 102.

9. *The Social Evil, with Special Reference to Conditions Existing in the City of New York. A Report Prepared* [in 1902] *under the Direction of the Committee of Fifteen*, ed. Edwin R. A. Seligman, 2nd ed., revised with new material (New York, G. P. Putnam's Sons, 1912), pp. 148–149; Jane Addams, *A New Conscience and an Ancient Evil* (New York, Macmillan, 1912), p. 122. See also Vice Commission of Chicago, *The Social Evil in Chicago* (Chicago, Gunthorp-Warren Printing Co., 1911), p. 245.

10. See, e.g., Lubove, *The Progressives and the Slums*, p. 132 (quoting Lawrence Veiller); Henry C. Wright, *The American City: An Outline of its Development and Functions* (Chicago, A. C. McClurg, 1916), pp. 169–170; and Joel A. Tarr, "From City to Suburb: The 'Moral' Influence of Transportation Technology," in *American Urban History: An Interpretive Reader with Commentaries*, ed. Alexander B. Callow, Jr., 2nd ed. (New York, Oxford University Press, 1973), pp. 202–212.

11. Barbara Rotundo, "Mount Auburn Cemetery: A Proper Boston Institution," *Harvard Library Bulletin*, 22 (July 1974), 268–279; Andrew Jackson Downing, "A Talk about Public Parks and Gardens," *Horticulturalist*, 3 (Oct. 1848), 153–158, and "Public Cemeteries and Public Gardens," ibid., 4 (July 1849), 1–12; Thomas Bender, "The 'Rural' Cemetery Movement: Urban Travail and the Appeal of Nature," *New England Quarterly*, 47 (June 1974), 196–211; George F. Chadwick, *The Park and the Town: Public Landscape in the Nineteenth and Twentieth Centuries* (London, Architectural Press, 1966), pp. 163–183 (Downing).

12. Julius G. Fabos, Gordon T. Milde, and V. Michael Weinmayr, *Frederick Law Olmsted, Sr., Founder of Landscape Architecture in*

America (Amherst, University of Massachusetts Press, 1968), pp. 12, 18; Chadwick, *The Park and the Town*, pp. 183–191.

13. William H. Wilson, *The City Beautiful Movement in Kansas City* (Columbia, University of Missouri Press, 1964), pp. 13, 38, 40–52, 120–125; Mel Scott, *American City Planning since 1890* (Berkeley, University of California Press, 1969), p. 15.

14. Thomas S. Hines, *Burnham of Chicago, Architect and Planner* (New York, Oxford University Press, 1974), p. 319; Scott, *American City Planning*, pp. 18–22; Andrew W. Crawford, "The Development of Park Systems in American Cities," *Annals of the American Academy of Political and Social Science*, 25 (1905), 218–232, esp. pp. 223–226.

15. Henry Ward Beecher, *Eyes and Ears* (Boston, 1869), p. 284; Clarence C. Cook, *A Description of the New York Central Park* (New York, 1869), p. 18 (quoting the mayor's 1851 message). One need hardly even call attention to the irony that these great city parks, whose moral potential once aroused such high hopes, are today among the more dangerous and crime-ridden regions of some cities.

16. Frederick Law Olmsted, "Public Parks and the Enlargement of Towns" (1870) in *Civilizing America's Cities: A Selection of Frederick Law Olmsted's Writings on City Landscapes*, ed. S. B. Sutton (Cambridge, Mass., MIT Press, 1971), p. 54; Olmsted, "Observations on the Progress of Improvements in Street Plans, with Special Reference to the Parkway Proposed to be Laid Out in Brooklyn" (1868), ibid., p. 36.

17. Ibid., p. 56.

18. Ibid., pp. 65, 73, 78.

19. Albert Fein, *Frederick Law Olmsted and the American Environmental Tradition* (New York, Braziller, 1972), p. 24; idem, "The American City: The Ideal and the Real," in *The Rise of An American Architecture*, ed. Edgar Kaufmann, Jr. (New York, Praeger, 1970), pp. 51, 67; Geoffrey Blodgett, "Frederick Law Olmsted: Landscape Architecture as Conservative Reform," *Journal of American History*, 62 (Mar. 1976), 869–889; Olmsted, "Observations on the Progress of Improvement of Street Plans," in Sutton, ed., *Civilizing America's Cities*, p. 36. On Olmsted's ties with liberal Protestant thought, especially that of Horace Bushnell and Henry W. Bellows, see Laura Wood Roper, *FLO; A Biography of Frederick Law Olmsted* (Baltimore, Johns Hopkins University Press, 1973), pp. 247, 249, 151–152.

20. Fein, *Frederick Law Olmsted and the American Environmental Tradition*, p. 16.

21. Olmsted, "Public Parks and the Enlargement of Towns," pp. 80, 81.

22. Ibid., pp. 75, 76, 96. A very high-strung man, Olmsted worked best in the silence of the dead of night. In describing urban life as a "prolific source of morbid conditions of the body and mind, manifesting themselves in nervous feebleness . . . and various functional derangements" (Fabos, Milde, and Weinmayr, *Frederick Law Olmsted, Sr.*, p. 47), he was surely in part projecting his own fragile nervous system upon the urban population as a whole. At some level, it would seem, the tranquil urban park was not only an instrument of moral

control, but almost literally a guarantor of sanity in the city. Ironically, Olmsted spent his final years at McLean Hospital, a mental institution near Boston, which he himself had landscaped years before (Roper, *FLO*, p. 474).

23. Cook, *Description of Central Park*, p. 107.

24. C. Walker Hayes, "Public Morals and Recreation," *Social Hygiene*, 3 (July 1917), 334. Rauschenbusch, *Christianity and the Social Crisis*, p. 377; [George Kessler], *Report of the Board of Park and Boulevard Commissioners of Kansas City, Missouri* (Kansas City, Hudson-Kimberly, 1893), excerpted in *The American City; A Documentary History*, ed. Charles N. Glaab (Homewood, Ill., Dorsey Press, 1963), p. 260; [Charles Eliot], *Report of the Board of Metropolitan Park Commissioners* (Boston, Wright and Potter, 1893), excerpted in *The Urban Community; Housing and Planning in the Progressive Era*, ed. Roy Lubove (Englewood Cliffs, N.J., Prentice-Hall, 1967), p. 52.

25. G. Washington Eggleston, "A Plea for More Parks, and the Preservation of the Sublimities of Nature" (n.p., n.d. [but early twentieth century from internal evidence]), p. 10; Glaab, ed., *The American City*, p. 260 (Kessler); Lubove, ed., *The Urban Community*, p. 52 (Eliot). See also Wright, *The American City*, p. 167, for similar sentiments. On the survival of arcadian ideas in this period see Peter J. Schmitt, *Back to Nature: The Arcadian Myth in Urban America* (New York, Oxford University Press, 1969).

26. Schmitt, *Back to Nature*, p. 74 (quoting Joseph Lee). Here my conclusions somewhat parallel those sketched out by Thomas Bender in the final pages of his insightful study *Toward an Urban Vision: Ideas and Institutions in Nineteenth Century America* (Lexington, University of Kentucky Press, 1975). However, I would question his interpretation of Olmsted's thought as part of a "lost heritage" of nineteenth-century urban social thought that was "obliterated during the Progressive Era" and then "rediscovered" by Lewis Mumford around 1930 (p. 185). This interpretation blurs the continuity between Olmsted's ideas on the social role of the park and those of the Progressive park planners. Certainly, there were important differences between the two. As Bender notes, and as the work of the Progressive-era park and playground spokesmen amply bears out, Olmsted believed in the power of "nature" to mold social behavior and to promote the restoration of a sense of "organic community" in the city, whereas the Progressives placed their hope in bureaucratic strategies and more active forms of environmental manipulation. But this does not mean, as Bender suggests (pp. 192–193), that the Progressives believed in "social control" while Olmsted did not. As we have seen, the "natural" oases he sought to create in the cities were in fact the product of a sophisticated set of aesthetic and social ideas, and in translating those ideas into reality he ascribed a central role to a public-spirited professional elite. Indeed, Bender himself acknowledges (p. 179) that Olmsted "combined a sincere feeling for the less fortunate with a somewhat manipulative concern for raising them up to middle-class standards." Nor can I agree that the Progressives' more open concern with social control involved an abandonment of Olmsted's "social

vision and moral commitment" (p. 192). Though their fascination with "efficiency" and the "scientific" tone of their writings often blurred the fact, the Progressives yielded to no generation in the moral passion and visions of social harmony that underlay their urban reform efforts.

27. *Parks: A Manual of Municipal and County Parks*, ed. L. H. Weir (New York, A. S. Barnes, 1928), pp. 1, 2, 6, 7.

28. Ibid., pp. 4, 5, 6 (italics added), 7, 11.

29. George Burnap, *Parks: Their Design, Equipment, and Use* (Philadelphia, Lippincott, 1916), pp. 69, 82, 84, 88, 122.

30. Ibid., pp. 102, 104, 106, 110.

31. Everett B. Mero, ed., *American Playgrounds: Their Construction, Equipment, Maintenance and Utility* (Boston, American Gymnasia, 1908), p. 240; Ross E. Paulson, *Radicalism and Reform: The Vrooman Family and American Social Thought, 1837–1937* (Lexington, University of Kentucky Press, 1968), pp. 80–81; Lee, *Constructive and Preventive Philanthropy*, p. 120.

32. Ibid., p. 128; Charles Mulford Robinson, "Improvement in City Life," *Atlantic Monthly*, 83 (Apr. 1899), 533–534; James B. Crooks, *Politics and Progress: The Rise of Urban Progressivism in Baltimore, 1895 to 1911* (Baton Rouge, Louisiana State University Press, 1968), p. 179.

33. Lee, *Constructive and Preventive Philanthropy*, p. 123; Luther Halsey Gulick, "Play and Democracy," *Charities and the Commons*, 18 (Aug. 3, 1907), 481–486; Mero, *American Playgrounds*, p. 240; Henry S. Curtis, *The Play Movement and Its Significance* (New York, Macmillan, 1917), pp. 15–18; *Dictionary of American Biography* (Luther H. Gulick); ibid., supp. II (Joseph Lee). For an instance of the PAA field secretary's role in arousing playground interest at the municipal level see William D. Miller, *Memphis during the Progressive Era, 1900–1917* (Memphis, Memphis State University Press, 1957), p. 105.

34. Curtis, *Play Movement and Its Significance*, p. 12; Graham R. Taylor, "How They Played at Chicago," *Charities and the Commons*, 18 (Aug. 3, 1907), 473–474; Henry S. Curtis, "The Growth, Present Extent and Prospects of the Playground Movement in America," *American City*, 1 (Sept. 1909), 32.

35. Gulick, "Play and Democracy," p. 486; Roy Lubove, *Twentieth Century Pittsburgh; Government, Business, and Environmental Change* (New York, John Wiley and Sons, 1969), p. 51; Amalia Hofer Jerome, "The Playground as a Social Center," *American City*, 5 (Aug. 1911), 33.

36. Curtis, *Play Movement and Its Significance*, pp. 6, 8, 119. Curtis had worked as a summer playground director in New York City in 1898–1901, and in 1905 had been appointed superintendent of playgrounds in Washington D.C. *Who Was Who*, 3 (Chicago, Marquis, 1963), 203.

37. Harriett Lusk Childs, "The Fourth Annual Play Congress," *American City*, 3 (July 1910), 20; Curtis, *Play Movement and Its Significance*, pp. 8, 36; idem, "Athletics in the Playgrounds," *American City*, 3 (July 1910), 25.

38. William B. Forbush, *The Boy Problem*, 6th ed. (Albany, Sab-

bath Literature, 1901; rewritten, Boston, The Pilgrim Press, 1907), pp. 75, 76; Walter Vrooman, "Playgrounds for Children," *Arena*, 10 (July 1894), 287.

39. Kessler quoted in Nelson P. Lewis, *The Planning of the Modern City* (New York, John Wiley and Sons, 1916), p. 146; Lee, *Constructive and Preventive Philanthropy*, p. 166. See also, for criticism of the playground movement, Burnap, *Parks*, p. 150.

40. Howe, *The City*, p. 228; Riis, *Peril and Preservation of the Home*, p. 168; Lubove, *The Progressives and the Slums*, p. 72 (quoting Riis); Charles M. Robinson, *The Improvement of Towns and Cities* (New York, G. P. Putnam's Sons, 1901), p. 179; DeForest and Veiller, *The Tenement House Problem*, I, 47; Calkins, *Substitutes for the Saloon*, p. 192.

41. J. Horace Macfarland quoted in *City Planning; A Series of Papers Presenting the Essential Elements of a City Plan*, ed. John Nolen (New York, D. Appleton, 1916), pp. 139–140; Mero, *American Playgrounds*, p. 219; Jane Addams, "Public Recreation and Social Morality," *Charities and the Commons*, 18 (Aug. 3, 1907), 494; Elmer E. Brown (United States commissioner of education), "Health, Morality, and the Playground," ibid., 500–501; "Playgrounds," in *The New Encyclopedia of Social Reform*, ed. W. D. P. Bliss (New York, Funk and Wagnalls, 1908), pp. 898–899; Theodore Roosevelt, *An Autobiography* (New York, Macmillan, 1913), p. 174.

42. Lubove, *Progressives and the Slums*, p. 71.

43. J. Adams Puffer, *The Boy and His Gang* (Boston, Houghton Mifflin, 1912), quoted in Steven L. Schlossman, "G. Stanley Hall and the Boys' Club: Conservative Applications of Recapitulation Theory," *Journal of the History of the Behavioral Science*, 9 (Apr. 1973), 144; Dorothy Ross, *G. Stanley Hall, The Psychologist as Prophet* (Chicago, University of Chicago Press, 1972), pp. 279–308, esp. 299–301, 371; Dom Cavallo, "Social Reform and the Movement to Organize Children's Play During the Progressive Era," *History of Childhood Quarterly*, 3 (Spring 1976), 510 (on Curtis).

44. Calkins, *Substitutes for the Saloon*, p. 77; the Reverend John T. Stone and Allan Hoben quoted in *The Child in the City: A Series of Papers Presented at the Conferences Held during the Chicago Child Welfare Exhibit* (Chicago, Department of Social Investigation, Chicago School of Civics and Philanthropy, 1912), pp. 427, 433.

45. Joseph Lee, "Play and Playgrounds," National Recreation Association pamphlet (New York, 1908), p. 3; *DAB*, supp. II (Joseph Lee).

46. Lee, "Play as an Antidote to Civilization," National Recreation Association pamphlet no. 89 (New York, n.d.), pp. 6, 8, 11, 12; reprinted from the *Playground*, July 1911.

47. Ibid., p. 6.

48. Ibid., pp. 4, 14.

49. Lee, "Play and Playgrounds," p. 29.

50. Lee, "Play as a School of the Citizen," *Charities and the Commons*, 18 (Aug. 3, 1907), 489.

51. Lee, *Constructive and Preventive Philanthropy*, pp. 140, 141, 180; idem, *Play in Education* (New York, Macmillan, 1915), p. 335.

52. Ibid., pp. 382–383.

53. Lee, "Play and Playgrounds," pp. 22, 28; *Constructive and Preventive Philanthropy*, pp. 171, 172.

54. Clarence E. Rainwater, *The Play Movement in the United States* (Chicago, University of Chicago Press, 1922), p. 239.

55. Jerome, "The Playground as a Social Center," p. 35; Curtis, "Growth of the Playground Movement," pp. 28, 31; Allan Hoben quoted in *The Child and the City*, p. 434. See also Henry S. Curtis, "Athletics in the Playground," *American City*, 3 (July 1910), 21–25, a strong plea for a "trained body of play leaders" (p. 21).

56. Newton D. Baker, "Expression versus Suppression," *Social Hygiene*, 4 (July 1918), 312.

57. Quoted in Mero, "How Public Gymnasiums and Baths Help to Make Good Citizens," p. 71 (quoted passage); Rainwater, *The Play Movement in the United States*, pp. 232–233; Mero, *American Playgrounds*, pp. 112–116, 212–219. See also Gulick, "Play and Democracy," p. 482, and Herbert E. Weir, "The Playground Movement in America," *American City*, 6 (Mar. 1912), 579.

58. Quoted in Mero, "How Public Gymnasiums and Baths Help to Make Good Citizens," pp. 70–71.

59. Mero, *American Playgrounds*, p. 256.

60. Quoted in ibid., p. 100; Lawrence Veiller, "The Social Value of Playgrounds in Crowded Districts," *Charities and the Commons*, 18 (Aug. 3, 1907), 509; Curtis, "Growth of the Playground Movement," p. 28.

61. Delos F. Wilcox, *The American City: A Problem of Democracy* (New York, Macmillan, 1904), pp. 113, 121; Curtis, *Play Movement and Its Significance*, p. 109; Calkins, *Substitutes for the Saloon*, pp. 164–78, quoted passage p. 172. Although I have focused on the playground movement, it was only a part of a larger Progressive reform effort aimed at the social control of city children. Playground leaders welcomed the juvenile-court movement and such organizations as the Boys' Clubs of America (1906), Boy Scouts of America (1910), and Campfire Girls (1910) as valuable supplements to their own efforts. They also responded favorably to the suggestion of Boston settlement-house leader Robert A. Woods that, with proper guidance from social workers, the neighborhood could become the basis of a stable urban social order. The playground, they suggested, with its supervisory staff, was the ideal nucleus for the kind of neighborhood development Woods suggested. See Anthony M. Platt, *The Child Savers: The Invention of Delinquency* (Chicago, University of Chicago Press, 1969); Steven L. Schlossman, *Love and the American Delinquent: The Theory and Practice of "Progressive" Juvenile Justice, 1825–1920* (Chicago, University of Chicago Press, 1977), pp. 124–193 (an in-depth examination of the functioning of the juvenile-court system in the Progressive era); Amalia Hofer Jerome, "The Playground as a Social Center"; Robert A. Woods, "The Neighborhood in Social Reconstruction," *Proceedings of the American Sociological Society, Eighth Annual Meeting, Minneapolis Minn., Dec. 27, 29, 30, 1913* (Chicago, University of Chicago Press, 1913), pp. 14–28.

62. Rainwater, *The Play Movement in the United States*, pp. 90, 293, 323, 326.

17 THE CIVIC IDEAL AND THE URBAN MORAL ORDER

1. Waring quoted in Delos F. Wilcox, *The American City: A Problem of Democracy* (New York, Macmillan, 1904), p. 118; Henry Drummond, *The City without a Church* (New York, 1893), quoted in Gregory H. Singleton, "Protestant Voluntary Organizations and the Shaping of Victorian America," in *Victorian America*, ed. Daniel Walker Howe (Philadelphia, University of Pennsylvania Press, 1976), p. 56.
For some brief but suggestive reflections on the rise of a rhetoric of "urban community" in the 1890s, and its function in promoting social cohesion, see Michael Frisch, "Social Particularity and American Political Culture: The Two-Edged Sword of Community," in "The City and Sense of Community" (Ithaca, N.Y., Center for Urban Development Research, Cornell University [mimeographed occasional paper no. 6] April 1976), pp. 32–37, esp. pp. 34–35.

2. Henry B. F. Macfarland, "The Twentieth Century City," *American City*, 5 (Sept. 1911), 138; John Ihlder, "The New Civic Spirit," ibid. (Feb. 1911), 127; Jean B. Quandt, *From the Small Town to the Great Community: The Social Thought of Progressive Intellectuals* (New Brunswick, N.J., Rutgers University Press, 1970), p. 20.

3. Frederic C. Howe, *The City, The Hope of Democracy* (New York, Charles Scribner's Sons, 1906; reissued, Seattle, University of Washington Press, 1967), pp. 23, 282; Richard T. Ely, *The Coming City* (New York, T. Y. Crowell, 1902), p. 73. See also, for similar sentiments, the 1909 hymn of Walter Russell Bowie, "O Holy City, Seen of John," in the Presbyterian *Hymnbook* (Richmond, Va., 1955), p. 508.

4. Newton M. Hall, *Civic Righteousness and Civic Pride* (Boston, Sherman, French, 1914), pp. 4, 61, 185, 186.

5. Ibid., pp. 8, 10.

6. Delos F. Wilcox, *Great Cities in America* (New York, Macmillan, 1910), p. 8; Hall, *Civic Righteousness and Civic Pride*, pp. 112, 151; Macfarland, "The Twentieth Century City," p. 138. Wilcox was an official of the New York Public Service Commission.

7. Josiah Strong, *The Twentieth Century City* (New York, Baker and Taylor, 1898), pp. 124, 125; Woodrow Wilson, "The Need of Citizenship Organization," *American City*, 5 (Nov. 1911), 266.

8. Herbert Croly, *The Promise of American Life* (New York, Macmillan, 1909; reprinted, Indianapolis, Bobbs-Merrill, 1965), pp. 152, 153.

9. Simon N. Patten, *The New Basis of Civilization* (New York, Macmillan, 1907), p. 214; Macfarland, "The Twentieth Century City," p. 139. In his perceptive recent monograph *The Urban Ethos in the South, 1920–1930* (Baton Rouge, Louisiana State University Press, 1975), Blaine A. Brownell discusses the "civic loyalty" rhetoric in its somewhat debased 1920s form, when it had largely degenerated into the kind of chamber of commerce boosterism lampooned by Sinclair Lewis in *Babbitt* (1922). Even in the twenties, however, as Brownell notes (p. xix), the "urban ethos" in cities like Atlanta was never

merely a crude rationalization of economic interest, but "a complex of social views" which "functioned as justifications of municipal policy and social control." See also Charles Garofalo, "The Atlanta Spirit: A Study in Urban Ideology," *South Atlantic Quarterly,* 74 (Winter 1975), 34–44.

10. Ely, *The Coming City,* p. 60; Hall, *Civic Righteousness and Civic Pride,* p. 137.

11. Clarence E. Rainwater, *The Play Movement in the United States* (Chicago, University of Chicago Press, 1922), pp. 267, 281 (quoted passage).

12. Percy MacKaye, *The Civic Theatre in Relation to the Redemption of Leisure* (New York, Mitchell Kennerley, 1912), pp. 82, 87, 161–171 (the Saint-Gaudens's pageant), 254; and *Community Drama: Its Motive and Method of Neighborliness* (Boston, Houghton Mifflin, 1917), pp. 45, 47.

13. Roger N. Baldwin, "The St. Louis Pageant and Masque: Its Civic Meaning," *Survey,* 32 (April 11, 1914), 52; Charlotte Rumbold, "The St. Louis Pageant and Masque," ibid., (July 4, 1914), p. 372; *Pageant and Masque of Saint Louis, 1914. Reports of the Chairmen of Committees* (Saint Louis, 1916), p. 5.

14. *The Book of Words of the Pageant and Masque of St. Louis* (Saint Louis, 1914), pp. 85, 91; *Pageant and Masque,* p. 16.

15. *Book of Words,* pp. 90, 96, 103.

16. Ibid., p. 103.

17. Ibid., p. 104; *Pageant and Masque,* p. 85.

18. Rumbold, "The St. Louis Pageant and Masque," p. 372; Gundlach quoted in *Pageant and Masque,* pp. 5, 10. Information on Gundlach from Saint Louis Public Library.

19. *Pageant and Masque,* pp. 14, 19.

20. Ibid., pp. 14–15, 85.

21. Ibid., pp. 16, 17.

22. Ibid., p. 17. For further local reactions in this vein see MacKaye, *Community Drama,* pp. 16–18. Another epic civic drama, Percy MacKaye's *Caliban,* was given a series of performances at the stadium of the City College of New York in 1916, drawing a total of 135,000 spectators. It was hailed by the *New York American* as the overture to a new urban era when "all the people will cooperate to make the common life more beautiful until the communal life itself shall become a work of living art." Ibid., pp. 53–54.

18 THE CIVIC IDEAL MADE REAL

1. Woodrow Wilson, "The Need of Citizenship Organization," *American City,* 5 (Nov. 1911), p. 267.

2. Herbert Croly, *The Promise of American Life* (New York, Macmillan, 1909; reissued, Indianapolis, Bobbs-Merrill, 1965), p. 443; *Proceedings of the New York Conference for Good City Government and the Eleventh Annual Meeting of the National Municipal League* (Philadelphia, National Municipal League, 1904), p. 381 (Adler).

3. Mel Scott, *American City Planning since 1890* (Berkeley, University of California Press, 1969), pp. 69–70; Josiah Strong, *The Chal-*

lenge of the City (New York, Eaton and Mains, 1907), pp. 82, 83; James Bryce, *The American Commonwealth*, 2 vols. (New York, 1888; new ed., New York, Macmillan, 1919), pp. 880–881; John Nolen address in *City Planning. Sixty-first Congress, 2nd session, Senate document, vol. 59, no. 422*, Proceedings of the First National Conference on City Planning, Washington, D.C., May 1909 (Washington, D.C., Government Printing Office, 1910), p. 74.

4. Jon A. Peterson, "The City Beautiful Movement: Forgotten Origins and Lost Meanings," *Journal of Urban History*, 2 (Aug. 1976), 415–434, esp. pp. 416, 417, 419–420, 423, 425, 429. For a sense of the varied manifestations of city beautiful enthusiasm, see Robert Dale Grinder, "The War Against St. Louis's Smoke, 1891–1924," *Missouri Historical Review*, 69 (Jan. 1975), 191–205; Martin V. Melosi, " 'Out of Sight, Out of Mind': The Environment and Disposal of Municipal Refuse, 1860–1920," *Historian*, 34 (Aug. 1973), 621–640; and almost any issue of *American City* magazine for these years. The term "City Beautiful," which became current in New York art circles around 1899, appears to have been coined by the Arts and Crafts Exhibition Society of London in 1896. Peterson, "City Beautiful," p. 419.

5. J. Horace McFarland, "The Great Civic Awakening," *Outlook*, 73 (Apr. 18, 1903), 917, 920.

6. Scott, *American City Planning*, p. 67.

7. Peterson, "City Beautiful," p. 417.

8. Thorstein Veblen, *The Theory of the Leisure Class* (New York, 1899; reissued, New York, Funk and Wagnalls, Minerva Press, n.d.), p. 107.

9. Thomas S. Hines, *Burnham of Chicago, Architect and Planner* (New York, Oxford University Press, 1974), pp. 160, 316.

10. *Dayton Daily Journal* (May 16, 1901) quoted in Peterson, "City Beautiful," p. 424.

11. Harvey N. Shepard, "Municipal Housekeeping in Europe and America," *American City*, 6 (May 1912), 713.

12. *City Planning*, Proceedings of First National Conference on City Planning, p. 77 (Pope); Municipal Art Society quoted in Joseph Lee, *Constructive and Preventive Philanthropy* (New York, Macmillan, 1902), p. 88.

13. Charles Mulford Robinson, *Modern Civic Art; or, The City Made Beautiful* (New York, G. P. Putnam's Sons, 1903), pp. 35, 26, 229. See also, by the same author, "Improvement in City Life: III. Aesthetic Progress," *Atlantic Monthly*, 83 (June 1899), 771–785.

14. Robinson, *Modern Civic Art*, pp. 34, 245, 247, 260, 261.

15. Ibid., pp. 261, 262.

16. Ibid., p. 170; Charles Mulford Robinson, *The Improvement of Towns and Cities* (New York, G. P. Putnam's Sons, 1901), p. 219.

17. Robinson, *Modern Civic Art*, pp. 81, 82, 91.

18. Ibid., pp. v, 4, 17; idem, *Improvement of Towns and Cities*, p. 294.

19. Herbert Croly, "What Is Civic Art?" *Architectural Record*, 16 (July 1904), reprinted in *The Urban Vision: Selected Interpretations of the Modern American City*, ed. Jack Tager and Park Dixon Goist

(Homewood, Ill., Dorsey Press, 1970), pp. 78–82, quoted passages, p. 79; George B. Ford, "Digging Deeper into City Planning," *American City*, 6 (Mar. 1912), 559.

20. Manfredo Tafuri, *Architecture and Utopia: Design and Capitalist Development* (trans. Barbara Luigia La Penta, Cambridge, Mass., MIT Press, 1976), p. 23; John W. Reps, *The Making of Urban America: A History of City Planning in the United States* (Princeton, Princeton University Press, 1965), chaps. 4–7; Frederick Law Olmsted [Jr.], "The Town-Planning Movement in America," *Annals of the American Academy of Political and Social Science*, 51 (Jan. 1914), 172–181.

21. Scott, *American City Planning*, pp. 45, 50–55, 89–90; George F. Chadwick, *The Park and the Town: Public Landscape in the Nineteenth and Twentieth Centuries* (London, Architectural Press, 1966), p. 213 (on influence of German city-planning movement); "Garden City Movement," in *The New Encyclopedia of Social Reform*, ed. W. D. P. Bliss (New York, Funk and Wagnalls, 1908), p. 532; Benjamin C. Marsh, *An Introduction to City Planning* (New York, n.p., 1909), pp. 113–119 (on English "garden cities" and model towns for workingmen). For an instance of Ebenezer Howard's influence in America, see Kim McQuaid, "The Businessman as Social Innovator: Nelson O. Nelson as Promotor of Garden Cities and the Consumer Cooperative Movement," *American Journal of Economics and Sociology*, 34 (Oct. 1975), 411–422, esp. p. 415.

22. *Patrick Geddes: Spokesman for Man and the Environment*, ed. with an introduction by Marshall Stalley (New Brunswick, N.J., Rutgers University Press), 1972. Encountering Geddes's work in 1915, the young Lewis Mumford formed what would prove a lifelong interest in urban matters. Lewis Mumford, *City Development: Studies in Disintegration and Renewal* (New York, Harcourt Brace, 1945), p. 2.

23. Walter D. Moody, *What of the City? America's Greatest Issue —City Planning* (Chicago, A. C. McClurg, 1919), p. vii; Reps, *Making of Urban America*, p. 514; Hines, *Burnham of Chicago*, chap. IX; Harvey A. Kantor, "The City Beautiful in New York," *New-York Historical Society Quarterly*, 57 (Apr. 1973), 149–171; Chadwick, *Park and Town*, p. 213; Scott, *American City Planning*, pp. 63–65, 80, 163, 182; *The Report of the New York City Improvement Commission to the Honorable George B. McClellan, Mayor of the City of New York* (New York, n.p., 1907); *City Planning*, Proceedings of the First National Conference on City Planning.

24. Marsh, *Introduction to City Planning*, unnumbered prefatory page entitled "Some Reflections."

25. Moody, *What of the City?* pp. 9, 40, 48, 49, 217. At the Washington city-planning conference of 1909 (see note 3 above for citation), the moral-control theme was especially prominent in the addresses of Henry Morgenthau (pp. 59–62), George M. Sternberg (pp. 62–63), Frederic L. Ford (pp. 70–73, esp. p. 72) and Robert A. Pope (pp. 75–79, esp. pp. 76–77).

26. Walton Bean, *Boss Ruef's San Francisco* (Berkeley, University of California Press, 1967), pp. 12–66, 124; Hines, *Burnham of Chicago*, pp. 175, 178.

27. Henry A. Morgenthau, "A National Constructive Program for City Planning," *City Planning*, p. 59; Hines, *Burnham of Chicago*, p. 163.

28. Cass Gilbert and Frederick Law Olmsted, Jr., *Report of the New Haven Civic Improvement Commission* (New Haven, Tuttle, Morehouse and Taylor, 1910), p. 15. Frederick Law Olmsted, Jr., son of a famous father, was himself a landscape architect and city planner of considerable repute.

29. Joseph Lee, *Play in Education* (New York, Macmillan, 1915), pp. 388–389; John Ihlder, "The Development of Civic Spirit," in *Proceedings of the Cincinnati Conference for Good City Government and the Sixteenth Annual Meeting of the National Municipal League* (Philadelphia, National Municipal League, 1909), p. 432; *Report of the New York City Improvement Commission*, p. 7. See also Clinton R. Woodruff, Introduction, in *City Planning; A Series of Papers Presenting the Essential Elements of a City Plan*, ed. John Nolen, New York, D. Appleton, 1916), p. xxvi.

30. Quoted in ibid., pp. 1, 2.

31. Charles Zueblin, "The Making of the City," *Chautauquan*, 38 (Nov. 1903), 275.

32. Richard Watson Gilder, "The Vanishing City," *Century*, 46 (Oct. 1893), 868–869.

33. George McAneny, quoted in Nelson P. Lewis, *The Planning of the Modern City* (New York, John Wiley and Sons, 1916), p. 9. Cf. the comments of New York Mayor George B. McClellan in accepting an award from an architectural society in 1908 for his role in promoting city planning: "It is the city beautiful that compels and retains the love of her people. It is in the city beautiful that civic spirit is at its best." (Quoted in Kantor, "The City Beautiful in New York," p. 166.) Even when such plans ran afoul of urban economic realities and did not advance beyond the drawing board stage, many believed they could be a force for good. As one newspaper observed when the Minneapolis city plan was unveiled in 1912, "Some said it bolstered their civic loyalty just to look at the drawings." Vincent Oredson, "Planning a City: Minneapolis, 1907–1917," *Minnesota History*, 33 (Winter 1953), 336.

34. Quoted in Wilbert R. Hasbrouck, introduction to Daniel H. Burnham and Edward H. Bennett, *Plan of Chicago* (Chicago, The Commercial Club, 1909; reissued, New York, Da Capo Press, 1970), p. v; Hines, *Burnham of Chicago*, p. 4.

35. *The Meanings of Architecture: Buildings and Writings by John Wellborn Root*, ed. with an introduction by Donald Hoffmann (New York, Horizon Press, 1967), p. 141; Hines, *Burnham of Chicago*, xvii, 4–72; Jack Tager, "Partners in Design: Chicago Architects, Entrepreneurs, and the Evolution of Urban Commercial Architecture," *South Atlantic Quarterly*, 76 (Spring 1977), 204–218, esp. pp. 210, 214–215. My thanks to Jack Tager for allowing me to read this perceptive article in manuscript.

36. Hines, *Burnham of Chicago*, chap. XIV, esp. pp. 314–321.

37. *Plan of Chicago*, pp. 1, 48, 108; Hines, *Burnham of Chicago*, p. 328.

38. *Plan of Chicago*, pp. 1, 8.

39. Ibid., pp. 53, 108, 109.

40. Ibid., p. 36.

41. Ibid., pp. 4, 111, 121 ("love of order").

42. Hines, *Burnham of Chicago*, p. 315 (quoting an 1897 address by Burnham); *Plan of Chicago*, pp. 4, 29.

43. Ibid., p. 30.

44. Ibid., p. 29.

45. Ibid., pp. 111, 113, 115, 116.

46. Ibid., p. 118, caption of plate CXXX following p. 112.

47. Ibid., p. 116.

48. Reps, *Making of Urban America*, p. 524; Scott, *American City Planning*, pp. 107, 108.

49. Hines, *Burnham of Chicago*, chap. VIII, "The Paradox of Progressive Architecture," pp. 158–173 (quoted phrase, p. 173); Chadwick, *Park and Town*, p. 216; Vincent Scully, *American Architecture and Urbanism* (New York, Praeger, 1969), p. 140; John Burchard and Albert Bush-Brown, *The Architecture of America, A Social and Cultural History*, abridged ed. (Boston, Little, Brown, 1966), pp. 212–213. For a more sympathetic discussion of *The Plan of Chicago* see Carl W. Condit, *Chicago, 1910–1929: Building, Planning and Urban Technology* (Chicago, University of Chicago Press, 1973). Noting the pervasive emphasize on social harmony and the desire to idealize civic loyalty which underlay Burnham's plan, Condit writes (p. 79): "The vision was essentially a true one, but unfortunately the American—and particularly Chicago's—experience gave it a bitter, ironic quality: by 1970 the city was mortally sick, its problems overwhelming, and its primary aim was to heal rather than to memorialize itself."

50. Hines, *Burnham of Chicago*, pp. 334–335. Although challenging Hines at certain points, I have benefited from his careful, scholarly biography and his insightful discussion of Burnham's career.

51. In a parallel development, a number of industrialists of the Progressive era revived the idea associated with the Lowell mill owners of the 1830s: that the physical conditions of industrial life could be modified to promote the moral welfare of workers. In the early 1900s, for example, the National Cash Register Company of Dayton, Ohio, erected a group of light, airy, and well-landscaped factory buildings on which were engraved such elevating (if sometimes rather Delphic) aphorisms as "Labour is a Girdle of Manliness." See Burchard and Bush-Brown, *The Architecture of America*, p. 179.

52. *Plan of Chicago*, pp. 120, 123. For an interesting contemporary counterpoint to Burnham's philosophy of city planning see Kevin Lynch, *The Image of the City* (Cambridge, Mass., MIT Press, 1960). Focusing on three American cities (Boston, Jersey City, Los Angeles), Lynch examines the "poetic and symbolic" qualities of each, and what he calls its "imageability": "the ease with which its parts can be recognized and . . . organized into a coherent pattern." While Burnham's

generation saw in city planning a means of objectifying the civic ideal and thereby influencing private behavior, Lynch is more interested in the power of the total urban physical environment to enrich the "sensuous enjoyment of life" and enhance "every human activity that occurs there." Few Americans realize, he writes, the value of "harmonious surroundings" as a source of "daily delight, . . . a continuous anchor for their lives, or as an extension of the meaningfulness and richness of the world" (Lynch, *Image of the City*, pp. 2, 3, 119). For some slightly earlier speculations along the same lines see R. Richard Wohl and Anselm L. Strauss, "Symbolic Representation and the Urban Milieu," *American Journal of Sociology*, 63 (March 1958), 523–532.

53. Tafuri, *Architecture and Utopia*, p. 16.

54. Michael P. McCarthy, "Chicago Businessmen and the Burnham Plan," *Journal of the Illinois State Historical Society*, 63 (Autumn 1970), 255; Hines, *Burnham of Chicago*, p. 326.

55. McCarthy, "Chicago Businessmen and the Burnham Plan," pp. 248, 254, 255. Burnham's plan had official standing in these years, having been approved by the voters in a 1910 referendum and in 1917 adopted by the Chicago City Council as the city's official plan. Condit, *Chicago, 1910–1929*, p. 64.

56. Ibid., p. 84, n. 21, quoting a speaker at a dinner honoring the publication of the *Plan of Chicago*; Charles H. Wacker, "The City Plan," in *The Child in the City. A Series of Papers Presented at the Conferences Held during the Chicago Child Welfare Exhibit* (Chicago, Department of Social Investigation, Chicago School of Civics and Philanthropy, 1912), p. 465–466; McCarthy, "Chicago Businessmen and the Burnham Plan," p. 256 (quoting Bernard W. Snow).

57. Scott, *American City Planning*, pp. 102, 120–26, quoted passage, p. 121. In contrast to my interpretation, Scott places the origins of this narrower technical focus in the Progressive period itself. Zoning, too, of course, can and sometimes did have its moral-control dimension, but when contrasted with the soaring vision of the Progressive city planners, it represented a much diminished and far more defensive expression of the goal of controlling the urban moral order by reshaping the city's physical aspect.

19 POSITIVE ENVIRONMENTALISM AND THE
URBAN MORAL-CONTROL TRADITION

1. Edward A. Ross, *Social Control; A Survey of the Foundations of Order* (New York, Macmillan, 1901; reissued, Cleveland, Case Western Reserve Press, 1969), pp. 432, 435.

2. Geoffrey Blodgett, "Frederick Law Olmsted: Landscape Architecture as Conservative Reform," *Journal of American History*, 62 (Mar. 1976), 869–889, esp. pp. 872 and 888.

3. Frederic C. Howe, *The City, The Hope of Democracy* (New York, Charles Scribner's Sons, 1905; reissued, Seattle, University of Washington Press, 1967), p. 229.

4. "Gilder, Richard Watson," *Dictionary of American Biography* (New York, Charles Scribner's Sons, 1929), VII, 275–278; "Gulick, Luther H., [Sr.]" and "Gulick, Luther H., [Jr.]," ibid., VIII, 46–48; Neva

R. Deardorff, "Lee, Joseph," ibid., *Supplement II* (New York, 1958), 374–375; Roy Lubove, *The Progressives and the Slums: Tenement House Reform in New York City, 1890–1917* (Pittsburgh, University of Pittsburgh Press, 1962), p. 89n.

5. Ross, *Social Control*, p. 222.

6. Meredith Nicholson, "Indianapolis, A City of Homes," *Atlantic Monthly*, 93 (June 1904), 839.

7. Samuel P. Hays, "The Politics of Reform in Municipal Government in the Progressive Era," *Pacific Northwest Quarterly*, 55 (Oct. 1964), 157–169; idem, "The Changing Political Structure of the City in Industrial America," *Journal of Urban History*, 1 (Nov. 1974), 6–38, quoted phrase, p. 33.

8. Daniel H. Burnham and Edward H. Bennett, *Plan of Chicago* (Chicago, The Commercial Club, 1909; reissued, New York, Da Capo Press, 1970), p. 4; Charles Mulford Robinson, *Modern Civic Art; or, The City Made Beautiful*, 2nd ed. (New York, G. P. Putnam's Sons, 1904), p. vi; Charles H. Wacker, "The City Plan," in *The Child in the City: A Series of Papers Presented at the Conferences Held during the Chicago Child Welfare Exhibit* (Chicago, Department of Social Investigation, Chicago School of Civics and Philanthropy, 1912), pp. 461–62. See also Michael P. McCarthy, "Chicago Businessmen and the Burnham Plan," *Journal of the Illinois State Historical Society*, 63 (Autumn 1970), 228–256; and Vincent Oredson, "Planning a City: Minneapolis, 1907–1917," *Minnesota History*, 33 (Winter 1953), 331–339.

9. Hays, "The Changing Political Structure of the City in Industrial America," p. 23.

10. Howe, *The City*, p. 241.

11. Frederick Law Olmsted, Jr., in *City Planning: A Series of Papers Presenting the Essential Elements of a City Plan*, ed. John Nolen (New York, D. Appleton, 1916), p. 15 (italics added).

20 GETTING RIGHT WITH GESELLSCHAFT

1. John G. Thompson, *Urbanization: Its Effects on Government and Society* (New York, E. P. Dutton, 1927), pp. 490, 531, 617.

2. *The Twenties: Fords, Flappers, and Fanatics*, ed. George E. Mowry (Englewood Cliffs, N.J., Prentice-Hall, 1963), p. 1. I am, of course, aware of the view, most fully articulated by Morton and Lucia White, that a "powerful tradition of anti-urbanism" has remained the controlling force in America's response to the city down to the present day. Although evidence of antiurban sentiment may certainly be adduced from the post-1920 period as well as before, I find the center of gravity of urban social thought moving from fear, uneasiness, and hostility toward a more complex and fundamentally positive assessment around the time of the First World War. Further, when one does encounter antiurban expressions in the post-1920 period, they are most often directed at the city's presumed capacity to stamp a sterile and standardized conformism upon mass humanity, rather than its power to destroy moral cohesiveness and homogeneity. From the perspective of my study, the precise nature of the antiurban sentiment, rather than its mere presence, becomes crucial. The rather broad brush

strokes of the Whites' interpretation tends to obscure such distinctions. Morton and Lucia White, *The Intellectual Versus the City* (Cambridge, Mass., Harvard University Press, 1962; reissued, New York, Mentor, 1964), quoted phrase p. 15.

3. Herbert Asbury, *The Gangs of New York; An Informal History of the Underworld* (New York, Alfred A. Knopf, 1928); idem, *The Barbary Coast; An Informal History of the San Francisco Underworld* (New York, Alfred A. Knopf, 1933); Dashiell Hammett, *The Continental Op*, ed. with an introduction by Steven Marcus (New York, Random House, 1974); idem, *The Maltese Falcon* (New York, Alfred A. Knopf, 1930); Lincoln Steffens, *The Shame of the Cities* (New York, McClure, Phillips, 1904; reissued, New York, Sagamore Press, 1957), p. 163.

4. Robert Park, "The City: Suggestions for the Investigation of Human Behavior in the City Environment," *American Journal of Sociology*, 20 (Mar. 1915), 577–612, quoted passage, p. 584. See also Park Dixon Goist, "The Urban Theory of Robert Park," *American Quarterly*, 23 (Spring 1971), 46–59, esp. pp. 54–55. Morton and Lucia White, predictably, stress the antiurban elements in Park's work. *The Intellectual Versus the City*, pp. 160–170.

5. Louis Wirth, "Urbanism as a Way of Life," *American Journal of Sociology*, 44 (July 1938), 1–24, quoted passage, p. 2; Pitirim Sorokin and Carle C. Zimmerman, *Principles of Rural-Urban Sociology* (New York, Henry Holt, 1929), pp. 400 (quoted passage), 402–404, 608–609; Niles Carpenter, *The Sociology of City Life* (New York, Longmans, Green, 1931), p. 262. For contrasting interpretations emphasizing the negative aspects of Wirth's view of urbanization see James B. McKee, "Urbanism and the Problem of Social Order," *Centennial Review*, 10 (Summer 1966), 392–395; and Herbert J. Gans, "Urbanism and Suburbanism as Ways of Life: A Re-evaluation of Definitions," in *American Urban History: An Interpretive Reader with Commentaries*, ed. Alexander B. Callow, Jr. (New York, Oxford University Press, 1973), pp. 507–508.

6. Zane L. Miller, *The Urbanization of Modern America* (New York, Harcourt Brace Jovanovich, 1973), p. 149.

7. Arthur S. Link, "What Happened to the Progressive Movement in the 1920s?" *American Historical Review*, 64 (July, 1959), 833–851.

8. Milton M. Gordon, *Assimilation in American Life: The Role of Race, Religion, and National Origins* (New York, Oxford University Press, 1964), p. 144. Kallen had been associated with the concept of cultural pluralism—if not this precise term—since 1915. See his "Democracy Versus the Melting Pot" in the *Nation*, 100 (Feb. 18 and 25, 1915).

9. Park, "The City," pp. 595, 608–609.

10. Ibid., pp. 610, 611.

11. Lewis Mumford, *The Culture of Cities* (New York, Harcourt, Brace, 1938), pp. 481, 482, 492; Wirth, "Urbanism as a Way of Life," p. 2. Writing in the context of fascist successes in Europe, Wirth also noted the political hazards of a process of urbanization that uprooted people from their traditions and customs and reduced mass man to "virtual impotence as an individual" (ibid., p. 22). But as a German-

Jewish immigrant who spent his childhood in a Rhineland village and his adult years in Chicago, he more than balanced his reservations with a positive assessment of urbanization. He was, his daughter writes, keenly aware of the "deficiencies of the rural setting," and "never tempted to romanticize rural life or to bemoan the rural-urban migration." Elizabeth Wirth Marvick, "Louis Wirth: A Biographical Memorandum," in *Louis Wirth on Cities and Social Life*, ed. with an introduction by Albert J. Reiss, Jr. (Chicago, University of Chicago Press, 1964), pp. 333–340, quoted passages p. 334.

12. Luther Lee Bernard, *Social Control in Its Sociological Aspects* (New York, Macmillan, 1939), p. 16; Carpenter, *Sociology of City Life*, p. 327; Park, "The City," p. 600.

13. Ibid., pp. 582, 579.

14. Mumford, *The Culture of Cities*, p. 485.

15. Ibid., pp. 485, 486, 489. For a contemporary restatement of Mumford's ideal see Richard Sennett, *The Uses of Disorder: Personal Identity and City Life* (New York, Alfred A. Knopf, 1970).

16. For a critical discussion of the preoccupation of sociologists with the mass media in these years, see Richard T. LaPiere, *A Theory of Social Control* (New York, McGraw Hill, 1954), pp. vi, 18–19, 266n., 518–519. LaPiere suggests that his predecessors overemphasized the social-control role of the mass media and failed to recognize the degree to which, even in cities, individual behavior was still shaped largely with reference to primary groups, out of the need for the "kind of status that only such groups provide" (p. vi).

17. Edward L. Bernays, *Crystallizing Public Opinion* (New York, Boni and Liveright, 1923), pp. 125–126, 218 (italics added). See, in the same context, Walter Lippmann's *Public Opinion* (New York, Harcourt, Brace, 1922), which recommends that government play a conscious, activist role in shaping mass perceptions and opinions on complex political and foreign-policy issues.

18. Norman F. Harriman, *Standards and Standardization* (New York, McGraw-Hill, 1928), p. 209. Harriman, a metalurgist and expert in designing tests for metals, was assistant to the director of procurement of the United States Department of the Treasury. *New York Times* obit., July 1, 1949, p. 19.

19. Carpenter, *Sociology of City Life*, pp. 204, 445; Sorokin and Zimmerman, *Principles of Rural-Urban Sociology*, pp. 55, 287.

20. Frederick E. Lumley, *Means of Social Control* (New York, Century, 1925), pp. 13, 145, 398.

21. Ibid., p. 395.

22. A. B. Hollingshead, "The Concept of Social Control," *American Sociological Review*, 6 (Apr. 1941), 217–224, quoted passages, pp. 219, 221.

Index

Handbook of Charity Organization (S. Gurteen), 146, 150
Handy, Robert T., 81, 216–217
Hanover Street Association of Young Men. See Association of Young Men (Boston)
Hansen, George, 179, 338 n.12
Harriman, Norman F., 290
Hartford, Conn., city planning in, 267
Hartford Vice Commission, 216, 222
Hartley, Robert, 86, 88–94, 98–99, 130, 145, 292
Hatch, Alfred S., 135
Haussmann, Georges, 274
Havens, Richard N., 84
Hawes, Joel, 322 n.8
Hawthorne, Nathaniel, 70
Hay, John, 126
Haymarket bombing (1886), 125, 126, 128, 131, 135, 151, 177, 242
Hays, Samuel P., 212, 281, 282
Henry, Alexander, 36
Hewitt, Abraham S., 106
Higham, John, 163
Hill, Octavia, 144–145
History of Human Progress Under Christianity (C. Brace), 106
Hobbes, Thomas, 256
Hobsbawm, Eric, 69
Hofstadter, Richard, 195, 212
Holli, Melvin G., 172
Hollingshead, A.B., 291
Home of the Guardian Angel (Boston), 319
Homestead strike, 126
Homosexuality, 207
Hone, Philip, 20, 67, 70, 76, 112
Hoover, Herbert, 218
Hopkins, C. Howard, 115
Horrors of the White Slave Trade (C. Roe), 195
House of Refuge movement, 94–95
Housing reform. See Tenement housing reform
Howard, Ebenezer, 267, 363 n.21
Howe, Frederic C., 190, 197, 235, 245, 253, 279, 282
Howells, William Dean, 214
How the Other Half Lives (J. Riis), 127, 233
Hull House (Chicago), 155
Hull-House Maps and Papers (1895), 157

Humanity in the City (E. Chapin), 72
Human Nature and the Social Order (C. Cooley), 225, 227–228
Hume, John Ferguson, 129
Hunt, Richard M., 264

If Christ Came to Chicago (W. Stead), 184–188, 202
Ihlder, John, 253
Image of the City, The (K. Lynch), 365 n.52
Immigrants and immigration: in antebellum period, 4, 67, 85, 310 n.4; in Gilded Age, 123–124, 146; in Progressive era and after, 189, 285, 286; German, 77, 165; Irish, 67, 69, 77, 124, 125; Italian, 154; Jewish, 124, 133, 138, 244; Polish, 134, 137; Protestantism and, 11, 136–138; urban moral reform and, 24, 77, 80, 85–86, 165, 169, 205, 271; Anti-Saloon League on, 205; Robert Hartley on, 90; J. S. Lowell on, 147–148; Sunday school writers on, 35
Improvement of Towns and Cities, The (C. Robinson), 265
In Darkest England (W. Booth), 140
Independent (New York), 125–126
Indianapolis, Ind., 78, 280
Infant school movement, 305 n.22
Ingraham, Joseph Holt, 71, 72
In His Steps (C. Sheldon), 167, 172, 173, 176, 177, 178, 181–182
Institution Church League, 138
Institutional church movement, 138–140, 330 n.21
Intellectual Versus the City, The (M. and L. White), comment on, 367 n.2
Intemperance, 5, 13, 14, 53, 76. See also Temperance movement; Prohibition movement
Introduction to City Planning (B. Marsh), 267
Irving, Washington, 106

Jackson, Andrew, 7, 297 n.20
Jackson, Miss., votes dry, 212
James, Henry, 262
James, William, 270
Jefferson, Thomas, 3, 5
Jehovah's Witnesses. See Zion's Watchtower Society

bian Exposition, Louisiana Purchase Exposition

World War One: and prohibition, 193; and antiprostitution, 195

Wright, Carroll D., 163

Young Men's Bible Society of New York, 24

Young Men's Christian Association: origins and growth, 112–113, 324 n.30; leadership, 113–114; local organization, 114–115; middle-class orientation, 115; social goals and tactics, 116–120; coercive aspects, 119–120, 216; criticized by playground leaders, 244; mentioned, 102, 203, 255, 269, 277, 279. See also entries for specific cities

Young People's Society of Christian Endeavor, 164

Zimmerman, Carle C., 286, 290

Zion's Watchtower Society, 329 n.8

Zueblin, Charles, 269

LaVergne, TN USA
12 January 2011
212191LV00002B/130/P